ON THE BRINK

ON THE BRINK

*Americans and Soviets Reexamine
the Cuban Missile Crisis*

JAMES G. BLIGHT &
DAVID A. WELCH

With a foreword by McGeorge Bundy

SECOND EDITION

THE NOONDAY PRESS
Farrar, Straus and Giroux
NEW YORK

For Janet and Melissa:
our wives, friends, and colleagues

Acknowledgments

This book is the result of a collaboration between a psychologist with historical interests (Blight) and a political scientist also trained in philosophy (Welch). As a result of this quadridisciplinary effort, we probably owe more debts of gratitude to more kinds of people than do most authors. In the list of our debts that follows, therefore, there are bound to be significant, inadvertent omissions. We apologize for these oversights, claiming only imperfect memories in our defense.

Our first and most substantial debt is to a man we both consider our mentor: Joseph S. Nye, Jr., director of Harvard's Center for Science and International Affairs, where we have been in residence throughout the preparation of this book. He has supported this project every step of the way—as well as offered his helpful and pointed criticism. Not least importantly, Joe Nye was the moderator of the Hawk's Cay and Cambridge conferences (Chapters 1 and 5). This was a necessity, not a convenience. We know of no one with a comparable talent for guiding a complex discussion through a given range of issues without unduly constraining it or allowing important topics to slip through the cracks.

A project as ambitious as this one cannot occur without a good deal of financial support. Our salaries during the past few years have been paid by the Carnegie Corporation of New York, under a grant to Harvard's Project on Avoiding Nuclear War. Support for the conferences and for travel connected with the interviews was provided by separate grants from the Carnegie Corporation of New York, the Alfred P. Sloan Foundation, and the Ford Foundation.

This book has benefited from discussions with dozens of people, including Scott Armstrong, Robert P. Beschel, Stephen Biddle, Kurt M. Campbell, Ashton B. Carter, Abram Chayes, Ray Cline, Jorge Dominguez, Daniel Ellsberg, Peter Feaver, Hans Fenstermacher, Alexander George, Fen Osler Hampson, William Hyland, Robert Jervis, Carl Kaysen, Peter Kornbluh, Richard Ned Lebow, Jeffrey Legro, Murrey Marder, Ernest R. May, Leonard C. Meeker, Frederic A. Mosher, Richard Neustadt, John Newhouse, Benjamin Read, Scott Sagan, Arthur Schlesinger, Jr., Enid C.B. Schoettle, Arthur L. Singer, Jr., Allison Stanger, William Taubman, Marc Trachtenberg, and Stephen Van Evera. For other valuable assistance we thank CBS for permission to use

Anatomy of a Crisis at Hawk's Cay; Elizabeth Deane of WGBH–TV Boston for producing the videos that proved to be so provocative at the Cambridge conference; Marie Allitto-Hadley for supervising the conference arrangements in Cambridge; Melissa Baumann for assisting us in constructing the chronology; William Jarosz for logistical assistance at the Cambridge conference in addition to sage Sovietological advice; and to Judith Vassilovsky and Lisa Schweig for secretarial and organizational help far beyond the call of duty.

Several people deserve special thanks. Graham Allison, our dean and colleague, challenged us to try to make his study of the crisis, *Essence of Decision*, irrelevant. We failed, but we appreciated the extra incentive. Bruce Allyn conducted personal interviews in Moscow during the process of choosing which Soviets we wished to invite to Cambridge, and he has provided knowledgeable, energetic assistance throughout the latter part of the project. McGeorge Bundy played a central role in convincing his former colleagues on President Kennedy's ExComm to join us in our enterprise, and has provided much-needed intellectual and moral support. Albert Carnesale, who has tried for years to convince us that psychology, history, political science, and philosophy are merely palliatives for those who could not be physicists and engineers, has been an entertaining and incisive interlocutor. Raymond Garthoff of the Brookings Institution has been an indispensable source of information and advice. The manuscript has had the benefit of his close reading and rigorous criticism. Morton Halperin has provided more stimulation than he can possibly be aware of. Linda Healey, our editor, has given us superb guidance. Robert McNamara has given us something that any innovative endeavor must have: the conviction that what we are doing is important. Richard E. Neustadt has helped us repeatedly to interpret what we have been told, and we have appreciated the many hours he has spent puzzling over our material. Thomas C. Schelling has for several years served as a gadfly extraordinaire to our effort to look inside the Cuban missile crisis, and has repeatedly prodded us into finding better ways to defend and express ourselves. And William Taubman has been an inexhaustible source of insight; his practical experience in dealing with Soviets helped make the Cambridge conference a reality.

Finally, our wives, Janet M. Lang and Melissa S. Williams, deserve special mention. Janet was an active participant in the planning for the Hawk's Cay meeting; she assisted Blight in an important follow-up interview with George Ball; she was co-interviewer of Douglas Dillon in Welch's absence (see Chapter 3); and she has criticized and improved every chapter in the book. A psychologist by training, an epidemiologist by profession, she has now added the Cuban missile crisis to the repertoire of subjects about which she is expert. Melissa provided invaluable organizational assistance at Hawk's Cay, actively participated in the discussions which helped shape the focus and direction of this book, and scrupulously read and criticized every line of the manuscript. Without both of their contributions, this volume would not have been possible.

This book is the result of a collaboration in the fullest sense of the word. From the selection of materials to the analysis and commentary, we have carefully observed an equal division of labor. The opinions expressed herein are therefore equally ours—and, of course, those of the people who speak on the pages that follow. They should not necessarily be understood as the opinions of the organizations that supported this project.

J.G.B. and D.A.W.

Contents

Foreword

This book is a clear demonstration of the proposition that any student of nuclear danger who thinks we know all we need to know about the Cuban missile crisis is wrong. By the new light it sheds on American behavior, the book shows that the parts of the story that are relatively familiar can be understood more clearly and deeply, and by its new light on Soviet behavior, it shows us not only how much help a student can get from Soviet discussion that is not confined to a narrow party line but also how much remains to be learned in the new dialogue made possible by Gorbachev's *glasnost*.

The book begins with questions that are both familiar and puzzling, and it ends with questions that are puzzling and new. On both kinds of questions it sheds so much light that it becomes at once an indispensable addition to the serious student's shelf on the missile crisis.

The book is also full of interest for those who are not specialists. It is based on three different experiments in what the authors call critical oral history: first, a conference that brought American participants and scholars together in Florida for a weekend of intense exchange; second, a set of four interviews with senior participants who hold strongly different views on the role and meaning of the strategic nuclear balance during this crisis; and third, a meeting in Cambridge which produced the first sustained and serious exchange of assessments between Soviet and American observers. In these meetings and interviews, things were said that graphically exhibit the differences to be found between scholars and decisionmakers, between "hawks" and "doves," and between those who are inside the Soviet system and all the rest of us. The attentive reader will find evidence in each of the three sets of encounters that no single vantage point is always the best.

I particularly commend the three chapters of analysis and commentary by Blight and Welch. These two younger scholars, drawn to the problem of nuclear danger from different backgrounds and disciplines, were the moving spirits in the triple inquiry on which they report. In their own commentaries they exhibit the combination of intelligence, sympathy, and fairness which marked their work in the organization and management of the two conferences and the four special interviews. No reader is likely to find every one of their judgments compelling; there are too many for that, and the protean character of the crisis itself forbids easy unanimity. But the chance to match wits and judgments with writers so bright and generous and straight is one that I have found rewarding, and I think the reader who chooses to accept the challenge will not regret the choice.

Blight and Welch have done a great service by producing their book quickly. They are the first to insist that it is not the last word on the subject. Indeed, they are already at work with Soviet colleagues on plans for a further conference in Moscow in 1989. Meanwhile, we learn more, month by month, from American scholars addressing American evidence. There is hope for a new openness from Cuba, too.

Of course, the missile crisis, important as it was, is not the only possible source of new understanding. The task of thinking straight about moments of danger in the nuclear age is much larger than the study of any single episode. But the crisis was indeed a time of learning for all concerned, and this book can help us all to learn still more.

McGeorge Bundy

June 8, 1988

Preface to the Second Edition

On the Brink was published in January 1989, simultaneously with the third in our series of conferences, in Moscow, which brought together high-level delegations from all three principals in the Cuban missile crisis: the United States, the Soviet Union, and Cuba. That conference, and a series of follow-up interviews conducted in both Moscow and Havana, shed new light on many issues discussed in the original volume, especially those concerning Soviet and Cuban decisionmaking, and Soviet–Cuban relations. We incorporate this information here.

The most significant change is the addition of an afterword that summarizes our findings since the publication of the first edition. We have chosen not to reproduce extended portions of the Moscow conference transcript or our follow-up interviews, since they lack, for the most part, the conversational give-and-take of the Hawk's Cay and Cambridge transcripts and the interviews presented in Chapter 3. The Moscow conference was very large and necessarily somewhat formal, while the interviews were targeted on highly specific questions raised in the Moscow conference. The afterword is therefore our attempt to pull together this new information into a concise narrative of Soviet and Cuban decisionmaking relevant to the causes, conduct, and outcome of the Cuban missile crisis. In addition, we have expanded the chronology and corrected mistakes in the original text in light of subsequent disclosures. Readers may judge for themselves whether, as we believe, our central theses have withstood more recent testimony; indeed, many seem to us to have been powerfully reinforced.

We would like to acknowledge the indispensable role our friend and colleague Bruce Allyn played in the organization of the Moscow conference, and in the research that followed it. Without his facility with the Russian language, his rapport with prominent Soviet participants, and his knowledge of the Soviet Union, this revised edition would not have been possible. We would also like to acknowledge the valuable assistance of Jorge Domínguez, Alexander George, Scott D. Sagan, and Rafael Hernández for their insights and criticisms; the Institute of World

Economy and International Relations (Moscow), the Center for the Study of the Americas (Havana), and the National Security Archive (Washington) for ongoing institutional support; and the Carnegie Corporation of New York, the John D. and Catharine T. MacArthur Foundation, the Ploughshares Fund, George Keros, and Carl Sloane for invaluable financial assistance in the latter stages of our research.

J.G.B. and D.A.W.

The written word has taught me to listen to the human voice, much as the great unchanging statues have taught me to appreciate bodily motions. On the other hand, but more slowly, life has thrown light for me on the meaning of books.

But books lie, even those that are most sincere. The less adroit, for lack of words and phrases wherein they can enclose life, retain of it but a flat and feeble likeness. Some . . . make it heavy, and encumber it with a solemnity which it did not possess; others, on the contrary . . . make life lighter than it is, like a hollow, bouncing ball, easy to toss to and fro in a universe without weight. . . . Historians propose to us systems too perfect for explaining the past, with sequence of cause and effect much too exact and clear to have been ever entirely true; they rearrange what is dead, unresisting material. . . . I should take little comfort in a world without books, but reality is not to be found in them because it is not there whole.

MARGUERITE YOURCENAR
Memoirs of Hadrian

ON THE BRINK

Prologue

The historian not only re-enacts past thought, he re-enacts it in the context of his own knowledge and therefore, in re-enacting it, criticizes it, forms his own judgement of its value, corrects whatever errors he can discern in it. The criticism of the thought whose history he traces is not something secondary to tracing the history of it. It is an indispensable condition of the historical knowledge itself.

R. G. COLLINGWOOD
The Idea of History

Many people recall the Cuban missile crisis of October 1962 as one of the most terrifying events of their lives. At 7:00 p.m. on October 22, President John F. Kennedy went on television to announce to the nation and to the world that the United States had discovered Soviet nuclear missile bases under construction in Cuba, scarcely ninety miles from the coast of Florida.* Stressing that the deployment was undertaken secretly, in defiance of Soviet assurances that no offensive weapons would be shipped to Cuba, and in evident disregard of the President's attempts to deter such a move, Kennedy declared that he would do whatever was necessary to force the missiles out of Cuba. He announced his intention to impose a naval "quarantine" of the island, and in order to drive home the seriousness of his commitment, he unequivocally proclaimed that a Soviet missile launched from Cuba against any nation of the Western Hemisphere would be regarded as an attack by the Soviet Union upon the United States, requiring a full nuclear response.

Around Cuba, the President assembled an awesome display of military power: hundreds of ships, nearly a thousand aircraft, and more than a hundred thousand troops. The Strategic Air Command went to its highest level of alert ever. Evidently shocked at the American discovery of the missiles and outraged at the President's announcement, Soviet Chairman Nikita Khrushchev ordered construction crews at the half-finished missile sites to work day and night until the sites were completed, and

---

* Readers unfamiliar with the events of the crisis should refer to the chronology in the Appendix.

denounced Kennedy's piracy in the strongest possible terms. The superpowers had locked horns.

The world sat glued to television sets and radios as Soviet ships steamed inexorably toward the quarantine line, awaiting the inevitable confrontation. Just before 10:00 a.m. on Wednesday, October 24—the hour the blockade was officially to go into effect—the Soviet ships stopped dead in the water and turned back. For two days, there was stalemate; but work proceeded at the missile sites as American troops and planes streamed into southern Florida. On October 26 came an apparent break in the crisis: Khrushchev privately offered what seemed to the President and his advisors to be acceptable terms for resolving the confrontation. He would withdraw the missiles in Cuba in return for an American pledge not to invade the island. But before Kennedy could reply, Khrushchev demanded publicly, on the morning of October 27, that the United States withdraw its fifteen Jupiter missiles from Turkey—first-generation missiles deployed under the aegis of NATO —as a quid pro quo for the withdrawal of the Soviet missiles from Cuba. Meanwhile, over Cuba itself, an American U-2 reconnaissance plane was shot down and its pilot killed. The Soviets had drawn first blood, and the tension rose to a crescendo.

The President decided to "accept" Khrushchev's October 26 "offer," and to ignore his latest demand. His brother, Attorney General Robert Kennedy, arranged to meet Soviet Ambassador Anatoly Dobrynin at the Department of Justice to deliver the President's message, and to press upon him the urgency of a resolution. Meanwhile, final preparations for military action were made; Soviet and Cuban intelligence determined that an American attack was imminent. The United States and the Soviet Union seemed to be on the brink of war. The next morning, Khrushchev gave in.

Thus ended the most dangerous crisis in history, an unforeseen event with an unexpectedly swift and peaceful conclusion. By turns angry, confused, and terrified, the leaders of the superpowers, and the whole world, emerged deeply sobered by the experience. How did it happen? How did two governments, each of which fully realized the consequences of a nuclear war, find themselves entangled in a crisis that brought them perilously close to a catastrophe neither wanted? Why did Khrushchev attempt to deploy missiles surreptitiously in America's back yard? Why did he think he could get away with it? Why did the President feel compelled to force the missiles out? Why did he choose a quarantine as his initial response, rather than an air strike against the missiles on the one hand, or quiet diplomacy on the other? Why did Khrushchev accept a non-invasion pledge in return for Soviet withdrawal of the missiles? What would the President have done had he refused?

These are some of the questions explored in this volume. They are not, for the most part, new questions. The Cuban missile crisis has attracted an enormous amount of attention, and the literature on it is vast.[1] But, for all the ink devoted to the event, it is far from well understood. Until we understand the intentions and actions of both sides in the confrontation, we will be unable to see clearly how the experience of it can help us avoid or handle another.

Prior to *glasnost*, there was no meaningful dialogue between Americans and Soviets on the causes, conduct, or lessons of the Cuban missile crisis, and the few Soviet accounts that have been written are difficult to take seriously.[2] The Soviet side of the crisis, therefore, has been almost entirely opaque. Though there has been no shortage of analysis and commentary on the American side, we have yet to arrive at a balanced understanding; for our main sources of information have been the retrospective accounts of the participants—in memoirs, or as told to journalists and historians.[3] The weaknesses of retrospective accounts are obvious: human memories are unavoidably selective, subjective, and often unreliable. It is easy to overemphasize one's own role when recounting a story, and it is easy to allow one's present agenda to affect the way in which one recalls past events. As a rule, also, recollections generally prove to be insufficiently self-critical, when they are checked against the facts.[4]

Recently, students of the crisis have gained access to a large body of previously classified material which has challenged the conventional wisdom of the event in fundamental ways.[5] With documents in hand, we can now understand more clearly than before the way events unfolded. Yet documents have a weakness of their own: they do not supply their own context. We now know a good deal about the details of the military options that were available to President Kennedy during the missile crisis, but they tell us nothing of what the President was going to do with them. We now have access to transcripts of some of the ExComm* meetings;[6] but they reveal only what was said by the participants, not necessarily what they were thinking—and, in many cases, it is becoming clear that what the President and his closest advisors were thinking was often at odds with, and possibly more important than, what was said in the Cabinet Room at the White House.

To a large extent, the memories of the participants can help supply the missing context to the documents, and the documents can supply many of the facts which human memories distort or forget. And in concert, several people's memories may test and correct each individ-

---

* Executive Committee of the National Security Council, the body convened by President Kennedy to advise him on the conduct of the crisis. Several variations on the acronym are in currency—ExComm, ExCom, Ex Comm, Ex Com, and EXCOMM, among them.

ual's memory, so that errors in recollection or egregious distortions can be reduced—all the more so if the parties to a discussion are known to have divergent views of the event. In a properly designed conversation, therefore, in which key participants discuss the event among themselves and with knowledgeable scholars, a more accurate picture can be reconstructed than would be possible if we relied solely on recollections or on documents alone.

We call our research method *critical oral history*. At the center of our inquiry is the belief that there is no teacher like hard experience. That is why an important aspect of critical oral history is the orchestration of meetings attended by people who actually lived through an event, with varying degrees of responsibility for its outcome. But, unlike conventional oral history, in which such people merely tell their stories, critical oral history subjects these stories to multidimensional criticism. The procedure is to begin with a meeting attended by scholars and policymakers, for which all participants prepare by familiarizing themselves with hundreds of pages of carefully selected primary and secondary documents. This ensures that the stories are told within the constraints of the facts (such as they are known). The scholars and other policymakers present are instructed to interrupt the storyteller whenever his recollections seem to be at variance with the facts. Thus, a particular story—not only a policymaker's recollection of his experience but also, perhaps, a scholar's favorite theory—must answer to three judges: the documentary record, the expertise of specialists in the field, and the recollections of those who lived through the event in positions of official responsibility. If necessary, in-depth follow-up interviews may supplement a conversation where it proves impossible to extend the scope and reach of the conference itself.

The Hawk's Cay Conference, March 5–8, 1987

The first such conversation was the Hawk's Cay conference, March 5–8, 1987, in the Florida Keys, where several members of the ExComm met with scholars noted for their work on the Cuban missile crisis for three days of intense discussion. The idea for the Hawk's Cay conference was born at a meeting sponsored by Harvard's Project on Avoiding Nuclear War in Jackson Hole, Wyoming, in July 1986. It was the brainchild of one of the present authors, James Blight, and the shape of the enterprise was worked out by a group consisting of Blight, Joseph Nye, Graham Allison, Albert Carnesale, Robert McNamara, Alexander George, David Hamburg, Ernest May, and Frederic Mosher. David

Welch joined the project in early fall, and in addition undertook to produce the conference transcript.

It was decided very early on that the proceedings of the meeting should not be tape-recorded, as we were likely to deal with some very sensitive documentary material and it was felt that microphones might unduly constrain the conversation. Instead, Welch reconstructed the discussion from shorthand notes and circulated a draft for revision and elaboration (by way of footnotes). In retrospect, we believe this choice of procedure was correct, for the participants had the chance to ensure that they go on record saying precisely what they intended to say, and nothing else. The risk we ran, of course, was that the revision process might be abused. But all of the participants acted in perfectly good faith, and did not use their right of review to alter the substance of their remarks in any way whatsoever. We were so impressed with the usefulness of the procedure that we repeated it at the Cambridge conference in October.

Chapter 1 presents an edited version of the Hawk's Cay transcript. It represents roughly two-thirds of the unedited text. The omitted portions are neither as important nor as interesting as what is presented here. Care has been taken to indicate all places where material has been omitted, so that students of the crisis who may wish to consult the unedited transcript may easily compare the two documents.[7] Chapter 2 provides our own analysis and commentary, but of an interpretive rather than a purely historical kind. As the historical significance of the transcript has already been discussed in several places, and as it is already finding its way into the literature, we have chosen not to restrict our commentary merely to analysis of the "facts." We were impressed by what we believe to be an equally important feature of the document: the light it sheds on the differences between the scholars' and the policymakers' views of the Cuban missile crisis, and what those differences may mean in practice.

Hawks and Doves: The Interviews with Paul Nitze, Douglas Dillon, Dean Rusk, and Robert McNamara

The gulf between the scholars' and the policymakers' understandings of the crisis was only one conceptual divide evident at Hawk's Cay. The other was the division within the ExComm itself between the hawks and the doves. Seeking to explore the causes and consequences of this division further, we interviewed several principals after the Hawk's Cay meeting. Four of these interviews are presented in Chapter 3, again in edited form. Chapter 4 provides our analysis and commentary. There we search for the causes and consequences of what we discovered were two wholly incommensurable Cuban missile crises: one experienced by the hawks, and one experienced by the doves.

The Cambridge Conference, October 11–12, 1987

Though the Hawk's Cay conference and the interviews provided new windows on the Cuban missile crisis, they confirmed our opinion that the most glaring gap in our understanding of the event concerns Soviet motives and actions. As a consequence, we organized a conference in Cambridge, Massachusetts, bringing together three knowledgeable Soviets, three former members of the ExComm, and several American scholars. The procedure with the transcript was the same as with the Hawk's Cay document. Welch reconstructed the conversation from notes and circulated a draft for revisions. (The logistics of sending transcripts between the United States and the Soviet Union were difficult and complicated; the Soviets' revisions came back to us through a still-unidentified member of Mikhail Gorbachev's Washington summit entourage in December 1987.) Chapter 5 presents an edited version of the transcript.[8]

Chapter 6 presents our commentary and analysis of the Soviet views of the crisis as they appear in the transcript. Here we have allowed ourselves more space to explore some of the implications of what was said in that astonishing meeting. Even the anecdotal evidence therein is so much more detailed than any previous Soviet account to which we in the West have had access, so much more plausible and challenging to traditional American interpretations of Soviet actions, that we believe it represents a new departure for Soviet studies. The candor and intellectual curiosity of our Soviet participants—Fyodor Burlatsky, Sergo Mikoyan, and Georgy Shakhnazarov—are what made the meeting a success and paved the way for both the Moscow conference (January 1989) and unprecedented conversations with prominent Cubans, the results of which are presented in the Afterword. The seeds sown at the Cambridge conference continue to bear fruit.

Dramatis Personae

The participants in the dramas that follow are a diverse group of Cuban missile crisis veterans and scholars who have studied the event. Accordingly, we have divided the cast of characters below into former policymakers and academics. As will become obvious, however, the distinction is one partly of convenience, for their memberships often overlap.

BALL, George W.   Princeton, N.J.; Under Secretary of State in the Kennedy and Johnson Administrations (and a member of the ExComm), and former Ambassador to the United Nations; advisor, during the 1950s, to Jean Monnet and Adlai Stevenson, and to the White House under President Carter. George Ball was a prominent dove during the Cuban missile crisis, arguing repeatedly about the importance of avoiding irreversible actions that might have severe unintended consequences. As such, he was a strong proponent of the quarantine of Cuba and a critic of those advocating stronger military action, such as an air strike against the missile sites or an invasion of the island.

BUNDY, McGeorge.   Professor of History, New York University; dean of the Faculty of Arts and Sciences, Harvard University, 1953–60; Special Assistant for National Security under Presidents Kennedy and Johnson (and a member of the ExComm); president of the Ford Foundation, 1969–81. McGeorge Bundy's role in the Cuban missile crisis was varied and crucial. Bundy called the meetings of the ExComm; he played devil's advocate throughout the discussions, to prevent premature consensus; and he spoke for the ExComm as a whole in discussions with the President. Bundy participated in the Hawk's Cay and Cambridge conferences both as a policymaker and as a scholar who has written extensively on nuclear diplomacy and national security matters.

BURLATSKY, Fyodor.   Political commentator for *Literaturnaya gazeta* (Moscow) and head of the Philosophy Department, Social Sciences Institute, Moscow; Political Advisor for Socialist Countries of Eastern Europe and speechwriter for Chairman Nikita S. Khrushchev and General Secretary Mikhail Gorbachev. Several months before the crisis, in May 1962, Burlatsky traveled with Khrushchev to Eastern Europe; it was then, according to Khrushchev's memoirs, that he first thought of deploying nuclear missiles in Cuba. During the crisis, Burlatsky worked in Moscow with a team of political advisors responsible for informing and responding to Soviet allies. He also helped draft Khrushchev's important speech of December 12, 1962, in which the official Soviet account of the crisis first appeared.

CHAYES, Abram.   Felix Frankfurter Professor of International Law, Harvard Law School; State Department Legal Counsel during the Kennedy Administration; author of works on the theory and practice of international law, and of a memoir of the Cuban missile crisis. Chayes was in Paris when the American government confirmed the presence of Soviet missiles in Cuba. Called back to Washington by George Ball, Chayes was instrumental in crafting the legal justification for the quarantine of Cuba. Chayes participated at the Hawk's Cay conference as both a scholar and a former policymaker.

DILLON, C. Douglas.   New York City; Secretary of the Treasury under Presidents Kennedy and Johnson (and a member of the ExComm); Ambassador to France and Under Secretary of State during the Eisenhower Administration. Dillon had had wide experience with nuclear diplomacy. While in Paris, he handled the interchange between the French, who requested American nuclear assistance in Vietnam, and the Eisenhower Administration, which refused. Dillon was an acknowledged leader of the Republicans and a prominent hawk in the ExComm.

GARTHOFF, Raymond L.   Senior Fellow, Foreign Policy Studies Program, The Brookings Institution, Washington, D.C.; Special Assistant for Soviet bloc Political/Military Affairs in the State Department during the Kennedy Administration; Executive Officer of the first Strategic Arms Limitation Talks, 1969–73; Ambassador to Bulgaria, 1977–79; author of numerous works on U.S.–Soviet relations. During the Cuban missile crisis, Garthoff worked in the State Department, reporting to Walt Rostow and Under Secretary U. Alexis Johnson. He wrote several key memoranda during the crisis, including those on the military significance of the Soviet deployment and on the Soviet proposal for trading their missiles in Cuba for NATO missiles in Turkey. Garthoff participated in the Hawk's Cay and Cambridge conferences as both a scholar and a former policymaker.

McNAMARA, Robert S.   Washington, D.C.; president of the Ford Motor Company, 1960–61; Secretary of Defense in both the Kennedy and the Johnson Administrations (and a member of the ExComm); and president of the World Bank, 1968–81. McNamara was one of the most important players in the Cuban missile crisis, a dove throughout, and a firm advocate of the quarantine. President Kennedy relied more heavily on McNamara than on anyone else to manage the quarantine and the military, whose leaders uniformly advocated stronger action. McNamara is also one of the most articulate and forthright proponents of the view that crises cannot be "managed," and is well known for his argument that nuclear weapons serve no military purpose.

MIKOYAN, Sergo. Editor, *Latinskaya amerika* (Moscow); formerly personal secretary to his father, Soviet First Deputy Premier Anastas I. Mikoyan, a close associate of Nikita Khrushchev, and Special Envoy to Cuba at the conclusion of the Cuban missile crisis. Sergo Mikoyan worked closely with his father throughout the crisis, and remains close to Fidel Castro and the Cuban leadership. He is also an outstanding Latin American specialist and is therefore uniquely situated to discuss U.S.–Soviet–Cuban relations in 1962 both as a player and as a scholar.

NITZE, Paul H. Special Ambassador for Arms Control in the Reagan Administration; head of State Department Policy Planning under President Truman; Assistant Secretary of Defense under President Kennedy (and a member of the ExComm). Paul Nitze was primary drafter of National Security Council Memorandum 68 (NSC-68), which formalized the Truman Administration's doctrine of Containment. During the Cuban missile crisis, he was a forceful hawk who strongly believed that the United States' conventional superiority in the Caribbean, and its strategic nuclear superiority over the Soviet Union, assured an American victory. He also led the Berlin Task Force charged with constructing possible responses to an anticipated Soviet move against Berlin.

RUSK, Dean. Professor of Law, University of Georgia; director of the State Department's Office of Special Political Affairs under President Roosevelt; Deputy Under Secretary of State under President Truman; president of the Rockefeller Foundation, 1951–60; Secretary of State under Presidents Kennedy and Johnson (and a member of the ExComm). Dean Rusk's role in the Cuban missile crisis has long been the subject of controversy. Robert Kennedy, in particular, believed Rusk to have been too reticent in offering advice. But new information reveals Rusk to have been a key player, upon whom the President relied more heavily than has previously been known. Rusk's modus operandi within the ExComm was similar to Bundy's, playing devil's advocate and interlocutor to prevent premature closure.

SCHLESINGER, Arthur M., Jr. Albert Schweitzer Professor of the Humanities, Graduate Center of the City University of New York; White House aide during the Kennedy Administration; author of many works on American history, including best-selling biographies of John and

Robert Kennedy. Schlesinger's duties in the White House included over-seeing Latin American affairs, but his importance rests primarily with his historical accounts of the Kennedy Presidency (*A Thousand Days*, 1965) and Robert Kennedy's career (*Robert Kennedy and His Times*, 1978).

SHAKHNAZAROV, Georgy.   Senior Staff Member of the Central Committee of the Communist Party of the Soviet Union, and personal aide to General Secretary Mikhail S. Gorbachev; translator of the works of George Orwell into Russian. He is an outspoken advocate of Gorbachev's reforms, and is an associate of several Soviet officials instrumental in the Cuban missile crisis.

SORENSEN, Theodore C.   Attorney with Paul, Weiss, Rifkind, Wharton & Garrison, New York City; Special Counsel to President Kennedy (and a member of the ExComm); author of works on the Kennedy Administration and Presidency. Sorensen was President Kennedy's Chief of Staff, close political advisor, and confidant. During the Cuban missile crisis, Sorensen drafted most of the President's key letters and speeches. He was a dove throughout, and a cautious advocate of the quarantine. His book, *Kennedy* (1965), remains a standard account of the Kennedy Presidency.

TAYLOR, General Maxwell D.   Superintendent of West Point Academy, 1945–49; commander of the Eighth Army in Korea, 1951–53; Army Chief of Staff under President Eisenhower; chairman of the Joint Chiefs of Staff during the Kennedy Administration (and a member of the ExComm); Ambassador to the Republic of Vietnam, 1968–69. General Taylor described himself during the Cuban missile crisis as a "twofold hawk" who, like the other Chiefs of Staff, advocated stronger action against the Soviet missiles in Cuba. General Taylor died after a long illness, shortly after the Hawk's Cay conference.

*   *   *

ALLISON, Graham T.   Former Dean and Dillon Professor of Government, John F. Kennedy School of Government, Harvard University; author of works on bureaucratic politics, strategies for reducing the risk of nuclear war, and the Cuban missile crisis. His seminal work, *Essence of Decision: Explaining the Cuban Missile Crisis* (1971), is the most widely read scholarly account of the crisis in English and also one of the fundamental texts in American political science.

ALLYN, Bruce.   Research Fellow, Center for Science and International Affairs, Harvard University; author of works on Soviet crisis decisionmaking and Soviet approaches to crisis prevention. Allyn has been instrumental in organizing numerous U.S.–Soviet exchanges, both cultural and political.

BLIGHT, James G. Senior research fellow of the Center for Foreign Policy Development, Brown University; author of works on the psychology of crises, the history of psychology and psychoanalysis, and the Cuban missile crisis. His interest in the Cuban missile crisis is informed especially by previous work he has done on the relationship between academic psychology and governmental policymaking, the effects of fear on performance in crises, and the history of scientific revolutions.

CARNESALE, Albert. Academic dean and Professor of Public Policy, John F. Kennedy School of Government, Harvard University; member of the American delegation to the first U.S.–Soviet Strategic Arms Limitation Talks; presently advisor to the Departments of Defense, State, and Energy; author of works on strategic defense, nuclear strategy, the history of arms control and strategies for reducing the risk of nuclear war. A nuclear engineer by training and a nuclear-policy analyst by profession, he is a specialist on a wide range of topics relating to American defense policy.

GEORGE, Alexander L. Graham Stuart Professor of International Relations, Stanford University; author of works on international crises and crisis management, the theory and practice of nuclear deterrence, stress and decisionmaking, and on the history of international diplomacy. George is a pioneer in many branches of international-relations scholarship, including the application of social psychology to political science. His book, *Deterrence in American Foreign Policy* (with Richard Smoke, 1974), won the Bancroft Prize in American historical writing.

HORELICK, Arnold. Director of the RAND–UCLA Center for the Study of Soviet International Behavior; author of numerous works on U.S.–Soviet relations, on Soviet crisis decisionmaking, and the Cuban missile crisis. Horelick published studies, immediately after the crisis, on Soviet motivations and behavior, and concluded that Khrushchev's primary aim in deploying missiles to Cuba was to redress the strategic nuclear imbalance quickly and cheaply.

LANG, Janet M. Assistant Professor, Department of Epidemiology and Biostatistics, Boston University. Trained in both cognitive psychology and epidemiology, she maintains a strong avocational interest in the Cuban missile crisis.

LEBOW, Richard Ned. Professor of Government and director of the Peace Studies Program, Cornell University; author of many works on international crises, including several on the Cuban missile crisis, and on psychological stress in crisis decisionmaking. His *Between Peace and War* (1981) is widely regarded as the most important work in English on international crises. More than any other individual, Lebow has shifted the focus in American political science from the study of the deeper causes of wars to the precipitating causes as they manifest themselves in crises.

MAY, Ernest R. Charles Warren Professor of History, Harvard University, and co-director of the Nuclear History Program at the John F. Kennedy School of Government, Harvard University; author of works on American diplomatic history, the Monroe Doctrine, intelligence assessment, the uses of history for decisionmakers, and the Vietnam War. May brings to the study of the Cuban missile crisis a breadth of knowledge and familiarity with nuclear policymaking that is without equal. Of his many works, *The "Lessons" of History* (1973) is probably the most controversial and most pertinent to the crisis; he holds that the conduct of the Vietnam War was in part a function of Lyndon Johnson's errant reading of the lessons of October 1962.

NEUSTADT, Richard E. Douglas Dillon Professor of Government, Harvard University; White House staff member under President Truman; founding director of Harvard's Institute of Politics; co-director of the White House transition team of President-elect Kennedy; author of works on the Presidency, bureaucratic constraints on Presidential decisionmaking, and the uses of history for political decisionmaking. His book *Presidential Power* (1960) had a significant impact on Kennedy. As one of the nation's foremost students of the Presidency, Neustadt has a special interest in the Cuban missile crisis, in which, as he has written, the world and the Presidency moved into a "new dimension of risk."

NYE, Joseph S., Jr. Director of the Center for Science and International Affairs, and Dillon Professor of International Relations, Harvard University; Deputy Under Secretary of State under President Carter; author of many works on international political economy, international organization, energy and security, and ethical and strategic aspects of reducing the risk of nuclear war. Nye is widely known for his emphasis on inadvertent causes of wars. He was moderator of the Hawk's Cay and Cambridge conferences.

SAGAN, Scott D. Assistant Professor of Political Science, Stanford University; author of works on nuclear strategy and nuclear crises. His pioneering work on alerts during the Cuban missile crisis has opened up a whole new area of inquiry, shedding light on the relationship between Presidential decisionmaking and the operational details of crisis management.

SCHELLING, Thomas C.   Lucius N. Littauer Professor of Political Economy and director of the Institute for the Study of Smoking Behavior, John F. Kennedy School of Government, Harvard University; consultant to the Department of Defense during the Kennedy and the Johnson Administrations. Schelling is widely regarded as an intellectual founding father of nuclear strategy (*The Strategy of Conflict*, 1960), arms control (*Strategy and Arms Control*, with Morton Halperin, 1961), and the study of nuclear crises (*Arms and Influence*, 1966).

TAUBMAN, William.   Professor of Political Science, Amherst College; author of works on Soviet foreign policy, Soviet governance and culture, and a forthcoming work on the Soviet Union during the Khrushchev years. His *Stalin's American Policy* (1982) is the standard work on the subject and is required reading for anyone seeking informed analysis of the tradition inherited by Nikita Khrushchev.

TRACHTENBERG, Marc.   Associate Professor of History, University of Pennsylvania; author of works on World War I, the history of nuclear strategy, and the Cuban missile crisis. Trachtenberg was instrumental in publishing the edited transcript of the tapes of the October 16, 1962, meeting of President Kennedy and his advisors, and his familiarity with archival sources concerned with American defense planning makes him one of the most knowledgeable students of the crisis.

URY, William L.   Research Fellow, Center for Science and International Affairs, Harvard University; author of works on negotiation and on communication in crisis. Ury has been instrumental in U.S.–Soviet negotiations on risk-reduction centers, a subject he takes up in *Beyond the Hotline* (1985).

WELCH, David A.   Research Fellow, Center for Science and International Affairs, Harvard University; author of works on internationalism and on the Cuban missile crisis. His research interests include the relationship between international conflict and theories of justice.

Authors' Note

[　　]	Information or elaboration supplied by the editor.
. . . or	A segment of speaker's remarks has been omitted by the editor.
. . . . . or	The remarks of at least one speaker have been omitted by the editor.
—	Speaker has trailed off or been interrupted.
*	Footnotes at the bottom of the page: commentary supplied by the participants after a review of the transcript, and identifications. All purely documentary references, and all commentary by the authors, may be found in the endnotes.

PART ONE

Scholars
and Policymakers

The historian, investigating any event in the past, makes a distinction
between what may be called the outside and the inside of an event. . . .
His work may begin by discovering the outside of an event, but it can
never end there; he must always remember that the event was an action;
and that his main task is to think himself into this action, to discern the
thought of its agent.

R. G. COLLINGWOOD
The Idea of History

CHAPTER

I

The Hawk's Cay Conference

In March 1987, a group of scholars and former Kennedy Administration officials gathered at Hawk's Cay, Florida, to discuss the Cuban missile crisis on the eve of its twenty-fifth anniversary.[1] Among the participants were several members of President Kennedy's ExComm, the Executive Committee of the National Security Council, the group convened to advise the President on the conduct of the crisis. Also present were several scholars noted for their work on crisis management in general and the Cuban missile crisis in particular. The purpose of the meeting was to bring together those who know about the crisis primarily from books and those who lived through it in positions of responsibility, to engage each other in a discussion of the causes, conduct, and resolution of the crisis, with particular emphasis on the lessons it holds for the future.[2]

The conference began on Thursday evening, March 5, with welcoming ceremonies hosted by Graham Allison, dean of the Kennedy School of Government. Following brief introductory remarks by each participant, the lights were dimmed for a screening of a half-hour documentary put together by Charles Collingwood of CBS News entitled *Anatomy of a Crisis*, which had aired on Sunday, October 28, 1962—the day Chairman Nikita Khrushchev and President John F. Kennedy agreed to terms that brought the crisis to an end.

Collingwood's report, with its breathless sense of relief at the end of a crisis concluded only hours before, captured the feeling of nuclear danger as no written or verbal summary could have done. For most participants, it provided a chance to relive the missile crisis as they had the first time: through the eye of the television camera, and through the minds of the men who struggled to see what it all might mean. For a few, the former members of the ExComm, it was a chance to see the crisis from the other side of the camera for a change, watching themselves perform in front of newsmen, twenty-five years later. From the controlled, authoritative tone of President Kennedy's announcement of the discovery of Soviet missiles in Cuba to the urgency of journalists pressing Administration spokesmen for information, from the drama of American forces on full alert in the Caribbean to the confrontation between Ambassadors Adlai Stevenson and Valerian Zorin in the United Nations Security Council, those thirteen dramatic days in October 1962 were brought back to life in a banquet room at a resort in the Florida Keys. The palpable tension was broken only by the ironic comedy of the commercials hawking remedies for "iron-poor blood" and "simple nervous tension."

Collingwood's report was an impressive effort, given the extreme time constraints under which it was prepared, but it nonetheless put forward an interpretation of events that many in the room found objectionable and that immediately pointed up major differences of opinion among both the scholars present and those who had served in the Kennedy Administration at the time. Collingwood's view of what caused the Cuban missile crisis was captured concisely in the following statement:

> The United States could brook the hirsute harangues of a Castro; it could not brook the presence of Soviet missiles capable of changing the whole balance of power. Although Russia has long-range missiles capable of reaching every part of the United States, it does not have enough of them to wipe out our retaliatory power. But the addition of medium- and intermediate-range weapons in Cuba would give Russia vastly more first-strike power; enough, perhaps, to neutralize our ability to wipe out Russia in return. And it is this ability which is our deterrent. It was on the basis of such calculations, involving the very essence of power, that President Kennedy directly challenged the Soviet Union.

While viewers watched film clips of American reinforcements unloading at the American base at Guantánamo, in southeastern Cuba, Collingwood described the American response to the missiles as "an undeniable indication that we had power, that we did not lack nerve, that we had weapons and that we did not lack the will to use them."

The picture Collingwood painted was one of a President primarily concerned with maintaining a favorable strategic nuclear balance and willing to go to war to do so. Collingwood's description of events left no doubt that he believed war with the Soviet Union was narrowly averted—President Kennedy, presumably, was on the verge of launching it—only by what he obviously believed was Khrushchev's capitulation at the eleventh hour. This interpretation of events prompted an immediate reaction from several of the conference participants. Robert McNamara adamantly declared that "the assumption that the strategic nuclear balance (or 'imbalance') mattered in any way was wrong."

As far as I am concerned, it made *no* difference. Now, I don't recall that we had any hard evidence that there were Soviet warheads in Cuba, though I suppose it is likely they were there; but what difference would the extra forty have made to the overall balance? If my memory serves me correctly, we had some five thousand strategic nuclear warheads as against their three hundred. Can anyone seriously tell me that their having 340 would have made any difference? The military balance wasn't changed. I didn't believe it then, and I don't believe it now.

When you try to understand something like this, you have to begin with an understanding of what the problem is. Contrary to what Collingwood said, the problem was *not* a change in the strategic balance.

Immediately, Douglas Dillon disagreed with McNamara. "All I can remember is how we felt at the time. *I* felt—and so did the Joint Chiefs of Staff—that there *was* a change in the strategic balance." Theodore Sorensen agreed with McNamara, noting that "the President never mentioned a shift in the balance of power as his reason for wanting the missiles out. He never said it in any of his speeches, and as far as I know, he never said it in any of our meetings."

Sorensen, perhaps concerned that the discussion would turn prematurely to questions of lessons, said: "Beware of using Cuba as a precedent in the future; we live in a different world now, with a different role for military force, a different role for the President of the United States. We need to be very careful about making easy judgments about the present and the future based on a very different past." Dillon agreed: "It's a *totally* different world today, and as far as I can see, the Cuban missile crisis has little relevance in today's world."

At this point, Richard Neustadt noted that "the program does not merely invite us to consider Cuba as a *precedent*." Then, reminding everyone present of the central reason for gathering at Hawk's Cay, Neustadt said:

This is perhaps the last opportunity for researchers interested in the Cuban missile crisis—and what it means for us today and down the road—to deal face-to-face with those of you who went through

the thirteen days. I don't know if there will ever be such an opportunity again, but I don't think it's very likely. The researchers
have come here with the assumption that there remain things to
learn from your experience.

Now, my belief is that you people did not know at the time that
the crisis was going to go thirteen days until it was over. You are
the *only* people we have access to who have had to face the problem
of escalation in a nuclear crisis. You are the only people who on
day 11 or 12 had to think seriously about the following week as
people immediately consulting the country's principal decisionmaker. You are the only people there are to talk to about the
perceptions, the feelings, the psychology, and the concerns of people in that kind of position. We can argue about this later, but it
is just not so that this was a unique event. For any future leader
who has to face the prospect of a crisis escalating out of hand, you
have valuable lessons to offer.

Neustadt's remarks struck a responsive chord in McNamara:

To support Dick on that, let me say that the Cuban missile crisis
was not unique in two respects. First, we live in a world of fifty
thousand nuclear warheads. Two or ten or fifty would destroy
millions of American citizens. This was just as true then as it is
now, so this is common thread number one. Second, our country
has allowed, and presumably will continue to allow, presidents of
Ford Motor Company to be Secretary of Defense. What kind of
a qualification for the job is that? [Laughter.] At least people like
Helmut Schmidt* and Denis Healey† in a parliamentary system
have the chance to rise through government to positions of power
with some experience and expertise in defense and security matters
under their belts. But Americans are always putting people in
positions of high authority and responsibility who have almost
nothing in the way of prior qualifications, and that carries its risks.[3]

Arthur Schlesinger noted that President Kennedy himself was concerned
that people might draw the wrong lessons from the event—he worried
especially that people would conclude: Just be tough with the Russians,
and they will back down. Kennedy believed his policy had worked for
three reasons. First, the United States had overwhelming local conventional superiority; second, Soviet security was not at stake in Cuba, so

---

* Former Chancellor of the Federal Republic of Germany.
† Former leader of the British Labour Party.

they could afford to back down if necessary; and third, "they did not have a case they could plausibly sustain before the world."[4]

Sorensen then clarified his point of view: "I didn't say that there are absolutely *no* lessons to be learned. But there are several misconceptions about what occurred, and the wrong lessons have been drawn as a result. I don't believe, for example, that we were *ever* set for an immediate air strike or invasion, and that is one of the things that I would like discussed here this weekend." McNamara agreed with this emphatically: "Ted's right. The quarantine had only begun to do its work. There was a lot more we could have done with it, if necessary. For example, we could have added POL [petroleum, oil, and lubricants] to the embargo list, and this would have strangled Cuba economically. There's no denying that the pressure was on for a military confrontation, but I think we could have avoided it, and I believe the President would have. We still had other options."

As the conversation moved on, George Ball indicated his agreement with McNamara on the unimportance of the strategic balance. "The President and all the others agreed that the balance of power hadn't changed significantly. But the point was that the Soviets had done this thing deceitfully and surreptitiously. *This* was what we couldn't accept, not the change in the balance of power."[5] Ball was even more interested in the practical lessons the event held for crisis management, and the differences between the world of 1962 and of today.

> We didn't react immediately, of course, and that's very important. Today, the temptation is always to react immediately. If we had done that then, there's no doubt in my mind that the crisis would have unfolded differently. We had an entire week to think about things. I don't know if that could be done today; but we kept the secret and took the time to make a careful dissection of the problem and the various options before us. Some shifted their positions, others maintained their original views throughout—but most of us felt that we had no business taking an irretrievable action. The quarantine was not irretrievable, and the most important lesson of all was the importance of that.

Abram Chayes was more interested in a larger point about deterrence:

> The main lesson as I see it is this. We talk an awful lot about the American conventional and nuclear superiority and its importance in forcing the outcome. If we'd had that, we could have just invaded and overwhelmed Cuba. Well, why didn't we? It was because a small, ragtail nuclear deterrent on the other side was a powerful

deterrent to us. What impressed me was how worried we were
that one or two nuclear weapons might land on the United States
and how inhibiting that was on what we might have done. So when
people talk today about superiority, I think back on what the
President rightly worried about back then: the idea of one or two
nuclear weapons falling on the United States.

As the discussion wound down, the participants were left with a number
of issues to ponder for the conference's formal sessions, and were prepared to look once again at the most dangerous event of the nuclear
age.

Friday, March 6, 1987—Morning—Causes

JOSEPH NYE: . . . Before we open things up for a more general discussion on each topic, we will have a brief introduction of ten minutes
or less to set up the issue. The discussion is what we are primarily
interested in, but the initial remarks will help us organize our treatment.

The agenda orders a very complex subject. This morning, we will be
talking about the causes of the crisis; after lunch, we will turn to the
events of the first week; tomorrow morning we will be looking at the
second, or public week of the crisis; tomorrow afternoon we will discuss
the psychological aspects, what is referred to in the agenda as "the look
and feel of nuclear danger"; and we will wrap things up on Sunday
morning with a discussion of the lessons and implications of the crisis,
which we touched on last night. . . .

Unless there are any comments or questions, I propose that we turn
to Ernie May to make a few introductory remarks about some of the
puzzles that still exist with respect to the causes of the Cuban missile
crisis.

ERNEST MAY: There will be two parts to my introduction here. The
first concerns questions touched on last night; and the second concerns
several specific questions that pertain to the causes of the crisis itself.

With respect to the first, we can ask two things. First, is there anything
to learn from the crisis? And second, would it matter if there were?
Clearly the answer to the former is yes. . . . This group and this format
is particularly well suited to the search for answers to lingering questions,
because it can counteract the negative tendency, as witnesses on the
stand demonstrate, to recall *how you have told the story in the past*,
instead of what actually happened. Here we can test each of your recollections against those of others, improving collectively on the accuracy

of individual memory. Clearly, too, the answer to the latter is yes. It is true that conditions are very different today: the political situation is different; the military situation is different—there are even differences in how political events were covered, and with significant effects. . . . These are all very real changes—but they do not mean that we have nothing to learn from the Cuban missile crisis, an event considerably less remote than the wars between Athens and Sparta in the fifth century B.C., which we still learn from today.

Among the specific questions about the causes of the crisis are these: What did you *think* and *feel* about what did happen or what was going to happen? Could you have anticipated the Soviet move? Is there any way you could have avoided surprise? Would a different understanding of the Soviet Union have helped? . . . I hope we can entertain different suppositions about what was happening in the U.S.S.R. in 1962, and I hope we can discern what it was that you were all *thinking* was happening there, and why.

Take the argument Herb Dinerstein has made: that Khrushchev thought he had an edge and thought he could act with impunity.[6] Now, I don't believe that Washington really thought in these terms at all. American military supremacy was clear to *us*, and we thought it was clear to *them*, and expected them to act accordingly. What were your presumptions on this?

On developments in Cuba: Some predicted the Soviets *would* put missiles there—John McCone* and Senator Keating,† for example, just to name the two most prominent. Where did they get their information? Why didn't the Administration believe them? In testimony, Admiral Anderson‡ asserts that he knew in *September* that the Soviets were putting missiles in Cuba, possibly because of information he had through the Navy's own intelligence-gathering network, since disbanded. What information was the Administration going on? What information was ignored?[7] . . .

NYE: Arthur, do you want to start things off?

ARTHUR SCHLESINGER: I saw the President at ten o'clock Monday morning [October 22]. He told me he thought it odd that our intelligence community hadn't anticipated the Soviet move earlier. Of course, one reason they hadn't is that they didn't believe Khrushchev would be so stupid as to do something which as much as invited an invasion. The President thought that the Soviet Union had done it for three reasons: that it would help bring Russia and China closer together; that it would

---

* Director of the Central Intelligence Agency.
† Senator Kenneth Keating (R–N.Y.).
‡ Admiral George Anderson, Chief of Naval Operations.

radically redefine the setting in which the Berlin issue would be reopened after the election; and that it would deal the United States a tremendous political blow. I said that the Russians must have thought we would not respond. The President said they had us either way. If we did nothing, we would be dead. If we reacted, they hoped to have us in an embarrassed and exposed position, whether with regard to Berlin or Turkey or the UN.[8]

Looking back, it seems to me that the most plausible reason Khrushchev had for putting missiles in Cuba was to repair his own missile gap. Castro didn't want nuclear missiles, as he told me when I spoke with him a year and a half ago. He was only persuaded to accept them on the grounds of socialist solidarity, and he was furious about not being consulted on their withdrawal. It seems that Khrushchev saw the missiles as a quick fix that would, in addition, put him in a better position to reopen the Berlin question.

On the balance-of-power issue, let me just say that while the missiles might not have had much effect on the overall U.S.–Soviet military balance, they had a considerable effect on the world *political* balance. The emplacement of nuclear missiles in Cuba would prove the Soviet ability to act with impunity in the very heart of the American zone of vital interest—a victory of great significance for the Kremlin, which saw the world in terms of spheres of influence and inflexibly guarded its own. Both Khrushchev (in his memoirs) and Mikoyan* (in a secret meeting with bloc diplomats in Washington after the crisis) described the missile emplacement as an effort to redress the balance of power.[9] It was a bold move into the American political sphere which, had it worked, would have dealt a severe blow to the American position worldwide. The simple calculus of military power wasn't the only thing that mattered.

. . . . .

THEODORE SORENSEN: The only honest answer I have is: "I don't know now, and I didn't know then." None of us knew. We could only speculate about what Khrushchev was up to. We talked about a quick fix, but that didn't make much sense of Khrushchev's attempt to smuggle the missiles in there surreptitiously. He could have signed an agreement with Cuba and announced his intention to install missiles openly, and this would have severely constrained our ability to respond. But the surreptitiousness implied that he had some other motive. We didn't know what it was, and we could only speculate. As a result, we had to behave with extreme prudence.

---

* Anastas I. Mikoyan, Soviet First Deputy Premier.

NYE: Bob?

ROBERT MCNAMARA: . . . I don't know why the Soviets did what they did. Ted's right. But we should recognize that we didn't then (and we don't today) give much thought to how Moscow will read what we are doing. We'd carried out the Bay of Pigs operation never intending to use American military force—but the Kremlin didn't know that. We were running covert operations against Castro. We'd convinced them we were actively trying to overthrow the Cuban regime. We never had put adequate emphasis on how the Soviets were interpreting our actions and how they might respond.

I want to mention, too, that our reaction to the so-called missile gap in the fifties was a massive buildup of our own. By the time of the Cuban missile crisis, we had clear numerical superiority and we were *still* building up. People in the Pentagon were even talking about a first strike. In March of 1961, I went out to look at the SIOP* and found that there were four regular options, plus a fifth called 1(a) which was a first-strike plan. LeMay† talked openly about a first strike against the Soviet Union if the Russians ever backed us into a corner. In November 1962, I received a memo from the Air Force advocating budget allocations for enhancing first-strike capability. So the Soviets may well have believed we were seeking Castro's overthrow *plus* a first-strike capability. This may have led them to do what they did in Cuba.

. . . . .

GRAHAM ALLISON: Bob, let me push you on the American buildup, which is certainly a very important point here. We don't yet know all the details of American capabilities, but Scott Sagan has managed to get the SIOP-62 briefing declassified, and among the things discussed in it is the possibility of the United States going first.[10] The prospects of a successful American first strike were thought at the time to have been pretty good: there seemed to have been at least a reasonable possibility that the United States would have suffered *no* casualties.[11] So even though we weren't thinking much about the Soviet reaction, we knew there was a missile gap—this time in our favor—and we still expanded. Why?

MCNAMARA: Let me first say that I don't believe that the President or I *ever* thought that we would launch a first strike under *any* circumstances. Putting moral issues aside for a moment, there was no reasonable chance that we could get away with a first strike unscathed. We

---

* Single Integrated Operational Plan, the American master nuclear-war plan.
† General Curtis LeMay, Air Force Chief of Staff.

simply didn't know where all of the Soviet warheads were. And don't forget that our accuracy then wasn't what it is today. Even if we put ten warheads on each target, we didn't have a very high probability of getting *all* of the Soviets' nuclear forces.*

Instead of ordering the SIOP plans totally reworked, we insisted on a withholding and retargeting capability. We knew (but didn't tell the military) that we would never use the SIOP plans as they were formulated. But the Soviets, of course, had no way of knowing this.

Why were we still building up? Because the lead time for most weapon programs is five to seven years, and we had to anticipate what the Soviets would have in 1967 or 1968. One of the big weaknesses of our planning was the way in which we made that estimate. We asked the CIA to figure out what the Soviets would have by then, and they did it by assuming that the Soviets would use their full capacity at full tilt, which of course they didn't. So by 1967 we had built to meet a threat that wasn't nearly as great as we thought it would be. We were left with a massive numerical advantage.[12] . . .

. . . . .

DOUGLAS DILLON: I would like to make an historical note about the Soviet reaction to the Bay of Pigs. I didn't know anything about the planning for the operation after January 1961, but prior to that I was in charge of the conceptual planning at the State Department. Part of the original plan was that we would use our own naval air in support of the landing if the initial air strikes by the Cuban invaders did not succeed in destroying Castro's Air Force. The Soviets could have become aware of this intention of ours which we never went through with even though we had carriers in place. This could well have given the Soviets a reason to jump to the mistaken conclusion that Kennedy was weak.

On this question of the strategic balance—our five thousand warheads against their three hundred—what we should really be paying attention to is the number each could *deliver* on the other. Before the Soviets put missiles in Cuba, it was doubtful whether they could deliver any warheads from Soviet territory at all. So while the Cuban installations didn't add very much to their numbers or didn't change the overall balance very much, my impression at the time was that they radically altered

---

* [Scott Sagan adds:] General Lyman Lemnitzer, chairman of the Joint Chiefs of Staff, reported to President Kennedy on September 13, 1961, that execution of SIOP-62 "should permit the U.S. to prevail in [the] event of general nuclear war." Lemnitzer also noted, however, that "under any circumstances—even a preemptive attack by the U.S.—it would be expected that some portion of the Soviet long-range nuclear force would strike the United States." See "SIOP-62 Briefing," *International Security*, Vol. 12, No. 1 (Summer 1987), pp. 50–51.

the numbers of *deliverable* warheads, and in that sense, they significantly increased Soviet capability.

NYE: Let's spend a little time trying to nail down this factual issue. Just how much did the Soviet move in Cuba add to their capability? . . .

RAYMOND GARTHOFF: At the time, the Soviets had forty-four ICBMs,* and ninety-seven SLBMs† mounted on diesel-powered submarines. These SLBMs were rather short-range weapons, and in order to fire them, the subs had to surface, making them extremely vulnerable. More-over, at the time of the Cuban missile crisis, these were deployed out of range and should therefore be discounted. They also had 155 heavy bombers, mostly [Mya-4] Bisons and [Tu-95] Bears, and a fairly large number of medium-range bombers, but these were constrained opera-tionally because they would have had to go through forward bases in the Arctic that were severely limited in the numbers of aircraft they could handle and service at any one time.‡

On the other side, the American forces were literally growing daily. At the climax of the crisis, we had 156 ICBMs, 144 Polaris SLBMs, 1,300 strategic bombers—many of which were medium-range aircraft, but with a thousand tankers for midflight refueling. All told, we had several thousand generated weapons. The discrepancy in forces was on the order of what Bob has already said.

The memorandum on the military significance of the missiles in Cuba that I submitted to the ExComm on the 27th of October[13] noted that 40 percent of all American bombers were within range of the missiles in Cuba, and because of the limited number of Soviet ICBMs, this meant that the missiles in Cuba theoretically, in a successful first strike, could have reduced our SIOP force by 30 percent. But this still would have left us with a massive retaliatory attack capability against the U.S.S.R., even though, in the sense I have just indicated, the missiles in Cuba added appreciably to Soviet capabilities.

The main effect of the Cuban deployment was on perceptions. It seemed to us to have been intended largely to make up for the earlier missile gap bluff, which Deputy Secretary of Defense Roswell Gilpatric's speech of October 21, 1961, had called them on.

NYE: To summarize, is it correct to say that the ICBM number is the most significant, and that while the Cuban deployment effectively dou-bled the Soviet missile force, it still didn't give them a first-strike ca-pability? Scott?

---

* Inter-continental ballistic missiles.
† Submarine-launched ballistic missiles.
‡ For further discussion, see the Afterword, pp. 328–29.

SCOTT SAGAN: I think that the bombers are in fact more important than the missiles here, because both sides relied on them more heavily. Remember that there were only forty-six SAC bases in the continental U.S. If the Soviets had managed to get the SS-5 IRBMs* installed, these missiles could have covered almost all the bases. They couldn't have covered all the SAC bombers if they were dispersed or more highly alerted, but it still looked like a significant threat to our bomber force, and this is what the Joint Chiefs worried about.†

MCNAMARA: But don't forget the airborne alert. We had planes flying around the clock—

SAGAN: Only twelve.

MCNAMARA: But we *could* have kept 150 bombers in the air during an alert almost indefinitely. The Chiefs and I had an ongoing disagreement on this.

. . . . .

GARTHOFF: A Soviet first strike without the Cuban missiles at *best* could have destroyed four hundred or five hundred of the total five thousand warheads in the American strategic nuclear arsenal. With the Cuban missiles, at best they could have destroyed 80 to 85 percent, still leaving something more than five hundred American strategic weapons. If that is the *best* they could have done even after a fully successful first strike, it couldn't have been very comforting to the Soviets. The balance was changed greatly by the Cuban missiles, but the end result was still the same. The United States in either case had a considerable nuclear advantage.

. . . . .

ALLISON: The President had a "reasonable" prospect under SIOP 1(a) of "getting them all" on a first strike, at least according to the military folks. Penkovsky‡ had been giving us hard information on Soviet bases at least until September 1962. But *after* the Soviets put MRBMs and IRBMs in Cuba, things are no longer so easy. So, clearly, from the

---

* Intermediate-range ballistic missiles.
† [Scott Sagan adds:] According to a declassified Air Force history, General Thomas Power, Commander-in-Chief of SAC, referred to "the critical nature of the Soviet threat from Cuba" in the following manner: "The deterrent power of SAC had depended upon warning of sufficient length to launch the ground alert force. The Soviet missiles on Cuban soil had posed an immediate threat to this capability." *Air Force Response to the Cuban Crisis*, USAF Historical Division Liaison Office, Headquarters USAF, Center for Air Force History, p. 14.
‡ Colonel Oleg Penkovsky, an officer in Soviet Military Intelligence, who had been working for American and British intelligence until his arrest during the Cuban missile crisis.

position of the SAC planner and the Joint Chiefs of Staff, the Cuban move looks very, very big.

GARTHOFF: I remember a conversation I had with a three-star general during the crisis who said that we could be quite sure of getting a percentage of the Soviet strategic forces in the high nineties if we went first. So Graham is right; that was a view expressed to me by people at the time. . . .

. . . . .

ALEXANDER GEORGE: I have a question: To what extent did the President take into account the possible casualties in *Europe*? We know a very great deal about his concern for American casualties, but no one has ever said very much about the Europeans. What of the Soviets' capability for "hostage deterrence" there? Can any of you remember any consideration of this?

McNAMARA: SIOP 1(a) was a totally unreal war plan. If we had used it, it would have led to unacceptably high casualties both in Europe and the United States. It called, for example, for huge strikes on Eastern Europe to take out air defenses, and the Soviets could have inflicted massive casualties on Western Europe—much more than on the U.S.—in return. SIOP 1(a) was totally unreasonable *before* Cuba, and it was totally unreal *after* Cuba. . . . Does anyone believe that a President or a Secretary of Defense would be willing to permit thirty warheads to fall on the United States? No way! And for that reason, neither we nor the Soviets would have acted any differently before or after the Cuban deployment.

NYE: To return to Ernie's questions, let's ask why we were wrong on our estimates of Soviet behavior and why there were several apparent intelligence failures.[14] George?

GEORGE BALL: There is a problem of method here. We are putting ourselves in the shoes of the Soviet leadership and assuming that they had the same information that we have now. I don't believe they had it, or that they went through a profound and careful decisionmaking process before they made their decision to put missiles in Cuba.

Let's face it, Khrushchev was not an elegant thinker. He was very crude in his approach to these questions. He had an impression that Kennedy was weak, and that he was young; this was confirmed in Berlin and by the Bay of Pigs. So, sitting in the Kremlin, suspicious and vindictive, he figured that he could teach this young man a lesson. The fact that we didn't do what he thought we would do in the Bay of Pigs, despite his awareness of massive American nuclear superiority, led him to believe that he could bring the U.S. down a peg, strengthen his own position with respect to China, and improve his standing in the Politburo with one bold stroke. I can't imagine Brezhnev doing this, can you?— it just wouldn't have been in character. But Khrushchev was a man very sure of himself and not averse to an audacious gamble. He may have been thinking that the least he could get out of it was a humiliation of the United States, or a tit-for-tat deal on the American missiles in Turkey.[15]

I say all this to challenge the assumption that has been lurking in the background here that this was an act done in an atmosphere of cool rationality by a sophisticated man. I don't think it was.

MAY: That's a very good post-hoc reconstruction of what was going on; but was anybody thinking that way at the time?

BALL: Not before the missiles were placed in Cuba; but during the crisis, I remember very well that we thought Khrushchev was unpredictable, that he was a loose cannon, and that he was clearly demonstrating his audacity.

. . . . .

RICHARD NED LEBOW: As I look over the evidence, it becomes less and less clear to me why Khrushchev did this. All of the claims that he was impressed by Kennedy's youth, his weakness, his behavior in the Bay of Pigs, in Berlin, and so on, are either not supported by the evidence or the evidence cuts both ways. On the question of Kennedy's youth, the only remark we have of Khrushchev's on the subject is that "Kennedy is young and young people do brash things."[16] Brashness isn't weakness, and it makes Kennedy look too unpredictable for Khrushchev to form any firm expectation of his reaction to Cuban missiles. On Vienna, Khrushchev summarized it as a tough meeting, and even expressed admiration for Kennedy's agility. Only later did Scotty Reston* pick weakness out of this—

BALL: That's not true. We all thought that Khrushchev saw him as young and weak.

LEBOW: Hang on just a moment. On the Bay of Pigs, it didn't take an astute analyst to know that this was an Achilles' heel for Kennedy politically, and that a second Cuba would have to be different.

BALL: *Sophisticated* Russians might have thought that way, but not necessarily Khrushchev.

---

* James Reston, columnist for *The New York Times*.

LEBOW: But subsequent writing confirms the view that we were projecting our own views of Kennedy's weakness on Russian action without justification.

BALL: I was merely challenging the assumption of Khrushchev's rationality, that's all.

. . . . .

SORENSEN: George is right that Khrushchev didn't know all of the details of the military balance the way we do. But George is wrong that Khrushchev was acting out of a perception of American weakness.[17] At Vienna, as the transcript shows, Kennedy gave as well as he got throughout. So that wasn't it; but Khrushchev still put missiles in Cuba, and it sure surprised all of us. The Sovietologists in 1962 were convinced that the Soviets would never put missiles outside the Soviet Union.

. . . . .

WILLIAM TAUBMAN: Well, it wasn't entirely accidental that nobody predicted this move. George Ball is right; Khrushchev *was* different.

And yet, perfect 20/20 hindsight shows that Khrushchev had many reasons to put missiles in Cuba. . . . Look at the range of foreign policy objectives Khrushchev could have been pursuing—adjusting the nuclear balance, forcing a satisfactory solution to the Berlin problem, scoring points with the Chinese, and defending Cuba—but look also at Khrushchev's domestic political dilemma. . . . The key to Khrushchev's domestic situation was the problem of de-Stalinization and all of the risks that it entailed for his own position. In addition, he embarked in a half-baked way on a variety of other far-reaching reforms, and met considerable opposition and resistance from the system. By 1962, he had made an absolute mess of it, and his authority (though not yet his power) was eroding as a result.[18] He was in search of foreign-policy victories, though not only for the domestic political reason of needing to shore up his position—he also felt the ideological pressure of the historical march of socialism, the need for an expansion of Soviet influence, and the importance of making the world milieu safe for his domestic program.

Europe in general and Berlin in particular were the places he sought his foreign-policy victories. Time and time again he was stymied; he didn't get his '58 summit; the May 1960 Paris summit collapsed; in the spring of 1961 he failed to get movement from the Kennedy Administration on Berlin, which proved even less willing than the Eisenhower Administration to reach an agreement; the Berlin Wall was a mixed blessing—it stopped the flow of refugees, but Khrushchev still had to drop his ultimatum about signing a German peace treaty; the 1962 talks on the future of Germany and Berlin went nowhere; his relations with China were going very badly; Soviet agriculture was on the rocks—the man was absolutely *desperate* for a success.[19]

Here his uniqueness as a person comes in. He was hyperactive, he had an abiding faith in his power of persuasion, and he had a massive inferiority complex that he was trying to overcome. His character both contributed to his problems and shaped the solutions he devised. As he saw it, the answer to several of his problems lay in Cuba. He undertook a bold gamble, and probably had in mind both maximum and minimum goals that he honestly thought he had a reasonable chance of achieving. What he had hoped to do was come to the United States in November with Cuban missiles in his back pocket, and make a stunning foreign-policy victory out of it. How did he perceive the United States and President Kennedy? He felt pressured and frustrated by the American military buildup, but thought he could get away with putting missiles in Cuba partly because of his analysis of Kennedy's character.

To the extent that Khrushchev is a unique figure in Soviet history, we are clearly going to have to be careful about the lessons we draw from this episode. But there are aspects of the event and of Khrushchev's position which are and were repeatable, and from which we can probably draw valid conclusions for future purposes. Not the least of these is the dilemma of the reformer in the Soviet system and some of the pressures that role exerts on foreign-policy making—something we are seeing being played out today.

NYE: Let me ask the other Sovietologists if Bill speaks the truth.

ARNOLD HORELICK: I just don't know. Khrushchev's discomfiture was undoubtedly an important factor; he was aware that his predicament with respect to the strategic balance was of his own making, because of the Sputnik bluff, pretending that the U.S.S.R. had near-term operational ICBM capability long before the United States. I suppose he had plenty of domestic political reasons to try what he did. It wasn't that the Agency [CIA] misread things; it was that they were being systematically misled. Khrushchev was personally very vulnerable. When we blasted the missile gap myth, we seriously deflated his reputation.

I remember President Kennedy saying in a *Washington Post* interview after the Cuban missile crisis that he didn't think Khrushchev would put missiles in Cuba because it was imprudent—and it was.[20] We simply misjudged Khrushchev's capacity to make mistakes and to delude himself.

I've thought about this question since 1962, and I have concluded that there is no entirely plausible explanation of why the Soviets did what they did. All rationales seem to me relevant to one degree or another.

Different parts of the Soviet government and different organizations probably came to support the decision for quite different reasons, and I don't know if we'll ever be able to disentangle all of the motivations.[21]

I think that the main question from the Soviet point of view is the one Bob McNamara mentioned last night: Did the Soviets perceive a change in the balance of power as a result of the deployment? Ray Garthoff persuades me on this. I don't think the Soviets thought the United States would be inhibited from using its nuclear capability for humane reasons; they simply thought it unacceptable that the United States should have a first-strike capability, especially after we became aware of our superiority and let them know it.

As far as I am concerned, the essential calculation in the question of the balance was prompt ICBM capability, not bombers. And they knew even more about their vulnerabilities in this department than we did. Even a generated Soviet ICBM force may have required more preparation than they had time for if the Americans were attempting a first strike, and they might not have been able to get off a launch before their forces were hit. This clearly worried them. So it isn't surprising to me that Khrushchev thought missiles in Cuba would be useful. What is surprising is that they thought they could get away with it surreptitiously. Of course, we all know that the way they deployed their missiles doesn't appear to make any sense if they really wanted to spring a fait accompli on the world; Graham Allison has a pretty persuasive account of why they deployed in the way they did, enabling us to spot their preparations—it was probably just because they were following standard operating procedures for installing missile sites.[22] Of course, if some of the missiles were operational, there were payoffs to be had from the ambiguity of who controlled them. Cuban control would surely have been more deterrent than Soviet control.

So, in my judgment, even after the passage of time, the Soviet anxiety about the deteriorating balance had reached a point of both military and political danger. Khrushchev seized on this way as the best way to correct the problem in the short term.

· · · · ·

MCNAMARA: In their mind, they were taking countermeasures to forestall a possible American preemption. What they were really after was an improvement in crisis stability.* I suppose it's ironic that that led to a crisis, but the lesson from that applies today.

· · · · ·

---

* Crisis stability is a condition where neither side has a decisive military incentive to attack first.

GARTHOFF: I agree with Bill Taubman's sketch of the political background in Moscow, and I agree with Arnold Horelick's sketch of the
geopolitical situation. I am inclined to think that the Soviets' overriding
desire was to redress a serious *publicly revealed* strategic imbalance in
order to improve their position on other domestic and foreign policy
issues, Berlin possibly being foremost among them. Incidentally, the
fact that nothing came of Berlin during and after the crisis is really quite
interesting. The non-Berlin crisis of 1963 is in my opinion one important
overlooked consequence of the Cuban missile crisis.

I think, though, that I would emphasize Khrushchev's strong personal
stake in improving the Soviet position, because he was the one that had
got them in the predicament in the first place. His memoirs, though
suspect on several points throughout, are really quite revealing and quite
useful if we take account of the very strong personal interests and biases
that pervade them, as well as the fact that his recollections were fading
in certain respects when he wrote them. But there are some very useful
clues in there about what was going on. One of the things I think we
should credit is his claim that the idea to install missiles in Cuba was
his personal one, though he mentions that he canvassed the views of
others and that there was discussion and argument on the subject. Reading between the lines, I think it makes sense to say that his primary
motivation was to improve the Soviet military position and his own
standing—there is one particularly interesting reference there to a
change in the correlation of forces. We also know that Mikoyan briefed
Warsaw Pact Ambassadors in Washington on the issue and told them
that it had been done in order to improve the overall standing of the
socialist community of nations.

Khrushchev's claim that his aim was deterrence of an American attack
on Cuba is probably true to some extent; but this seems to me to have
been no more than a secondary consideration, even though it later
emerged as the official line. They later had to claim this because this
was the only line they could take which had any chance of justifying the
deal to remove the missiles from Cuba. We do have one previously
unavailable source on this, which was a presentation on the Cuban
missile crisis made to the Soviet military in the confidential Soviet General Staff organ *Military Thought* in late November 1962, before Khrushchev's speech to the Supreme Soviet. . . . It was published under the
title "Be on Guard—Keep Your Powder Dry,"[23] but that was not really
the main theme. The explanation offered there included the deterrence
of invasion rationale which Khrushchev gave as the official explanation,
and argued that the United States had been stirring up a Cuban crisis
for which the Soviet missiles were merely the pretext. It referred to the
crisis as the most severe trial since World War II, and openly described

it as a confrontation that could have developed into thermonuclear war.

The main theme of the discussion is that the outcome of the crisis was a "reasonable compromise" based on "mutual concessions." The action in agreeing to the settlement was "the only correct course under contemporary circumstances," and on the Soviet side was an example of "Leninist firmness and flexibility." But "sound-thinking" Americans, too, understood that "in our time one must not take any problem of international affairs to the brink of war," and that this experience gave the concept of peaceful coexistence "a new, deep meaning." Finally, the discussion suggested that the crisis may have opened "a new page in the postwar history of international relations," rather than constituting merely "another incident in the 'cold war.' " I find that rather interesting for an article in the confidential Soviet General Staff journal in late November 1962. . . .

This leads to the question of calculation and miscalculation, particularly with respect to the decision to try for a fait accompli. They didn't need to do it that way, and things might have come out very differently if they hadn't. We wouldn't have liked it, of course, but the range of possible responses we could have made would certainly have been different. But they thought they could get away with it; they thought it was legal; and they thought it was equitable, because the United States had installed comparable weapons in Turkey and elsewhere in Europe. While they clearly did mislead us on the issue of "offensive" missiles, I am persuaded that they seriously believed that a case could be argued that there was no meaningful offensive/defensive distinction to be made, and that they thought they could hold their own in a debate with us in the political confrontation which they thought would be inevitable.

They clearly gave too little thought to worst case possibilities. They probably thought that, at the very worst, they might suffer a local defeat and that the Americans might commit some act of aggression, such as an invasion, which would have played in the Soviets' favor in terms of world opinion. Of course, if the Americans tried an air strike which destroyed the missiles, the Soviets could have denied the whole thing and charged that the Americans were striking at phantoms. They probably did not anticipate the blockade.

Subsequent Soviet treatments come in two phases. First, we have Anatoly Gromyko's, which remarkably manages to reconstruct the event without ever mentioning Khrushchev by name.[24] There have been three more recent works, in the last of which, incidentally, Khrushchev's name *does* appear in a matter-of-fact way.[25]

GEORGE: A quick question to satisfy my curiosity: Why did the President refer to *offensive* missiles as intolerable in his September speech?

By doing so, he gave the Soviets some room to dicker on semantics. Why didn't he just say that the United States would not tolerate the presence of surface-to-surface MRBMs and IRBMs?

. . . . .

ABRAM CHAYES: Well, first, to back up a bit. On Ray's point about the legality issue, we never took the position that the Soviet deployment was illegal. In fact, *our* legal problem was that their action *wasn't* illegal. Second, the Soviets must have anticipated the blockade because people in Congress were calling for it all the time.

The offensive/defensive distinction grew out of a legal memo written by Norbert Schlei* in response to the question: What can we do if the Soviets put missiles in Cuba?[26] The answer was—nothing, if the missiles are defensive in nature. That's why the President chose to speak of "offensive" missiles in his September 4 statement, which I believe was the first time the distinction between offensive and defensive missiles was made. That language was chosen because we were anticipating a legal basis for a response just in case the Soviets did deploy missiles in Cuba.†

GARTHOFF: What is the legal basis for objecting to offensive missiles?

CHAYES: Well, the argument in the ExComm was that emplacement of offensive missiles could be interpreted as an armed attack under Article 51 of the UN Charter—a line we didn't take, rather importantly, I might add, from the international lawyers' perspective.

Why were intelligence reports of missiles ignored? We haven't yet referred to the American domestic political situation. There was a major partisan fight going on, and a struggle over public opinion. The Republicans were really heating Cuba up as the November elections drew closer. As early as August, there were demands for a blockade. The Administration's response was to try to dampen this all down, and one strategy that was pursued was to argue that the reports of missiles in Cuba referred only to SAMs.

Things in Congress were getting out of hand. An extreme resolution was even introduced which called for military action against Cuba![27] We managed to have this watered down, so in its final form it only warned of dire consequences if offensive missiles were introduced in Cuba. It embodied this offensive/defensive distinction, and stated that we were

---

* Assistant Attorney General, Office of Legal Counsel.

† [Douglas Dillon adds:] Also by that time we had a pretty good idea that the Soviets were in the process of deploying SAMs to Cuba, and the use of the word "offensive" or some similar word was necessary to make clear that the President was not referring to SAMs.

prepared to use military force in defense of our security if we had to. This resolution was used, by the way, as a justification for President Kennedy's quarantine proclamation.

But I'd like to make a personal statement about these supposed intelligence failures. I for one didn't believe the reports of offensive missiles in Cuba because I didn't *want* to believe them. I didn't want to be lying to senators when I reported on the Cuban situation, and I certainly wasn't inclined to take Keating and McCone at face value, because I didn't think they were reliable anyway. I don't want to accuse anyone else of this, but it was very easy for me to disregard Keating and the other hotheads who were screaming about missiles in Cuba.

GARTHOFF: Bear in mind that there were a couple of hundred reports received of which *two* turned out after the event to have been valid. Most of the reports of Soviet missile activity in Cuba were quite properly disregarded.

As for whether the Soviets should have anticipated the blockade, don't forget that the decision to deploy was made in May or June, long before there was any talk of a blockade. It isn't clear, either, whether the Soviets thought we had discovered what they were doing. There is mixed information on this. They may have thought that the President was going to change his tune on the offensive/defensive distinction, precisely because of American inaction.

. . . . .

ALLISON: . . . As late as October 14, the day our U-2 discovered the missiles, Mac Bundy was on TV claiming that the United States had no information on offensive missiles in Cuba. He was aware at the time that the Soviets had sent Il-28s to Cuba. So it is not inconceivable that a decisionmaker in Moscow could believe that the United States would be willing to accept offensive missiles in Cuba as long as they were put there quietly.

. . . . .

HORELICK: Graham's argument strikes me as persuasive. Suppose they had tried to deploy the missiles above the board; that would have been the riskiest move of all, from the Soviet perspective. It would have left them with absolutely no ambiguity to maneuver with; they either would have had to back down publicly or they would have gotten away with it. By October 22, there was every reason for the Soviets to believe that we knew, so the big risks looked like they were over. The Soviets were stunned on Monday night when the President announced the blockade.

. . . . .

GARTHOFF: McGeorge Bundy was asked on the 14th about the possibility of Soviet missiles in Cuba, and he said that he doubted they would install any significant capability. He denied that we had any hard information on missiles there, and though he was aware of the presence of Il-28s by indirection, he said that they were of marginal value. Il-28 deployments had been accepted by the United States in both Egypt and Indonesia without any reaction, and so it is not entirely unlikely, putting all of these things together, that the Soviets thought the Americans were sending signals saying, in effect, that they would tolerate missiles as well.

CHAYES: I think you're right, Arnold, that a fait accompli looked best from the Soviet point of view for all the reasons you gave. But from the American point of view, it would have been very difficult to generate world support or an effective operational plan if the Soviets had deployed above the board. The net benefit for the Soviets might very well have been greatest with an open deployment. After all, the fact that there was a crisis over the issue increased our possibilities.

NYE: Alex?

GEORGE: . . . The September 4 statement seems to have been made largely as an effort to calm the hawks at home. The Soviets weren't the primary target because it wasn't expected that the Soviets would deploy. Of course, someone mentioned it to Dobrynin—but we don't know how strongly the point was stressed privately. The Soviets could have taken the September 4 statement as something intended solely for domestic consumption.
    A second point on this concerns the U-2 overflights. The public record tells us that early in September, when a Nationalist U-2 was shot down over mainland China, the decision was made that U-2 flights over western Cuba were too risky because of the improved air defenses there. We therefore gave up our best method of checking on what we thought to be a low-probability risk. It is possible that we could have discovered appreciably earlier what was going on, so we must be careful not to draw the wrong lessons.[28]
    I have a question for those of you who participated in these decisions: Did we ever seriously attempt to convince the Soviets that we wished to deter them from deploying missiles?

SCHLESINGER: In September, Robert Kennedy undertook to explore the issue of Soviet surface-to-surface missiles in Cuba, and he reported that he believed the President's statement made it very difficult for the Russians to deploy them. So I am not sure I agree with you, Alex, that the target of that statement was the American public.

. . . . .

SORENSEN: Let me say here that the line between offensive and defensive weapons was drawn in September, and it was not drawn in a
way which was intended to leave the Soviets any ambiguity to play with.
I believe the President drew the line precisely where he thought the
Soviets were not and would not be; that is to say, if we had known that
the Soviets were putting forty missiles in Cuba, we might under this
hypothesis have drawn the line at one hundred, and said with great
fanfare that we would absolutely not tolerate the presence of more than
one hundred missiles in Cuba. I say that one believing very strongly
that that would have been an act of *prudence*, not weakness. But I am
suggesting that one reason the line was drawn at zero was because we
simply thought the Soviets weren't going to deploy any there anyway.

THOMAS SCHELLING: When Joseph Stalin promised at Potsdam* that
there would be free elections in Poland, Truman decided to take his
promise at face value. If the elections were held, there would be a
democratically elected regime in Poland; if they were not, he could call
Stalin on it later and the world would blame Stalin for spoiling East–
West relations. Averell Harriman† counseled against it, however, and
he told Truman: "Stalin doesn't *believe* you take him at face value; so
if you don't call him on it now, he'll take your silence as tacit consent
and your later challenge as a breach of promise not to call him on it."
     Now maybe this was what was going on between Gromyko and Ken-
nedy. Gromyko probably did know what was going on in Cuba, and he
probably thought Kennedy knew, and he may have thought that the
fact Kennedy didn't bring up the subject with him indicated that they
had a gentleman's understanding of the matter.

HORELICK: That's plausible. I've thought about that. If it were otherwise, the expectation would have been that Kennedy would have
raised it with Gromyko.

CHAYES: Walter Lippmann wrote a column raising exactly that point.
There would certainly have been a professional diplomatic expectation
that Kennedy raise the issue with Gromyko.

HORELICK: One thing that strikes me is that time after time the
U.S.S.R. is a residual category. We only get around to asking what the
Soviets might think about something late in the game, as though we
expect them to understand what we are doing precisely as we do. All
Administrations care less and know less about the Soviets than the

---

* July 17–August 2, 1945.
† Then U.S. Ambassador to the Soviet Union.

domestic political situation. We need people who know about the U.S.S.R. to think about Soviet perceptions and responses before we get into confrontations with them.

NYE: But if we'd listened to Chip Bohlen* and Tommy Thompson† on the likelihood that the Soviets would deploy missiles in Cuba, we'd have been just as surprised, because they were wrong.

HORELICK: I'm not saying Sovietologists are infallible. There are no guarantees; but at least we'd be giving some informed thought to the subject.

. . . . .

GARTHOFF: . . . The Soviets *were* trying to deceive us, and they assured us that they were *not* deploying ground-to-ground missiles. I am not convinced that they would have gone to all of the trouble of making embarrassing assurances if they believed they were deploying with our tacit blessing. The Soviets had also gone to special pains to deceive us by having Georgy Bolshakov,‡ upon his return from Moscow, tell Robert Kennedy that Khrushchev had assured him that there would be no Soviet missiles in Cuba.[29]

As far as the photo reconnaissance is concerned, I really doubt whether we could have known about the missiles any earlier. One week earlier, maybe, although, as you know, the weather prevented over-flights the week before we actually found out about the missiles; two weeks earlier, probably not, simply because it is unlikely that the sites would have been prepared enough to be recognized for what they were; three weeks, definitely not. If we had taken photos of western Cuba two or three weeks before we did, it is conceivable that we would actually have discovered the missiles *later* than we did, because there would have been some delay before the next flight; it would probably not have taken place until some time after October 14.

As for Gromyko, it isn't clear that he knew about the missiles. He wasn't then a member of the Politburo, so he might not have, though I suppose we will never know for sure whether he did or not.[30] It is interesting that all subsequent Soviet accounts of the affair stress the fact that Kennedy did not raise the matter explicitly with Gromyko, and

---

* Charles E. ("Chip") Bohlen, newly appointed Ambassador to France and a former Ambassador to the Soviet Union.
† Llewellyn C. Thompson, former U.S. Ambassador to the Soviet Union and a member of the ExComm.
‡ Bolshakov was an official at the Soviet Embassy in Washington, and had been used as a regular channel of communication between Kennedy and Khrushchev. In Moscow in January 1989, Bolshakov claimed he had not been aware of the deployment at the time.

thus they have interpreted this as an *American* deception intended to enable us to spring the crisis on them.[31]

. . . . .

SCHELLING: I was at a conference about a year ago on the subject of permissive action links.* There I heard several specialists on Soviet custodial arrangements who said some things which led me to believe that there were no warheads in Cuba for those Soviet missiles. Given the fact that the Soviets had never deployed any nuclear missiles outside the Soviet Union before, and that they do not even trust their own military with custody of warheads in the Soviet Union, it seems almost inconceivable to me that they would then have trusted the warheads with anybody outside their borders. If they were worried about unauthorized use, then the smart thing for them to do would have been to keep warheads out of Cuba until absolutely necessary, when an attack is imminent.

What I would like to know is, do we know if there were warheads in Cuba? Why do we think that Bohlen and Thompson were *wrong* in their assessment that the Soviets would never put nuclear weapons in Cuba?[32]

GARTHOFF: Well, we never confirmed that there were warheads in Cuba. The storage facilities were certainly there, and we had some information that they were preparing to bring the warheads in. The IRBMs, as you know, had not yet been brought in, and these as well as some of the MRBMs were on the way when the quarantine was imposed.

SAGAN: What evidence did you have that they were preparing to bring warheads in? Did you have unusual radioactivity detections?

GARTHOFF: We had some indications from inside the Soviet Union that preparations were under way to move warheads to Cuba. This movement was, however, interdicted by the quarantine. I'm afraid I shouldn't say more than that. Of course, we didn't know that there were *no* warheads in Cuba, we merely never confirmed that there were. Prudence dictated that we had to assume that they did have at least some of the warheads there.

. . . . .

---

* PALs, electronic or mechanical locks on nuclear warheads, designed to prevent unauthorized use.

Friday, March 6, 1987—Afternoon—The First Week

NYE: This afternoon we will try to grapple with some of the issues surrounding the first or "private" week of the crisis, from October 16, when the missiles were discovered, to October 22, when President Kennedy went on television to proclaim the quarantine. I have asked Alex George to make some remarks in the same vein as Ernie's remarks on questions of causes. Alex?

GEORGE: . . . There are several groups of questions that I would like to raise for discussion. The first concerns consultation with Congress. We know what happened when the President met congressional leaders on October 22 just before his speech to the nation: he met with considerable opposition, and several objections were raised to his proposed course of action. Was the possibility of earlier consultation with congressional leaders discussed within the ExComm? Why wasn't there any? Were you worried that the hawks in Congress would unduly influence your judgment and choices? Were you worried that consulting congressional leaders would weaken your control of the decisionmaking process? Leaks? . . .

Second, the diplomatic option was considered in the ExComm and set aside very early. What more can you tell us of the possible variations on the diplomatic option that you could have tried, and your reasons for not trying them? To give you an example, one variant of the diplomatic option was to negotiate while building up forces, and another was to negotiate *without* building up forces. Did you weigh the merits of these different approaches? What aspects of the diplomatic option worried you most? Was it a concern that if you got involved in negotiations with Khrushchev too early in the crisis his price tag for removing the missiles might be too high? Did you perceive that he would have the bargaining advantages if you chose the diplomatic option? Were you worried that starting with the diplomatic option would lead to endless delays, or an inconclusive outcome?

The third group of questions concerns the choice of the blockade. This choice put you in what Tom Schelling has called a "compellent" relationship with the Soviets. It was an exercise of "coercive diplomacy."[33] What would have been the *next coercive steps* after the blockade, which everyone agreed could not be expected to remove the missiles? The public record shows an unresolved disagreement between those in the ExComm who thought the next step was going to be graduated escalation—a slow turning of the screw (as Bob McNamara puts it)—and those who foresaw a rapid escalation, presumably to an air strike. Which was it going to be? How would the decision have been made? Or had it already been made?

The public record shows that President Kennedy's eventual resort to an "ultimatum" on the last Saturday of the crisis was taken reluctantly. An ultimatum has three components: first, a demand on the opponent; second, a time limit for compliance; and third, a threat of punishment for non-compliance that is sufficiently credible and sufficiently potent to overcome the opponent's reluctance to comply with the demand.[34] Is it true that the President was finally forced into making the full ultimatum? By what or whom?

The fourth group of questions concerns the use of Soviet experts. The public record indicates that you all thought the contribution of Llewellyn Thompson enormously important—but there's very little documentation of this. What were the Soviet specialists saying? Did they help guide you to the choice of the blockade? What did they say about the likely Soviet response? Did they anticipate a countermove somewhere else, such as in Berlin? Were they asked, and what did they say? What was their prediction of the Soviet reaction to an air strike against the missile sites? Dean Acheson* was asked, and he said he believed the Soviets would respond to an air strike against the missile sites in Cuba with their own attack on the Jupiter missiles in Turkey, which would have to be followed by a NATO response of some kind against the Soviet Union! But what did the Soviet experts say about the likely Soviet response to an air strike?

Fifth, what were the effects of crisis-induced stress and pressure on your deliberations? In Bobby Kennedy's *Thirteen Days* and in Ted Sorensen's book, there are cryptic remarks about stress-induced breakdowns of some kind.[35] What happened? What was the effect of this on perceptions, and on decisionmaking? Was there any use of drugs or medication, and if so, what were their effects?

Sixth, what can those of us who wish to know more about crisis management learn from the Cuban crisis about the tension between "military logic" and "diplomatic logic"? What constraints did this tension impose on managing the crisis? What were the risks it carried? Did you anticipate them, and did you have well-formulated ideas about how you would cope with them? . . .

NYE: Thanks very much, Alex. You've given us a great deal to sink our teeth into. Once again, why don't we start with the participants. Arthur?

---

* Secretary of State under President Truman.

SCHLESINGER: First, let me make a few remarks on the issue of Soviet experts. Chip Bohlen had just been appointed Ambassador to Paris, and to President Kennedy's dismay, he decided that he had to go on as scheduled to Paris to avoid sending a signal to the Soviets that something was up. Tommy Thompson played a vital role, but we didn't fully exploit our resources of Soviet experts. For example, on Wednesday the 24th I was in New York working with Governor Stevenson on the UN presentation, and Averell Harriman called me, saying that Khrushchev was sending "desperate signals" to us to help get him off the hook. His letter to Bertrand Russell* and his meeting with Knox† in Moscow seemed to indicate he was fishing for a way out.[36] The signals were very similar to those sent out after the U-2 affair. We had to give him a way out, Harriman said, because otherwise he would escalate the crisis. I asked him whether he had been talking to Dean Rusk about this, and he said that Rusk hadn't asked him about it—he only consulted him on matters dealing with the Far East. But clearly his contribution would have been invaluable.

On the questions of the references to breakdown and the outrage some people felt at the apparently soft line we were taking, the names are all in my Robert Kennedy book, and I don't think there's much more to say about it.[37]

. . . . .

BALL: The reason why Dean Rusk didn't call on Averell Harriman is because he had complete confidence in Tommy Thompson, who was a known quantity who had a reputation for good judgment. Averell was thought of as being more rash, and the prevailing mood was to err on the side of prudence. Anyway, we didn't think of Averell as being primarily a Soviet expert. His expertise was in the Far East, and Tommy's advice proved to be very good. In retrospect, it seems to me that had we consulted more with Averell, it probably wouldn't have mattered much because he and Tommy had very similar readings of what was going on.

. . . President Kennedy was fully prepared to hold off consulting [Congress] until he had made up his mind about what we were going to do. He felt he needed a solid executive-department decision, not only because of the dangers Alex mentioned, including the possibility of leaks (which was a real worry), but because he wanted to exercise his privilege to make fundamental decisions of that kind. Another reason why he

---

* British philosopher Lord Bertrand Russell, who on October 24 appealed to Kennedy and Khrushchev to avoid a confrontation. Khrushchev responded on October 25 in conciliatory terms.
† William Knox, an American businessman traveling in Moscow.

didn't consult earlier was that most of Congress wanted stronger action, and that didn't accord with the President's mood. He didn't want to hear more of that kind of advice, because he feared its implications.

On the diplomatic option, our bargaining position did seem to us to be very weak. We needed a fait accompli to meet theirs. We needed more cards in our hand. We didn't want to be in the position of giving them an ultimatum, because we didn't want to run the risks of nuclear war that we would have done had we forced their hand.

I don't think that President Kennedy was prepared to make an air strike. I think Bob and Dean would agree with me on that. An air strike was the last thing we wanted because it was an irrevocable act. The greatest virtue of the quarantine was that it wasn't an irrevocable act.

Finally, on the question of stress, I know *I* felt ten years older afterward. I'll never forget walking through the rose garden with Bob McNamara on Sunday morning [October 28]; it was such a beautiful morning, and it reminded me very strongly of that Georgia O'Keeffe painting of a rose growing through a skull. It was a very intense period of time; but I don't think there were any permanent effects. I think I got over it. Remember that we had one enormous advantage, and that was a Secretary of Defense who was more than just a spokesman for the military. I hate to think what would have happened if we'd had one like the present Secretary of Defense.*

NYE: Doug, do you have any recollections on this question of the air strike?

DILLON: I am one of the last of the hawks who advocated the air strike; it's hard to find any around anymore. What motivated me was this: we had agreed at the very first meeting that the one thing we were all committed to was that the missiles must be removed, and it seemed to me that the most direct and effective way of doing that was with an air strike.† We were influenced by the military's assessment of the threat, but not by their assessment of what was required to remove it. We were

---

* Caspar Weinberger.

† [Douglas Dillon adds:] While everyone at our first ExComm meeting, specifically including the President, agreed that the emplacement of Soviet MRBMs and IRBMs in Cuba was totally unacceptable and that they had to be gotten out one way or another, I do not recall any specific discussion then or at later meetings of the ExComm as to just why they were unacceptable. It just seemed obvious to all of us. To me, at least, it seemed that one reason for our unanimous feeling was that those missiles in Cuba changed the strategic balance in the Soviets' favor by greatly increasing their ability to hit or threaten the United States with missiles. However, I agree that, in the ExComm meetings themselves, there was no discussion of the strategic balance and the effect or lack of effect the emplacement of these missiles in Cuba had on it. [Editor's note: Cf. "White House Tapes and Minutes of the Cuban Missile Crisis," *International Security*, Vol. 10, No. 1 (Summer 1985), which reveals that there was in fact some inconclusive discussion of the issue.]

thinking of very limited attacks on the missile sites, where there were only Russian and Cuban soldiers—no civilians of any kind. I also thought it was very important that something be done before the missiles were operational, and the air-strike option was certainly the best way to ensure that. The quarantine certainly didn't do it.

Dean Acheson kept to that line throughout. I changed my opinion on Friday [October 19] at the meeting in George Ball's office when Bobby Kennedy brought out the parallel with Pearl Harbor. That impressed me a very great deal.[38] I felt that we just couldn't live with that, so I moved into the camp advocating the blockade, and decided that the air-strike option could be reserved as a later resort to be used only if absolutely necessary.

Finally, I did not believe that the Russians would respond to an air strike with a nuclear attack on the United States. I'll always recall the summer of 1960 when I was Under Secretary of State and the Russians shot down one of our reconnaissance planes in international waters. We didn't do anything about it, we just yelled a lot. They knew that they were in a similar situation in Cuba. Many of us felt that the missiles could only be removed by forceful action or in response to a serious threat of force; and, of course, that is what happened in the end. The Russians reached the conclusion, after Bobby Kennedy's meeting with Dobrynin, that we would strike. He had told Dobrynin that if they didn't take the missiles out, we would do it for them. That's why they were so quick to give us a hurried radio response accepting our terms.*

But since Cuba wasn't one of their vital interests, and since it all occurred in a different time and with a very different military balance, I don't expect that kind of threat to work again.

. . . . .

SORENSEN: . . . Bob and I were reminiscing last night about the night of Saturday the 27th. We had just dispatched Bobby Kennedy to Dobrynin, expecting the so-called ultimatum to be rejected. The only word which can describe the meeting that night is "rancorous"—we *did* show the effects of stress and fatigue, and the air strike *was* gaining strength, and its proponents were becoming more and more vigorous. The President was under *tremendous* pressure at this point, and I think it's highly speculative to say that the President would "never" have gone ahead with the air strike.

But to turn back to the original questions: . . . the diplomatic option was never totally abandoned. We pursued it concurrently with the quarantine. But we couldn't conceive of a *purely* diplomatic approach which would succeed in getting the missiles out. We never fully resolved the

---

* Cf. the discussion on this issue in the Afterword, pp. 340–42.

tensions between the surgical air strikers and the massive air strikers and all the others, which is one of the reasons we didn't opt for the air strike.

As far as the ultimatum is concerned, I don't believe we made one. We don't know precisely what Bobby Kennedy told Dobrynin, but I seriously doubt that he put it in those terms.[39] On the Soviet experts, Tommy Thompson *was* invaluable, and his advice and his judgment were always on target. He was convinced that war could be avoided, and he thought it possible that the missiles could be removed. . . . Harriman's hands were full in the Far East, which was his assignment at the time, not the Soviets. Finally, people performed with varying degrees of endurance and skill and reaction to stress—I knew nothing of any drugs, and I doubt they were a factor—but I still feel that we were essentially a harmonious group and that we never had any serious lapses or succumbed to any pressure to "cave in."

. . . . .

MCNAMARA: I don't think we've quite succeeded in re-creating the atmosphere at the time. The questions Alex asked simply weren't framed that precisely back then. There were deep differences of opinion among us, and very strong feelings about Cuba, and the fact is that we weren't going through an unemotional, orderly, and comprehensive analytical decisionmaking process.

There were tremendous political and military pressures to *do* something. Max Taylor,* who was one of the wisest, most intelligent military men ever to serve, called himself a "double hawk" at the time, but he was a *dove* among the military people. After Khrushchev had agreed to remove the missiles, President Kennedy invited the Chiefs to the White House so that he could thank them for their support during the crisis, and there was one hell of a scene. LeMay came out saying, "We lost! We ought to just go in there today and knock 'em off!"

Right from the beginning, there was tremendous tension between those who wanted to use the opportunity to get rid of Castro and those who thought it too dangerous, and between those who thought that the Soviet deployment meant a massive shift in the strategic balance and those who didn't. There was a great difference of opinion on everything, including among the advocates of the air-strike option on the form it should take and how it should be followed up.

Now, I don't believe that the military *ever* gave us a surgical air strike option. They always emphasized the necessity of having an invasion follow the strike, and they told us we could expect thousands of casualties. No one ever agreed on what the Soviet response would have

* General Maxwell Taylor, chairman of the Joint Chiefs of Staff.

been. As far as I know, none of us thought that a response in Berlin was likely, but we thought Soviet action in some other area was highly probable.

So our deliberations were more crude than Alex's questions imply. In the end, there never was a consensus on what to do. The majority by the end of the second week clearly favored action, but the President was of a different mind.

What would have happened if Khrushchev hadn't accepted President Kennedy's terms? I don't know. I believe we still could have done a lot more with the blockade. We could have continued to turn the screw for quite some time, and I believe that's what we would have done. I *don't* believe that Bobby Kennedy ever told Dobrynin anything as bald as "You take them out or we'll take them out." That's not the way we were thinking.

We were all uncertain of what was going to happen, and with hindsight, there were great gaps in our thinking. Let me give you an example. About six weeks ago, I was talking with a retired admiral about what would have happened if there had been nuclear warheads in Cuba and we had attacked them. He said that if they'd been NATO missiles without PALs, then the NATO officers, acting without Presidential authorization, would have been likely to use them rather than lose them. The fear that Soviet or Cuban officers might have reacted the way NATO officers might have was one reason I was extremely reluctant to risk the air strike. However, it was not until the admiral and I were discussing the matter that either of us realized that the ExComm, when discussing the air-strike option, had given no consideration to how we would respond to such a nuclear attack. Our only "plan" was the SIOP, which would have destroyed us as well as the Soviets, so I don't think there's any way we would have used it, though we didn't discuss the matter.*

. . . . .

CHAYES: . . . I agree with Bob on his point about the crudeness and the difficulty of deliberation. One thing was done properly: people *did* discuss the law. And I say that not because of my own concerns about

---

* [Marc Trachtenberg adds:] The issue apparently did come up at an ExComm meeting on October 20. What if the blockade failed to bring about the withdrawal of the missiles? The Sieverts Report—which, it must be emphasized, is a secondhand account—paraphrases the discussion as follows: "If after several days there was a continuation of missile site construction an air strike might be necessary against a minimum number of targets to eliminate the main nuclear threat. It was held unlikely that the Soviets would retaliate, especially since the Strategic Air Command would be in a full alert condition. If surviving Cuban missiles after an air strike were used against the U.S., it might be necessary to invade Cuba, but not to use nuclear weapons against Cuba. However it might be necessary to make a compensatory attack against the USSR." Frank Sieverts, "The Cuban Crisis, 1962," pp. 75–76, Box 49, National Security Files, John F. Kennedy Library.

that—it's more than a lawyer's quirk. The legal position was very important in the diplomatic context, and Tommy Thompson was the one who triggered our concern about it because of his interesting remark that the Soviets were very legalistic.[40] Tommy was the unsung hero, no doubt about it—Chip Bohlen, incidentally, would have had a slightly different effect.

The technical issue revolved around the question of whether we were going to take unilateral action or get OAS* approval ahead of time. Put in that way, the question had a spin in the direction of the blockade, because there was no way we were going to get OAS approval for an air strike. The State Department, the Department of Defense, and the Attorney General's Office all agreed that we needed OAS approval, and that meant that we had to consider what we could get the OAS to approve. Having to consider the legal position carefully contributed, I think, to the wisdom of our choices.

. . . . .

GARTHOFF: Arthur Schlesinger's remarks about Averell Harriman reminded me of the fact that Harriman submitted a memorandum to President Kennedy on October 22, making the point that Khrushchev was under pressure from his military and from hard-liners, and that he had been *pushed* into putting missiles in Cuba.

SCHLESINGER: Just a footnote on that. This question of whether it was Khrushchev's initiative or not is interesting, and I think unresolved. I was talking recently with Fyodor Burlatsky—*glasnost* and the improved climate of free speech in the Soviet Union, by the way, are having a wonderful effect on serious East–West discussion—and I asked him where Khrushchev got the idea for deploying missiles in Cuba. He told me that he thought the idea came from Malinovsky.†[41] If so, Averell Harriman might have been right.

NYE: Burlatsky wrote a very interesting play [*Burden of Decision*] on the Cuban missile crisis not too long ago which embodies a very interesting portrayal of a civil-military crisis, with the apparent purpose of telling the Soviets that they must be very careful about letting such a thing get out of hand. It wasn't entirely accurate history, but intriguing nonetheless.

SORENSEN: Actually, it wasn't all that distorted.

NYE: Ray?

---

* Organization of American States.
† Rodion Ya. Malinovsky, Soviet Minister of Defense.

GARTHOFF: There's no question that Tommy Thompson was a key factor, but the ExComm had to choose what to make of his rather oblique and guarded analysis, so his influence was indirect. I can't say for sure whether the original idea was Khrushchev's or Malinovsky's, but I can tell you what the intelligence community thought at the time. They thought it was Khrushchev's initiative, but they were split on his motivations, some thinking he was trying to shore up the strategic balance, and others thinking he was mostly trying to shore up his own political position. I have always believed the idea was Khrushchev's own.

. . . . .

HORELICK: I have a question. In the first week, time after time, the idea that the missiles were becoming operational figured heavily in your discussions. What was the image in your minds of what that meant? Did it mean to you that the missiles could be fired on short notice? Did it mean that they could be fired, but only on a long fuse? What did the term "operational" mean to you?

. . . . .

MCNAMARA: We knew those missiles were obsolete, and that they required substantial preparation time before they could be fired—

GARTHOFF: Four to six hours, roughly.[42]

MCNAMARA: But I don't think we put great weight on the date on which they might become operational. At least, I didn't. I know the later writing on the subject makes it sound like an important issue, but it had no effect on my decisions.

SCHLESINGER: The CIA report of October 23 estimated that four MRBM sites were operational, but it didn't indicate whether there were warheads there.

SAGAN: But just this morning you said you assumed they were there.

SCHLESINGER: Well, we did.

MCNAMARA: . . . I think the literature is simply wrong in reporting our concern about the date on which the missiles would become operational.

NYE: But if you felt that time was running out quickly—

MCNAMARA: I didn't think time made any difference.

ALBERT CARNESALE: But wait a minute. Time pressure is what makes a crisis! Now you're telling us that there was no time pressure—so why was there a crisis? I don't understand.

ALLISON: The CIA report of the 27th speaks of missiles being "fully operational" without any explicit reference to the nuclear warheads. In Khrushchev's conversation with William Knox, he asserted that the Soviets had nuclear warheads in Cuba.[43] If you worried about the possibility of a launch from Cuba, then the question of whether the missiles are operational and what you understood by that is very important.

McNAMARA: Well, we put very little trust in CIA estimates of when the missiles would be operational. It is possible that the missiles were operational by the 15th of October, for example. We had to assume they might have been and we weren't going to go a route that risked millions of lives. We just weren't going to risk it.

NYE: But, Doug, you said that you thought time was running out. Did you share Bob's view on this at all?

DILLON: Well, "operational" is a vague word, and we did have to assume the worst. I remember that on the first Friday the report that the missiles were "becoming operational" made a big difference to our deliberations.

. . . . .

BALL: One reason there's confusion here is the split between the air-strike advocates and those who advocated the quarantine/diplomatic approach in the ExComm. The air-strike advocates were using the issue of the missiles becoming "operational" to buttress their case for urgency.

McNAMARA: But those who initially favored the air strike *continued* to favor it even after it became clear that the missiles *were* operational.

HORELICK: Did the technologically unsophisticated in the crowd request a briefing on what "operational" meant?

McNAMARA: No, they didn't.

NYE: Ray, what did the intelligence community mean by "operational" when they reported on Cuba?

GARTHOFF: We understood it to mean that everything was there that was needed to fire the missiles. Nothing was operational in that sense on October 14, but the MRBMs rapidly became operational shortly after that.

SCHLESINGER: Everything was there except possibly the warheads, you mean.

GARTHOFF: Well, you could fire the missiles without warheads if you really wanted to. [Laughter.] By the 26th and 27th, the MRBMs had all the support preparations they needed. The IRBMs were on a slower track, but it was estimated that by mid-December they would have become operational.

But this was only one consideration, and it didn't necessarily prejudge our options. One problem we had to worry about was the fact that as time wore on, Soviet missiles in Cuba became more and more a feature of the status quo, gradually improving their bargaining position. . . .

SCHELLING: Bob said earlier that he had worried about a Soviet unauthorized launch. It seems to me fairly clear that Moscow would have worried about that, too. For that reason, I very seriously doubt that the warheads were there; or if they were there, they would have had to have been under custodial arrangements that did not risk unauthorized use.

Anyway, Bob mentioned some concern about Soviet PALs. What was the Soviet version of a PAL at the time? Inert weapons? KGB people with police dogs patrolling storage bunkers? Something else?

McNAMARA: I don't know what they had. We had *zero*.

ALLISON: You knew nothing about them?

McNAMARA: Absolutely nothing.

GARTHOFF: We did know that the Soviets normally gave the KGB custody of all nuclear warheads, though we did not know what the particulars of the Cuban custodial arrangements would be. We did not know whether the Soviets there were KGB or Army, because they were all wearing the same type of sport shirt and slacks, not uniforms. They were heavily armed, presumably because they wanted to be prepared for any contingency, an American commando raid, even a Cuban attempt to seize control of the missiles. In fact, on October 28, the Cubans *did* surround the missile bases for three days, and they didn't pull back until Mikoyan arrived.

. . . . .

MARC TRACHTENBERG: I'm a little confused by what Secretary McNamara said about not being concerned that the missiles were becoming operational. The reason is that there's a passage in the October 16 transcript where you make the opposite argument:

[B]efore commenting on either the unknowns or outlining some military alternatives, there are two propositions I would suggest that we ought to accept as, uh, foundations for our further thinking. My first is that if we are to conduct an air strike against these installations, or against any part of Cuba, we must agree now that we will schedule that prior to the time these missile sites become operational. I'm not prepared to say when that will be, but I think it is extremely important that our talk and our discussion be founded on this premise: that any air strike will be planned to take place prior to the time they become operational. Because, if they become operational before the air strike, I do not believe we can state we can knock them out before they can be launched; and if they're launched there is almost certain to be, uh, chaos in part of the east coast or the area, uh, in a radius six hundred to a thousand miles from Cuba.[44]

I don't understand why you say that the question of the missiles becoming operational had no effect.

McNamara: That was the very first day, Tuesday the 16th. We were forming our initial reactions to the news. But after we began to think about it, that restriction began to look irrelevant.

Trachtenberg: Why? If that's a *premise*—

McNamara: Because some of the missiles had become operational while we were still thinking, and the *second* guideline became more relevant [that any air strike would have to include SAM sites and air bases as well as MRBM and IRBM sites]. An air strike *would* have imperiled the East Coast once the missiles were operational, and that's one of the main reasons we weren't going to risk it. I agree with Al when he says that the time urgency was brought on the ExComm by itself. We had to get the thing resolved quickly on that second weekend, because by Monday the pressure for an air strike would have been *tremendous*.

. . . . .

Sorensen: I don't think anyone thinks this was totally unimportant. We just didn't know what the Soviet command and control situation was. But that doesn't mean time was running out. We knew that if we were going to go through with the blockade option, it could have stretched out for months—and we were prepared for that. We weren't committed to any offensive military action. When the U-2 was shot down on October 27, although we'd already decided that our policy would be to retaliate against the SAM site responsible, we held off and didn't do it—wisely, as things turned out.

. . . . .

ALLISON: How much thought was there about the probable leak date and hence the period of time you had to play with? Were you prepared to forfeit the initiative if there had been a story in the *Post* or in the *Times*?

SORENSEN: Our deliberations just weren't that orderly, so there isn't any real answer to the question. I remember that the President expressed surprise to me that the story hadn't leaked on Wednesday [October 17]!

CHAYES: The story had leaked by Sunday [October 21], but it wasn't printed.

BALL: That's right, Scotty Reston had the story Sunday, but we talked him out of printing it. We were concerned about finding the right course of action, and we probably wouldn't have jumped the gun just because the story leaked. We simply hoped it wouldn't.

SCHELLING: Do you have any guess as to how the story leaked?

BALL: Reston was a very smart man, and the *Times* had its antennae out. There were troop movements, and you couldn't entirely conceal that sort of thing. We did all we could, but we couldn't prevent a smart observer from catching on.

SCHELLING: So it wasn't really a leak.

. . . . .

SAGAN: Two questions. First, according to the CIA, on the 27th, and according to Roger Hilsman's account, Khrushchev had said that there were warheads in Cuba but that they couldn't be fired without his orders.[45] Did the ExComm get that report? Second, we had threatened a full retaliatory strike on the Soviet Union if a single weapon was fired from Cuba. Why did we do that?

. . . . .

McNAMARA: Well, on your second question, that simply appeared to be the kind of deterrent we needed at the time. But I guarantee you that the President would not have responded using any option available in the SIOP.

SAGAN: What about Hilsman's report?

McNAMARA: That was communicated to the ExComm.

CHAYES: You have to remember that we couldn't take that at face value, because even though Khrushchev might have been the only one with the authority to order a launch from Cuba, it didn't follow that he was the only one with the ability to do it.

McNAMARA: I put very little weight on Khrushchev's statement for that very reason.

HORELICK: An interesting aspect of that statement is that it indicates Khrushchev was willing to take responsibility for a Cuban launch.

GARTHOFF: Yes, that's right, we noted that at the time. He must have been fairly sure of his ability to control the missiles.

NYE: Well, it has been a fascinating tour of the area, and I'd like to thank Alex George for prodding us in all the right directions. We may not have answered all of your questions, Alex, but we gave most of them a fairly good look.

That's it for today; we have been a little liberal with our schedule, so tomorrow I would like to ask that we all try to observe our starting and ending times as closely as possible. We'll see you at 9:00 a.m.

Saturday, March 7, 1987—Morning—The Second Week

NYE: This morning we are going to have a look at the second, or "public," week of the crisis, followed this afternoon by a discussion of some of the psychological aspects—what Jim Blight has referred to as "the look and feel of nuclear danger." . . . Marc Trachtenberg and Scott Sagan will start us off this morning. . . .

TRACHTENBERG: There are a lot of things Scott and I would like to bring up. . . . The basic problem, as we see it, is the interplay between the political and the military sides of the crisis. You're all probably familiar with Clausewitz's dictum that war has its own grammar but not its own logic[46]—that has to be supplied through outside political direction. The central problem of escalation turns at its core on this interplay between "military grammar" and "political logic"—between the way military action can have a momentum of its own and the efforts to make sure that military power is controlled for political purposes. And this problem of escalation lies at the heart of the great riddle of the nuclear age: how can nuclear forces carry political weight—how can nuclear risk even exist—if no one would ever actually want to go first with the use of these weapons?

How does all this relate to the Cuban missile crisis? We'd like to learn more about what was going on, especially in the military sphere, that was forcing the pace—that is, how was momentum being generated, and how were these pressures being controlled? Were things building up to a climax? If there was an increasing sense of urgency, what was it rooted in?

Let me lay out some of the evidence on both sides of this question. On the one hand, there is this idea that until the very end—and maybe not even then—there was no great sense of urgency. Alex George lays out an argument of this sort in *The Limits of Coercive Diplomacy*. The virtual ultimatum that led to the end of the crisis, he says, was "improvised at the last minute by President Kennedy himself" in reaction to the downing of Major Anderson's U-2, and marked a complete change from the "try-and-see" approach that had been American policy up to that point.[47] The basic evidence for this sort of interpretation—in addition to what Secretary McNamara told us yesterday—was the reference to a crisis lasting for "months," at the end of the October 22 speech, and all the talk about extending the blockade to include POL.

On the other hand, there was also a lot of talk about the blockade as a "first step," that it was to function mainly as a political signal: as the italics and exclamation point in the American insistence that the missiles be withdrawn. And there is a lot of evidence, even prior to the attack on Major Anderson's U-2, that there was a sense of urgency— a lot of concern in particular about the missiles becoming operational. And certainly during the final weekend, there was a strong feeling that matters were coming to a head. Bobby Kennedy, for example, on that Saturday, wanted to avoid a confrontation at the quarantine line: "He urged that we buy time now in order to launch an air attack Monday or Tuesday." Later that day, Secretary McNamara, according to the ExComm minutes, said that a "limited airstrike on Cuba was now impossible because our reconnaissance planes were being fired on. He felt that we must now look to the major airstrike to be followed by an invasion of Cuba." And at the end of the meeting: "Secretary McNamara said that we must now be ready to attack Cuba. . . . Invasion had become almost inevitable."[48]

On a related issue: Is there anything you can tell us about President Kennedy's instructions to his brother before the meeting with Dobrynin, beyond what we already know from books like *Thirteen Days*?

If it is true that people had a sense that things were coming to a head, what exactly was generating it? In particular, was there a feeling that the American military was not fully controllable? I'm not talking about a coup, or anything like that, but I wonder if there's even a germ of truth in the account Khrushchev gave in his memoirs. . . . Ted Sorensen made a comment yesterday when Joe Nye was talking about Burlatsky's picture of a crisis brewing in U.S. civil-military relations at the time: "I have to say it wasn't all that distorted, Joe." Was Sorensen's remark meant seriously? . . .

. . . . .

SAGAN: I would like to focus attention on some of the operational details of military activities undertaken in the second week. For example, the ExComm was constantly keeping tabs on the operations of surface ships at the quarantine line, and was tracking the positions and the procedures of every vessel in the area. But, curiously, there seems to have been much less in the way of direct monitoring by the civilian political leadership of other important activities. One of these was the area of ASW* operations. During the quarantine, the Navy forced four or five F-class submarines to the surface by riding on them, pinging them with active sonar, and in at least one case, dropping practice depth charges. Now, these ASW actions were neither unauthorized (the Secretary of Defense authorized them) nor unknown at the time (they were announced to the press and the Soviets); but I would like to know three things. First, were the ASW rules of engagement reviewed? How dangerous did you think these operations were? Was anyone informed of the fact that one Soviet sub was crippled during these operations, and had to be towed back to the Soviet Union? Second, why did we do it? Was it a coercive signal? Were you suspicious of, or did you have knowledge of, submarines carrying warheads to Cuba? Third, what were the rules of engagement for our SSN† barriers further out? On October 27, a barrier was set up south of Newfoundland.[49] Were our people there authorized to shoot first?

Another operational area that seems to have been very important is reconnaissance, which was intimately linked with the execution of SIOP-63 and the possibility of preemption. The SIOP-62 briefing is presented in the briefing book, and we know that nuclear-war plans under Gates‡ and Eisenhower embodied virtually no genuine options, allowed minimal withholding capability, and called essentially for a massive, coordinated attack against both military and industrial targets in all the nations in the Sino—Soviet bloc. Secretary McNamara had ordered changes made for SIOP-63, which was briefed to Kennedy in September '62. Two important points about that plan are now known because of declassification: first, the new SIOP had five options, at least one of which provided for preemption on unambiguous warning; second, SAC had very specific pre-SIOP reconnaissance options.

---

* Anti-submarine warfare.
† Nuclear-powered submarine.
‡ Thomas S. Gates, Jr., Secretary of Defense under President Eisenhower.

My questions are these: What was "unambiguous warning" taken to be? Was the ExComm informed of what that meant? How much attention was paid to Soviet nuclear-readiness activities inside the Soviet Union itself? Was there any attention paid to the possibility that American reconnaissance activities might be read by the Soviets as preparation for a nuclear strike? What about the U-2 which strayed into Siberian airspace on the 27th, and which was reported to be on an air-sampling mission? Why wasn't that mission turned off? Was it in fact part of a pre-SIOP reconnaissance? How would you have turned it off if you had wanted to?

Our air defenses had recently acquired nuclear weapons for the first time. Did Air Defense Command have predesignated authority to use nuclear weapons in an air-defense role? What details can you give us on this? Should the crisis be considered to have lasted thirteen days or thirty, after the Il-28s are finally removed? The alerts were maintained until then—what would have happened if the Il-28s had not been removed?

Finally, on the first and second letters that came in from Moscow, how were these communicated? Do you have any information on who was supporting what in the Kremlin?

NYE: Thanks, Scott. Ernie, did you want to add something?

MAY: Yes, another question in that same vein. What consideration was given to the status of nuclear weapons in the NATO area? Were you confident that they were not going to be used without authorization? Did they seem to you to pose any serious risks of provocation?

SAGAN: We do know that the President on the 25th issued a NSAM* authorizing the loading of nuclear weapons on SACEUR† aircraft. USAFE‡ was told to take measures to increase readiness, but without doing anything provocative. But who defined what is and is not provocative?

. . . . .

McNAMARA: First, let me say that I don't think there was any danger of the military coming out from under civilian control whatsoever. The military voices were very restrained in the ExComm. There was no extreme pressure from the military for action before or after the President's decision. Don't forget that some civilians were just as pro-air

---

* National Security Action Memorandum.
† Supreme Allied Commander, Europe.
‡ U.S. Air Force, Europe.

strike as the military were; but, in any case, Max Taylor had complete control of the military.

I'd like to make another general remark, which is that in military operations you must recognize the importance of the unpredictable and the uncontrollable—everything you can't foresee. I talked with Harold Brown* about this a couple of weeks ago, and he said, "You know, Bob, the first information I ever had in any situation was always wrong." Just think about what that means when you're dealing with the SIOP!

Henry Kissinger† is an old friend of mine, and when I was president of the World Bank, he once asked me how I could have served seven years as Secretary of Defense and left the SIOP in such an unusable form. I told him there wasn't much of anything anybody could do with it. Eight years later he had the grace to say that he agreed. SIOP-63 was absolutely *useless*. Under *no* circumstances would I have used it. And, as you know, I said to both President Kennedy and to President Johnson that I couldn't imagine *any* circumstances in which I would recommend they initiate the use of nuclear weapons. The people who would advocate initiating the use of nuclear weapons have to meet one hell of a burden of proof that it would be in our interest.

As far as the U-2 incident is concerned, we just didn't know it was up there collecting air samples. We didn't know at the time that we'd injured a Soviet submarine, either. There are some things you can't foresee, and you can't process all the relevant information at once. We did know that we were putting U.S. servicemen at risk, and that there were Soviet subs near the quarantine line. We discussed what to do if submarines came into the area near our surface ships, and we issued guidelines that said that they should be monitored and that incidents should be avoided if possible, though obviously our ships had to be able to protect themselves; for that reason, they were authorized to force the Soviet subs to surface. What else can you do?

The point was that our quarantine was intended to be a political signal, not a textbook military operation, and trying to get that across to the military caused us all a lot of headaches. For twelve days I lived in the Pentagon, from the 16th to the 27th, because I feared that they might not understand that this was a communications exercise, not a military operation.

One evening, to try to ensure that this difference was understood, I met with the Navy people. . . . We had pinpointed the location of every single Soviet ship approaching the quarantine line, and it was clear one of the ships would reach the line the next day. I asked Admiral An-

---

* Secretary of Defense under President Carter.
† Secretary of State and National Security Advisor under Presidents Nixon and Ford.

derson, "When the ship reaches the line, how are you going to stop it?"

"We'll hail it," he said.

"In what language—English or Russian?" I asked.

"How the hell do I know?" he said, clearly a little agitated by my line of questioning.

I followed up by asking, "What will you do if they don't understand?"

"I suppose we'll use flags," he replied.

"Well, what if they don't stop?" I asked.

"We'll send a shot across the bow," he said.

"Then what, if that doesn't work?"

"Then we'll fire into the rudder," he replied, by now clearly very annoyed.

"What kind of ship is it?" I asked.

"A tanker, Mr. Secretary," he said.

"You're not going to fire a single shot at anything without my express permission, is that clear?" I said. That's when he made his famous remark about how the Navy had been running blockades since the days of John Paul Jones, and if I would leave them alone they would run this one successfully as well. I rose from my chair and walked out of the room, saying this was not a blockade but a means of communication between Kennedy and Khrushchev; no force would be applied without my permission; and that would not be given without discussion with the President. "Was that understood?" I asked. The tight-lipped response was "Yes."

The point of all this is that you can't anticipate all the details of any operation. Admiral Anderson was a patriotic American who was only doing his job. But we wanted to use the quarantine in a very precise way for a very precise purpose, and the military had not run a blockade in that way before. The risk of unanticipated things happening out there was very great, and when you're in a situation where you are dealing with the possible eventual use of nuclear weapons, you just cannot afford to take risks which can be avoided.

. . . . .

SCHLESINGER: . . . I do think President Kennedy was worried about control of the military. Now, Khrushchev's memoirs mention something about Bobby Kennedy expressing to Dobrynin worries about a possible military coup; that really wasn't a worry from our point of view, but Bobby did express some concern about controllability in some form. A more measured account of that meeting, I think, appears in Anatoly Gromyko's articles. There he writes that Bobby communicated to Dobrynin that there were "hotheads" who were pressing for action and that the situation could get out of control.[50] There's an enormous difference between the *situation* getting out of control and the *military* getting out of control. Bobby Kennedy's own MemCon* doesn't include mention of this remark, but on Monday, after the resolution of the crisis, the President told me that the military were hopping mad and that it was lucky for us that we had McNamara over there to keep things under control.

NYE: Ted, on the remark you made about Burlatsky's play—was that facetious?

SORENSEN: Not entirely. He'd clearly done his homework.[51]

. . . . .

McGEORGE BUNDY:† The distinction between the situation and the military getting out of control is crucial. . . . The Chiefs were unanimous that we act immediately.

. . . . .

McNAMARA: There was *tremendous* pressure to think about getting ready for military action that week, from the civilians as well as from the military. But that didn't mean that we were going to do it right away. We had lots of time left to turn the screw on the blockade, and a lot of pressure to take that route, too.

ALLISON: Let me push you on that for just a minute, Bob. The minutes Marc Trachtenberg cited a few moments ago indicate that you yourself thought that military action was imminent, and Bobby Kennedy's memoirs clearly state that in his meeting with Dobrynin he said that if the Soviets didn't pull out the missiles, "we would remove them."

SCHLESINGER: All he said was that we had to have a commitment that the bases would be removed. It wasn't an ultimatum.

CHAYES: But the very next sentence says very clearly—"we would remove them."

SCHLESINGER: He didn't report it as an ultimatum.

NYE: Ray, do you have any information on this?

GARTHOFF: . . . As far as an American military coup is concerned, there's nothing of this in official Soviet accounts. What they do say in recent writings is that Bobby Kennedy told Dobrynin that there were military "lamebrains" itching for a fight—I suppose you could translate

---

* Memorandum of conversation.
† This is Bundy's first appearance in the Hawk's Cay conference transcript, as his arrival was delayed by pressing business in New York.

that as "hotheads," if you like—and that the "situation" could slip out of control. So Moscow probably heard Bobby Kennedy saying that the military wanted action, but not that the military were threatening to take over.

NYE: Let's keep on this question of the meeting between Bobby Kennedy and Dobrynin for a minute. Did the meeting convey to the Soviets the idea that an attack was imminent?

GARTHOFF: The latest Soviet account quotes a Congressional Research Service study which says that there was "practically unanimous" agreement among the President's advisors to strike the next morning. That was written on the 27th. But Moscow would have formed its judgment based on information it had from three sources: first, the meeting between Bobby Kennedy and Dobrynin; second, Castro himself; and third, their own intelligence.*

. . . . .

GEORGE: I'd like a clarification. Someone said that the brief to Bobby Kennedy did not authorize him to give an ultimatum. Has anything been declassified that would confirm that?

. . . . .

DILLON: I was there, and I don't recall the ExComm telling Bobby Kennedy anything very specific about what he should say to Dobrynin.[52] He got his last-minute and final instructions from the President and only from the President. There would be no written record of this.

ALLISON: This may be a semantic red herring. We have Bobby's own recollection of the meeting, and we can get his MemCon; it seems fairly clear what he said. The important point is how the Soviets chose to take it.

   He also gave them an account of what would eventually be done with the Turkish missiles. He put to them the proposition that the missiles would ultimately be removed, though not as part of any deal. That wasn't.discussed in the ExComm, as far as I know.

   The next morning, over the *radio*, Khrushchev accepts Kennedy's terms. Isn't this powerful circumstantial evidence that Bobby had convinced the Russians that an air strike was imminent?

. . . . .

McNAMARA: I really don't know what Bobby told Dobrynin. It is likely that he'd been briefed by his brother beforehand. But if President Kennedy were going to strike on Monday or Tuesday, then he would have

---

* See the Afterword for further information, pp. 342–44.

told me about it so that we could make the necessary preparations. He hadn't told me, so I don't think he was going to strike.

BUNDY: The transcript of the meeting on the 27th gives a very short account of what Bobby was going to say. It was very clear that Bobby gave the Soviets warning that tough decisions were coming fast, but the President kept his options open.

. . . . .

GARTHOFF: I have no doubt that Khrushchev took Bobby Kennedy's message to be an ultimatum, but one which was coupled with an offer to resolve the crisis on the basis of his letter. His sense that there was a high probability of military action undoubtedly increased his willingness to settle.

NYE: Bill?

TAUBMAN: Khrushchev's memoirs, though not a perfect guide, seem to indicate that he got the message of an ultimatum. On page 414 of the briefing book, the passage reads: "President Kennedy issued an ultimatum, demanding that we remove our missiles and bombers from Cuba," and the next passage seems to indicate that he got the message from the meeting between Bobby Kennedy and Dobrynin.[53]

HORELICK: That would be consistent with his speech to the Supreme Soviet,[54] but note that he has to say that because he's got to justify caving in. He has a very strong rhetorical interest in depicting the situation as being just hours away from war.

. . . . .

SORENSEN: I agree with that last statement, but not with much else of what's been said so far. The main message Khrushchev got was from Kennedy's letter. The threats weren't new—they'd heard those all along—and the letter did not contain anything which sounded like an ultimatum. . . . . . The main offer President Kennedy made was both peaceful and conciliatory. It was an agreement not to invade if the missiles are withdrawn. That's hardly an ultimatum.

NYE: But my experience has been that the best way to deliver an ultimatum is to say, "It's out of my hands! I'm just trying to help you"— not, "Do this or else!" Wouldn't Bobby's message to Dobrynin have played like a sophisticated ultimatum, no matter what was intended?

CHAYES: Giving an ultimatum has a very precise meaning in diplomatic history, and the level of communication is always very important. I believe that Bobby was instructed *not* to give an ultimatum, and he was eager to relate that he hadn't. He'd given a warning, not an ultimatum—and that's important, both practically and semantically.

. . . . .

SCHELLING: As we know from negotiations with terrorists, divorce lawyers, and labor unions, to say "This is not an ultimatum" can mean either of two things: one weaker than an ultimatum, one stronger than an ultimatum. It can mean, "This is not my final offer—I'm still negotiating"; or it can mean, "This is a fact—I don't have any further control over the matter." And this latter stronger form of the statement often doesn't come across as a hostile act, merely as a communication of information. Part of the communication that Bobby Kennedy gave Dobrynin was, "Things are fast getting out of hand." I can certainly interpret this as a communication given in a friendly spirit.

. . . . .

GEORGE: I have a factual question related to Khrushchev's motivation for accepting Kennedy's terms. Perhaps he, too, was worried about inadvertent escalation, especially once the U-2 is shot down. I have heard that the Cubans actually had control of the SAMs; is that correct?

SORENSEN: Later there was a transfer of control, but my recollection is that, during the crisis, the SAMs were manned by Soviets.

SCHLESINGER: Some have claimed that Cubans controlled them, but it seems ludicrous that the Soviets would have allowed that. The claim we've all heard that Castro personally fired the SAM that brought down Major Anderson is just ludicrous.

SAGAN: Wasn't the issue whether the Cubans had *taken* control of the SAM sites?[55]

GARTHOFF: They were still under Soviet control. The story I had heard about Castro's claim was that he was being given a tour of one of the SAM sites, and he asked which button fired the missiles. He was told, he pushed it, and the missile coincidentally brought down the U-2. I think it's pretty clear that the story is apocryphal.

. . . . .

NYE: Scott, you wanted to rephrase one of your questions?

SAGAN: Yes, on the issue of civilian knowledge of the details of operational plans—the Secretary of Defense was pushing for all of the details on the quarantine, but what about the details of the SIOP?

McNAMARA: I did not push at that time for additional details of the SIOP. I *knew* what I was going to do with the SIOP. *None* of the options was going to be used at all. I had procedures in place for withholding, which, of course, would have given the military a fit; but before the Cuban missile crisis, I had recommended to President Kennedy that he never make use of the SIOP under any circumstances. Then as now, no human being could perceive all the contingencies and, in advance, decide exactly how to respond to them. We certainly didn't.

SAGAN: But what you had planned for is what they would have had to do had it been necessary.

McNAMARA: Not with respect to nuclear weapons.

SAGAN: In January 1961, McGeorge Bundy had communicated to the President his concerns that predesignated authority might have resulted in unauthorized use if communications failed between the President and certain commanders. Actions were taken by President Kennedy to reduce that risk.[56] But, in any case, you had to worry about the war plans on the shelf, theirs as well as ours. That's why the issue of pre-SIOP reconnaissance is so important. In a 1961 exercise called "Pine Cone," the SIOP was ordered executed by the Secretary of Defense in response to a reported large radar penetration by Soviet bombers.[57] What if they read our reconnaissance activities in a similar vein? What if we picked up a significant radar penetration? Wasn't there a risk the SIOP would have been used?

McNAMARA: No, I don't think so. We simply weren't going to use the SIOP no matter what. It's just not true that what was exercised would also have been authorized. The prior exercises can set up some possibly dangerous momentum, but that doesn't mean that reality is always going to unfold like an exercise.

SAGAN: But on this question of reconnaissance, few details of American operations were reaching you and you seem to have been relatively unconcerned about them. Did you have any information at all during the crisis about what the Soviets were doing and how they were reacting to our reconnaissance? Were they doing anything that increased their readiness for nuclear war?

Also, you might not have been willing to preempt, but you certainly considered the threat of preemption useful.

McNAMARA: Well, that might have been unwise. But what we were worried about was their preemption. They had three hundred soft weapons against our five thousand. It worried us that they might feel they had to use them or lose them.

NYE: What was the effect of the two U-2 events on your fears of loss of control? I'm referring to the shoot-down and the stray. The second you said you'd simply forgotten to turn off, and the air-sampling missions were expendable. What of the first?

MCNAMARA: My memory is weak on this; but we never intended to put either of those planes at risk, and we didn't think it either useful or necessary to respond to the shoot-down.

NYE: But was it worrisome, as far as loss of control is concerned?

MCNAMARA: Sure, it was worrisome. But we could have kept things under control.

NYE: We know from a memo that Adam Yarmolinsky later wrote that the Soviet strategic nuclear forces were not at a high level of alert.[58] Did that have any effect on your decision?

MCNAMARA: Not on mine.

NYE: Mac?

BUNDY: At no time did any consideration of nuclear alerts affect us in *any* way. That just wasn't part of our sense of danger.

SAGAN: Then why the fear of preemption?

BUNDY: There wasn't any.

MCNAMARA: We wanted to make sure the Soviets didn't have any incentives to launch, though we didn't expect that they would. I remember very clearly later when we first started getting reports that the Soviets were beginning to harden their silos, the story broke and I was quoted in print as saying that I was very glad to hear it. I was damn near lynched for saying it, but I thought it was a tremendous boost to crisis stability. It is very important to make sure that there are no incentives to launch, and the softness and vulnerability of the Soviet forces worried us for that reason.

BUNDY: We never thought there was any chance anyone was going to push that button deliberately.

BALL: Although the *momentum* of events was something of a worry.

MCNAMARA: Not a momentum toward strategic nuclear war, mind you—just the momentum toward the use of military force of whatever kind. When you look at two countries like the United States and the Soviet Union, you realize that a military conflict of any kind is something to be avoided.

ALLISON: But why the urgency? I still don't understand.

. . . . .

SCHLESINGER: Max Taylor had said on Saturday [October 27] that the Joint Chiefs wanted military action on Monday. That doesn't mean that there would have been military action on Monday, but the President plainly wanted to head off the pressure for it by getting Bobby Kennedy to get an answer from the Soviets before then.

. . . . .

SORENSEN: I'd like to say that I am completely convinced that the President was determined not to step on that ladder of escalation at all. But I don't know exactly what would have happened if we hadn't had an answer right away. It's very easy for us to sit here and say that we had a strong-minded President who didn't want war, and so there wouldn't have been a war; but there was enormous pressure for us to do something.

As far as the U-2 shoot-down is concerned, I think it is important to realize that the President didn't reverse his earlier policy; he merely postponed taking action in accordance with it.

MAY: What was Maxwell Taylor saying, and why was he saying it?

. . . . .

BUNDY: Max Taylor was merely reporting the Joint Chiefs' recommendation. As far as they were concerned, time was getting a little tight because you just can't keep an elaborate military apparatus in high gear indefinitely, and you can't keep flying surveillance missions over Cuba without increasing the risks that more planes are going to be shot down.

McNAMARA: Of course, low-flying reconnaissance planes were an alternative to the U-2s. I don't think the probability of further shoot-downs was very high, but you just don't want to take any unnecessary risks.

Max was a vigorous advocate of the Chiefs' position, but it would have been a mistake if we had allowed ourselves to be pushed into premature action. I'm just glad that not all the Chiefs were in the ExComm.

. . . . .

JAMES BLIGHT: . . . What was it that you were most worried about toward the end of that second week? Was it the domestic political situation? The fear of losing control of the military? Stress? Inadvertence? Was it something else?

. . . . .

DILLON: My impression was that military operations looked like they were becoming increasingly necessary. We were drifting without wanting to into becoming victims of a fait accompli, and some of us felt that that could not be permitted and that we had to do something about it. Military action was beginning to look like it was going to be the only way to do it, and when the U-2 was shot down, it added enormously to the pressure to act. By Saturday the 27th, there was a clear majority in the ExComm in favor of taking military action. . . . I quite agree that the President had not made a decision to use military force and that he was going to make his decision on his own with the advice of his inner group, which included the Secretary of Defense, the Secretary of State, and the Attorney General. It doesn't make much sense to ask questions like: Why not wait for action until Wednesday or Thursday?—because that's not how things worked. The pressure was getting too great. Some final decision had to be made very soon. Personally, I disliked the idea of an invasion, because of the lives that would be lost, the resistance we would meet in Cuba, and the loss of political support we would suffer around the world and especially in Latin America, where Yankees would be seen to be fighting Cubans who were, after all, fellow Latin Americans. Nevertheless, the stakes were so high that we thought we might just have to go ahead. Not all of us had detailed information about what would have followed, but we didn't think there was any real risk of a nuclear exchange.

. . . . .

DAVID WELCH: I still don't see how you thought you were going to manage to limit a conflict and prevent escalation once military action began. What thought had you given to this? How did you think you were going to keep things under control? What contingencies had you planned for? How and where were you going to draw the necessary lines?

NYE: Bob, do you want to handle that?

McNAMARA: Well, that's a very big question. So I think we ought to postpone it until this afternoon.

NYE: All right, are there any comments from other members of the ExComm? Ted?

SORENSEN: . . . I don't agree with Doug that we were all drifting toward an invasion. That isn't to say that the advocates of the quarantine weren't under pressure—we were, because the evidence was mounting that it hadn't worked. It was beginning to look like a failure. An invasion wasn't the only alternative, but we were thinking that we had to come up with *something*.

Now as far as the question about the expected length of the crisis is concerned, when we made the decision to opt for the quarantine we literally expected it to go on for months, though as the crisis wore on our expectations shortened. In retrospect, I would say that the crisis lasted thirteen days, not thirty. Once Khrushchev accepted our terms on the missiles, the pressure lifted right away.

. . . . .

BALL: It's extremely hard to reconstruct the feeling in the ExComm, and the receipt of the second letter was intensely dismaying. The hawks were gaining strength and momentum, that's for sure; but I was confident the President would make his own decision.

If it weren't for Bob McNamara and the prudence of the President, I would have been even more concerned at the time. But as Bob has mentioned, there was still a good deal of flexibility left in the quarantine. We could have extended the embargo to cover POL, and we could have gone even further than that if we had to. But if we were going to do an air strike at all, we could only avoid making a decision so long.

. . . . .

LEBOW: Some of you seem to be saying that the pressures you felt were a function of the fact that the missiles were becoming operational; others have said that they were a function of military demands; others have said that they were a function of fears of inadvertence; and still others worried about the international political context and the fact that there was a solidifying status quo of missiles in Cuba. But what of domestic public opinion and its pressures? To what extent was this important in the first week, and once the cat is out of the bag, what sorts of pressures and constraints did you feel from public opinion?

. . . . .

BUNDY: I've listened to the tapes of the October 27 meetings, and I can say with a high degree of confidence that I don't think there was any worry of that kind whatsoever. I have no recollection of anyone voicing any fear of being lynched over the affair in Cuba.

. . . . .

SORENSEN: Are you referring to the public opinion that was in favor of invasion or the public opinion that was in favor of our backing down?

There were both of those views, and it's misleading to suggest that all of the pressures of public opinion were in any one direction.

LEBOW:　But there would have been a dominant direction, and I would like to know how it was read and how it affected the decisions.

SORENSEN:　There was always pressure on all sides. We knew we were subjecting ourselves to heavy public pressure when we opted for the quarantine route, and we were prepared to accept whatever reaction there was to later decisions as well.

NYE:　If the suggestion is that public opinion was leaning generally toward a more active response, that doesn't seem quite obvious to me. Remember that we had just gone through four years of nuclear allergy since Sputnik and the alleged missile gap—

CHAYES:　There were very large demonstrations in New York City and people had banners calling for the end of the blockade, and saying, "We don't want to be nuked." There was a lot of opposition to stronger action.

NYE:　But let me push you on Ned's question just a bit. On the 27th, did you feel at all pushed by public opinion one way or the other? Doug?

DILLON:　Well, first, I don't accept the premise that we were swayed by the question of public opinion at all. I agree with Mac Bundy totally; I never heard in the ExComm any comment about public opinion or how our choices would fly politically or anything else like that. Obviously, every President has to consider that sort of thing, but that wasn't our job. Maybe the Attorney General paid a certain amount of attention to that, because he was so close to his brother; but we others—Bob McNamara, Mac Bundy and I, and the rest—that wasn't our role, and we didn't discuss it.

· · · · ·

BUNDY:　We started out feeling pressure because of the need we perceived to get the missiles out before they became operational. But by the second Saturday the pressures were coming from other directions— from the U-2 shoot-down, from the possibility that the Russians were going to be taking a harder line. Did the second letter indicate that hard-liners were taking over in Moscow? Tommy Thompson didn't know, but it was certainly a possibility. We were worrying more and more about the possibility of an intense confrontation at a non-nuclear level as a result of deliberate Soviet action.

· · · · ·

GARTHOFF: I have just one thing I would like to note about this question of urgency, and that is that the Soviet Embassy began burning its archives on the 27th. Usually, this should be taken as a sign that things are very late in the game and that they expect the worst momentarily.*

The general points made earlier about what Clausewitz called friction and the fog of war seem to me to have been valid, and extremely important as far as managing the crisis was concerned. To illustrate this, I'm going to tell you about three developments on October 22 that even the ExComm didn't know about at the time; and each of these had the potential to profoundly affect the outcome of the crisis.

First—and this is a story a colleague of mine has exhaustively researched and which he plans to publish in the fall, so I would appreciate it if none of us scooped him on it[59]—the Jupiter missiles in Turkey formally became operational and were handed over to the Turkish foreign minister on, of all days, October 22, 1962. The Turks knew that this was when the missiles were going to become operational, and presumably they thought that the Americans knew. But Rusk didn't, and when he spoke with the Turks long before the crisis about the possibility of dismantling the missiles, they didn't understand what he was talking about because he thought they were already operational and they knew they weren't.

Second—this is something that will come as a surprise to Mr. McNamara—the Commander-in-Chief of the Strategic Air Command, General Power, sent out the DefCon 2 alert instructions to all SAC units *in the clear*, without authorization, just so the Soviets could pick it up.[60] They did. The ExComm thought that the signal had gone out in code, which would have been the proper procedure. General Power had simply taken it upon himself to rub the Soviets' noses in their nuclear inferiority.[61]

Third, on the 22nd of October, Colonel Penkovsky was arrested. He had been under surveillance for some time, but the Soviets did not know what he had told us about their nuclear dispositions and capabilities, and perhaps about the Cuban missiles. . . . The Soviets knew there had been a serious breach of security, and they could only guess what Penkovsky had told us.

NYE: Can you elaborate that last point? What had Penkovsky given us?

GARTHOFF: He did not give us any advance information on the deployment of missiles to Cuba. . . . He *had* contributed to our knowledge of the SS-4s and SS-5s, and of Soviet military thinking and the military establishment up through September. . . .

---

* See Afterword, p. 344.

ALLISON: One more point. Penkovsky did provide important information on Soviet ICBMs, and the Soviets could have believed that he had given us enough information to allow us to target their nuclear forces if we went first.

GARTHOFF: That's true, and he also gave us some information on Soviet order of battle which wasn't relevant in this case. But Penkovsky didn't provide us with our best information on the location of Soviet ICBMs. That came from satellite photos.

. . . . .

SAGAN: It's vitally important to think of how Khrushchev was reading all of this. The U-2 overflight probably wasn't pre-SIOP reconnaissance—

MCNAMARA: No, it certainly wasn't.

SAGAN: But if I were Khrushchev, it certainly would have added to my sense of urgency.

. . . . .

CHAYES: I'd like to make a statement orthogonal to the topic at hand, if I may. We've been discussing the strategic interaction in rather formal, chess-like terms; but another very important element of the whole thing was the international political aspect. . . .

The Soviets were shocked by the OAS response, and I think that had something to do with their own. They simply misjudged the political costs of what they were doing. . . . The OAS support helped us in the UN. Previously, the Soviets had exploited our Latin American situation there after the Bay of Pigs, and we suffered a real defeat on that. The ExComm this time around appreciated the international-organization dimension of the affair—President Kennedy refused to sign the quarantine proclamation until after the OAS resolution, and then he cited it for support—and the result was that we had a surprisingly strong international political position, and we presented the Soviets with a united political front. . . . Let's not forget the importance of taking world opinion seriously, because that was something that was working in the Kremlin as well.[62]

. . . . .

Saturday, March 7, 1987—Afternoon—The Look and Feel of Nuclear Danger

NYE: . . . We are going to begin this afternoon's discussion by having a look at excerpts from an interview Dick Neustadt did with General Maxwell Taylor a few years ago. I'm sure you'll hear a few things in this tape which will provoke a good discussion of those aspects of the crisis that involved assessments of risks and dangers, as well as the purely psychological dimensions of the position some of you were in.

. . . . .

NEUSTADT: General Taylor, in the first week of the Cuban missile crisis, what was your perception of the problem, and the alternatives—the options to deal with it?

TAYLOR: Well, fortunately, there was no question about the problem. The President announced his objective within the hour after seeing the photographs of the missiles: it was to get the missiles out of Cuba. That solved so many things, because if you're drawing up a policy, it should consist of an objective and ways to get there. I find in Washington, more argument is expended on the first, they never get to the second.

Once we got such information as was available—and of course, the information is never complete, or entirely satisfactory—I would say we grouped ourselves around three possible alternatives. I call them (facetiously) to "talk the missiles out," to "squeeze the missiles out," or to "shoot the missiles out." The first was to use negotiation: get in touch with Khrushchev and tell him, "We know you're there, now you have to get out, let's talk about it." The second one turned out to be the quarantine solution: using a naval blockade, or something resembling one, again, to show the seriousness of our intent to Khrushchev, but avoid doing anything that might escalate rapidly to points in the sky, one knew not what. The third was to shoot them out, which was a surprise attack on the missiles in Cuba at the outset, without any notification to Khrushchev. And the question, I suppose, will be, why was I for shooting them out?

NEUSTADT: Sure.

TAYLOR: For the following reason. As an artilleryman, when I saw those missiles, with their transporter vehicles alongside of them, my immediate thought was they can pull them out and hide 'em any time they want to. And that was certainly the case. So if that's the case, and we announce to Khrushchev, "We gotcha down there," certainly at a minimum he'll hide those missiles in the jungles of Cuba, and we can never get 'em out unless we invade the island. Well, invading the island was the last thing I thought we should do, in our interest.

NEUSTADT: Tell me why.

TAYLOR: We were having trouble in Europe; Berlin was being threatened by Khrushchev; in the Far East we had the Laotian problem; the Vietnam problem was just burgeoning; and our forces were (relatively speaking) low, in numbers and readiness. And once you invade Cuba, what are you going to do with it? You gonna sit on it for eternity? You could have the seed of guerrilla warfare against our occupying forces, and again tie down a large part of our conventional strength. Of course you shouldn't want that. So there's a possibility if you hit the missiles before they got hidden, at least you'd have that many accounted for, in a positive sense. But furthermore, you will have really shaken Khrushchev; he will know we're moving right in. He doesn't want us to invade, either; and I felt there was a fair chance of him giving way on that point. So that was the reason why the Joint Chiefs, from the outset, recommended the "shoot 'em out" [approach].

It was argued very eloquently by Bobby Kennedy that that would be our doing the act of the Japanese in attacking Pearl Harbor. I never felt my conscience [one bit; it was] completely clear, because the President on the 9th of September, I believe it was, warned the Soviets that "if there are indeed offensive missiles in Cuba and you say there are not, I will take whatever measures necessary."[63] So he was warned, and he should have taken the consequences.

Now, having said that, we found the quarantine, as you know— the world knows now—the President, after listening to all the pros and cons of these three points, the first one dropped out very quickly. It really [came down to choosing between] the "squeeze 'em out" or "shoot 'em out" [options]. Not until the 21st, so far as I know, had he finally made up his mind. And then it was not to eliminate the "shoot 'em out," but to use the lesser method first, and then meanwhile the military were told to get ready for an attack on the missiles, and also ready for an invasion of Cuba.

NEUSTADT: Now, did you remain, as long as the issue was open, in favor of the "shoot 'em out" [option]?

TAYLOR: I never wavered until my Commander-in-Chief took another decision. And I add, I'm glad he did, because it proved to be enough.

NEUSTADT: General, you were loyal to the decision, but I take it you didn't think that the quarantine was going to work.

TAYLOR: I thought it had dangerous possibilities, because Khrushchev could simply bring his ships just short of the quarantine line and stand there and scream to the world over the violation of international law we were indulging in, and meanwhile start that argument going while his missiles completed their readiness in the island. That was certainly a possibility.

NEUSTADT: If one then had to turn to the air strike, which Mr. Kennedy apparently reserved as an option, what's the disadvantage of doing it later?

TAYLOR: Well, Khrushchev could have done two things with the missiles: continue to build 'em up, or hide 'em, which was always the option which I thought most likely.

NEUSTADT: That's what worried you most?

TAYLOR: Yeah.

NEUSTADT: All right; had you worried, in the first week, about the possibility that the air strike wouldn't suffice? Some other reason why it would have to be too big, would lead to invasion, or something of the sort?

TAYLOR: Yes. We analyzed very carefully the military require-ments of an air strike, and like most military requirements, the longer we studied, the more we needed. I believe that the total number of aircraft which the Air Force wanted to use was around five hundred. Well, that was a good way to kill the project! But then it was an honest estimate, because not only would you have to get the missiles on the ground, but meanwhile Cuba was prickly with SAM missiles—surface-to-air—many of which we knew were operational. So you had to protect your aircraft attacking the ground missiles [by eliminating] the anti-air threat.

So yes, that was thought about, and the President, very wisely, had General Sweeney,* a three-star general who would be re-sponsible for the outcome, and he came up and he gave a very frank statement. Yes, he would undertake it without any question,

---

* General Walter C. Sweeney, Commander of the Tactical Air Command.

but [he said] "you can't expect me to get 'em all; some of the missiles would get away." And these other requirements of collateral use of aircraft—yes, that was a requirement. So, really, Sweeney, at the last minute, by a straightforward statement—which the Joint Chiefs did not disagree with one minute—certainly tilted the President, if he needed any real tilting, to the quarantine option as the initial option, to be followed, if necessary, by the second.

. . . . .

NEUSTADT: Was it unexpected to you? Was [the final] outcome [of the crisis] unexpected to you?

TAYLOR: I was so sure we had 'em over a barrel, I never worried much about the final outcome, but what things might happen in between.

NEUSTADT: The outcome to which I'm referring is Khrushchev's acceptance of our—

TAYLOR: Well, at some time he *had* to accept. I never expected it on that particular day.

NEUSTADT: Okay, you thought it was going to go a while longer—

TAYLOR: Unless he was crazy and full of vodka. But I assumed his colleagues in Moscow would take care of him.

NEUSTADT: You have written in your retrospect in *The Washington Post* on October 5, '82, as I remember—the twentieth year—that you don't recall any concern about the strategic balance, or any fear of nuclear exchange in this whole period. Now, some of the civilians do recall worries about the time of that second Saturday; worries that really run to two or three steps up the ladder of escalation. The Soviets don't accept our demand; there follows an air strike; the Soviets then feel impelled to strike the missiles in Turkey; the Turks call on NATO for support; we feel we have to do something in Europe; the Soviets then launch a nuclear exchange—something like that was in some of their minds. I take it not in yours?

TAYLOR: They never expressed it to a military ear, I'll say that.

NEUSTADT: That's interesting.

TAYLOR: Not at all. It's the nature of some people [that] if they can't have a legitimate worry, they create them. Apparently they had some of that in the group you're speaking of.

NEUSTADT: In your mind, there was no legitimacy in this worry?

TAYLOR: Not the slightest.

NEUSTADT: Because Khrushchev could look up that ladder—

TAYLOR: If he was rational. If he was *irrational*, I still expected his colleagues to look after him.

NEUSTADT: And at the top of the ladder, if I understand what you saw correctly, the imbalance between the damage we could do to the Soviets and they could do to us in a nuclear exchange was so—

TAYLOR: Oh, of course.

NEUSTADT: —so enormous—

TAYLOR: Of course.

NEUSTADT: —that that would restrain them.

TAYLOR: Yeah; but why, oh why, didn't Khrushchev see this at the outset?[64] Because he was bound to lose with conventional forces right on our doorstep. He couldn't win! Except [the] only explanation that I can find that has a certain appeal is that the meeting of Khrushchev with President Kennedy in Vienna had so impressed him with the unreadiness of this young man to head a great country like the United States, plus the experience that he had seen in the Bay of Pigs, [led him to believe that] he could shove this man around any place he wants. Well, he was wrong.

. . . . .

NEUSTADT: Incidentally, when President Kennedy finally decided on the second Saturday to disarm the missiles in Turkey—those old missiles in Turkey—I take it, having disarmed them, he was going to announce it to try to demonstrate that we weren't there, that there was nothing there worth the Russians bombing. Did that trouble you at all?

TAYLOR: Yes, it would have been a great mistake to do it right in the middle of this thing. I was not aware of the fact [that] the President had discussed with State the desirability of getting the missiles out of Turkey until this time. And I opposed it, obviously.

When you've got the guy on the run, why say, "Come back, we'll give you a piece of cake!" Why do that? No sense in it whatever. It would again show, these uncertain Americans, they're not sure of themselves. It's quite true, the missiles were outmoded, and I was very happy to get 'em out after very careful negotiations with Turkey and [replace] them by the presence of a nuclear submarine.

NEUSTADT: But you were not persuaded by whatever concerns the President had to do this precipitous act in the middle?

TAYLOR: I didn't know he was going to do anything. I thought we'd talked him out of it.

NYE: Mac Bundy has kindly consented to start things off for us this afternoon.

BUNDY: It was a real treat to hear from Max Taylor. The clarity with which he represented his opinions strikes me as just a little different from the way in which he represented them in the ExComm, but there his job was to represent the views and opinions of the entire American military to the Commander-in-Chief. His concern in our meetings was with an effective military result, and of course that does leave out an awful lot of political considerations.

Let me start by saying that his recollection of Saturday afternoon [October 27] is a little different from mine. I don't believe he was at our ExComm meeting that day, because he was with the Chiefs working on their problems, not in the White House.[65]

The question of danger as perceived by the President is very important, and it is something that should never stray too far from our minds. It became particularly acute after Khrushchev's switch in messages. His second letter may have been one last ploy to hold together the people in the Politburo who didn't know about the first letter, or it may have been a simple toughening of their position. But it made us worry about the effectiveness of the quarantine and the possibility of Russian pressure elsewhere, such as in Turkey. The President worried a very great deal about the effects on the NATO alliance if our action in the Western Hemisphere led to Soviet action against Turkey. He was worried about what was going to happen if the Trollope Ploy* didn't work, and what we would have to do if the pressure increased any further. He was worried heavily about the level of unity in Europe, and he came back to this theme time after time. Some thought the worst outcome of all

---

* Kennedy's decision to "accept" Khrushchev's October 26 "offer" and ignore his October 27 missile-trade demand has come to be known as the Trollope Ploy. See Welch and Blight, "The Eleventh Hour of the Cuban Missile Crisis," p. 11.

would have been our selling out Turkey because of a problem in the Western Hemisphere, and that's probably how it would have been read had he agreed to swap Turkish missiles for Cuban ones. Some thought that would have been the end of the alliance. Others thought that the worst outcome possible was a geographic escalation of conflict.

I don't think, looking back, that the pressure was as great as the President thought at the time. But what if Bobby Kennedy's message hadn't been enough? This is why Bob is right that the real choice would have pressed itself forward on us in a way that would push us to build on our success already. Had we looked at the course of events since the 16th, both political and military, we would have recognized that the quarantine had been effective and that the danger to Khrushchev of trying to get warheads through the blockade would have explained why the blockade was never seriously challenged. We know what the Soviets would have thought if our quarantine had picked up warheads, all right.

So the shift from guarded optimism to the possibility of an even more serious encounter led to a profound sense of despair on that Saturday when the second letter came through. There was the threat of further action plus the sweetener of a proposed trade on the Turkish missiles, and the President had been making it clear all day long that he didn't want the Turkish missiles to stand in the way of a resolution of the crisis.[66] Dean Rusk was the prepared mind which was receptive to that point of view, and I have just been speaking with him on this very subject. Rusk and the President worked out in fifteen or twenty minutes the basis of a settlement which the President could resort to if Khrushchev's reply to his letter were negative. It indicates that he was prepared to go the extra mile to avoid a conflict, and to absorb whatever political costs that may have entailed.

I'm going to read you part of a letter Rusk wrote to Jim Blight about this, though I want you to understand that this is off the record until Dean Rusk says otherwise. The letter says this:

[T]here is a postscript which only I can furnish. It was clear to me that President Kennedy would not let the Jupiters in Turkey become an obstacle to the removal of the missile sites in Cuba because the Jupiters were coming out in any event. He instructed me to telephone the late Andrew Cordier,* then at Columbia University, and dictate to him a statement which would be made by U Thant, the Secretary General of the United Nations, proposing the removal of both the Jupiters and the missiles in Cuba. Mr. Cordier was to put that statement in the hands of U Thant only after further

---

* President of Columbia University; former United Nations parliamentarian.

signal from us. That step was never taken and the statement I furnished to Mr. Cordier has never seen the light of day. So far as I know, President Kennedy, Andrew Cordier and I were the only ones who knew of this particular step.[67]

Now, it's important to underline that this wasn't a decision; it was the necessary preparation for a possible future decision. But the direction of thought is clear enough.

NYE: When was this instruction given to Cordier?

BUNDY: The night of the 27th, after Bobby Kennedy was dispatched but before the response. It's interesting to note that this proposal wasn't going through the U.S. Mission. Cordier was a friend of U Thant's as well as of Dean Rusk's. The intention was to make it sound like a UN proposal, not an American one.

This doesn't mean that we know how great the risk of nuclear war was at the time. That is, this doesn't definitively show that there was *no* risk. In fact, I hope Ted will talk a bit about Kennedy's assessment that the risk of war was somewhere between one out of three and even. But it does show that the underlying risk was one of loss of control, rather than deliberate choice, and it's very hard to quantify that.[68] The closer you get to nuclear war, the greater the importance of small deterrents.

NYE: Thanks very much. . . . . . Let me note that there are at least five questions that have already been raised that we should try to give more detailed consideration to this afternoon. As I have them, they are as follows. First, what degree of risk did you perceive, and what was it risk of? Douglas Dillon said earlier that he felt there was no risk of nuclear war, and Max Taylor seems to have agreed. He spoke only of risks of *conventional* war. Others expressed their greatest anxieties precisely in terms of the risk of nuclear war. Why did people perceive the risks so differently? Second, what difference, if any, did nuclear weapons make? Imagine that this had been a crisis over events in Cuba but in a non-nuclear world—would things have unfolded differently? Was there anything unique about this crisis that had to do with the fact that it was a nuclear crisis? Third, what was the effect of fear? Recall the title of this session—"The Look and Feel of Nuclear Danger." When psychologists look at the Cuban missile crisis, they tend to assume that the effects of fear are universally negative. But are they? Darwin thought that fear was both functional and adaptive, and it may be that it can lead to a heightened sense of prudence. Maybe fear is helpful in a crisis, even if it is non-rational. Fourth, what was the effect of stress? Stress isn't the same thing as fear, although the two are, clearly, closely related: stress can come from fear or from fatigue, which were both present to some degree. What were the practical effects of stress? Finally, fifth, what would the crisis have looked like had it gone on longer—say, for sixty days instead of thirteen? What happens to the minds of a very small group of people and their ability to cope? . . .

SCHELLING: . . . In the late fifties and early sixties, I designed a series of "crisis games" to simulate what might happen under various scenarios in which military alerts, preparations for military action, and even uses of nuclear weapons all seemed plausible responses. I remember that I designed one for a crisis in Berlin, another for the Persian Gulf, a third for Laos, and so on. The participants included men like Paul Nitze, Charlie Hitch,* John McCone, Dick Bissell†—people who were basically comparable to members of the ExComm. They spent a very intense couple of days from 8 a.m. to 6 p.m. on each of these crises. . . . . . The participants did not play roles; everyone on a team was jointly responsible for the decisions they made. . . .

There were two properties that were common to all of these games: the first was that all teams—Red, Blue, or Yellow (which was what a Chinese team was called at the time)—exhibited extraordinary caution, prudence, and care at all times; the second was that there was no way you could have told from the participants' behavior who were civilians and who were military. The military men behaved indistinguishably from the civilians. Maxwell Taylor provides a good illustration of this. If in that interview we just saw he made, say, twelve judgments—four of them would have been military judgments, five political, and three diplomatic. The judgment that the missiles in Cuba were mobile was a purely military judgment; the judgment that the missiles would have been moved if we hadn't destroyed them in a surprise air strike was a political judgment, as was the judgment that we had Khrushchev over a barrel. He clearly didn't limit himself to military judgments in that interview, nor did the military men limit themselves to military judgments in my crisis games.

Why is it, then, that the Chiefs were in a tank or a cage through the missile crisis, having no contact with the President except through Max Taylor's occasional visits to the White House or General Sweeney's briefing on the air-strike option? Why did they feel so estranged, and why were they so suspicious of the Administration's judgment? My

---

* Charles Hitch, Comptroller of the Pentagon.
† Richard Bissell, Jr., CIA Deputy Director for Planning early in the Kennedy Administration. He and his boss, Allen Dulles, were forced to resign in May 1961, following the Bay of Pigs fiasco, which they had supervised.

hunch is that if they'd been present at the ExComm meetings, they would have stopped suspecting the President of being overly averse to the military and they would have had to concern themselves more with the political and diplomatic dimensions of the problem, possibly with moderating effects on their views. One of the most significant aspects of our "team" in this was, except for Taylor, who thought of himself as one of the Chiefs, no one else who was part of this collegial group was responsible for any military planning. That probably explains a very large part of their sense of estrangement. If we ever have need of a group like this again, consideration should be given to bringing people in from the military service and insisting that they take a full role in considering the various alternatives.

One final point. Late in Kennedy's Presidential campaign, several Chiefs proposed the pre-delegation of nuclear authority to SACEUR because of the weakness of communications in wartime. It occurred to me that if SACEUR had predesignated authority, the extra weight of responsibility might make them less rather than more likely to use nuclear weapons without orders from above. So I would like to suggest that the estrangement between the civilians and the military may have been a function of the fact that the military did not have any real responsibility for making the crucial decisions. . . .

. . . . .

McNamara: I still think, looking back on it, that we shouldn't have had more people in the ExComm, though perhaps it would have been okay to have more military people involved. But I would like to state that I for one didn't feel any sense of estrangement at all.

Schelling: Not even with the admirals?

McNamara: Well, that was a very narrow issue—we were talking about the fine details of the quarantine operation. I didn't mean to imply that we had a lot of wild men in the Pentagon, because we didn't.

. . . . .

Ball: It seems to me that if we'd had all the Chiefs in the ExComm, they would have had one big collective opinion on what to do, don't you think?

McNamara: Possibly. On the major issues, we might have just had five views like Taylor's.

Sorensen: Though, after the Bay of Pigs, the President had asked for written opinions from the Chiefs about what to do in Laos, and he got very different answers.

SCHELLING: Anderson wasn't acting like a Chief in one of my games when he was thinking about striking Soviet bases north of Iran. He had succeeded in breaking out of his real role then, and it's possible that the Chiefs would have done the same if they'd been full participants in the ExComm meetings.

SORENSEN: But you can carry that too far. You want the opinion of the military men as military men. When we wanted advice on the air strike, we brought in Sweeney. When we wanted advice on the quarantine, we talked to Anderson. These people participated and made a positive contribution as it was.

NYE: Ted, what about this question of the perception of risks? Did you share the assessment in that famous quotation that the risks of nuclear war were somewhere between one out of three and even?

SORENSEN: That quote has been misinterpreted. It doesn't refer to the probability of nuclear war; it refers to the probability that the Soviets would go all the way to war against the United States.

I think the fact that the crisis occurred in the nuclear era made all the difference in the world. Both sides behaved with extreme prudence as a result, and both avoided taking irreversible steps. None of us ever expected a nuclear first strike from the Soviet Union, nor did we intend one ourselves.

NYE: So what you felt was a diffuse fear of nuclear danger, not a specific one. Do the others agree? What about you, Douglas? You said this morning that you thought there was no risk of nuclear war whatsoever.

DILLON: The fact that we were in the nuclear age led me to believe that the likelihood of any Soviet military action was very small. I didn't think they'd directly initiate military action even after an air strike against Cuba. I was more worried about what Max Taylor referred to: an invasion of Cuba, becoming mired down, and the Latin American reaction that would have followed. The second letter made us all wonder what the Soviets were trying to do, and it seemed to me that we were being forced into military action.

The only time I felt a fear of nuclear war or a use of nuclear weapons was on the very first day, when we'd decided that we had to do whatever was necessary to get the missiles out. There was always some background fear of what would eventually happen, and I think this is what was expressed when people said they feared they would never see another Saturday; but that wasn't a logical thing.

. . . . .

BALL: I'd like to make a small qualification of what Doug just said. I thought *any* kind of shooting war with the Russians was dangerous because we didn't know it wouldn't go out of control. It's possible that one side or the other would have felt compelled to resort to nuclear war. We just couldn't tell for sure.

McNAMARA: At no time did I feel that strategic nuclear war was probable, even after a conventional clash.

NYE: What does "probable" mean there, Bob?

McNAMARA: Enough to cause me concern. What caused me concern was the feeling that if we initiated military action, something would follow. There would have been a Soviet response somewhere—and that was simply unforeseeable. I didn't expect a strategic nuclear exchange, but I just didn't know where things would go.

Sweeney had said on Sunday [October 21] that he was prepared to undertake an air strike and invasion, but that he couldn't guarantee that an air strike would get all the missiles. That caused me a great deal of concern. The probability was very low that they'd have been used—

NYE: How low? If you had to put a figure on it, what would you say?

McNAMARA: I don't know; maybe one in fifty, something on that order of magnitude. But the point is that I didn't want to risk millions of American deaths on a one-in-fifty chance when we could get those missiles out another way without running that risk at all, by turning the screw further. We had to make decisions from day to day, but we couldn't foresee everything, and I wasn't prepared to run unnecessary risks.

. . . . .

ALLISON: I remember interviewing you when I was working on my dissertation, and you said to me that on the 27th you worried that it might be the last Saturday you saw. So you must have been worried about some paths to nuclear war; what were they?

McNAMARA: If we'd not gotten the response we did from Khrushchev, I would have proposed an extended blockade. I didn't know what would have happened, but that course of action ran lower risks of loss of control.

It's true that we were all under a lot of stress. There's no denying it. But as far as I'm concerned we could have gone for days, even weeks, without serious problems. I was all right, and I could have handled the stress.

NYE: Mac?

BUNDY: In my opinion, the "turn of the screw" view would have won out. That would have kept the stress going longer, of course, and it's a good question what the effects of that would have been if the crisis had gone on for thirty days. I know there are stories of some people in the ExComm breaking down during the second week, but let me ask you: Would a man at the end of his rope behave with the wisdom and circumspection Rusk did on that second Saturday? I don't think so. Besides, most of us were under fifty—

SORENSEN: Hell, some of us were under forty! [Laughter.]

BUNDY: Stress and strain and fatigue might very well have been more of a problem for men in their sixties or seventies, but they weren't debilitating in our case.

NYE: Ned?

LEBOW: Granted, Bob, that the least likely scenario for a nuclear war beginning was missiles being fired from Cuba, you said that you expected a Russian response somewhere, and that that would lead to escalation. The question arose this morning: How and where did you expect to be able to stop it?

MCNAMARA: Right there on the blockade. Turn the screw on the blockade and avoid the air attack and invasion, which would probably lead to escalation. But even though there was a high probability of *conventional* escalation, there was a very low probability of *nuclear* escalation.

LEBOW: Those firebreaks seem awfully rigid in your mind. Why?

MCNAMARA: We could have accepted a lot of conventional conflict before we felt pressed to go nuclear—and, unless we stimulated Soviet preemption, we certainly couldn't imagine a Soviet first use given the tremendous nuclear imbalance. The danger wasn't one of nuclear war but of uncontrollable conventional war.

NYE: But in *Hawks, Doves, & Owls*, we concluded that the most likely scenario for a nuclear war was escalation from a conventional war.[69]

CARNESALE: It all seems too analytical in retrospect. If nuclear-armed missiles in Cuba are the problem in the first place, it seems hard to believe that you weren't concerned about the prospect of a nuclear war. It also seems a little funny that you worried about conventional escalation but not escalation to nuclear war, since you had massive conventional superiority in the Caribbean, and conventional inferiority in Europe that you had to shore up with nuclear weapons.

But I have a question on the nuclear balance. You've said that the balance didn't matter one bit. Suppose we'd had three hundred nuclear weapons and they'd had five thousand? Now what happens? Do things come out differently? It seems to me that nuclear weapons were very relevant. Am I wrong?

MCNAMARA: You're wrong, in my mind. I had no idea of how to use our five thousand nuclear weapons with benefit to the U.S. Set aside the question of whether or not there were nuclear warheads in Cuba; if we'd tried a first strike, the Soviets might have had 25 percent of their original three hundred left, and that was enough of a threat to keep us from going to nuclear war in the first place. Maybe you're very glad that I'm not Secretary of Defense now, but that's the way I believe you have to think of these things.

. . . . .

TAUBMAN: What did the risk of nuclear war seem like to the Soviets? The first place to look for evidence is at Marc Trachtenberg's article in *International Security*.[70] According to Marc, the Soviets were not engaged in anything like the nuclear preparations we were. What does that mean? Maybe it means they were having technical difficulties on their side. I prefer to think it has a political meaning.[71] Recall Khrushchev's account of how he felt upon discovering the capabilities of nuclear weapons. He says that he couldn't sleep for several days, until he finally decided that they couldn't be used, and then he could sleep again. Maybe the Cuban crisis changed his mind; maybe American nuclear preparations convinced him that nuclear weapons could be used after all, and maybe this scared him out of his wits. Or maybe he was just bluffing all along and was willing to keep up the pretense until the 28th when his bluff was called and he caved in, which wouldn't have been out of character for him at all. If so, then Soviet nuclear preparations were simply beside the point, because they were irrelevant to the psychological game he was playing.

. . . . .

HORELICK: I can't prove it, but everything I know leads me to believe that the Soviets worried more about nuclear war than you people did. They were just too scared to issue a general alert, for fear of provoking an American attack, just like Stalin was in 1941. It's the last thing they would have done. . . .

GARTHOFF: I agree very strongly with Arnold. We never observed any Soviet alerts, though in *Pravda* it was mentioned that Soviet forces were put on a general alert. All they did was cancel some scheduled leaves and troop rotations. They recalled to Moscow foreign diplomats who were traveling around the Soviet Union, but they went ahead with scheduled rehearsals for the military parade on November 7. Overall, they made a very low-level response to avoid provocation.

I think now, as I thought then, that the odds of a Soviet military reaction to a strike on the missiles in Cuba were extremely low. I believe they would have tried to come up with some sort of political counter-measure, but they were simply too scared to risk a military response.

. . . . .

BLIGHT: On Joe's question of the difference between this event and a similar one happening in a non-nuclear age: if you'd replayed this in a pre-nuclear era, would the outcome have been the same as if you had had positive information that there were no warheads in Cuba? In a similar vein, you've all indicated to me that the nuclear context made all the difference in the world. If you'd really feared loss of control, would it have made any difference to your choice of actions if you knew ahead of time that there would have been no Soviet response?

. . . . .

SORENSEN: Well, for prudential reasons, [President Kennedy] had to assume that there were warheads in Cuba. But obviously it would have mattered a great deal whether your loss of control problem was with a howitzer or with a nuclear missile. All-out conventional war was not unthinkable, whereas all-out nuclear war was.

Now, what if the nuclear balance was the other way around? Since we were unwilling to take any unnecessary risks in the face of such a small Soviet nuclear capability, it seems probable to me that it would have worked the same way if the shoes were on the other feet.

. . . . .

MAY: In the transcript of the first ExComm meeting, the fear of nuclear war is very evident. There is talk of chaos on the East Coast; Rusk says that if they shoot those missiles, "then we're in a nuclear war," and so on.[72] It seems unimaginable that the fear of nuclear war played no role in your deliberations.

I interviewed Curtis LeMay in the seventies on the question of the SIOP during the Cuban missile crisis, and he said to me then that it was his belief that at any point the Soviet Union could have been obliterated without more than the normal expectable SAC losses on our side—

DILLON: That's why he wasn't in our meetings. [Laughter.]

MAY: My question is: How did Khrushchev see the message from the United States? He had a lot of public and private signals coming from all sorts of channels. Did he read things the way LeMay did? What did he think we were going to do? I'm sure a certain amount of what the Navy was doing had nothing to do with the missiles in Cuba, but would have been read differently in Moscow. They must have seen our dispositional changes, SACEUR activity, the increased volume of military and diplomatic messages back and forth, and the signs of increased military readiness; their agents in Britain and the German Defense Ministry must have picked up a lot of distressing signals. Khrushchev must have felt extremely threatened.

CHAYES: I wasn't even in the meeting room, and I sure as hell felt scared. What we've been trying to do here is reconcile our emotions at the time with a retrospective calculus of probabilities. That's not how things worked. At the time, calculations of that kind wouldn't have made any difference—we were just scared.

   So what about Khrushchev? Of course he was scared! He *told* us so. The reason things settled out the way they did is because he was scared and we were scared; the reason the President was willing to go the extra mile on the Turkish missiles is because he was scared. There's only so far you can press an analysis of probabilities on fear.

NYE: Abe, do you think that fear had a positive effect?

CHAYES: Yes, I do. And in a non-nuclear era, our inhibitions would have been very different. Don't forget that we had complete local superiority. Our five thousand to their three hundred definitely had an effect on the Kremlin; but their three hundred also had an effect on us!

· · · · ·

ALLISON: It does look unlikely that any rational calculation could have led you to nuclear war. But to the extent that you had worries about controllability and projected those on the Russians, you must have worried a very great deal about nuclear war in any case. The *Guns of August* scenario rested on a combination of accident, misunderstanding, and miscalculation, and my own understanding of the event is that you all thought the *Guns of August* scenario was a plausible one.[73]

· · · · ·

HORELICK: What I hear from you resonates well with what I know of the Soviet side. The great fear there seems to have been loss of control. For that reason, the quarantine was vital; it didn't risk loss of control as much as the strike option did, though it did force them to make some tough choices. The question of what was going to follow the quarantine was a vital question; Bobby Kennedy's threat of further action forced Khrushchev's hand because of this.

BALL: We'd looked at the various steps to escalation for two weeks, and that's why we opted for what we did.

NYE: Ted?

SORENSEN: Let me make this a little more concrete. We'd had one of our U-2s shot down, but we were going to continue our surveillance. If we had a second or third or fourth U-2 downed, it would have been extremely hard to keep up our surveillance without taking military action to protect our planes, and the risks of inadvertent escalation would have increased as a result.

. . . . .

NYE: . . . We are out of time, so we will have to call it a day. Tomorrow morning is our final session, and we will concentrate on the lessons of the missile crisis. . . .

Sunday, March 8, 1987—Morning—Lessons

NYE: What we are going to try to do this morning is to determine what the lessons and implications of the Cuban missile crisis are for future policymakers. . . . Perhaps the most interesting place to begin is with Bobby Kennedy's book, which ends with the account of the meeting between von Bülow* and Bethmann-Hollweg.| "At the outbreak of the First World War the ex-Chancellor of Germany, Prince von Bülow, said to his successor, 'How did it all happen?' 'Ah, if only we knew,' was the reply." Bethmann-Hollweg had merely expected the Bosnian crisis all over again; von Bülow had warned him not to try to repeat it. One lesson we might learn from the Cuban missile crisis is the importance of not trying to repeat it.

We should start with the null hypothesis that there are no lessons for us to learn . . . that present conditions are so radically different from those that obtained in 1962 that we would be very dangerously misled if we tried to apply the apparent lessons from that context in the current one. There are five areas which are seen as preventing us from drawing

---

* Bernhard von Bülow, Chancellor of Germany during the Bosnian crisis of 1908.
† Theobald von Bethmann-Hollweg, Chancellor of Germany at the outbreak of World War I.

useful lessons. The first is the strategic situation: in 1962, we had a massive nuclear and local conventional superiority, as well as asymmetrical stakes. We are unlikely ever to be able to repeat this conjunction of circumstances. The second is the international political situation; world opinion was on our side. How many of you think that we could get anything like a quarantine measure through the OAS today? What about virtual unanimity in NATO? A favorable UN reception? Third is the domestic political situation: pre-Vietnam and pre-Watergate. Congress and the Presidency were very different then. Why didn't somebody try to leak the fact that Kennedy was about to cave in, to try to constrain his options? How was a leak prevented? Could it possibly be prevented today? Fourth is the area of nuclear operations: some things have gotten better now (for example, use-control measures such as PALs), and some things have gotten worse. But, more generally, things have gotten vastly more complex, especially nuclear operations—command and control are in some ways more tenuous, and now that we have prompt hard-target kill capability, there is considerably greater time urgency. Fifth is the change in the Soviet political situation: we know that Khrushchev was probably bluffing, and this explains why a risk-averse nation committed to an expansionist policy would back down. But what if Gorbachev had been in charge, or one of his successors, whatever they may be like? What about the effect of political and economic changes in the Soviet Union—are they likely to increase or decrease future risk-aversion?

So let's begin with the assumption that, for these negative reasons, there are no lessons to be learned, and let's see if we can find any which aren't ruled out by these considerations. We'll start with the seven lessons mentioned in Bobby Kennedy's *Thirteen Days*.[74]

First, take time to plan; don't go with your first impulse. George Ball reminded us of the importance of this on Friday. It seems to me that this one still holds, although it may be a good deal more difficult to do today than it was in 1962.

Second, it is important to make sure that the President is exposed to a variety of opinions. The Bay of Pigs was a disaster, Kennedy notes, in part because of the fact that everyone had been of a unanimous opinion and insufficient critical thought was given to the risks and implications of the action. This one still seems to hold, though, again, it might be more difficult to observe because time constraints are tighter today.

Third, use your Soviet expertise, and avoid mirror-imaging or projection. This one would seem to hold up well, and we have heard this repeated several times during this conference.

Fourth, keep civilian control and beware of the limited outlook of the military. This one is particularly interesting in the light of the debate Tom Schelling and Bob McNamara had on the issue, and I think the issue is still unresolved, though worth thinking about further.

Fifth, pay attention to world opinion. Abe Chayes has reiterated this for us a couple of times; I think the appropriate response to this one is "yes, but." That is, it is important to do this, but our ability to do this has atrophied, and for that reason, it is somewhat vitiated.

Sixth, don't humiliate your opponent. This is a good old classic lesson of crisis management; as the Chinese proverb has it, "Build golden bridges behind your enemy."[75] This holds up well today, but recall the point Maxwell Taylor made—that when you have your enemy on the run, sometimes it doesn't make sense to offer him a piece of cake. Perhaps we might have avoided some later problems with the Soviets and deterred them from adventures in places like Angola if we'd been tougher on them in Cuba.

Seventh and finally, beware of inadvertence—the *Guns of August* scenario. This one seems to hold as clearly today as it did then.

Now, why is it that some of these lessons still hold and others do not, especially in the light of the various respects in which the world has radically changed that I noted earlier? Because some things don't change all that much. One of these is human psychology; people still react to stress, fear, and fatigue the way they did in the 1960s. Another is the dynamics of small-group politics; the way in which personalities and organizational interests interact doesn't change much over time. A third is the wisdom of classical diplomacy; building golden bridges behind your enemy is as valuable and as important in the nuclear age as it was in the age of the great Chinese dynasties. A fourth is the awareness of nuclear risks and the importance of the crystal-ball effect. If the Kaiser the Czar, and the other leaders of Europe had been able to see in 1914 what the world was going to be like in 1918, there would have been no World War I; nuclear weapons provide a powerful crystal ball. They did in 1962, and they do all the more in 1987. That continuity remains— we can see when we embark on military conflict with another superpower that the end of the nuclear road is too disproportionately destructive to justify heading down it.

This suggests that nuclear war is not likely to come from rational action, but from loss of control—and this is the central claim made by what we have called "owls" in our earlier book. Among the lessons that owls would draw from the Cuban missile crisis are these: First, beware of the danger of misperceptions. Bob McNamara referred to the quarantine earlier as a signal to the Soviets. We know that it was only one among a very great number, several of which the ExComm didn't even know about, such as the DefCon 2 order going out over an open channel.

It is as important now as it was then to know how one's actions are being read by the other side. Second, organizational procedures are not fully controllable by small groups of men. We heard a great deal about the problems of micromanaging complex military operations such as a quarantine, ASW activities, and reconnaissance. Third, be sensitive to the risks of accident, as illustrated by the stray U-2 over Siberia. Fourth, be sensitive to the effects of stress and fatigue. It is interesting to me how much this was downplayed here—I don't know if that was done out of politeness or whether it was an accurate rendering of history. But when we look at the debilitating effects of stress, we often miss some of the beneficial effects of fear, and this is something that must be borne in mind.

Other lessons that seem to me worth taking from the Cuban missile crisis include these: Beware of being too clever by half—the uncertainties surrounding any crisis make it both impossible and unwise to attempt to craft and pursue a delicately nuanced strategy that relies heavily on your own virtuosity for success. Also, nuclear crises are different, as Ted Sorensen's earlier remark about howitzers and nuclear missiles aptly shows. This means that the First World War or *Guns of August* analogy is only valid up to a point, largely because of the crystal-ball effect of nuclear weapons. Finally, a little nuclear deterrence goes a long way. The United States was deterred from taking certain actions by the prospect of just a few Soviet nuclear weapons striking the U.S., despite an overwhelming nuclear superiority. This is a fascinating finding, and it leads to the question: Is this effect symmetrical? In other words, if the balance had been the other way around, would the Soviets have likewise been deterred? Our Sovietologists have given us some reason for thinking that the answer may be yes. One last observation: the Cuban missile crisis does not tell us how much nuclear deterrence is enough, or what form a deterrent should take; but it does make us think twice about relying on purely conventional deterrents, because these have readily broken down in the past.

So it seems that there are lessons that can be drawn from the missile crisis, and this conference has succeeded in reconfirming my biases in that regard. But let me now turn the discussion over to you, because I'm sure a number of you have different views. Graham?

ALLISON: . . . When they speak of power or strength, the Soviets use a good distinction between subjective factors and objective factors. The subjective factors seem to me to be at least as important to the outcome of a crisis like this as the objective ones. Take a group like the ExComm; the way they met and the experiences they brought to the crisis were major factors in the determination of the choices made. This comes out quite clearly, for example, when you try to explain why the blockade was chosen over the air-strike option. Now take the same group and look at the Bay of Pigs, or imagine that the Cuban missile crisis had happened in April 1961. What choices would have been taken, and with what outcomes? I suspect that things would have been very different. The relations among the members of the ExComm, their experiences on the job, and their relations to the President seem to me to be critical. These factors vary quite widely over time. Don't lean on a single case to derive lessons for crisis management and prevention, because when we do that, we overlearn.

Secondly, a few remarks about the issue of time. Joe and I teach a course in which we pose to the students the hypothetical situation in which the Soviets have installed cruise missiles in Nicaragua, and we ask them questions like: "When is the probable leak date?" The President asks his advisors: "How long do we have to decide?" The answer invariably seems to be: "Today; forty-eight hours, maximum, if you want the initiative of the first move." If that's right, because of changes in communication and the media and the Administration's ability to keep things secret, imagine that the Cuban missile crisis had occurred today. Suppose President Kennedy had forty-eight hours to make up his mind before the story leaked. He could either choose to make up his mind in forty-eight hours or forfeit the initiative. Imagine the former, which seems to me likely—George Ball has said that he thinks the choice would have been different. Is that correct? Would Khrushchev's reactions also have been different?

The frame of reference you bring to the issue is vital—the factors you think are important and the weights you attach to them—and this reinforces Joe's point. I remember very clearly when Herman Kahn offered a $1,000 prize to anyone who could come up with a plausible scenario leading to nuclear war between the United States and the Soviet Union. I thought I should have won it, because I could think of several plausible scenarios. Of course, he reserved to himself the right to decide what was and was not a plausible scenario, and his criterion of plausibility was rationality. It's very hard to get to nuclear war if the framework you bring to the question is purely rational. But if irrational factors are important in your frame of reference, things look very different. Even Bob McNamara made a remark yesterday which he prefaced with a comment something like, "Set aside the risk of warheads in Cuba . . ." That struck me as very revealing. The temptation is always there to "set aside" certain considerations, and this can have a powerful influence on the decisions that are made.

NYE: Ted?

SORENSEN: Joe, I thought your analysis was brilliant. First-rate. I'd like to comment on three observations and add some others.

First, on the question of our knowledge of Soviet politics, my sense is that things aren't very much different today than they were then. We still don't know very much about it. Second, on the question of world opinion, our concerns that we expressed then were not limited to what the UN might think of what we did, or what the man in the street might think; we were talking about the long-term stature of the United States in the world and how our actions would affect that. This is the real importance of world opinion, and it strikes me that it's just as significant now as it was then. Third, on your claim that "a little deterrence goes a long way"—that was certainly true as far as our group was concerned, but I don't know that it's necessarily true for all groups. Some of our military people, for example, weren't deterred in the least by what the Soviets had at the time, and it may be that people in future Administrations will or will not be deterred by different things.

Finally, let me add a few lessons, which aren't entirely new. First, you should begin dealing with a crisis with a course of action that is limited, flexible, and reversible. A number of us have come back to this theme again and again, and I think it holds up well today. Second, keep open your channels of communication with the other side, and keep the dialogue going. When you stop talking, things can begin to go seriously wrong. Third, make damn sure you elect the right President of the United States.

. . . . .

BUNDY: I agree that your opening statement was extraordinarily good, Joe, but I think *Thirteen Days* was a little optimistic about some things. It seems to me that the book is a little black-and-white where there ought to be shades of grey.

I'd like to add that I don't think the world would have been in a really bad mess if we had gone ahead with the Achesonian air strike. The nuclear context was vital, and as Joe suggests, the crystal ball might have kept order once we'd taken action. I also don't think that we learn an awful lot from the details of the Cuban missile crisis, because most things have changed in important ways since then. I agree with Graham that there is a great deal more time pressure now, but if you take Ted's point about finding a flexible first step which leaves your options open, you can deal with it because you won't be irreversibly committing yourself right at the outset.

On how much is enough, it is interesting to note that the missile crisis did not spread to any of the areas we expected it to. We had a respectable but, as it turns out, wrong fear of a third Berlin crisis. It doesn't seem that the Soviets were thinking in terms of escalating the crisis to Berlin, probably because of their own very great fear. The caution they exhibited was no doubt a function of the crystal-ball effect. That impulse to be very cautious is something that is becoming ingrained today. There are still people around in important positions of authority on both sides who have a collective memory of the Cuban missile crisis; sooner or later they will disappear, so it's very important to keep people afraid. Even a one-in-fifty risk is too much to take, and I think you're absolutely right, Joe, that a little deterrence goes a long way.

The most important part of crisis management is not to have a crisis, because there's no telling what will happen once you're in one. The fact that the Commander-in-Chief of the Strategic Air Command sent out an alert over the open channels without authorization was an extremely arrogant and undisciplined thing to do, and failures like that can have devastating consequences. So, more than anything else, the enduring lesson of the Cuban missile crisis is the importance of avoiding superpower confrontation.

. . . . .

BALL: Ted made a point that I would like to emphasize, which is the importance of not taking irrevocable action, or action which forces the Soviets to react in a particular way. Once you get into a fixed action/reaction dynamic, you can't predict where it's going to go.

I agree with what you said about the crystal-ball effect; it gave us an element of caution that just wouldn't have been there if we'd been in a non-nuclear world. You ask what would have happened if the crisis had occurred today? I'll tell you what would have happened. It would have leaked quickly, that's what. You couldn't count on the *Times* to be as responsible today as it was then, and not only because Dryfoos* and Reston were two of the most responsible people in the industry; Watergate changed the whole relationship between the press and the Administration, and today, with a fiercely competitive environment, the importance of being the first with the story would have overridden any sense of responsibility.

. . . . .

DILLON: I think Ted is right about his reading of the importance of world opinion; that's why I was unique among the so-called hawks in changing my mind. This was a unique situation, because the Soviet move was shocking to all of the American states. It's very difficult to imagine

---

* Orville Dryfoos, publisher of *The New York Times*.

that there would be the same kind of outrage today over, say, shipments of weapons to Nicaragua.

The main point I would like to make is this: there were real fundamental differences between the views of the hawks, including myself, and the views of those who were reluctant to take strong military action. The so-called hawks did not want war with the Soviets any more than the doves. But they had very differing perceptions of the risks involved in the use of force in the nuclear age. I didn't believe there would be any Soviet military reaction to an air strike even if accompanied by an invasion of Cuba, because of their awareness of our military superiority; I agree completely with Maxwell Taylor on that. This was something that they had started in our back yard, and they knew it was dangerous. I thought they might possibly blockade Berlin again, but I really didn't see any military confrontation beyond that. I think the Soviet perception of the importance of the strategic imbalance was different from ours, and that they put great weight on it. They were more deterred by far than we were to start anything that would cause trouble. The so-called hawks did not think that they were running any substantial risk of war with the Soviets, and certainly not of nuclear war.

I think there were very few on the ExComm who really expected further military confrontation if we'd gone ahead with military action after a Soviet rebuff of our final offer on October 27. Different groups worried about our taking military action, but for different reasons.

NYE: That's very interesting, Doug; it suggests that both hawks and doves had a similar view about the likelihood that nuclear war would come about through rational choice, but differed in their assessments of the risks of inadvertence.

DILLON: Well, that may well be right, but we (the so-called hawks) didn't worry about that, because we didn't think the Russians would start anything anyway.

McNAMARA: I don't think the Cuban missile crisis *was* unique. The Bay of Pigs, Berlin in '61, Cuba, later events in the Middle East, in Libya, and so on—all exhibit the truth of what I'll call "McNamara's Law", which states: "It is impossible to predict with a high degree of confidence what the effects of the use of military force will be because of the risks of accident, miscalculation, misperception, and inadvertence." In my opinion, this law ought to be inscribed above all the doorways in the White House and the Pentagon, and it is the overwhelming lesson of the Cuban missile crisis. "Managing" crises is the wrong term; you don't "manage" them because you *can't* "manage" them. . . . And that holds whether or not you're talking about a nuclear crisis. Even if we hadn't had nuclear weapons, conflict with the Soviets was something to be avoided because of the massive power of the two blocs.

And another thing: it's very dangerous to bring in the president of Ford Motor Company—or even worse, General Motors [Laughter]—to be Secretary of Defense. I'm only being half facetious here. I really think it is vitally important to have people in top Administration positions who have some prior expertise in national-security matters, and it's at least as important to have people who understand the Soviets available when you need them.

Another lesson I would take away from this is that each Administration, early in its term, should get all the relevant people together to draw preliminary guidelines for the use and non-use of nuclear weapons, first, in retaliation to one's opponents' use of nuclear weapons, and second, in all other cases. That would at least help reduce some of the risks of inadvertence.

. . . . .

DILLON: I agree with Bob on the importance of expanding our understanding of Soviet thinking. That should be an ongoing process.

I want to note that everything I've said about what I thought we should have done at that time doesn't apply today, mostly because of the changes in the military situation. If the Cuban missile crisis happened today, I'd react in much the same way as Bob McNamara, and I would like to make that absolutely clear.

. . . . .

GARTHOFF: I agree with Bob McNamara's main conclusion that it's more important to avoid crises than to plan to deal with them. From the Soviet writings I have seen and the conversations I have had with Soviets, it seems to me that they would strongly agree. . . .

I agree that it's important to try to emphasize Soviet thinking, and to try to understand it as far as you can, though I disagree with Ted Sorensen's suggestion that we know as little about the Soviet Union now as we did then. On the contrary, I think we know the internal Soviet situation quite well; but I agree there will always be uncertainties and gaps in our knowledge that will loom large, particularly during crises.

I think the Soviet leadership knew how unusual the move into Cuba was, and felt a certain amount of responsibility as a result. I think it's right to say that they felt justified in deploying missiles there, especially in view of the apparent symmetry with NATO's nuclear weapons; but they still felt that they were responsible for the mess they had gotten themselves into.

We have overstated the cautionary effect of nuclear weapons, I think, because the historical record shows that when we warn them against doing something, sometimes they back off and sometimes they do not. I didn't believe that a Soviet move against Berlin was likely even if we had taken stronger action, partly because, despite the fact that there were the symmetries we have been talking about, we had a treaty commitment to Europe and they didn't have a treaty commitment to Cuba, not accidentally. I think that's very important. . . .[76]

. . . . .

CHAYES: . . . We should obviously use our Soviet specialists, but there's a problem with relying on expertise too heavily, and that is that these people often have a very particular reading of the Soviet Union. Nothing substitutes for a little direct experience of the Soviets, and I think for that reason there is a strong argument for much wider contacts with them. Of all the members of the ExComm, only Tommy Thompson had gone to the U.S.S.R. Any ExComm today would include a lot of people who did have extensive contacts with the Soviets.

Secondly, as far as world opinion is concerned, it would be a mistake to overemphasize this today. In 1962, NATO was less suspicious of the United States, and we had a base of support in the OAS because the Alliance for Progress had worked to some extent. We had considerable stature worldwide. Since Vietnam, we have lost the reputation for responsible leadership and we have lost a lot of sympathy around the world. You don't garner world opinion in the last week of a crisis; you need to have it going in.

Last point, going back to the Jupiters. Max Taylor said that there were three options—talk the missiles out of Cuba, shoot 'em out, and squeeze 'em out. There was a fourth: buy 'em out. This one gets talked about much less than the others because of the power of the Munich stigma and because it sounds a lot less courageous. But in fact we did, in part, buy 'em out, and the President seems to have been willing to go even further than he did in this direction if need be. He was willing to pay an enormous price in world opinion and in his domestic standing, but the other options had prices, too, and who's to say that this one was the highest? An invasion carried with it the price of all those lost lives, and possibly even a bigger political price around the world and at home than a Jupiter swap would have incurred. . . . I have a distinct recollection of a meeting on Saturday the 20th in the Situation Room— Bob, I think you were there, and Bobby was, too; it was a meeting of Indians, not Chiefs, because we were preparing for some of the organizational details of the quarantine—anyway, the President had rejected Stevenson's idea of a trade, and somebody polled the group on whether we thought we were going to get out of this thing without trading the Jupiters—I think it was you, Bob—and not a single person thought we were![77]

The tendency is for us to compartmentalize the different options. In fact, we used *all* of the options except the air strike. We used an orchestrated approach on a wide variety of fronts. The mixture of options is what did the trick, not any one of them, and in my opinion the buy-out option—the one mentioned in Dean Rusk's letter—played at least as important a role as anything else.

. . . . .

BALL: Just a note on world opinion. At the time of the Cuban missile crisis, the United States had never cast a single veto in the UN Security Council. Up until that time, the Soviets had cast 109. Our first veto was in 1970, and since then, the U.S. has cast over forty—more than half of those during Reagan's Presidency—while the Soviets have cast only nine. That's a pretty clear indication of trends in world opinion of the superpowers, if you ask me.

. . . . .

CARNESALE: Before we go too far drawing lessons from a data set of one event, imagine that there had been a successful air strike, and let's go through Bobby Kennedy's list of lessons and see what they might have looked like. First, on the question of time: Suppose the presence of the missiles had leaked, but not in time to foil the air strike because it was chosen and implemented fairly quickly. The lesson? "Act quickly and decisively." Second, instead of "bring all options onto the table," the lesson that would have been drawn might be: "Don't waste time exploring implausible options. Make your choice, and have the responsible staff do its work." Third, on the use of Soviet experts: Bobby might have said, "You can't predict Soviet behavior any better than you can predict American behavior, and besides, you can find a Kremlinologist who will support any particular view." The lesson? "Don't pay attention to so-called Soviet experts." Fourth, on the importance of keeping civilian control: Of course you should keep civilian control; but once a military option is chosen, let the military professionals implement it, not civilian amateurs. Fifth, on paying attention to world opinion: World opinion accommodates to power, as we saw in Grenada and Libya. The lesson? "Keep American vital interests in mind, and don't worry so much about what the rest of the world thinks." Sixth, on the importance of not humiliating the opponent: "Either make the adversary believe that the alternative to your preferred outcome is humiliation, or make clear to him that the alternative to humiliation is nuclear war." Seventh, on being wary of inadvertence: Of course you should beware of inadvertence; but notice how much of it there was in the Cuban missile crisis, and it didn't matter at all with regard to the outcome! Maybe we should add an eighth as well, which is: "Nuclear weapons are not usable; therefore, we needn't fear escalation. A little deterrence goes a long way."

Now, all that's unfair to Bobby Kennedy, but not to the conference. For instance, what he meant to emphasize was the importance of thinking of all the options, not taking a lot of time to do it. There are other things that are even more important than any of these. First, figure out what's at stake! It's remarkable how little agreement there was on this here this weekend. And second, don't have a process that creates a crisis unless you want one. The crisis was caused by the United States because of the way it reacted to the missiles in Cuba. The fact that there was a time deadline, unless you believe that the question of when the missiles were going to become operational was important, was entirely self-generated.

. . . . .

SCHELLING: I want to state something I firmly believe that hasn't been mentioned yet, and that is that the Cuban missile crisis was the best thing to happen to us since the Second World War. It helped us avoid further confrontation with the Soviets; it resolved the Berlin issue; and it established new basic understandings about U.S.–Soviet interaction. Sometimes the gambles you take pay off.

If I took the risks of nuclear war to be McNamara's one in fifty, I'd conclude that the risks were worth taking if the risks were greater than one in fifty with things going on as they were in Berlin and elsewhere. The answer to Al's question, "Do we want this crisis?" is yes. Now, that doesn't make me a hawk; I worry enough about nuclear war that I am willing to take a one-shot risk to reduce the risks over the long run.

Take Khrushchev's profession of his desire to prevent the invasion of Cuba at face value, for a moment. If that is what he wanted to do, then he would have preferred that he secure Cuba against invasion without having his nuclear missiles there if he could. As things turned out, he emerged better off than when he went in. He got his assurances, and he didn't even have to leave his nuclear missiles in. He also got his piece of cake, because the Turkish Jupiters were going to be coming out as well. But of course, this didn't play in his Peoria in '62.

I don't think the Cuban missile crisis should be repeated, but I do think it was a good crisis. That sounds like a strange view to some. But

I want to tell you about my reaction on the night of the 22nd, when President Kennedy gave his speech revealing that we knew about the Soviet missiles in Cuba. I was at a Harvard–MIT Arms Control Seminar that night at the Faculty Club, and we all gathered around the television to listen to what the President had to say. I remember after the speech we were left with a sense of gloating; we just couldn't imagine how Khrushchev could have done such a dumb, blundering act, and we knew that we had him on this one and the only question was how bad a fall we were going to give him. But my impression here is that this is not at all how people felt in Washington. Why not? Why did we react that way, while you didn't? It's not that you knew things in Washington that we didn't know; what we in Cambridge know now that we didn't know then about the huge superiority of the United States in nuclear weapons would have reassured us even more. My guess is that the difference is explained by the fact that you were the ones who suffered from the stress; you were the ones who were in the difficult position of having to make the decisions. The stress of *responsibility* may simply make a very great deal of difference. . . .[78]

As I said at the beginning, I'm surprised the conference hasn't gone the way I'd expected. Jim Blight has asked the question, "Why did crisis prevention fail?" and I want to ask the question, "Aren't we glad it did?" I think I agree with Bob McNamara that crises should be avoided at all costs in this day and age; but I'm glad *this* one wasn't.

BUNDY: I agree with you; it was a tremendously sobering event with a largely constructive long-term result.

I think putting the odds of nuclear war in the Cuban crisis at one in fifty is too high. If I had to put a number on it, I think it would have at least three figures. But, over the long haul, one in a thousand is too high if you aren't steadily reducing it as you go. On the other hand, one in fifty is acceptable at one time if running the risk results in a later risk of one in a hundred, then one in a thousand, and so on. I really do think that the Cuban missile crisis was a massive risk reducer.

. . . . .

LEBOW: . . . When we were trying to determine why the Soviets were putting missiles in Cuba, there was a difference of opinion between scholars and the members of the ExComm. The ExComm at the time of the crisis read it as an episode of Soviet expansion encouraged by their perceptions of Kennedy's apparent lack of resolve, while the scholars here have been describing the deployment as a defensive move, something Khrushchev had to do because of his own political needs. It's interesting to me that the ExComm people are coming around to this latter view in this conference; had they seen things that way in the first place, their responses would have been very different, I think. . . . As far as the outcome is concerned, I agree in retrospect that we were lucky and that the missile crisis lowered the long-run risks of nuclear war. But its damaging effects included Vietnam, where wrongly applied lessons had a disastrous outcome, as well as a long and sustained Soviet buildup. After Cuba, the Soviets were not willing to be caught in a position of such inferiority that they could be humiliated by the United States again. For these reasons, we might want to think twice about whether Cuba was the glorious event Tom Schelling seems to suggest.

. . . . .

GEORGE: . . . My studies have indicated that the perception of objectives is very important, because it determines how you can act. They also show that a basic rule of prudence essential to successful crisis management is that neither side should initiate the use of force against the other's military forces. An important corollary of this is: Don't exploit your advantages to force the other side into a choice between a serious defeat and the use of force.

What is crisis management? It is the management of the tension between the objective of protecting your most important interests and the objective of avoiding escalation. This is the basic tension and policy dilemma in all crises, and dealing with it requires a sense of strategy. Bob McNamara has been quoted as having stated after the missile crisis that henceforth there is no such thing as strategy, there is only crisis management. As I see it, however, the problem in a crisis is to devise a strategy which will allow you to achieve your objectives without a military confrontation. In the Cuban case, the strategy the United States employed was a coercive approach; in other crises, other strategies have been effective. The point is that if we are going to be able to manage crises successfully in the future, we need to build a repertoire of strategies to choose from.*

---

* [William Taubman adds:] On the issue of what lessons should and should not be drawn from the crisis with an eye to applying them in the future, I'd like to stress again the importance of what I see as Khrushchev's uniqueness. As I pointed out earlier, his singular character and approach are central to explaining both why he placed missiles in Cuba so recklessly and why he took them out again so readily. The implication of his uniqueness for crisis prevention is reassuring; namely, that no future Soviet leader is likely to get himself into a Cuban-style fix. But the implication for crisis management is not so reassuring; namely, that if and when a non-Cuban-style crisis does break out, a future Soviet leader may be more likely than Khrushchev to stay the course—motivated, in part, by the more "normal" (i.e., non-Khrushchevian) conviction that nuclear weapons are for use, not just for bluff.

. . . . .

SAGAN: The operational revelations we've heard at this conference reinforce my impression that the military machine is so complex that no ExComm can know and handle everything at once. An irony of the Cuban case is that that fact may have been helpful in bringing about a favorable resolution—but we shouldn't press our luck the next time.

Several quick points. First, I agree that we should avoid crises where we can; but that's not always our choice. Sometimes we just have crises thrust upon us. Second, it is extraordinarily important that we do something to institutionalize what Bob McNamara did with the admirals. Alex George has given some thought to using the NSC* in this way, and I have given some thought to the possibility of using civilians in operational roles. Third, we ought to try to find some way of getting people in positions of authority to pay attention to these sorts of things ahead of time. I realize it's difficult to do this, particularly with busy and self-confident people. Fourth, some of the remarks that were made about exercises and war games were very interesting, and I wonder what can be done to encourage nuanced exercises for people in positions of responsibility. . . .

. . . . .

NEUSTADT: I get a depressing underlying lesson from the Cuban missile crisis, which is that the President of the United States is very isolated in the thinking he has to do and the concerns he has to take under consideration, even in the presence of a group like the ExComm. . . .

The President is the only person constitutionally responsible for foreign policy and for national security, and it would be very nice if he had some comprehensive advice to match the mix of demands placed on him by virtue of his position. Doug Dillon made the interesting remark that the ExComm didn't advise the President on the politics of the event. *Somebody* should have been able to do that; it's part and parcel of his responsibility. . . .

[President Kennedy's] subjective estimates of risk may be opaque, but let me give you a concrete example of the kind of thing he had to think about. In the Civil War, out of a total population of 31 million, 600,000 people died. Bob McNamara's account of the prospective civilian deaths that could have been anticipated if Soviet nuclear weapons fell on the United States was roughly proportionate to that. It took this country a hundred years to recover from the Civil War. President Kennedy saw nothing worth even a low risk of that. At the end of a TV interview he did in 1962, Kennedy said, "The President bears the burden

---

* National Security Council.

of the responsibility; advisors can move on to fresh advice." I have been tremendously impressed at how you participants have been able to do that and at how the academics present cannot resist thinking of this affair as one of Tom Schelling's games. I'm sure Kennedy didn't.

The President's recollection of the control problem was, I think, a little different than has been recounted here. He is reported to have asked at one point, "Suppose Khrushchev has the same degree of control over his forces as I have over mine?" The prospect horrified him (to judge from one short conversation some months later); his fear was of a *mutual* loss of control, and I think that this explains why there was such prudence in his choice of actions. Look at what he did with Rusk that Saturday night. Kennedy was preparing then to take a hell of a lot of heat on the Hill in order to avoid any escalation of the crisis. But if he'd gone into a third week just fiddling with the blockade, I think the heat for that would have been even worse. Maybe he thought so, too. When military officers tell congressmen that the Administration is not doing its duty to the country, you know you're awfully close to a loss of control. Shades of Douglas MacArthur, the classic case; President Kennedy, I take it, was prepared to take the heat on a trade for the Turkish missiles rather than allow the crisis to go into a third week and run that risk, never mind the risks of escalation per se. Moreover, a week before, J.F.K. had virtually committed himself to an air strike if the blockade didn't work. The air-strike advocates were heating up, and if things had gone into a third week, the blockade would no longer have flown politically—not many days, in my judgment.

I am also impressed that it was Rusk, a man accused of seldom being there, that the President finally turned to on the night of the 27th. He was the man who would have been called up to Capitol Hill to explain why they had sold out an ally; he was prepared to draft the trade and to take heat for it. . . .

The President's office is a lonely one, and the burden of responsibility is very personal. If we expect so much of the Presidency, we should also provide it with the advice it needs. . . .

. . . . .

SORENSEN: . . . I'd like to say a concluding word to a weekend that I've enjoyed very much; and that is that the gap between research and participation is aptly symbolized by the gloating in the Faculty Club Tom Schelling told us about earlier. And I think the difference is, as he aptly said, a difference of responsibility.

. . . . .

BUNDY: To be fair, the people in the Faculty Club were just going on the basis of that speech. We sure didn't feel as good as that speech sounded. . . . [Laughter.]

NYE: Marc Trachtenberg and Graham Allison will be our last two speakers. You both have an impossible task, summing up what we now know that's new, and where we need to go from here. Marc?

TRACHTENBERG: . . . Let me start by talking about how I've changed my mind as a result of what's been said here—those issues where I now think I was wrong.

First, I really did think, until a few days ago, that an invasion of Cuba was imminent at the end of October. But now—if only because of the new information from Rusk—this issue seems much less clear-cut.

But still, that final weekend there was a real sense of urgency. What was it rooted in?[79] I had thought that the whole issue of when the missiles were becoming operational had created a sense of a deadline for action that remained pretty constant over the whole two-week course of the crisis. But now I see this was wrong. The key thing was the narrowing of the time constraint during the second week. What exactly was driving things—why were things coming to a head? It's not that the question of missiles becoming operational counted for nothing. The important thing is that it was just one issue, embedded in a whole complex of issues. And it was the complexity of the situation—the impossibility of anyone understanding, let alone controlling, everything that was going on, especially in the area of military operations—that seems to have generated a sense of uncontrollability, and thus a feeling that the matter had to be resolved very quickly. . . .

The next point relates to the whole question of Soviet military preparations—or really their failure to do anything like what the United States was doing at the time. What is striking here is not just the asymmetry in this area, but the fact that our top officials didn't seem to care very much about it. You'd think that we'd have been looking for every possible indicator of Soviet intentions—

BUNDY: That *was* going on—

TRACHTENBERG: *Every* possible indicator? I don't think so. What strikes me as incongruous about all this is that from the very beginning of the crisis, the U.S. side paid a good deal of attention to the kind of signals *our* military moves were giving. Even as late as November 12, Secretary McNamara opposed any relaxation of the extraordinary U.S. alert level, saying that "any reduction in the state of readiness of U.S. forces would be a sign to the Soviet Union."[80] We think that what is important is the message that *we're* giving, what *we're* doing and saying.

But sometimes how we listen—how well we listen—is equally important.

There's one final point—a basic issue that we skirted around but never really focused in on. Ted Sorensen said that it would have complicated things for us if the Soviets had deployed the missiles in Cuba openly. There is this basic problem of symmetry: What gives us the right to have missiles in Turkey, but doesn't give them the right to have missiles in Cuba? I'm not saying there's no answer to that question, only that it should have been faced directly—

BALL: We did discuss it in the ExComm.

TRACHTENBERG: That was too late. Why wasn't it done earlier?

BUNDY: We'd also decided in '61 to take the Jupiters out.

TRACHTENBERG: This issue had been around for a long time. Even in 1959, when the original decisions were being made, Eisenhower had remarked that while it was okay to put missiles into the core NATO area in Western Europe, deploying IRBMs on NATO's southern flank was "very questionable," and would be similar to the Soviets putting missiles into "Cuba or Mexico."[81] A little while ago, Alex George quoted Secretary McNamara's famous remark: "There's no such thing as strategy any more, only crisis management." I'm not sure that I'd go so far as to reverse it completely, but I do think that more attention has to be paid to these basic issues of policy *before* you get into a crisis.[82]

. . . . .

ALLISON: . . . I think we've learned a lot about the Cuban missile crisis, but less than should have been expected in twenty years. First, on causes: We have more information on Khrushchev's motivations, American first-strike capability, attempts to subvert Castro, and how things were being seen in Moscow. Given these factors, I now believe that reckless action was more probable than I'd thought in the 1960s. We weren't thinking enough about the effects of our actions on the Soviets. Clearly, this is an aspect of American policy that needs much more thought. . . .

I don't know whether the McNamara/Bundy view that the next step would have been another turn of the screw rather than an air strike is a revision of history, but I suppose there is a chance that POL would have been added to the embargo list and even that it might have done the trick. I wonder, though, whether the President would even have opted for this, given the preparations being made for a public deal on the Turkish missiles. He may have gone for the quick exit.

The risks of inadvertence seem to me now to have been even more impressive than I'd thought then, given Ray Garthoff's numerous revelations. It's obvious now that there were a number of fuses to war, many of which the ExComm didn't even know about, let alone have control over.

On the sense of danger, I think I agree very strongly with Ted Sorensen's view, and my prejudices on this have been confirmed. As we get further away from the crisis, it seems less and less conceivable that we were running any serious risks; but at the time the Administration had plenty of reasons for feeling the heat.

Bobby Kennedy's lessons are interesting ones, and not the less so for having been made by a man in his position. If we listen to Bobby, President Kennedy explained what he was doing in terms of responding to a Soviet violation of a precarious status quo and tenuous rules of the road. One of the main additions I would make today to my dissertation would concern the importance of the rules of the road and the precariousness of the status quo, and how they affect expectations, perceptions, and assessments of risk.

In conclusion, let me make note of President Kennedy's quotation from which I borrowed the title of my book, that "the essence of ultimate decision remains impenetrable to the observer, and even to the decider."[83] There are always dark, impenetrable corners to every event of this kind; and so, for the cottage industry of missile-crisis studies, may there always be dark corners.

The View from Washington and the View from Academe

The meeting of scholars and former policymakers at Hawk's Cay originated in our belief that two very different kinds of knowledge inform our collective understanding of the Cuban missile crisis and that these two modes of comprehending this pivotal event are seldom, if ever, encouraged to confront one another directly. Together, they epitomize Kierkegaard's famous dictum: "It is perfectly true, as philosophers say, that life must be understood backwards. But they forget the other proposition, that it must be lived forwards."[1]

On the one hand are the scholars, journalists, and other commentators, in search of explanations for judgments made and actions taken, who begin their studies with facts and theories and with the retrospective realization that the crisis lasted but thirteen days, ended without a war, and was, on the whole, a positive turning point in U.S.–Soviet relations. On the other hand are the participants in the crisis, whose understandings of the event begin with the lived experience of it, not knowing its outcome at the time, but knowing with painful certainty that a critical failure or misjudgment on their part, or even a bit of bad luck, could conceivably have resulted in the worst catastrophe the world had ever seen. Scholars understand the event backwards; the participants themselves lived it forwards. We presumed that this difference would make it extremely difficult for scholars and policymakers to see the crisis in the same light. At the same time, we realized that it is of crucial importance for members of each group to move closer to a common understanding of the crisis. The discussion at Hawk's Cay confirmed our judgment that this gap exists and that it is clearly in need of a bridge.

In organizing the meeting at Hawk's Cay, we sought to create a situation in which the points of view of both groups, analysts and former policymakers, would collide in useful ways.[2] We hoped two things would happen. First, and by far most important, we hoped the former Kennedy Administration officials would, under scholarly criticism, provide a more complete picture than we have had of what it was like to try to manage the most dangerous crisis in history, and, in the process, challenge the scholars—whose models and interpretations of the event largely ignore the role of subjective factors in its conduct and resolution—into rethinking their views. Second, we hoped that the scholars would force former policymakers, whose recollections would inevitably have changed in various ways over twenty-five years, to revise their narratives in the light of the facts as they are presently known in the scholarly community. By means of an exercise in critical oral history, we sought to enrich our understanding of the Cuban missile crisis as it comes to us from books *and* from life, from scholarship *and* from experience, in the hope that such enrichment would provide some assistance to those who seek to better understand the nature of nuclear crises in general, and the Cuban missile crisis in particular.

The "Rusk Revelation": Mountain or Molehill?

As the discussion indicates, many scholars present at Hawk's Cay hoped to provoke the policymakers into providing information that would lead directly to *the* answers to a host of lingering questions about the crisis. Many of these questions are very basic ones: Why did the ExComm think Khrushchev had decided to deploy the missiles in Cuba? Why did they believe he chose to do so surreptitiously? Why did President Kennedy find Khrushchev's action intolerable? Why did he plunge the world into a dangerous confrontation without first trying a diplomatic solution? What would have happened had Khrushchev not backed down? Why *did* Khrushchev back down? Were we in fact on the brink of nuclear war? Other questions probed at a finer level of detail: Were there nuclear warheads in Cuba? Did the ExComm know what was happening in the anti-submarine campaign? Who controlled the surface-to-air missiles (SAMs) in Cuba, and who shot down Major Anderson's U-2? Was it shot down on Moscow's orders? Just what did Robert Kennedy tell Dobrynin on the night of October 27?

Questions such as these evoked a great deal of earnest debate at Hawk's Cay, yet not a single one was answered definitively. Instead, the ExComm members repeatedly *opened* possibilities, explored alternatives, and rejected scholars' interpretations, frequently without offering substitutes. In this way, the discussion at Hawk's Cay often complicated rather than simplified our view of the crisis. And this is due mainly to the success of the former ExComm members in communicating the complexity and uncertainty of the crisis itself.

Yet their success was quite incomplete. One aspect of the Hawk's Cay meeting pointedly illustrated the difficulty everyone had in bridging the chasm between the views of those who have learned about the Cuban missile crisis from books and the views of those who lived through the crisis in positions of responsibility: Dean Rusk's startling revelation that on the evening of October 27, 1962, President Kennedy had instructed him to open up a channel to the United Nations through which a public trade of missiles—SS-4s and SS-5s in Cuba for NATO Jupiters in Turkey—might have been consummated. Reactions to this information were swift and powerful. In the corridors and at meals, the scholars expressed shock and amazement at what they regarded as a piece of news worthy of front-page coverage. Indeed, the Rusk revelation did eventually appear on the front pages of many American newspapers, beginning with a piece in *The New York Times* on August 28, 1987.[3] The public discussion that followed mirrored many private discussions about it at Hawk's Cay. Many observers focused on the fact that the President's initiative was secret, and that it had been kept secret for twenty-five years. Many jumped to the conclusion that it proved President Kennedy had secretly been a dove all along, just like Adlai Stevenson, who had been publicly excoriated for proposing a public missile trade during the first week of the crisis.[4] Still others believed that Rusk had supplied them with the answer to the question: What would have happened if Khrushchev had not met the terms given to him on the evening of October 27? Many now believed that Rusk's revelation definitively showed that the President would have traded missiles, despite the appearance it would have given that he was capitulating to the Soviets and selling out Turkey and the other NATO allies to bail himself out of a local difficulty in the Caribbean.[5]

The excitement surrounding the revelation, however, obscured Rusk's own opinion of it. Rusk believed that the information he provided to the Hawk's Cay meeting "was not all that much of a big deal. It was simply an option that would have been available to President Kennedy, had he wanted to use it."[6] "No one can possibly know what President Kennedy's decision would have been," Rusk maintained. "I think we've made a mountain out of a molehill."[7] McGeorge Bundy also expressed dismay at those who leaped to the "mountain" interpretation, worrying that they did not fully grasp the distinction between a contingency and a firm decision to act.[8]

In order to get an idea as to why Rusk prefers the "molehill" interpretation, consider the letter drafted by Theodore Sorensen from President Kennedy to Chairman Khrushchev, dated October 18, 1962, and declassified in 1978:

> Dear Mr. Chairman,
> For the first time since the Korean War, the United States is confronted with a hostile development to which we have an inescapable commitment to respond with military action. . . . Consequently, the purpose of this note is to inform you that, shortly after the close of your conference with my emissary, I have no choice but to initiate appropriate military action against the island of Cuba. . . . Should those in your government who fail to grasp the meaning of total war urge upon you any countermeasures or threats which affect other vital interests of this nation, I ask you to remember that the United States possesses both the will and the weapons to take whatever action is needed in the defense of those interests.[9]

The central fact about this bellicose letter is that it was never sent, and the options it contained simply were not exercised. The former members of the ExComm considered dozens of such options during the missile crisis, ranging from those represented in the harsh Sorensen draft letter of October 18, to the conciliatory Rusk initiative of October 27. Only a very few were acted upon.

If we begin our assessment where the former policymakers begin, in the recollected process of decisionmaking, then the information provided by Rusk becomes just another possible action the President would have considered. And rightly so. Events on that second weekend were fluid and unpredictable; the Soviets were sending conflicting signals; things began to look as if they were spinning out of control. From where the President sat, it would have seemed foolhardy not to prepare the machinery for what was, after all, a guaranteed way out of the confrontation, just in case he needed one.

This does not mean that the Rusk revelation is unimportant. When placed in context, it adds a great deal of weight to the argument that President Kennedy would in fact have opted for a public trade of missiles, rather than an air strike or an invasion of Cuba, if events had forced him to choose between the two. This is an argument that we have made elsewhere and that we still find persuasive.[10] But events did not force him to choose between the two, and the contingency lay fallow. Clearly, how one sees it depends upon how one approaches it, and scholars and policymakers approach it quite differently. But the Rusk revelation is not the only illustration of this difference in approach.

What Caused the Crisis?
The View from Somewhere and the View from Nowhere

There would have been no Cuban missile crisis in October 1962 if Nikita Khrushchev had not decided to deploy MRBMs and IRBMs in Cuba; nor would there have been a crisis if he had done so and President Kennedy had decided that he could tolerate Soviet missiles ninety miles from Florida.[11] It is unlikely that there would have been a crisis if Khrushchev had foreseen the premature discovery of the missiles and the American reaction, for he might have chosen not to go ahead with the deployment; and it is consequently unlikely that there would have been a crisis if, in a timely fashion, Kennedy had unambiguously communicated to Khrushchev what the American reaction would be.[12] This was a crisis neither leader wanted; it was a crisis neither one expected.

The first question to ask, then, is: Why did Khrushchev decide to deploy the missiles? What was his motivation? A number of hypotheses have been advanced over the years, most of which were discussed at Hawk's Cay:

1. *Defense of Cuba.* Khrushchev had reason to believe that the United States was a serious threat to the Castro regime. An American invasion may have appeared likely, even imminent. Given the military asymmetry in the Caribbean, there was no conceivable way for the Soviet Union to defend Cuba, and therefore an American invasion had to be deterred beforehand. Khrushchev may have believed that the only effective form of deterrence would be nuclear deterrence.[13]

2. *Missile-gap repair.* In October 1961, Deputy Secretary of Defense Roswell Gilpatric delivered a speech in which he revealed the American government's knowledge that the "missile gap" favoring the Soviets had been a hoax and that in fact the United States enjoyed substantial superiority in strategic nuclear weapons. The Soviets did not have a long-range ICBM which could be produced in numbers sufficient to redress the imbalance rapidly, but it did have medium- and intermediate-range SS-4s and SS-5s available which could only reach key targets in the United States if deployed outside the Soviet Union. The only friendly country close enough was Cuba.[14]

3. *Bargaining chip.* Khrushchev may have been extremely concerned by the presence of American nuclear missiles on the Soviet periphery, particularly in Turkey. He may have seen a symmetrical

deployment as the only useful lever for securing a negotiated withdrawal of these weapons.[15]

4. *Berlin gambit.* Khrushchev had been stymied in his attempt to settle the Berlin issue. He needed a way to fractionate the NATO alliance, divert American attention away from Berlin, and either provoke the U.S. into taking some military action which would justify a seizure of Berlin or present the U.S. with a hemispheric threat serious enough to force a quid pro quo in which a favorable Berlin settlement would be the Soviet payoff.[16]

5. *Socialist hegemony.* The Soviet Union was losing its position as the socialist community's *primus inter pares.* The rift with China, long in the making, was becoming wider, uglier, and more public. A deployment of missiles in Cuba would be a spectacular coup against "imperialism," would rally the socialist world back to the Soviet standard, and would help Moscow's campaign against Chinese nuclear armament.[17]

6. *Cold War politics.* A successful Cuban deployment would have boosted the morale of the Soviet bloc, weakened American morale, put the United States on the geopolitical defensive, distracted the Americans from Europe, and impressed the non-aligned countries. In case the Soviets chose later to press the Berlin issue, or the issue of American nuclear deployments, or the issue of leadership of the socialist world, the Cuban deployment would be a useful preliminary step.[18]

7. *Soviet domestic politics I.* Khrushchev was on the defensive at home. His domestic program was in shambles, and his foreign policy record was dismal. He may have felt he desperately needed a bold foreign-policy success to bolster his position against hardliners and his rivals in the Presidium for the sake of his own political health.[19]

8. *Soviet domestic politics II.* Khrushchev may have been under pressure from his hard-liners to take bold action for one of the purposes mentioned in the other hypotheses, and he may have reluctantly agreed to deploy missiles, fearing for his position should he resist.[20]

One of the striking features of the discussion at Hawk's Cay was how ready the scholars were to stake out positions on the issue of Khrushchev's motives and how reluctant the policymakers were to do so. Moreover, when dealing with the possibility that Khrushchev was operating on the basis of more than one motive, the scholars were eager to try to assign relative weights to them, while the policymakers shied away from doing so.

William Taubman staked out the clearest position on the issue, arguing very eloquently for the Soviet domestic politics I hypothesis.[21] Arthur Schlesinger asserted that the "most plausible" motivation was missile-gap repair (reinforced by Cold War politics),[22] a view which Graham Allison evidently found attractive, assigning great weight to Soviet fears of American first-strike capability.[23] Scott Sagan likewise appeared to subscribe to a strategic-nuclear rationale, though he was alone in arguing that the primary value of missiles in Cuba was as a threat to the American bomber force.[24] Raymond Garthoff voiced the opinion that the Soviets' "overriding desire was to redress a serious *publicly revealed* strategic imbalance in order to improve their position on other domestic and foreign policy issues, Berlin possibly being foremost among them."[25] All the scholars present, of course, were sensitive to the likelihood that more than one motivation was at work. Garthoff, for instance, saw the defense of Cuba as a secondary consideration, and he qualified his statement about their "overriding desire" to include some consideration for Khrushchev's personal standing.[26]

In contrast, the policymakers emphasized their ignorance and confusion. Theodore Sorensen made the baldest confession: "The only honest answer I have is, 'I don't know now, and I didn't know then.' None of us knew. We could only speculate about what Khrushchev was up to."[27] Robert McNamara immediately concurred: "I don't know why the Soviets did what they did. Ted's right."[28] Not a single ExComm member present staked out a firm position on why Khrushchev deployed the missiles; the only one who came close to doing so was Douglas Dillon, who believed that the deployment was of considerable strategic value to the Soviets, and who evidently interpreted it primarily as an attempt to repair their missile gap.[29]

George Ball's exchange with Ernest May was particularly revealing on this point. Ball grasps immediately the extent to which the detached mode of scholarly assessment of relative Soviet motivations may have been quite irrelevant, in the event, to both the Soviet deployment and the American attempts at the time to explain it.

> **BALL:** There is a problem of method here. We are putting ourselves in the shoes of the Soviet leadership and assuming that they had the same information that we have now. I don't believe they had it, or that they went through a profound and careful decisionmaking process before they made their decision to put missiles in Cuba. . . . I say all this to challenge the assumption that has

been lurking in the background here that this was an act done in an atmosphere of cool rationality by a sophisticated man. I don't think it was.

MAY: That's a very good post-hoc reconstruction of what was going on; but was anybody thinking that way at the time?

BALL: Not before the missiles were placed in Cuba; but, during the crisis, I remember very well that we thought Khrushchev was unpredictable, that he was a loose cannon, and that he was clearly demonstrating his audacity.[30]

Here Ball challenged the very idea that the Soviets went through a careful and rational decisionmaking process, implying very strongly that there may be no real answer to the question at all.[31] Khrushchev's motivation was entirely inscrutable to the ExComm. As a result, they worried that the Soviet leader may have been simply and profoundly irrational.[32] The implication of this is that post-hoc motivational assessment of Khrushchev's action bears little relation to the ExComm's assessment and sheds but dim light on the ExComm's reaction to it.

A very great deal was at stake in the ExComm's assessment of Khrushchev's motivations. If the President chose to seek a negotiated solution, he would need to gauge those motivations in order to identify an acceptable bargain. If Khrushchev had deployed the missiles to defend Cuba, for instance, he might have accepted a non-invasion pledge in return for withdrawing them, but he probably would have rejected an offer of a missile trade. If the President chose instead to remove the missiles by military means, then he needed to gauge Khrushchev's motivations in order to provide some basis for forecasting likely Soviet reactions.[33] If Khrushchev had deployed under pressure from hardliners, for instance, there may have been reason to think that an air strike or invasion carried comparatively little risk of Soviet retaliation, because Khrushchev could blame an American attack on his domestic opponents and use the opportunity to secure his political position and enhance his reputation as a peacemaker. If his main motivation was to provoke an American action to justify a move against Berlin, on the other hand, then a subsequent move against Berlin would seem a more likely response.

Why were scholars so eager to judge Khrushchev's motivations, and why were policymakers so reluctant to do so? We believe the answer to be straightforward but significant. Scholars are in the business of explaining things. Facts are their grist, logic their mill, and explanations and interpretations their products. But policymakers are in the business of steering the ship of state and navigating treacherous waters, an awesome responsibility with profound implications for their actions, particularly in unexpected squalls we call crises. They have neither the time nor the detachment to work through the scholars' puzzles, and, unlike scholars, they often cannot afford to be wrong.

But there is more to it than this. When men like Sorensen and McNamara say they do not know why the Soviets deployed the missiles, they are conveying a key piece of the psychological reality of living through the Cuban missile crisis in its earliest phases: it was a profoundly disorienting experience. Many ExComm members hold that their three greatest assets in the missile crisis were a cautious President, sufficient time to consider their options, and the cogent advice of the ExComm's Soviet expert, Llewellyn Thompson. These factors, it seems, gave them the leadership, the time, and ultimately the information and advice they needed to reorient themselves, to get over the initial shock, and, finally, to begin to try to explain the Soviets' behavior in rational terms. This process of psychological disorientation and reorientation, inevitable in the earliest phases of any truly nuclear crisis, profoundly affects the perceptions, judgments, and choices of decisionmakers. No explanation or understanding of the Cuban missile crisis can be complete without a recognition of this fact.

Khrushchev's decision to deploy missiles in Cuba was only one half of the reason why there was a crisis in October 1962. The other half was the Kennedy Administration's unwillingness to tolerate them. On this issue, there was also a profound difference in approach between scholars and policymakers. The latter, it appears, never seriously debated the issue. For them, it was simply axiomatic that the missiles could not be tolerated.[34] Hawk's Cay conference participants heard Maxwell Taylor put the issue to them with perfect clarity: "There was no question about the problem," he said. "The President announced his objective within an hour after seeing the photographs of the missiles. It was to get the missiles out of Cuba."[35]

When pressed by the scholars, the policymakers appealed to a variety of considerations to explain why the missiles could not be tolerated. Some, such as Dillon, were obviously impressed by the difference he believed the Soviet deployment made to the strategic balance.[36] Others, however, were not—McNamara being the most vocal among them.[37] To McNamara, the problem was purely political, not military.[38] George Ball argued that the *way* in which the Soviets deployed was what could not be tolerated—secretly, and in contradiction to their many public statements professing that they had neither the need nor the intention to base nuclear weapons in Cuba.[39] Other remarks by ExComm members suggest that still other considerations may have been in the back of their minds—that the Soviet deployment was a violation of a long-standing pillar of American foreign policy, the Monroe Doctrine;[40] that it set a bad precedent for deterring future Soviet actions in the hemisphere; that it could only be read as a direct challenge to the U.S. But, for whatever reasons, it is clear that no one in the ExComm argued that the missiles did not have to be removed from Cuba.

Many scholars, on the other hand, repeatedly called this into question. Some of their arguments were these: while the deployment would have eased the Soviets' strategic nuclear predicament, it did not change the fundamental fact of American strategic nuclear superiority;[41] the Americans had deployed nuclear missiles on the periphery of the Soviet Union, and there was no particular reason why the Soviets should not have been entitled to do the same with respect to the United States;[42] there was nothing in international law which prohibited the Soviet action, though clearly the manner in which it was undertaken involved an unprecedented level of deceit on the part of the Soviets.[43]

Differences on this issue between scholars and former ExComm members illustrate the extent to which scholarly analysis seeks relentlessly to achieve what Thomas Nagel has called "the view from nowhere," while volitional action must always take place "somewhere," in a particular place and at a particular time.[44] Scholars who doubted the inevitability of the assumption that the missiles had to be removed seemed perplexed and dismayed by what they took to be a striking lack in the policymakers of the capacity for self-criticism. The former ExComm members, on the other hand, were amazed to discover what they believed was disregard for the realities they faced in October 1962: a bitter Cold War; their repeated public statements declaring offensive Soviet forces in Cuba unacceptable; the frightening novelty of American nuclear vulnerability; and the shock of Communist penetration of the hemisphere. To question the unacceptability of Soviet missiles in Cuba seemed to the ExComm members an abstract, ahistorical, and naïve exercise.[45]

The Conduct and Resolution of the Crisis: Nuclear Threat and Nuclear Danger

The Kennedy Administration considered the Soviet deployment intolerable and it had no confidence in its ability to explain why the Soviets did it. These two facts, taken together, explain why the ExComm chose the course of action it did: a limited naval quarantine; a slowly increasing threat of further action; and an improvised ultimatum (or something that may have looked rather like an ultimatum in Moscow) coupled with an offer consisting, first, of a public guarantee against an invasion of Cuba and, second, of a private assurance that the Jupiter missiles in Turkey would soon be withdrawn. At no time did the Administration pursue a course of action premised on one (and only one) theory of Khrushchev's motivations for deployment, and at no time did the Administration undertake a course of action which irrevocably committed it to military action against Cuba or the Soviet Union. Instead, American actions were designed to allow its leaders the greatest flexibility and the greatest possible opportunity for on-the-job learning, minimizing the consequences of an error in judgment about Soviet motivations and needs.[46] Premised as it was on a recognition of their own ignorance and the size of the potential stakes, this was a sober and prudent strategy under the circumstances.

Alexander George, both at Hawk's Cay and in his writing, has described the Administration's handling of the affair as an example of "coercive diplomacy."[47] Those wielding such a strategy, according to George, seek "to create in the opponent the expectation of unacceptable costs of sufficient magnitude to erode his motivation to continue what he is doing."[48] They may do so in a variety of ways. The weaker variant of the strategy—the "try and see" approach—is to communicate concern and resolve, but not to issue a specific threat with a time limit attached for compliance. The stronger variant—the "tacit ultimatum" approach—relies on an explicit threat of further action.[49] George claims that the Kennedy Administration tried both versions of the strategy in the missile crisis, switching from the former to the latter on Saturday, October 27, when Robert Kennedy communicated an "ultimatum" to Anatoly Dobrynin, threatening that if the Soviets did not agree to remove their missiles from Cuba immediately, the U.S. would remove them by force.

When George opened the discussion at Hawk's Cay, he posed questions about the range of strategies he believed were open to President Kennedy, and about the coercive strategy George believes he ultimately decided to pursue. In particular, George asked whether the merits and risks of the various versions of the diplomatic approach were considered before the quarantine option was selected; he asked what the "next coercive steps" would have been had the blockade failed to secure a withdrawal of the missiles; he asked if President Kennedy had been "forced" to issue an ultimatum on Saturday, October 27, and if so, by whom; he asked for details of the advice given by Soviet experts on the likely Soviet reactions to American moves; he asked about the effects of crisis-induced stress and fatigue on the ExComm's deliberations; and he asked, finally, if there were any lessons to be learned about the tension between "military logic" and "diplomatic logic."[50]

Robert McNamara's reaction to George's presentation and to his list of questions laid wide open the enormous chasm between the scholars' and the policymakers' approaches to understanding the event. Mc-Namara responded:

> I don't think we've quite succeeded in re-creating the atmosphere at the time. The questions Alex asked simply weren't framed that precisely back then. There were deep differences of opinion among us, and very strong feelings about Cuba, and the fact is that we weren't going through an unemotional, orderly, and comprehensive analytical decisionmaking process.[51]

Abram Chayes concurred: "I agree with Bob on his point about the crudeness and the difficulty of deliberation."[52] And when Graham Allison asked a question—"How much thought was there about the probable leak date and hence the period of time you had to play with? Were you prepared to forfeit the initiative if there had been a story in the *Post* or in the *Times*?"—Theodore Sorensen's response made exactly McNamara's and Chayes's point: "Our deliberations just weren't that orderly, so there isn't any real answer to the question."[53]

Remarks such as these astonished and troubled many of the scholars present. Some could be overheard in the corridors wondering why the Kennedy Administration did not ask itself basic operational questions about the alternatives open to it. They were perplexed as to why the ExComm did not seem to work through all, or at least some, of the various possible paths to an acceptable solution. In a very interesting and quite unexpected development, therefore, the scholars at Hawk's Cay began to ask questions of the ExComm that the ExComm had once asked of Khrushchev and his colleagues: Were they really rational in October 1962? Or did this exceptionally bright and talented group of men simply forsake, in that moment of crisis, the rationality and good sense of which they were clearly capable?

Several other aspects of the discussion perplexed the scholars present. Consider three:

Contingency planning and resistance to hypotheticals. The Kennedy Administration had a complex goal in the crisis: to get the Soviet missiles out of Cuba, but at an acceptable (preferably minimal) cost. The strategy selected carried risks of escalation; those risks entailed unacceptable costs. The scholars present at Hawk's Cay clearly expected these risks to have been explored, and they expected the ExComm to have played out possible escalation scenarios in their minds, considering in advance the various options available for dealing with them. To the great surprise of the scholars, and apparently contradicting George Ball's assertion that President Kennedy and his advisors made "a careful dissection of the problem and the various options,"[54] the ExComm members showed little or no evidence of having done this.

Robert McNamara provided the clearest examples of this lack of interest in the hypothetical details of a war with the Soviet Union. Having stated both that nuclear war was possible and that it was unlikely, McNamara was challenged repeatedly on how he (or the ExComm as a whole) thought escalation might be contained if shots were fired. But McNamara did not take up these challenges:

WELCH: I still don't see how you thought you were going to manage to limit a conflict and prevent escalation once military action began. What thought had you given to this? How did you think you were going to keep things under control? What contingencies had you planned for? How and where were you going to draw the necessary lines?

NYE: Bob, do you want to handle that?

McNAMARA: Well, that's a very big question, so I think we ought to postpone it until this afternoon.[55]

. . . . .

LEBOW: Granted, Bob, that the least likely scenario for a nuclear war beginning was missiles being fired from Cuba, you said that you expected a Russian response somewhere [to an American air strike], and that that would lead to escalation. The question arose this morning: How and where did you expect to be able to stop it?

McNAMARA: Right there on the blockade. Turn the screw on the blockade and avoid the air attack and invasion, which would probably lead to escalation.[56]

. . . . .

ALLISON: I remember interviewing you when I was working on my dissertation, and you said to me that on the 27th you worried that it might be the last Saturday you saw. So you must have been worried about some paths to nuclear war; what were they?

McNAMARA: If we'd not gotten the response we did from Khrushchev, I would have proposed an extended blockade. I didn't know what would have happened, but that course of action ran lower risks of loss of control.[57]

McNamara was not unique in his resistance to scholarly hypotheticals; the transcripts of the October 27 ExComm meetings clearly show that there was no meaningful discussion about contingencies in the event of war.[58] While there were occasional, vague worries expressed that the Soviets might respond to an American air strike with reprisals in Turkey and Berlin, nowhere in that document does any ExComm member discuss options for containing and arresting a conflict. It is McNamara himself who comes closest to engaging in a concrete, step-by-step exploration of likely moves and countermoves up the ladder of escalation, though it is clear that he had no idea of what to do about it.[59] But if fear of a major war with the Soviet Union was the main source of anxiety during the missile crisis, why, scholars wondered, did the ExComm not explore this matter more fully?[60]

Interpretations of documentary details. At the session on the management of the second week of the crisis, the week of the public confrontation, Marc Trachtenberg and Scott Sagan attempted to probe the policymakers on several perplexities that arise in the body of American primary documents, formerly classified, which have recently become available. No one is more familiar with this material than Trachtenberg and Sagan, who assisted us in the preparation of the briefing book for the meeting, and who led off the session with long lists of detailed questions.

Scott Sagan pointed to the fact that the documents seemed to show that the ExComm was disproportionately concerned with managing the details of interception procedures on the quarantine line.[61] He noted that comparatively little attention was being paid to anti-submarine operations, reconnaissance missions and how these would be interpreted in the Kremlin, the provisions of the SIOP and the conditions specified in it for American preemption, the status of Soviet forces,[62] and air-defense operations. Correctly noting that risks arose from each of these quarters, Sagan pressed for information as to why they received relatively little attention, or, in some cases, no attention at all.

Marc Trachtenberg noted that the record of the October 16 ExComm meeting indicated that McNamara believed that a "premise" in American deliberation should be that if an air strike were to be undertaken against the missiles in Cuba, it would be scheduled prior to the time the missiles became operational.[63] Yet an air-strike option was still on the table long after most of the MRBMs had already been reported to be operational by the CIA. What had happened to McNamara's premise? Why did he change his mind?

Trachtenberg's query is related to an apparent perplexity in the documentary record concerning the meaning of the term "operational."

The ExComm had from the very beginning attached a great deal of weight to the operational status of the Soviet missiles in Cuba, presumably because a single Soviet missile fired from Cuba could kill millions of Americans.[64] Yet they seem never to have understood what "operational" meant. Clearly, if there were no warheads in Cuba for these missiles, then of course this particular risk would have been negligible. According to CIA Deputy Director of Intelligence Ray Cline, President Kennedy inevitably asked about the presence of warheads at the daily intelligence briefing; he was inevitably told that there was no hard evidence of warheads present.[65] Yet the CIA nevertheless continued to report that some of the MRBMs were already operational, and that more and more were rapidly becoming operational.[66] And as the transcript of the October 27 meetings shows, the members of the ExComm used the word "operational" (or "operable") in a way which clearly indicated that they attached some importance to it.[67] But in response to Arnold Horelick's question at Hawk's Cay—"Did the technologically unsophisticated in the crowd request a briefing on what 'operational' meant?"—McNamara astounded many scholars present when he replied, "No, they didn't."[68]

The policymakers present at Hawk's Cay clearly had little patience for these puzzles. For example, when Sagan asked Robert McNamara—"What about the U-2 which strayed into Siberian airspace on the 27th, and which was reported to be on an air-sampling mission? Why wasn't that mission turned off?"[69]—McNamara brusquely replied, "We just didn't know it was up there collecting air samples. . . . There are some things you can't foresee, and you can't process all the relevant information at once."[70] It was clear that McNamara considered it a question with an obvious answer, and equally clear that McNamara's answer left Sagan entirely unsatisfied.

The sense of urgency and the need to resolve the crisis. At 7:00 p.m., October 22, 1962, President Kennedy delivered a short televised address in which he reviewed the Soviet military buildup in Cuba, revealed the presence there of Soviet nuclear missiles, and announced the initial American response—a naval quarantine of Cuba. Toward the end of his address, the President also revealed in broad outline what, at that point, he believed would be required to resolve the crisis peacefully and on terms acceptable to the American government. He concluded:

> My fellow citizens, let no one doubt that this is a difficult and dangerous effort on which we have set out. No one can foresee precisely what course it will take or what costs or casualties will be incurred. Many months of self-sacrifice and self-discipline lie

ahead—months in which many threats and denunciations will keep us aware of our dangers.[71]

Yet, scarcely six days later, Kennedy and Khrushchev had found a way to resolve the crisis peacefully and on mutually acceptable terms. It is clear from memoirs of the missile crisis that by the eleventh and twelfth days, decisionmakers on both sides felt that the pressure to reach a resolution, so unexpected just a few days before, was almost unbearable. The event was not the chronic, months-long struggle anticipated by the members of the ExComm when they helped draft the President's speech.

But this radical departure from the ExComm's initial expectation has never been satisfactorily explained, and the scholars at Hawk's Cay were keen to have the puzzle solved. Why the feeling that time was running out? In his introductory remarks to one of the sessions, historian Marc Trachtenberg made this issue central. "There is a lot of evidence even prior to the attack on Major Anderson's U-2 that there was a sense of urgency. . . . If it is true that people had a sense that things were coming to a head, what exactly was generating it?"[72] This elicited one of the most revealing dialogues at Hawk's Cay. Yet the fascination of the ensuing discussion lay primarily in answers not given, in closure not achieved, and in perplexity not diminished. At one point, for example, Joseph Nye asked McNamara whether the U-2 overflight of Siberia and the U-2 shoot-down in Cuba had been the sources of worry and urgency. McNamara responded that they had not.[73] Scott Sagan then asked whether they had feared a Soviet preemptive strike, to which Bundy responded that they had not, that in fact they had never worried at all that anyone on either side would "push that button deliberately."[74] Ball then noted that "the *momentum* of events was something of a worry," but McNamara immediately added the caveat that the momentum he worried about was not toward strategic nuclear war but rather "toward the use of military force of whatever kind."[75] Graham Allison eventually threw in the towel for the scholars: "But why the urgency? I still don't understand."[76]

The inability of scholars and policymakers to engage in a mutually satisfying exploration of the conduct and resolution of the crisis can ultimately be traced to basic differences in their ways of understanding the event. To the scholars, Hawk's Cay was a laboratory in which to test and generate hypotheses connecting causes and effects. They were familiar with the documentary record; all they needed from the former policymakers was a certain amount of information to fill in gaps and resolve lingering puzzles. But the information they were looking for was information of a certain kind: reconstructions of logical trains of thought,

estimates of costs and benefits, judgments of probabilities—rational reconstructions of rational processes of deliberation. What they found was
that the cerebral dimensions of the ExComm's experience could not be
separated from, and in some sense were subordinate to, the visceral
dimensions.

Underlying McNamara's, Sorensen's, and Chayes's response to
George's list of questions was their subjective experience of what the
crisis was really like. From where they sat, strategy was clearly secondary
to muddling through.[77] Most of their time was spent trying to keep their
balance as the ship of state pitched and rolled, rather than meting out
precise measures of sanctions and incentives according to a blueprint of
crisis management. Though the ExComm certainly may be said to have
engaged in an exercise of coercive diplomacy, the term only describes
their activity in a unidimensional and abstract way. They were also
locked in the most dangerous and fearsome confrontation of the nuclear
age, in which the fate of the world rested in their hands—an awesome
responsibility for mortal men. The information they were working with
was often incomplete and inaccurate; their adversary was inscrutable
and unpredictable; and events seemed increasingly difficult to control.
Their judgments and decisions could not fail to be affected by the psychological texture of the context in which they were made.

Alexander George came closest of all the scholars to grappling with
the subjective dimension of crisis management when he inquired about
the effects of stress and fatigue on the ExComm's deliberations. His
questions were important ones; psychological research indicates that,
up to a point, stress can have a beneficial effect on performance, but
that periods of prolonged, intense stress can result in dysfunction or
breakdown, with ominous implications for sound decisionmaking in crisis.[78] The way in which scholars understand the effect of stress is as a
degradation of rationality—an impediment to the weighing of costs and
benefits and the assessment of risks and probabilities. All the ExComm
members who chose to respond to George's question acknowledged
feeling stress and fatigue, but they all maintained it was "manageable";
they denied suffering a degradation in rationality. And as far as we can
tell, they may be right.[79] But "stress"—if we are to use the term as a
shorthand for the subjective dimension of managing a major nuclear
crisis, the whole package of fears, anxieties, and uncertainties—shaped
the policymakers' entire view of the event. It was precisely because of
the effects of stress that the ExComm viscerally realized that the lexicon
of rationality was adequate for describing only a part of their experience;
it was precisely because of this stress that their minds were focused on
the unpredictability of events and the horrifying consequences of a mis-

step; it was precisely because of this stress that handling the crisis seemed to require more circumspection than strategy. The ExComm members may have been right in denying having suffered from a degradation of rationality; but they were keen to make clear that the stress of the crisis powerfully affected the way in which rationality operated

The subjective element so powerful in the ExComm members' understandings of the crisis, and so obviously absent from the scholars', also explains why the policymakers refused to play the scholars' game of hypotheticals. One possibility is that the policymakers were simply protecting their flexibility in light of the dynamism and fluidity of the situation in which they found themselves. When there is a premium on flexible and reversible action, and when a situation is as unpredictable as was the Cuban missile crisis, there is an advantage in not thinking through hypotheticals and contingencies in too much detail, for doing so may constrain the later exploration of the options, or may lead to operational decisions which unnecessarily restrict them. A second possibility is that the unpredictability and dangerousness of the situation caused some of them—the doves—to dismiss certain actions from their minds a priori. The ExComm had a limited amount of time to deliberate; it was constantly having to deal with shocks and surprises. Under circumstances such as these, there is little point in spending time and effort exploring the various possible firebreaks up the ladder of U.S.–Soviet military escalation if one is already committed to avoiding that ladder in the first place.[80]

The difference in viewpoint also seems to account for the scholars' and the policymakers' inability to connect on interpretations of documentary details. Documents do not supply their own context. Only the decisionmakers know what they thought or intended when they uttered the words recorded in the minutes of a meeting or in the transcript of an audio tape. Clearly it is the thought or the intention, so difficult to recall and to paraphrase, that mattered to the policymakers.

Consider the question of the operability of the missiles in Cuba. "We started out feeling pressure because of the need we perceived to get the missiles out before they became operational," McGeorge Bundy recalled. "But by the second Saturday the pressures were coming from other directions."[81] The ExComm soon realized that the problem of proving the presence or absence of warheads in Cuba was simply insoluble, a kind of decision reached daily by policymakers but hardly ever by scholars in their work. And against the backdrop of what seemed to be the rising probability of inadvertent war, the operational status of the missiles in Cuba gradually dimmed in importance. The President and his closest associates concerned themselves less with the nuclear threat posed by the activity of the Soviets at the missile sites in Cuba, and concerned themselves more with what Bundy calls the nuclear danger of two superpowers inadvertently stumbling into disaster.[82]

As the quarantine began to look like a failure, the members of the ExComm had to make up their minds about the course of action they should try next. Their deliberations occurred against the backdrop of fears and uncertainties compounded by the fluidity of the confrontation. Many premises asserted on October 16 had become irrelevant by October 27. A U-2 had strayed into Siberia, a U-2 had been shot down over Cuba, and unforeseen developments at the anti-submarine barriers could not be controlled and simply had to be taken in stride; the President had to position himself for other shocks and surprises, possibly in Turkey or Berlin. Through the *Sturm und Drang*, the ExComm's energies had to be focused on making its main signal, the quarantine, as clear as possible. This, the policymakers told us, was what managing the crisis was like; and managing the crisis was nothing like documenting the crisis. The puzzles that arise in the documentary record seem to the policymakers a function of this simple fact.

These same considerations also account for the sense of urgency on the final weekend of the crisis. When the President forecast on October 22 that the crisis might take months to resolve, he had no real sense of what the coming six days would be like, of the dangers and uncertainties he would have to face. He had to *experience* the crisis before he could sense the urgency of ending it.

The inability of scholars and former policymakers to find common conceptual ground on which to base an explanation of the sense of urgency on October 27 illustrates a significant deficiency in most attempts to use the missile crisis as a historical laboratory within which to study the psychological requirements of nuclear-crisis management. What seems to have happened is that scholars have fashioned an image of the crisis "from the neck up." Thus, decisionmakers on both sides are seen as weighing options, calculating probabilities, assessing risks, and estimating costs.[83] Many analysts regard the presence of feelings, moods, and emotions—especially fear—as deficiencies to be overcome, so that rational information-processing might resume, on the theory that the removal of fear from the psychology of the situation results in better, safer decisions.[84] In our view, this approach to the psychology of nuclear crises is mistaken on two counts: first, because fear in the missile crisis was demonstrably adaptive in generating a peaceful solution; and second, because fear and other powerful emotions are ineradicable aspects of crises of this kind. How could it be otherwise? Can one imagine a nuclear crisis not dominated by surprise, shock, confusion, fatigue, and a riveting sense of nuclear danger? We cannot. Accordingly, traditional,

purely cognitive scholarship on these questions will never be very true
to the psychological life of nuclear crises. The crises that scholars reconstruct and analyze are not the crises that policymakers live through.

There is policy-relevant work to be done in this area, but work that
begins with fear, with feelings that require a scholarly apparatus capable
of making sense of psychological factors that influence nuclear crisis
decisionmaking. This doesn't mean that policymakers are portrayed as
having lost their heads, but rather that nuclear crises are lived through
and managed by whole persons.[85]

The Challenge of Hawk's Cay:
Understanding the Burden of Responsibility

Is the gap between a scholar's understanding of an event from books
and a policymaker's understanding of it from experience important?
The policymakers at Hawk's Cay believed that scholars have missed
both the essence and the point of the Cuban missile crisis. For if the
scholars cannot appreciate the significance of the subjective dimensions
of crisis management, they will continue to explain and prescribe purely
in terms of the balance of forces, the strength of relative interests, the
clarity of threats and commitments, the distribution of costs and gains.
These objective factors are important, but they clearly provide only a
partial view of what crisis management is like, and alone they do not
provide a full description of causes and effects in any given case, or a
determinate set of principles of action for future use. The accuracy and
policy relevance of crisis-management scholarship will be impaired as
long as it fails to come to grips with subjective factors.

The tools and methods of scholarship, of course, put a spin on attempts
to understand crises in the direction of objective factors and away from
subjective ones. Whereas the goal of evoking a personal memory may
well be partial reentry into a given feeling at a given place and time,
careful scholarship as normally understood requires just the opposite:
movement as far as possible from such an individually constrained point
of view, and toward the grandest, most comprehensive synthesis available. We have seen this made manifest repeatedly in the discussion at
Hawk's Cay. But can the gap between an understanding attained by
living forwards and an understanding attained by looking backwards be
narrowed? Can reality as understood by academics be brought closer
to reality as lived by statesmen? We are all well aware, of course, that
no one can ever have the experiences of another; no one will ever know
precisely what it is like to be anyone other than oneself. There will
therefore always be some difference between a scholar's understanding

and a policymaker's understanding. But this does not mean that the gap cannot be narrowed and its effects better understood.[86] Nor does it mean that we should always defer to the policymaker's understanding whenever it is in conflict with the scholar's. After all, scholars have several offsetting advantages: they are less emotionally invested in a particular rendition of an event; their wide reading and comparative study well prepare them to draw lessons from history; and, as relatively objective students of events, they may be more persuasive, and their conclusions more credible, to present and future generations of potential nuclear-crisis managers. The method of critical oral history is designed to make use of these advantages. The meeting at Hawk's Cay was itself an experiment to see whether progress can be made in narrowing the gap by bringing scholars' and policymakers' comparative advantages to bear on each other's understandings of nuclear-crisis management.

We feel it was a partial and encouraging success: the discussion clearly and powerfully highlighted the very gap we sought to bridge, and a dialectic was successfully generated. At the same time, no grand fusion of perspectives was achieved. But there was movement in that direction. This may be seen most vividly in the heroic effort of Thomas Schelling to bridge the gap in one compact and very revealing statement:

> I want to tell you about my reaction on the night of the 22nd, when President Kennedy gave his speech revealing that we knew about the Soviet missiles in Cuba. I was at a Harvard–MIT Arms Control Seminar that night at the Faculty Club, and we all gathered around the television to listen to what the President had to say. I remember after the speech we were left with a sense of gloating; we just couldn't imagine how Khrushchev could have done such a dumb, blundering act, and we knew that we had him on this one and the only question was how bad a fall we were going to give him. But my impression here is that this is not at all how people felt in Washington. Why not? Why did we react that way, while you didn't? It's not that you knew things in Washington that we didn't know; what we in Cambridge know now that we didn't know then about the huge superiority of the United States in nuclear weapons would have reassured us even more. My guess is that the difference is explained by the fact that you were the ones who suffered from the stress; you were the ones who were in the difficult position of having to make the decisions. The stress of *responsibility* may simply make a very great deal of difference.[87]

Schelling is the game theorist par excellence, the man who had, many years before, brought coherence and precision to the theory of nuclear deterrence. He is a scholar noted for his ability to think abstractly, even mathematically, about nuclear war. And here was Schelling coming to grips with the personal, subjective dimensions of the missile crisis as it was experienced by its American managers. Theodore Sorensen, a former ExComm member who was normally quite uninhibited in his criticism of the "cottage industry" of Cuban missile-crisis studies, approved of Schelling's conclusion: "The gap between research and participation is aptly symbolized by the gloating in the Faculty Club Tom Schelling told us about earlier. And I think the difference is, as he aptly said, a difference of responsibility."[88]

However, a clear indication that the gap had not quite been bridged arose when Schelling attempted to draw some policy implications from his experience as a designer of war games for the Pentagon. In particular, he recalled a series of games he conducted in which several officials who later became members of the ExComm participated, and which required all players, civilian and military, to share equally in the burden of responsibility for making all decisions. Under these conditions of shared responsibility, according to Schelling, all players exhibited extraordinary caution. Based on these findings, Schelling suggested that it might have made sense to include all the military chiefs in the ExComm, not just their chairman, General Maxwell Taylor, and that in another such crisis a variety of military people should perhaps be included in the President's decisionmaking circle. Schelling's point was that by bringing such people into the highest level of decisionmaking, one could moderate the tensions between the military and civilian leadership by making them share responsibility.[89]

McNamara, Ball, and Sorensen rejected Schelling's suggestion out of hand.[90] Yet it remained for a scholar, Richard Neustadt, to explain the weak link in Schelling's chain of thought. The problem, according to Neustadt, is that whereas responsibility can be shared, increased, or even removed in games, it cannot be manipulated, shifted, or abdicated in a major national crisis. Ultimate responsibility is constitutionally the President's alone, and the experience of that awesome personal responsibility has virtually nothing in common with the manufactured responsibility of Schelling's games—games which, by design, lasted only a weekend. What President Kennedy saw was the prospect of a catastrophe at least as devastating as the Civil War, an event from which the country took a century to recover. Citing President Kennedy's own reflection on the missile crisis, Neustadt said, "The President bears the burden of the responsibility; advisors can move on to fresh advice."[91] Neustadt concluded: "The President's office is a lonely one, and the burden of responsibility is very personal."[92] Only his closest advisors, sharing in a portion of it vicariously, can truly understand how heavy that burden was.

Thus we saw evidence of movement to close the gap, as participants in the discussion began to reconsider their understandings of the event. Hawk's Cay brought several differences between scholarship and policymaking into sharp relief, and demonstrated both the difficulty and the importance of trying to narrow those differences, bringing analysis more into line with the psychological reality of bearing the burden of responsibility in the Cuban missile crisis. It showed that progress is possible in that direction, and vindicated the assumptions undergirding the method of critical oral history. But Hawk's Cay did not indicate how far the gap between scholarship and policymaking can be narrowed, and it raised new questions: Why did the experience of managing the most dangerous crisis in history affect hawks and doves in different ways? Do the differences between hawks and doves undermine the conclusions we have reached about the differences between scholars and policymakers? Why, or why not? These questions were explored in the follow-up interviews with two hawks—Paul Nitze and Douglas Dillon—and two doves—Dean Rusk and Robert McNamara.

PART TWO

Hawks and Doves

Recollection is a treacherous guide. . . . Politicians . . . remember very well the impacts and emotions of a crisis, but are apt, in describing the policy they then advocated, to contaminate it with ideas that belonged in fact to a later stage in their career. And this is natural: because thought is not wholly entangled in the flow of experience, so that we constantly reinterpret our past thoughts and assimilate them to those we are thinking now.

R. G. COLLINGWOOD
The Idea of History

CHAPTER

3

The Interviews: Paul Nitze, Douglas Dillon, Dean Rusk, and Robert McNamara

We had expected substantial differences of opinion and perspective between policymakers and scholars to emerge at Hawk's Cay. Those expectations provided the rationale for the first phase of our critical oral history of the Cuban missile crisis. And the differences did emerge, as the transcript of the meeting shows. But an interesting counterpoint was apparent even at the beginning of the meeting, and it became very pronounced at certain stages: the multidimensional tension that still exists, after a quarter century, between the views of those policymakers who became known shortly after the crisis as "hawks" and "doves."[1]

The tension was clearest in the discussion immediately following General Maxwell Taylor's videotaped interview. A self-described "double hawk," Taylor evidently believed that the crisis contained little, if any, risk of nuclear war; that American military superiority both locally and at the strategic nuclear level gave the United States a virtually free hand in dealing with the Soviet missiles in Cuba; and that the event was only a crisis because of an unwarranted level of anxiety among the President's principal civilian advisors.[2] The contrast between Taylor's view of the crisis and Dean Rusk's letter, read to the participants by McGeorge Bundy immediately after Taylor's interview, was striking. The President, it seemed, was sufficiently frightened by the confrontation to lay the groundwork secretly for a rapid resolution on unfavorable terms. In his view, the crisis was dangerous. It did run some risk of nuclear war. In rapid-fire sequence, two ExComm members too ill to attend the meeting at Hawk's Cay in person presented us with two very different Cuban missile crises.

Though the tension between hawks and doves was powerfully present in the Hawk's Cay discussion from time to time, it did not dominate.

This was because Douglas Dillon alone represented the hawks, and—by design—the conversation focused on the differences between the scholars' and the policymakers' views. But in the belief that discussion of these two missile crises left much unsaid, we decided to pursue it in individual interviews. Paul Nitze and Dean Rusk, one hawk and one dove, did not have the opportunity to participate in the discussion at Hawk's Cay, and so we decided to bring them into the conversation.[3] Dillon and McNamara rounded out our foursome.[4]

The interviews were undertaken in an order and manner that illustrate our attempt throughout this enterprise to keep the oral history critical.[5] First, we interviewed Nitze and Dillon, whose story is largely untold. None of the major histories or biographies relating to the Cuban missile crisis is by, or primarily about, any of the hawks: Dean Acheson, Douglas Dillon, John McCone, Paul Nitze, and Maxwell Taylor. In our discussions, we sought to probe for the set of issues on which hawks and doves disagreed, as seen by the hawks themselves. We then took the conversation to Rusk and McNamara and presented them with the hawks' story, again with the aim of highlighting the points of disagreement, this time as seen by the doves. This vicarious group discussion produced interesting results. Uninhibited by the presence of their colleagues and interlocutors, all four interviewees were more forthright and critical than they would have been in the reunion atmosphere of Hawk's Cay. In fact, the sharpness of their disagreements in our interviews stands in marked contrast to the collegiality of the actual ExComm meetings themselves.[6]

The philosopher Karl Popper has said that knowledge grows only in proportion to the degree of criticism that is directed at received wisdom.[7] Here, in these interviews, hawks and doves engage in an unprecedentedly candid and revealing mutual criticism. As we shall see in Chapter 4, our understanding has been advanced proportionately.

Interview with Paul Nitze, May 6, 1987, Washington, D.C.

JAMES BLIGHT: At the meeting that you were coming to if you hadn't been called away, we walked our people through a number of issues: what caused the missile crisis, why they felt the missiles were placed in Cuba by the Soviets, how the crisis was managed, and so forth. We have some specific questions that we could ask, or you could start off if you prefer.

PAUL NITZE: I can start off. . . . My recollection is the following. First of all, before the Cuban missile crisis, Gromyko arrived here to negotiate.* At that time, it was early in the game and we didn't know whether the missiles were there or whether they weren't. Obviously we didn't have any photographs at that time as to whether they were there or whether they weren't, but there was a lot of discussion about it.[8] Senator Keating, you remember, was saying the missiles were there. But it was more than that. I can remember going to a meeting with McNamara in the "tank" with the Joint Chiefs—we used to go once a week to the tank with the Chiefs, McNamara and I, and Ros Gilpatric—and we were briefed at the beginning of each one of those meetings by somebody from the JCS† intelligence section. Week by week we got information on all the bits and pieces of intelligence that had come in about what was going on in Cuba. And from that intelligence it became more and more clear that the missiles were there prior to the time of the first U-2 flights. I became persuaded that the missiles were there well before—I don't know how many days before—the first photographs. . . .

I became convinced that the missiles were there, and told Chip Bohlen that I'd come to this conclusion. Chip was skeptical of it. Then on the Sunday night, was it, when we had dinner here in this building?—

AIDE: I think it was Monday night—the Secretary's dinner.

NITZE: The Secretary's dinner was for Adenauer, wasn't it?[9] I've forgotten now. In any case . . . we were discussing what the Russians were apt to do next. I said I thought that they were going to convert the Berlin crisis, which we had just lived through, into a crisis in Cuba. And [one of the German guests] thought I was talking nonsense and we argued about this for a while. . . . Rusk went out to talk to Hilsman on the telephone;‡ when he came back into the room he looked quite suddenly pale. This was at the end of the eating. He rose from the table, signaled to me to go out on the terrace here on the eighth floor, and there described to me what it was Hilsman had told him: that the photographs had confirmed that the Soviet missiles were in Cuba. Rusk turned to me and said, "What do we do next?" And I said, "I would think that the first thing we do is to tell the President about this, and second we ought to figure out what it is the Russians are up to and why they're up to it, and then figure out what is the best course of action for us, which we can't do just off the cuff." And I guess that we must have gossiped about it for a good fifteen to twenty minutes. He thought that was probably the right thing to do, and so he went and took some action, as I remember, to see to it that the President was alerted. But

---

* Andrei A. Gromyko, Foreign Minister of the U.S.S.R., 1957–85.
† Joint Chiefs of Staff.
‡ Roger Hilsman was director of Intelligence and Research in the State Department.

I think Mac Bundy decided the President was not to be alerted until the next day.

BLIGHT: That's right. I think that's what Mac Bundy says, that he preferred to give him a good night's sleep before he digested that new piece of information—or something along those lines.

. . . . .

NITZE: I had to go down to Kentucky the next day, so I was not there. But while flying down to Kentucky I remember working on a piece of paper trying to figure out what the Soviets were up to—what process could have gone through the Soviet mind in deciding to do this? And what might be their maximum and minimum objectives? And then what general courses of action were appropriate for us? I don't think we've ever been able to recover that piece of paper.

. . . . .

DAVID WELCH: What did you decide their objectives were?

NITZE: I can't remember too clearly, but it seemed to me that their maximum objective would be to have us pour our scorn on Castro; then they could come onto the scene as the great protectors of Castro and posture themselves in the world as being protectors of a small country trying to defend itself against the pressures of an imperialistic country— an overwhelmingly powerful imperialistic country—and have us permit them to leave their missiles there. I thought their maximum objective was to do this, to get away with their deployment, not have a crisis, and improve their strategic posture. I differed with McNamara about the impact that these deployments would have on the relative strategic posture of the two countries. I thought it made a substantial difference and therefore that they would gain quite a lot—that they would gain a full offset to their defeat in the Berlin crisis. We'd outfaced them on the Berlin blockade threat, you remember, the very year before, and it would really have the effect, not of making the Soviets equal to us, but of greatly neutralizing the degree of nuclear superiority which we then enjoyed.

I thought their minimum objective was to trade their missiles for a U.S. concession concerning Berlin.

WELCH: Mr. Dillon said something very interesting after the conference. He said he never recalled any discussion in the ExComm as to why those missiles were unacceptable. Do you recall any discussion of that?

NITZE: Well, my recollection is that that happened on the first day when I was not there. That's when right away the decision was made that they were unacceptable. Certainly my view as to why the Soviet deployment was unacceptable was that militarily it would be a major step toward nuclear parity—effective nuclear parity, not in numbers but in military effectiveness—because their capability in an initial strike from those sites would be tremendous. After all, these could cover almost all targets in the United States. Between the MRBMs and the IRBMs there was hardly any part of the United States that wasn't vulnerable to these missiles. And if they really got off a first strike they could raise havoc. . . .

The other was that politically they would be a tremendous setback to the United States. We had just gotten through what I thought was really a major success with respect to the access routes to Berlin. Khrushchev threatened to turn over control of the access routes to Berlin to the East Germans by December 31 unless we did X, Y, and Z. And we did *not* do X, Y, and Z and he did *not* turn over the access routes to the East Germans. We called his bluff and it had been a real ultimatum. And we had achieved this success with respect to Berlin through the close collaboration we had with the Germans, the French, and the British. That's what I'd been doing most of my work on in the preceding year, heading the military committee of the interdepartmental group.[10] What did we call that?

AIDE: The military subgroup of the Washington Ambassador's—

NITZE: The Washington Ambassador's group. We did a lot of work and we had a great deal of support from our allies. We were together on all the aspects of that with our allies, and now, of course, to show weakness in this case would seem to me to set us back a tremendous amount. So I thought there were tremendous political consequences to accepting this. And, thirdly, I was frankly annoyed at Gromyko having outrageously lied about this. It was a question of the character of the opposition, so typical of the way in which the Soviets handle themselves; I thought that to knuckle under to this kind of thing was unacceptable. That's my recollection of it.

But then afterward, you know, we had these everlasting debates on the morality of a big country attacking a small country, and so forth. Wouldn't attacking the missile sites be like Pearl Harbor? and so on.

BLIGHT: How did that sit with you? That apparently had a lot of impact on some. Dillon, for example, said that it had a big effect on him, and of course George Ball, whom I talked to last week, said that it had a tremendous effect on him.

NITZE: Frankly, I thought it was all nonsense. . . . In the first place, it seemed to me that the thing to do was not to point the finger of scorn at Castro, but at the Soviets. Clearly what they wanted us to do was point the finger of scorn at Castro and then leap in as the peacemaker. The hell with this. It wasn't Castro who was doing this, it was the Soviets who were doing this. Castro might have thought it would be fine to do it because it had enabled him to get a security guarantee; but operationally the responsible character was in Moscow. It was Khrushchev, and we oughtn't to dodge that fact. If we did, we'd forever regret it.

WELCH: When we talked about the causes of the crisis at the conference, this idea that what they really wanted to do was to provoke us into a position that would enable them to "save Castro" wasn't expressed. Do you know of anyone else who shared your view on that?

NITZE: Well, I think they quickly came around to the other view. I forget when they came around to the view that we ought to point the finger at Khrushchev rather than at Castro, but I have the feeling that wasn't such a difficult battle to win and that we won that battle, but I forget when. I don't believe that we really settled it until after the speech.

BLIGHT: I think that's right. I remember speaking to Mac Bundy about this, and the decision to define it as a U.S.–Soviet problem that happens to be occurring in Cuba was very significant to him, and also, he believes, the right decision to make. It was not a Cuban problem, it was a problem of U.S.–Soviet relations.

NITZE: That's right, but I think it took some time for the group to come to that conclusion.

WELCH: Do you remember who was suggesting it was really a U.S.–Cuban problem?

NITZE: It was my view that that was the way Khrushchev would try to make it look. He would try to make it a U.S.–Cuban problem; I don't remember that anybody on the ExComm ever took that position. But it's my recollection the issue wasn't really determined. Most of the discussion in those early days was way up at the level of morality and this kind of thing, and not on the issue of who does what, with what, to whom, and when. You go through the record and that wasn't what was talked about. This argument about whether we ought to take out the missiles was what caused all this talk about morality—talk about a strike, and whether it should be a surgical strike. There I was very much on the side of doing as surgical an air strike as you could. But then when you got to talking with the Air Force and how surgical you could make it, they had a different view of what was prudent. The Air Force always likes to make sure you have enough force. They look at those who look at the political aspects of the use of force with contempt as advocating restrictions on the militarily intelligent course. Sometimes political considerations should bear on the proper military approach. But they ask, why worry about that when their job is to win a military victory? LeMay was a hell of a good military man. I was always glad he was on our side and not on the other side. But this attitude was part of the problem.

Then, when we got to the question of blockade, that led to a strenuous legal argument between Dean Acheson and Len Meeker, the State Department legal advisor.* Acheson stated his view unambiguously: "The hell with international law. International law gets made, it's just a series of precedents and decisions that have been made in the past. But this is a unique situation and this is one in which one can, and should, make international law rather than just follow past precedents. There aren't any real precedents for this. And if you're troubled with what the books say about the blockade, then change the name." And then somebody came up with "quarantine."

WELCH: But Acheson favored the air strike.

NITZE: He favored the air strike and I also favored the air strike. But I also favored the blockade. Then the question at issue was: How do you sort all this out? My recollection is that I was so annoyed at the failure of the main discussions to deal with who-does-what-with-what-to-whom-when, it wasn't really a planning session, it seemed to me rather to be a sophomoric seminar.

One person sympathetic to my view was Alexis Johnson.† So Alexis Johnson and I went off and agreed. "Let's look at this thing from the standpoint of a scenario, and let's make the central point of the scenario the time when a speech is made, because the one thing we know is that at some time the President is going to have to talk to the American public and to the world. There are certain things that will have to be done before he makes that speech, certain things that can be done after he makes that speech, and these things divide themselves into political and military actions. Why don't we sit down and write out a scenario in which S-hour is speech hour and then look at it from the standpoint of what needs to be done prior to S-hour and what can be done after S-hour, and let's fill in the time scales. Certainly we've got to do some consultation with the Organization of American States. How do we handle the UN? When do we tell the Russians about the speech? Do

---

* Leonard C. Meeker, Deputy Legal Counsel to the State Department.
† U. Alexis Johnson, Deputy Under Secretary of State and a member of the ExComm.

we deliver the speech without warning them about it, or what do we do? What do we do about our allies? What do we do about the Congress? What are all these political things that need to be done in advance of the President's speech and what are the things that can be done afterwards, and how long afterwards? And then what do we need in the way of military preparations? If you want to conduct a quarantine, what ships do you need, in what position, at what time, in order safely to do that? How much time does that take, and what orders do you need to put out and when? And what kind of a command structure do you need, and so forth and so on? How do you do all that? And if you want to do an air strike, what do you need in the way of planes and what do you need in the way of penetrating bombs and pilots and God-knows-what? And where do you want them? Where do they need to be and at what time? And how long is it going to take us to do that? When do you have to start this preparation and how do you maintain the security of it? And if none of this works, you may have to invade the Cuban island. If that, what forces do you need in order to conduct the invasion? What landing craft? Do you use the Marines or do you not? What air cover do they need, and so forth and so on? Where do you want them? When do you want them? How do you put all this together time-wise?" . . .

BLIGHT: . . . As you moved through the crisis, did you get the sense of a kind of hardening of position? There were people who were really attending to the detail who felt that we should get on with it, that we had certain responsibilities to carry out, and then another group—including, for example, people like McNamara, who once again told the story that implies that Washington would be bombed by the following Saturday and that he'd never live to see another Saturday sunset, and that the whole fate of the world is at stake and that we just had our hands tied, that we couldn't afford to do anything because the second lieutenant guarding the missile base in Cuba might feel like he had to use it before he lost it. I mean, there's a whole group of people who obviously were thinking in those terms, and if you think in those terms, I guess the morality thing must play an important part.

NITZE: My recollection is that I, for one, wasn't thinking that way. I was uncertain as to where we ought to go. I was uncertain about whether or not an air strike would be better than a blockade—or quarantine, as it came to be called—or whether you really had to invade the home island. But the main thing about this time-phase scenario was that it solved that problem, because the timed-scenario approach made clear that the thing that you should do at the earliest time was the quarantine—that was the most immediate thing that you could and should do. Then if the quarantine worked, you didn't need to do any of these other things. If the quarantine didn't work, it could be backed up by the air strike. If that didn't work, then, only then, did you have to contemplate the invasion of the home island. Therefore, by virtue of time phasing this thing, you could reconcile the three different options. They weren't really in conflict.

It was perfectly clear that what you needed to do policywise was to use the minimum force or threat of force necessary to accomplish the result. What you wanted was the result. You didn't want to have violence for violence's sake, you wanted to get the result and the result was to get rid of these damn missiles. And therefore you wanted to do the things in this time phase in order to produce this result with the minimum expenditure of force necessary and the minimum risk. That seemed to me to suddenly put this thing into an understandable framework.

Now, the problem we faced when Alexis and I got through with this was that we didn't have a draft of the speech. So when I returned the next morning the first thing I did was to talk to Sorensen and go over this with him and say we needed a draft of a Presidential speech right away, because otherwise the whole scenario didn't make sense. . . . And the moment we had an initial draft of the speech and a scenario, a time-phase scenario, hours for this and that and the other thing, we had the elements for translating what up to that time had been a bull session into a planning session, dealing with the pros and cons and adjusting this and changing the language in the speech: how many hours for deciding who should go talk to the French; who should deal with the British; when you need to do that and what is the relative time period you have to do it in; what you do in the UN.

Then a lot of the discussion, of course, switched to this question of what do you do with the Thors and Jupiters.[11] That became the second crucial problem, trying to get that thing straightened out. That's my recollection of the main outline of what happened during the early days.

WELCH: Some of the people at the conference expressed worries about the mobility of the missiles and worries about them becoming operational. Did either of those things bother you? Did you see those interfering with your time-phase approach?

NITZE: The point was, what could you do about it?

WELCH: Well, for instance, General Taylor, in the interview I sent you the transcription of, said that he was worried about the quarantine because it would give them a chance to hide the missiles in the jungle right away, and then we'd never be able to find them and take them out with an air strike at all. And so initially he favored an air strike. Did that seem to be a problem from your point of view?

NITZE: Well, from my standpoint, I found it hard to visualize hiding these in the jungle and then making them operational. It didn't seem to me that was an easy thing to do. And if you couldn't get rid of them, if you couldn't get the Russians to take them out, then you certainly could destroy the sites, and the missiles without a launch site didn't seem to be very useful objects. You might worry about them in the long run. You want to get them out. Your question would be whether you have an air strike and then invade the island; but I didn't think that was the major problem.

WELCH: But, at the time, many believed that the missiles were mobile and could be fired from temporary positions.

NITZE: We were keeping the missiles under pretty constant surveillance. But, you know, you had to make up your mind about what the main things to do were. There are all kinds of risks in an operation like this. The main decisions have to be made; you don't have an infinite amount of time. Why worry yourself to death about this objection and that objection? You've got to keep your mind on doing, within the requisite time, what needs to be done, or else you're lost.

WELCH: One of the striking things at the conference was everyone's admission that what you suggested you went through with Alexis Johnson wasn't in fact done for contingency planning. People weren't thinking, "If we do an air strike, what or where would the Russians respond and what would we respond to that with?"—and so on. Bob McNamara said that he just wasn't thinking in those terms at all. Did you have any conception of what the next steps would have been if there had been a response to an air strike? What do you think the Soviet response would have been?

NITZE: Well, certainly we thought about this. To my recollection, we alerted SAC, so that, you know, we could respond.[12] We were prepared to alert all the other services. I forget whether the DefCons went up or maybe it was a question of maintaining security by not alerting anybody as to what the problem was.[13] But within those considerations of security I think the military were thoroughly alert and ready for whatever might have resulted. We had to do that, because clearly the danger of war had gone up.

WELCH: Did you think the Soviets would blockade Berlin again if there were an air strike, or did you think that they would have attacked the Jupiters in Turkey? Did you think anything specific about that?

NITZE: We thought about all those possibilities. I, in particular, was worrying about that; I think I was given the task of worrying about it by Mr. Kennedy. So you try to put yourself in Mr. Khrushchev's shoes and try to decide what might be the West's most vulnerable positions, and how you could exploit them. Certainly the reinstitution of the blockade or in fact the invasion of Berlin was within the military capability of the Soviet Union. But, you know, you look at whether you would do that in light of the very great imbalance between our strategic nuclear capability and theirs. And, frankly, I thought it would be wholly unlikely that they would respond in that way because of our strategic nuclear capability—because of our undoubted superior nuclear capability. I think McNamara's figures as I saw them were wrong. I forget, he said something about the Soviets having only three hundred nuclear warheads?

BLIGHT: Five thousand to three hundred. I think those were the numbers that he used.

NITZE: I believe they bear little relationship to reality.

WELCH: What was your recollection of the balance?

NITZE: I think that at that time the number of U.S. missile launchers capable of striking the U.S.S.R. was somewhere around 350. The number of Soviet missile launchers capable of striking the U.S., apart from the forty being erected in Cuba, was then estimated to be approximately half that number. McNamara's figures appear to include a number of bombs for each U.S. bomber capable of an intercontinental strike and only one for each such Soviet bomber. Soviet MRBMs and IRBMs in the Soviet Union are excluded from these estimates.[14]

The spread, therefore, was very much in our favor. *Very* much in our favor. And certainly with respect to the seas, we had managed to cause all the Soviet submarines in the vicinity to surface. We had them under control. We had complete local tactical control of the situation. It was clear that the Russians could have had the same in Berlin; so, to my mind, the decisive factor was our undoubted strategic superiority. McNamara didn't believe in that, but I believed in its significance. And I therefore didn't think that the risk of the Russians responding in a way which would bring into action our undoubted strategic superiority was very great. Not infinitesimal, because you can never tell what people like the Soviets will do, and therefore you could well imagine that some irrational act could take place. But it seemed to me it would have to be an irrational act, a totally irrational act, on the Soviet side, to respond with an invasion of Berlin or even the institution of a blockade of Berlin.

Taking out the Jupiters and Thors, directing some kind of a strike against them, seemed to me to be the most reasonable response for Khrushchev to consider. But those Jupiters and Thors, although highly vulnerable, were further away from the U.S.S.R. than the Soviet missiles in Cuba were from the United States.[15] They would have had some problems carrying that out, although they were awfully vulnerable, the Jupiters and Thors. But, then again, taking those out didn't seem to me to be a sensible course for Khrushchev to take in the light of our strategic superiority. It seemed to me that we had both tactical superiority in the area of Cuba and we had overall strategic superiority; under those circumstances, we really were not running that great a risk. It was, as I say, not infinitesimal, but it wasn't that great a risk. It seemed to me the question at issue was: How do you handle this as intelligently as possible in order to get the result you want with the minimum use of force? That's my view of it. It's my recollection of my view then, and it's still my view.

BLIGHT: . . . Was there a point at which you concluded yourself that the quarantine just wasn't working, that more forceful action was required, probably an air strike? . . .

NITZE: My recollection is that I thought that McNamara was correct in viewing the quarantine and the way in which it was specifically executed as not only a military matter but a matter of very great political importance, and therefore I sided with McNamara . . . on his insistence that George Anderson should report minute by minute as to what happened when we were turning back the first ship. McNamara was quite right in proposing that he, in turn, talk with Mr. Kennedy minute by minute about that to see to it that the political as well as military risks were minimized. As far as the military risks were concerned, it was the task of the Navy and the commanders in the field to minimize them. But I came to the conclusion that McNamara was overdoing it. I thought that we were in a strong position, and that we ought to exploit it. I thought we should not let those deep-hulled merchant ships which I was sure had missiles aboard just turn around and go back. I thought we ought to go and stop them, board them and demonstrate that they had the missiles aboard and take them back to the United States. That was my personal view of it. And I also thought that we were being awful pantywaist about what it was we wanted to stop. We were letting all the tankers, and so forth, go to Cuba. I thought if we really wanted to bring pressure we should cut off the tankers and other things going to Cuba, and do that fairly promptly, for the same reasons that Max [Taylor] was talking about—that you didn't want this thing to take too long. And so it wasn't so much my feeling that the quarantine was wrong but that we weren't exploiting it with sufficient vigor. That was my particular view.

. . . . .

BLIGHT: Some people say—Bobby Kennedy says in his book, and George Ball told me again last week—that when General Taylor brought word into the meeting that Saturday [October 27] that the U-2 had been shot down over Cuba and the wreckage had been spotted and the pilot was assumed dead, that this was a critical point, that the normal thing to do would have been to retaliate against the offending SAM site, and that wasn't done.[16] And the way Ball remembered the meeting anyway was that it was quite different from some of the other meetings. It was very vehement and people had very different opinions. . . . He thought some people at that point had decided that enough is enough of the kind of slow, very slow squeeze, the dancing-on-eggs sort of business: "That's it really, they've just shot and killed an unarmed reconnaissance plane and they can't get away with this!" Other people felt: "Well, you still can't do anything. It's too dangerous." I gather you were in the former camp, or of the former view. Did that shoot-down change things as far as you were concerned?

NITZE: I don't have a firm recollection of what my view of it was on that day.[17] My general view was, as I've said earlier, that we should have taken firmer action. But I don't remember expressing any view on what we ought to do because of the shoot-down. The problem was a more general one, as to how aggressive could we afford to be and *should* be both from a military standpoint and a political standpoint. And from the political standpoint it was clear that we would lose by magnifying a thing beyond its true significance. From a military standpoint, I thought we were in a position where we could safely bring greater pressure and that we should bring greater pressure earlier. . . .

. . . . .

BLIGHT: . . . One other very interesting thing happened that took us aback at the dinner that you missed when we all sat down together for the first time before we had the official sessions. Everyone got to say a piece, and Ted Sorensen got up and said, "I don't really know why I'm here," roughly. "I don't think there are any useful lessons to learn from the Cuban missile crisis. Twenty-five years ago the world was different— the balance, everything's different." And then somebody challenged him on that and said, "You wouldn't have come, you know, you don't need a vacation in Florida that badly—there must be some reason why you came back." He said what he really meant was that he thought people had learned all the wrong lessons from the missile crisis, and the "wrongest" lesson of all was that the strategic balance matters when it comes time to manage these crises. Now, I don't—

NITZE: I think he's just dead wrong.

BLIGHT: —think for a moment that you would believe it.

NITZE: I think he's just dead wrong, and Mac Bundy's dead wrong. I think that whole school of thought is just—you know. They've come to a conclusion that a liberal policy toward the Soviet Union—in other words, unilateral disarmament with the Soviet Union—is the right policy, and therefore this has become—what do the psychiatrists call it, cognitive dissonance? You get so clear in your mind as to what the objective is that you just reject with true faith any evidence that is contrary to what supports that objective. It becomes not a question just of belief but of faith that the opposite is true. The opposite of what you see is true.[18]

WELCH: Isn't it possible that the strategic balance mattered a very great deal to the Soviets, but very little to McNamara, Bundy, and so on?

NITZE: I think it mattered a great deal to the Soviets, and I thought it properly mattered a great deal to the Soviets. And it mattered a great deal to me. But it did not matter to McNamara. I thought he was dead wrong about it. He's still dead wrong. That was my view at the time.

BLIGHT: Your view at the time was that—

NITZE: The extraordinary thing was that the one person who agreed with me was Garthoff. At that time he wrote a memorandum which supported my conclusion. He went through the numbers and the strategic significance of these IRBMs and MRBMs and he came out with the same conclusion I'd come to.[19]

WELCH: The one person apart from Max Taylor, you mean.[20]

NITZE: Well, Max Taylor is a great man, but I never thought Max was that good an analyst. Ray was then working for the CIA in an analytical function.[21] It's a different kind of a way of looking at things.

BLIGHT: . . . There were just very clearly different views of this situation, and they were represented really all up and down the government. There were people like McNamara who, interestingly, you say even at the time believed that the balance really mattered not at all. I've often wondered if that's a reconstruction, or—

NITZE: No, no, that was true at the time.

BLIGHT: He really believed that at the time?

NITZE: He believed it at the time, and I think he was just dead wrong

. . . . .

WELCH: What was your reaction to Dean Rusk's revelation that the President and he had actually planned for the contingency of trading off the Jupiters if Khrushchev's letter didn't accept his terms?

NITZE: It doesn't surprise me, because that's the way the President had been leaning all along. I forget what meeting it was at which the President decided in favor of offering to the Soviets formally in the letter a trade-off with the Jupiters and the Thors. My recollection is that he decided when Stevenson came down. . . . On that day, Stevenson came and made a strong pitch about his problems at the UN, and what world opinion would be, and so forth and so on, and he recommended we trade in the Jupiters and Thors. The President decided in favor of that, putting it in the speech.[22] And I objected strongly. After he had risen and everybody else had risen from the table, Doug Dillon came to my support. . . . So it turned out that there was quite a body of us that were just not in favor of that. And so we sat down again and the President—I forget exactly how he decided, but in any case, it wasn't put in the speech. My recollection is that I was told to get in touch with our Ambassador in Turkey and talk to him about it. Royal Tyler* and I tried to get through on the secure phone. The damn phone didn't work. We tried to get in touch with our Ambassador in Turkey and our Ambassador in Italy to discuss the reaction the Turks and the Italians would have. We couldn't get through to them. Those memories are dim.

BLIGHT: It's interesting that it was Stevenson's original idea, and that he was roundly hooted for it. And yet a week later this is exactly what the President seemed prepared to do.

NITZE: I've never been quite clear as to exactly what Bobby Kennedy did. I certainly didn't know about it at the time. I gather from what you tell me that others knew that Bobby Kennedy was going to go and talk to Dobrynin, but I didn't know about it and I gather Max Taylor didn't know about it. . . .[23]

---

* William R. Tyler, Assistant Secretary of State for European Affairs.

Interview with Douglas Dillon, May 15, 1987, New York City

BLIGHT: Dave Welch and I met with Paul Nitze a week before last.
. . . I remembered you saying that one of the reasons that we ought to
put our conversation off a little bit was so that we could talk to him
first.

DOUGLAS DILLON: I thought that would help because, for most of the
time during the missile crisis, with one real exception, I believe he and
I felt the same, and I knew that he would have a better memory and
he would have documents and things with which he could refresh himself. . . .

JANET LANG: What was the exception?

DILLON: The exception was this: I finally agreed with Bobby Kennedy
that a surprise attack on Cuba at that time was unacceptable because it
was too much like the Japanese attack on Pearl Harbor. If we attacked
like that, we would be forsaking the ideals for which I believed we had
fought World War II. . . .

. . . . .

BLIGHT: . . . I remember you said something at the meeting that a
bunch of us were talking about not long ago. . . . [The question arose]:
Did you, as some people have said, and as Bobby Kennedy wrote, think
that nuclear war was a real live possibility? And you stunned me a little
bit. But I think I understand it a little bit now. You said, "When I first
heard the news, the call came and I thought, what in the world is going
on here?" But, after that, you sensed that this could be handled. I mean,
we had to find a way to manage and handle this thing. Other people
seem to have had the idea that at first there seemed to be little reason
to worry about nuclear war but then, as the crisis wore on, the danger
seemed to increase. George Ball said to us a couple of weeks ago when
we talked to him that as the thing wore on he got more and more worried
about nuclear war coming about as an unintended consequence of some
irreversible action.

DILLON: I think part of the reason I got progressively less worried was
that I had been in the Treasury and not fully current for the last couple
of years on details of defense posture and so forth. I was not, when I
first heard about it, fully aware of the extent of the nuclear supremacy
that we had. And when I became aware of that, then I changed my
view entirely and, of course, I agree totally with Nitze and think the
McNamara thesis that our nuclear superiority made little or no difference
is dead wrong. Our nuclear preponderance was essential. That's what

made the Russians back off, plus the fact of our total conventional superiority in the region.

LANG: Could I ask a follow-up on that? I can sort of understand what you are saying, but at Hawk's Cay there was a comment that Abe Chayes made that was graphic in this regard. I think it was that first night after the dinner, he was talking about the nuclear capability of the Soviet Union and he said that that small, ragtail nuclear deterrent was nevertheless a powerful deterrent to us. What impressed me was how worried we were that one or two nuclear weapons might land on the United States and how inhibiting that was on what we all might have done.

DILLON: Well, that was probably true of a certain group and Chayes was talking about them. It wasn't true of others. It wasn't true of me; it wasn't true of the military; it wasn't true of Nitze. I think one reason for this difference was that we had had more to do with it before. I had had four years of service in the State Department during the Eisenhower Administration. I was convinced that the Russians were not crazy and that they would not do anything as crazy as provoke a nuclear war that would surely destroy them.

LANG: You believed they really would be restrained by that?

DILLON: Oh, very much, because all you had to do was to read the documents and their books and their military theory, which emphasized that nuclear weapons were a valid weapon and war could be won with them and they were trying to get them in a position where there was one they could fight and win. So, that being their thinking, and they'd see us with whatever it was, six or eight times their number of nuclear weapons or ten times, or whatever it was and they would behave accordingly.

BLIGHT: . . . You just mentioned something that I haven't thought of before, which is that those of you who are known as the hawks in the Cuban missile crisis—yourself, Paul Nitze, General Taylor, John McCone, and Dean Acheson—really did have more experience. I mean, I think of McGeorge Bundy, Robert McNamara, Ted Sorensen, the Kennedys—that was then a very new group to operational details in foreign policy and U.S.–Soviet relations. You people—the so-called hawks—had been through this many times before.

DILLON: I think most of the differences between the hawks and doves had something to do with this. I think simple inexperience led to an inordinate fear of nuclear damage, the fear of what *might* happen. McNamara, in particular, felt that way, I guess, although I wasn't so conscious at the time that that was his reason. You knew he was always holding back. But he had great influence on the President. The President thought very highly of him. And it may well be that because it was usually McNamara who described the situation to the President that the President felt that this was more dangerous than many of the rest of us did. Maybe it was McNamara himself who originally thought that the probability of nuclear war was about one chance in three or something like that.

BLIGHT: Nobody was going to take a one-in-three chance on nuclear war.

DILLON: No.

BLIGHT: So you believe hawks and doves differed mainly on what you thought the risks really were?

DILLON: Sure.

BLIGHT: So you think that President Kennedy had such great respect for McNamara that in a situation like this he was bound to depend heavily on him, and that he felt that McNamara was a sort of buffer between himself and the Pentagon? As you know, a lot of the doves in the missile crisis have said, as President Kennedy is reported also to have said, "Thank God for McNamara over there in the Pentagon." From statements like these, one almost gets the image of an animal straining to attack and McNamara holding the animal back. Are you saying that the President probably got that message from McNamara himself?

DILLON: Oh, I am sure he did. Of course, McNamara had some perfectly logical ideas for someone with less than two years' experience at the Pentagon. For example, when it came to stopping the tanker and that great fight he had with George Anderson, where Anderson was saying he was going to shoot at the tanker if it didn't halt, then McNamara asking Anderson about the cargo, or something like that—the idea obviously in McNamara's mind was that if you missed the rudder of the tanker, and hit the cargo—the oil—the tanker would blow up. But that's not true. Look at what happens when you shoot tankers in the Persian Gulf.

BLIGHT: They leak some oil. That's about it.

DILLON: Of course, if high-test gas was the cargo, that would be something else and you would have a real explosion. But McNamara didn't know the difference. I think, with more experience under his belt, McNamara might have worried less about accidents and things like that.

LANG: . . . All the way through the missile crisis, one gets the sense that McNamara believed things were getting out of control. You are saying that his worrying about loss of control might have been a function, in many cases, of simple lack of experience? He assumed that any little thing might lead to catastrophe?

DILLON: Yes.

LANG: Are you saying that more experienced people like yourself sort of thought, "Oh yes, these little things may get out of control. But it's no big deal; nothing significant really will result from an isolated event here or there?"

DILLON: That's right. If McNamara had known, for example, that shooting an oil tanker doesn't cause it to blow up, he wouldn't have been so worried and agitated about it. Of course, in the final analysis, we must remember that the quarantine proved sufficient to stop the Russian ships and to get the missiles out of Cuba without shooting anything. Some people say we should have gone further and used this as an opportunity to knock off Castro, but I disagree. I didn't like the idea of Americans fighting Latin Americans. That would have been very bad—maybe not for the first two days, but if you didn't get it done very quickly, you would be in a mess.

BLIGHT: Yes, we would be bogged down again in a war in a tropical jungle—fighting partisans in a guerilla-style war.

DILLON: What I mean is that Latin Americans would turn on us and say, "There's your Yankee imperialism again." I didn't want that at all. But I think people who fault the Kennedy Administration for not going straight to an invasion of Cuba are totally wrong. The gradual Mc-Namara approach worked. It proved to be enough. But I think someone ought to look into the relationship between the Cuban missile crisis and McNamara's conduct of the Vietnam War.[24] Someone, I think, has written a book saying that our troubles there were basically because of the McNamara philosophy of "graduated response."[25] Personally, I agree with that.

I only have one experience, right at the very beginning of the escalation of the Vietnam War, that relates to this. I was in a National Security Council meeting called by President Johnson in February of 1965, after the Vietnamese had attacked one of our training bases in South Vietnam, and some Americans were killed. It was the biggest attack up to that point on our base. They decided to do something about it. The way it was handled was typical of the way that President Johnson worked. He met first with the military people, McNamara, Dean Rusk, and maybe Central Intelligence people, and then decided what he was going to do. After that he would, for public-relations purposes, call a meeting of the National Security Council and have various other people around the table. I was there at this particular meeting; the President described what had happened and told us that we had to answer and that our answer was going to be the sending of two planes to bomb a certain bridge in North Vietnam. The idea was that this would send a signal to the North Vietnamese: that they couldn't get away with stuff like this. After that was finished, President Johnson went around the table and asked each person whether he agreed with him. Of course, you always wanted to do that if you could.

Now, you should know that by that time I had already resigned two or three times. It was clear I was going to be gone soon, so I said I had no objection on the condition that the use of force which we now were getting into for the first time—military force—would be followed by the application of a principle I had learned from President Eisenhower: Don't use force unless you are prepared to use all you've got. So I said sure, go ahead, as long as you are ready, if this raid doesn't do the job, to move right ahead and mine the harbor of Haiphong and do all the necessary things to win this war. President Johnson was quite angry. But next time they sent four planes, and so on, up the ladder. That was not the way to fight a war, as any military person will tell you.

BLIGHT: That's interesting. So you believe McNamara, and Johnson too, may have sort of overlearned a lesson of the missile crisis. You think they believed the gradual approach always works, but it didn't in Vietnam, where you should have used all the force necessary to win the war?

DILLON: That's right. That's part of it. But I also think Johnson should have learned a lesson in the Dominican Republic that he should have applied in Vietnam. He sent two divisions into the Dominican Republic [in 1965] when there was some trouble, when he only needed a regiment. He sent two divisions in there, and boy, it was all over in an instant. They pulled them out in two weeks and there has never been trouble since.

. . . . .

BLIGHT: . . . Did you really feel when you got into the missile crisis that you were in a deep and dangerous crisis? Was it clear to you that this was not an ordinary state of affairs? Or did it seem to you that the events of October 1962 were not that much different from some of these other things you had been through? I remember Mac Bundy telling me that he polled some of his former colleagues when he was writing his chapter on the missile crisis for his book, and they all told him it was the most profoundly intense and unforgettable experience of their public lives.[26] That's the way it affected them. I wonder if you feel that this kind of reaction derives from their relative inexperience in these matters?

DILLON: I think this is probably true. Of course, you must remember that all those other crises with the Russians were not close to home. All the other ones were overseas, and if they had led to a clash, the fighting and damage would be somewhere else. You weren't faced with this possibility of massive destruction right here at home. That was the immediate first reaction that I had where I heard for sure that the missiles had gone in. Others who favored the air strike felt this way, too. I certainly said that in Hawk's Cay. It was uppermost on my mind and I think it was on the minds of the others who felt the same way I did: that we should not permit these missiles to become operational, and that therefore we had to act quickly and that there was a real danger if they became operational. I was very surprised at Hawk's Cay to hear people like McNamara say that whether or not those missiles were operational didn't make any difference.

BLIGHT: Yes, I was surprised to hear that. I take it you disagree with McNamara on this?

DILLON: Yes, I think he is absolutely wrong to say that the operational status of the missiles made no difference. It made a tremendous difference, and I know the military felt that way, and that we hawks felt that way. As Paul Nitze said, this would have really changed the whole strategic balance and presented a very serious situation. I don't recall anyone at any time expressing the view in our ExComm meetings that the operational status of the missiles didn't matter. Of course, I cannot say that McNamara never felt that way at the time. All I can report is that neither he nor anyone else ever said anything like that. Frankly, I do find that statement [of McNamara's] hard to believe. How could it make *no* difference whether or not those missiles were ready to fire?

. . . . .

BLIGHT: Many of us were surprised by Bob McNamara's assertion in Hawk's Cay that the operational status of the missiles was relatively unimportant. I guess it just seems that a missile that's ready to fire is a whole lot different than one that isn't ready to fire because it doesn't have a nuclear warhead on it. It would seem to make a big difference as to what you are going to do about it, if you feel you must remove it.

DILLON: That's right, it makes a big difference. Bob McNamara is very good with figures and he uses them with telling effect, sometimes in a way that can mislead the uninterested. This occurred during the discussions at Hawk's Cay about relative numbers of U.S. and Soviet nuclear weapons. I pointed out that the important question was: How many did the Soviets have that could actually reach the U.S.? The missiles in Cuba made about a hundred percent increase.

BLIGHT: That's right. I remember you said that. Paul Nitze reiterated that to us, as did Ray Garthoff when I talked to him not long ago. Bob McNamara had said something like this: Before we discovered the missiles in Cuba, we led in strategic nuclear weapons by about five thousand to three hundred. After the missiles were discovered, it was five thousand to 340. In other words, he was saying the difference was insignificant. It meant nothing. Ray Garthoff's point, and your point, was that many more bomber bases could be reached by these missiles in Cuba. In other words, McNamara thought they were insignificant because there were so few. You thought they were very significant because, though they were relatively few in number, they could destroy so many more American strategic bombers than before. Is that right?

DILLON: Yes. And I believe my way—our way—was the right way to view the problem. That's the obvious strategic calculation of significance. Frankly, I think McNamara himself realizes this and that is why he tries to be so vehement with the sort of figures that he believes will back him up.

. . . . .

LANG: If Khrushchev hadn't agreed to remove the missiles by Sunday, October 28, would you have favored waiting another week, or two weeks, or a month, before abandoning the quarantine in favor of the air strike and invasion?

DILLON: Oh no, I wouldn't have wanted to wait anywhere near that long. Once we were ready, I thought that we should move. I thought that was what we were going to do and I was very surprised by a lot of statements at Hawk's Cay by people who were close to the President saying that we never would have done anything, and that we would have just stuck with the quarantine. I think they said that mainly to protect what they think President Kennedy's image ought to be. You know, they think he should be remembered as a man of peace that never would resort to war, and so forth. I think he was a strong man, and although he wouldn't have liked bombing and invading Cuba, I was fully convinced that if we had no answers from the Russians, or unsatisfactory ones on that Sunday, then at some point that next week we would have gone in. Frankly, I was a little confused by some of those arguments. On the one hand, they said the President never would have done it; and on the other hand, they said that pressures were building up and that we hawks were getting stronger, and so forth. Well, you can't have it both ways. The pressure *was* building: we *were* getting stronger.[27] I was convinced that we would have gone in the following week. Of course, what's much more important than my feelings or memory of what I was convinced of is that it is perfectly clear that the Russians were convinced that we were about to attack. That's why they stopped the crisis in such a quick way, broadcasting their acceptance of our terms over the radio the next morning. But of course the Russians were not only hearing what we were saying over the regular diplomatic channel. Now, what Bobby Kennedy told Dobrynin we will never know exactly, although I trust the account in his book. But the Russians also were undoubtedly aware in detail of all the military preparations we were making. They saw that we were ready to go in and they also saw that there was little or nothing they could do about it.

BLIGHT: Of course, that probably meant a lot more in the great scheme of things. That probably had more impact than any proclamation, public or private.

DILLON: Oh, yes. With a hundred thousand troops ready to cross from Florida, and with the planes to cover them—well, we were ready.

BLIGHT: Some people who knew Khrushchev felt he was a very impulsive person. Many people have told me that Llewellyn Thompson told them that in Khrushchev you were dealing with a guy who was a lot different than most Soviet leaders, a lot more spontaneous and risky. In fact, he was different enough to try a stunt like putting missiles in Cuba, and I gather that his affinity for risk taking worried people in the ExComm as the crisis wore on. They felt that if he'd do that, it wasn't clear what he would do. And this raises the question of why Khrushchev put the missiles into Cuba in the first place. Paul Nitze and McGeorge Bundy have said that their first reaction when they got the proof that there were missiles in Cuba was that Berlin was involved somehow, that Berlin, not Cuba, is what was really on Khrushchev's mind. We had not caved in on Berlin, in spite of the fact that he had applied pressure there intermittently since at least 1958, and he really didn't have that many options left open to him in his obsession with pushing the Allies out of Berlin. As I interpret Nitze and Bundy, they believed that the missiles were placed into Cuba to shore up the strategic balance all right, but then this new balance would, in Khrushchev's view, give him more leeway to throw his weight around in Berlin. As a further possibility, Dean Rusk feared a situation like that which developed in 1956, when Suez and Hungary occurred almost simultaneously, where one took your mind off the other and this allowed the Soviets to go on and crush the Hungarians.[28] Because of fears like these, I gather that many members of the ExComm were very surprised when, after the quarantine line went up, nothing happened around Berlin. The Soviets just didn't do anything. Did that surprise you at all? Did you think the missiles in Cuba were somehow a diversion from the real interest of the Soviets, which was Berlin?

DILLON: I didn't see it that way. I didn't think the missiles were a diversion, from anything. I think the belief that they were comes from the underestimation of the strategic importance of the missiles in Cuba, which, if left unchallenged, would change the nuclear balance in their favor all over the world and would therefore give the Soviets leverage everywhere.[29] So I didn't believe the missiles were specifically about Berlin. But I did think that if we had to take military action against the missiles, and they felt they had to react militarily somewhere, I thought it probably would have been around Berlin. I thought maybe they would try some sort of blockade against us, or something like that. But I didn't think they would react any more strongly than this anywhere. Berlin was the only important place they could react with a more or less passive use of force by blockading, so we would have to fight our way in and therefore become the ones who would have to initiate armed conflict. Also, we would be in trouble in Berlin because they had a big superiority in the area in conventional arms. That was the real problem in Berlin: they had a huge army close by and we didn't. That was my fear. I'm not sure where this idea came from that if we had gone into Cuba the Soviets would have struck at those ridiculous Jupiter and Thor missiles in Turkey.[30]

BLIGHT: Well, that's interesting, because, as you know, for the doves in the crowd, that fear of an attack on the bases in Turkey became, I gather, a kind of an obsession with them. My impression is that this was responsible for a good deal of their anxiety toward the end of the crisis. The scenario went something like this: If we strike at their missile bases in Cuba, they'll strike at our missile bases in Turkey. Turkey is a NATO ally. Our treaty says that an attack on one is an attack upon all. So NATO and the Warsaw Pact go to war. Inevitably, a move or two after that, we are in a nuclear holocaust.

DILLON: I gather that some people thought that way. But to me that scenario made no sense for two reasons. First, the Soviets weren't going to start something like that. They're not crazy. They know what would happen to them in a major war with us. And these missiles in Turkey were such a minor portion of our arsenal. I mean, why bomb a bunch of useless missiles in Turkey when we've got missiles and bombers all over the world that could hit them? By hitting our bases in Turkey, all the Soviets get is a war they don't want, and for no gain. Why would they do a thing like that? They wouldn't.

LANG: I would like to ask you about what many ExComm members remember as a crucial moment during the crisis: when the American U-2 was shot down over Cuba on October 27. The doves in your group tend to emphasize how important that event was in changing the course of the discussion, the nature of the decisionmaking process, even the outcome. What is your recollection of how things were moving along when this event happened, and what was its influence on later thinking and discussion in the ExComm?

DILLON: My recollection is that the U-2 shoot-down was sort of an isolated incident. Of course, it was a serious development, coming in the midst of a crisis, but, at least for me, it didn't change my thinking in any major way.

LANG: Was it troublesome to you that the President decided not to retaliate against the SAM site from which the missile had been fired that downed the American U-2? Were you pleased or disappointed with that decision?

DILLON: I think many of us thought that he would have to retaliate. I really didn't give it a whole lot of thought. But his decision didn't bother me, really. It didn't make much difference to me as long as I felt we were moving down the track to use whatever force would be necessary to get the missiles out of Cuba. And I was sure about that. The preparations were well under way.

. . . . .

BLIGHT: . . . I wonder whether you also believe we could have done much more in the missile crisis without, as the doves have maintained, risking blowing up the world. This then leads to what people have been calling the Rusk revelation at Hawk's Cay: that, at the President's order, Dean Rusk on October 27 opened up a channel to U Thant at the UN through which a public trade may have been negotiated—Soviet missiles in Cuba for American missiles in Turkey. . . .

DILLON: . . . The Rusk revelation that came out at Hawk's Cay really shocked me. I had no idea that the President was considering such a thing. If we had actually followed through on it, and publicly traded missiles, it would have been a terrible and totally unnecessary mistake.

. . . . .

LANG: . . . Can you recollect how you felt when you got the first letter from Khrushchev on Friday and then sort of follow that through to when the Saturday committee letter came through?

DILLON: When the first letter came through, it seemed like Khrushchev was ready to make a deal and that the crisis would soon be over. But then we got the second letter. It was like a dose of cold water in the face. I thought, we are back to square one. But, for some of us, this sort of thing had happened before when dealing with the Soviets. You had to get used to that kind of erratic behavior. It was Bobby Kennedy's idea, I think, to answer only the first letter and not the second and to go to the Russians with a strong ultimatum.[31] It was a brilliant way to handle it. I think he did a hell of a job of convincing the Russians that the roof was going to fall in on the President. That's what he was supposed to do, and he did it. Whether he said exactly what he says in his book seems to me unimportant. I believe that he successfully conveyed the message that, unless the Russians backed down immediately and agreed to withdraw the missiles, we would be forced to go in and destroy them ourselves. I was surprised to hear his former close friends say at Hawk's Cay that they didn't think Bobby had given the Russians an ultimatum: I think he *did!* And his own book clearly gives the impression that he did.*

. . . . .

LANG: . . . Did you get the sense that over the last few days of the crisis, especially the meetings on October 27, people were sort of hardening into their positions, and that there really was not a whole lot of switching going on? Were people sort of digging into the two positions and were they more ferocious in arguing for them? George Ball and Ted Sorensen remember it that way.[32] I wonder if you do, too?

DILLON: I don't remember the discussions being "ferocious." But I think that, as you discuss and discuss and events continue to move along, it becomes clearer that you don't have unlimited choices. What it really came down to was this: one side—mine—wanted to do something forceful and decisive about the situation, while the other wanted to put off making a decision. That's because we weren't nervous about the consequences, while they were.

---

* See Afterword, pp. 340–42.

. . . . .

BLIGHT: . . . The public at large also seems to have perceived the missile crisis as very, very dangerous—a close call to nuclear holocaust. There seems, for example, to have been a big run on the supermarkets during that week, and so forth. People seem to have had this visceral feeling that they were ever so close to annihilation. Did you feel this way?

DILLON: Yes and no. The crisis was unique in the sense that it was the first time that there was a real, imminent, potential threat to the physical safety and well-being of American citizens. Suddenly we were forced to realize that the threat was not to someone else but to us. That was unique and you could not help thinking about those missiles pointed at us just a few miles off the Florida coast. But, at the same time, I never thought the Soviets would use the missiles. I mean, if they had, they would have been committing suicide, and I never thought they'd do that. So I felt two ways at once. Irrationally, I thought, with the missiles so close, I'm not all that comfortable. But, rationally, they're not going to start a war. I think the people who at the time got very nervous focused too heavily on the potential threat, so close by, without giving enough thought to why the Soviets couldn't really use the missiles. By now, we've gotten used to living under this kind of potential threat, though not from Cuba. But in 1962 this was all new to us, and it was pretty scary.

. . . . .

LANG: During the crisis, George Ball slept at the State Department. Robert McNamara slept in the Pentagon. They recall being really engaged by the crisis to the point almost of exhaustion. Did the crisis affect you like this?

DILLON: No, it didn't affect me that way. I think McNamara had special problems because he was not only going to all these ExComm meetings, he was also supervising and worrying about all the detailed carrying out of everything at the Pentagon. He was terribly busy and involved. I was not, at least to that extent. I was called in from the Treasury by the President to listen, discuss, and offer advice. I was just an advisor in this case. There was no need for me to stay up nights worrying. McNamara faced a different, more difficult situation.

. . . . .

BLIGHT: . . . What do you think of McNamara's belief that, if the Soviets had not agreed to the American offer of October 27, the quarantine could have gone for weeks or months, and we would have done just that? Do you recall McNamara saying this at the time? And do you agree with the view that the quarantine would have, or could have, been extended and intensified for weeks or months?

DILLON: Well, I remember that our discussion toward the end seemed to turn on just how long we all thought the quarantine ought to be extended. It is possible that McNamara believed it could have gone on for months. But if he believed that, he was wrong, in my view. It was becoming clear to the President that enough is enough and that we ought to do something. I believe the President would have decided shortly after Sunday, October 28, that we would have to go in. If Khrushchev hadn't agreed, it would have been obvious that the quarantine had failed. We would have had to go in. The President knew that. And in spite of McNamara's powerful influence on him, I don't believe the President was as skittish about going in as McNamara was.

. . . . .

BLIGHT: Were you at all surprised by Robert Kennedy's role in the conduct and resolution of the missile crisis?

DILLON: I was surprised when I heard that a channel was set up between him and Dobrynin. It was an unusual channel. It was a channel direct to the White House rather than through the State Department and I think it was set up partly because of the President's lack of confidence in the State Department. The President wanted a strong and forceful representative dealing with the Russians. And he chose Bobby. On the whole, it was an excellent choice.

BLIGHT: At the meeting in Hawk's Cay, you opened the discussion by saying that you don't believe there are any useful lessons of the missile crisis. As I recall, you said something like, "It's a different world now." Can you elaborate on that?

DILLON: I just don't see another situation like the missile crisis arising, certainly not in our relations with the Soviets. Next time it would be governed by quite different principles. It just seems to me very, very unlikely that the Soviets and the U.S. will ever again find themselves locked in a crisis in which one side holds all the cards—both nuclear supremacy and conventional dominance in the area in dispute. I just can't conceive of it.

LANG: What difference do you think it would have made in the deliberations of the U.S. government if there had been something like nuclear parity in October 1962?

DILLON: That's a good question; and a hard one. But, postulating equality at 1987 levels, I think that we would have had to do the same thing. We would have had to tell the Soviets that this was unacceptable and we were going to use whatever conventional force was necessary to get the missiles out. We would want to make it crystal-clear that they, not we, would have to start a nuclear war, if there was going to be one. But we would also have to be clear that we were ready. By that I mean it would be obvious that the consequences for the Soviets of going to nuclear war would be the total destruction of the Soviet Union. Going to nuclear alert would accomplish that, just as it did in the missile crisis. But now, if they had something like a sixteen-to-one superiority in nuclear weapons over us, well—that's a totally different story. Then our hands would really be tied, just as the Russians' hands were tied in 1962.

BLIGHT: Paul Nitze told us in our interview last week that in order to address this question of the lessons of the missile crisis, the first thing you have to do is ignore the conventional wisdom of the doves that the nuclear balance made no difference. He said, roughly: "Look, I don't want to argue about that; it is just wrong." As if to emphasize the point, he reminded me that the Soviets put the missiles into Cuba precisely because the nuclear balance did matter. They put in the missiles, in Nitze's view, mainly to redress the nuclear imbalance. I think one implication of Nitze's position is that if the nuclear balance mattered that much to the Soviets, it should have mattered to us. And if it had, I believe he would argue, we probably would have taken the precautions necessary to prevent emplacement of the missiles in the first place.

DILLON: I am frankly flabbergasted at this notion that the nuclear balance made no difference in the missile crisis. Of course it made a huge, decisive difference. Now, some members of the ExComm may have come to believe over time that the balance didn't matter (though, for the life of me, I can't imagine why). But on the first day we were told about the missiles, and the pictures of them were shown, there was an absolutely unanimous opinion in the ExComm on two points: first, that the presence of these missiles greatly altered the nuclear balance;[33] and, second, that those missiles had to come out by whatever means necessary. I can say unequivocally that I never heard any questioning of those basic premises. Of course, I am perfectly willing to grant that McNamara and some of the others may have come to doubt that first premise (about the significance of the alteration in the nuclear balance), after arguing these things out for a week or two, and they may have come to conclusions different from mine. I guess they probably did. But certainly their first reaction—everybody's first reaction—was that the presence of those offensive missiles in Cuba was unacceptable because they were offensive. What could this mean, other than the fact that they gave the Soviets the ability to take out a far higher proportion of our own strategic forces than they ever could before?

. . . . .

BLIGHT: . . . The President had the luxury of taking the time to examine the consequences of destroying the missile sites with military force right away. . . . Wouldn't you want to conclude that a lot of this time wasn't really well spent, that the ExComm had the right idea in the beginning, and the more you did, the more queasy some of the members close to the President may have gotten?

DILLON: One of the things that I felt powerfully was that the longer our deliberations took, the more advanced the Soviet defenses became, as the SAM missiles became operational, and finally, as the MRBMs and IRBMs became operational, it would become necessary to do something much bigger and potentially more costly than would have been initially necessary. And that was something that I didn't particularly relish, because it would have had to involve fighting Cubans in a full-scale invasion of the island. I didn't think they would cave in right away. I thought they would put up fairly good resistance. Of course, they were not as well trained then as they are now, but they were trained well enough to cause us a lot of trouble. I still believe that the surgical strike would have worked, but only if it had been undertaken during the first three or four days of our deliberations. Once precious time slipped away, and we lost the advantage, what the Chiefs wanted to do was what I wanted to do, which was to follow the Eisenhower Doctrine (which *is* military doctrine). That meant that when we decided to use force, we ought to be prepared to do whatever is necessary to accomplish our goal.[34] But as time slipped away, and as the discussions bogged down in debates about taking this base out or that airstrip out and so on, then it quickly began to appear as if we had to do everything all at once. What the doves failed to realize was that we could have sent a signal, if you will, by a strong surgical first strike at the missile bases in Cuba. The signal would have been this: We know what you are up to and it won't work. Now get these damn missiles out of Cuba or else face the consequences. Let them draw their own conclusions about what the consequences would have been. They could have put two and two together, I think. I think the surgical strike would have conveyed the message that we meant business. I still think it would have worked. Of course, even in a surgical air strike you might have killed a lot of Cubans. I know this bothered the doves. But they fail to appreciate my point: that this very act of bombing the missile sites, knowing that collateral damage would occur, would have conveyed exactly the message we should have been sending: that we meant business; that they were not going to get away with this.[35]

BLIGHT: Your enthusiasm for the surgical air strike raises an interesting puzzle in my own mind. It has to do with the connection between that enthusiasm and your admiration for Robert Kennedy's analogy between a possible surprise air strike on the missile bases in Cuba and the Japanese attack on Pearl Harbor. I recall asking you about the Pearl Harbor analogy down in Hawk's Cay. I asked you why you thought it was so powerful and persuasive. You said, in so many words: "Well, for a person of your generation, it must be hard to appreciate why people of my generation would be so moved by that." The reason I ask about it again now is that, on the one hand, I can see part of you wanting to strike against the missile sites very quickly, and on the other hand, it is difficult to see how you could accomplish everything you wanted to accomplish with that and still publicize it in such a way that you were not engaging in the same sort of sneak attack that you associated with the Japanese attack on Pearl Harbor.

DILLON: You're right. At first, I didn't think of the Pearl Harbor analogy. It never occurred to me. I guess I focused on the provocation of the Soviets putting the missiles in and what I saw as the strong need to get rid of them as soon as possible, and certainly before they became operational. After the first day or two, Bobby Kennedy began talking about the analogy very passionately. I could see that this analogy could be exploited by the Soviets as a propaganda weapon that could be used against us. Because of this consideration, I concluded that it was probably worthwhile to give up the military benefits of the immediate air strike, but only if we were willing to commit ourselves to a course of action that might eventually end in an invasion of the island, the net result of which would be to get those missiles out of Cuba.[36]

LANG: In the interview with General Maxwell Taylor that was shown at Hawk's Cay, he pointed out that the longer the Air Force studied the problem of the surgical strike, the less "surgical" it became and the more aircraft appeared to be needed. I believe the total number of aircraft that the Air Force wanted us to use was eventually around five hundred. As Taylor said, that was a good way to kill the project. His feeling, I gather, was that once the Air Force started going into all the details of an air strike, it seemed too big and dangerous and the people who might have gone for something smaller were left without a suitable option.

DILLON: I think that's probably just what happened. I was in favor of a *surgical* strike, *before* the missiles became operational. Now, I am not a military tactician and I'm certainly no expert on air power, so I can't really know whether the Air Force was right. But Nitze, Acheson, Taylor, and myself were talking about, say, fifty or one hundred sorties, not five hundred. I never thought you could do it with ten or twenty, which is what Bob McNamara would have thought was adequate. I still believe the hawks weren't properly understood. We were talking about an air strike that would be relatively small, but still very damaging, that would convey unmistakably our seriousness, collateral damage or no. We needn't have worried about a few Cubans or Soviets, nor, if the missiles were being taken out before becoming operational, about the missiles being launched under attack.

. . . . .

LANG: One of the points that George Ball has made is that, toward the end of the missile crisis, increasing concessions were made to the hawks. He recalls that you and Paul Nitze, particularly, began to specify unmeetable deadlines, and so forth. He said he got very nervous because you hawks were setting these deadlines, and he felt as each new deadline failed to be met, the quarantine advocates' position weakened and the air-strike and invasion advocates gained ground.

DILLON: Well, Ball is right, in the sense that as time wore on, and the Russians sped up work on the missile bases, rather than dismantle them, those of us favoring the air strike and invasion gained ground. But this was simply a function of the situation. The quarantine was failing. Period.

BLIGHT: Of course, Ball had a different perspective than you did. The problem, as he saw it, was that the hawks kept saying, "If the Russians don't do this by time A, then bomb them." Well, then the Russians don't quite come around. Ball said that, by the end of the crisis, it really seemed to him that you and the other hawks were virtually obsessed with bombing the missile bases. He was afraid that you would somehow convince the President that the U.S. should do so, and that such an action might become the first step in an irreversible chain of events leading, in the worst instance, to nuclear holocaust. Like McNamara,

Ball was afraid something would happen—things would get out of control—after the air strike sought by you and the other hawks.

DILLON: I didn't see it that way at all. Not at all. I didn't understand then, and I don't understand now, why people worried so much about one limited, conventional action leading to nuclear war. The idea is preposterous! The only explanation I can think of is that Ball's (and McNamara's) relative inexperience in these matters caused them to draw unwarranted conclusions. I think they may have let their fears run away with them, mainly because they had never been through anything like this before.

. . . . .

BLIGHT: I asked Mac Bundy once, "Why do you think John McCone, among all the ExComm members, correctly predicted that the Soviets were putting offensive missiles in Cuba?" Remember the situation. He had this feeling; you said that McCone said he'd had this feeling for a long time. Bundy responded that it seemed to him that McCone thought like Khrushchev, in the sense that the nuclear balance mattered a lot to him. He thought in those terms, according to Bundy, and Khrushchev thought that way, too. He said so in his memoirs: that missiles in Cuba was the solution to many of his problems. Khrushchev thought somewhat as follows: We can do this in one stroke. We cannot mend the nuclear balance to the point where we are in a situation of parity, but will it ever make a big difference if we can get the missiles into Cuba and get the Americans to accept them as an accomplished fact! As Bundy recalls, he and the President, and the others in the ExComm who came to be called doves, just didn't think in those terms. The implication was that because the nuclear balance seemed politically unimportant to Bundy and his group, they fell into the trap of assuming, mistakenly, that it was also of little importance to the Soviets, or at least not important enough to take the bold step of putting nuclear missiles into Cuba. But they did, of course. McCone was right. What do you think of Bundy's hypothesis: that McCone, yourself, and the other hawks may have understood the situation better, because you had better insight, implicitly, into how the Soviets saw the problem?

DILLON: I think Bundy is right. In fact, I'm sure of it. But I would go further along these lines. I believe we not only understood the Soviet position before they put the missiles into Cuba, but also during the crisis. I never had any doubt that, if we chose to attack the bases and invade the island, they wouldn't have done anything drastic. They couldn't and they knew it. Don't you see—they put the missiles in Cuba in order to beef up their strategic position, which was grossly inferior to ours. But this meant that if we caught them in the act, that is, in their inferior position, and we took action to insure that they stayed inferior, they would have withdrawn. I mean, they acted rationally, in a way, by putting them in. If we'd struck at the bases, they'd have acted rationally and stayed put, I think, around Berlin and elsewhere. The Russians are rational. They're not like Khomeini or Qaddafi. I don't think McNamara and the others understood this.

BLIGHT: What you've just said reminds me that, for one group in the missile crisis, there was a kind of cloud—fear of nuclear war—increasingly hovering in the background. It went along with the feeling that somehow things would get out of control and that all hell would break loose. But for another group, the one to which you belonged, the Cuban missile crisis was, if not exactly ordinary, then also not as extraordinarily dangerous as legend would have us believe.

DILLON: That's right. You know, Bob McNamara, in particular, had that kind of feeling all through his career—the feeling that nuclear war was always just around the corner. I think one of the main reasons he didn't want to do more to try to win the war in Vietnam was his fear that somehow it would escalate to nuclear war. In fact, I've heard him say, "At least we avoided a world war." I draw basically the same conclusion in each case—Cuba and Vietnam. Because McNamara and people like him were so irrationally fearful of nuclear war, in each case we didn't come out nearly as well as we could have. And in Vietnam, of course, we were humiliated.

Interview with Dean Rusk, May 18, 1987, Athens, Georgia

· · · · ·

BLIGHT: Well, as you know, at our meeting we had your former colleagues and a lot of scholars who had been working on the Cuban missile crisis for the past twenty-five years. One of the things that came through to us is the great discrepancy in the views of this event between the people who are sometimes called the hawks and sometimes called the doves. We just spent some time with Douglas Dillon, and with Paul Nitze, and their views of this situation are on so many dimensions just so very different from others'. It's black turned to white, from my understanding of your view of it, as I gather from the tapes you did with Dick Neustadt here a few years ago.[37] And the reaction to your letter has focused that for us.

Just to give you an example, many of the people who read the significant paragraph [of your letter] at the meeting, when we were discussing the issue of the sense of danger on the last couple of days, thought that it was very reassuring to know that the President was thinking in those terms [of a public trade of Jupiter missiles in Turkey for Soviet missiles in Cuba]. It wasn't a policy decision, but it was an option that was being opened up, and it certainly seemed to them to show the direction of the President's thought. Doug Dillon told us the other day—he was at the meeting—that he hadn't known anything about it ahead of time, and when Mac Bundy read it, he said he was profoundly depressed.

DEAN RUSK: Depressed?

BLIGHT: Depressed and shocked that the United States government would even be thinking of caving in at a moment like that. . . .

RUSK: He overlooks the point that to me was crucial: that these missiles in Turkey were on the way out for U.S. and NATO reasons. They were not really relevant to the missiles in Cuba. To drag those missiles into the Cuban problem was a red herring, because the missiles in Turkey were coming out in any event as a U.S. matter. To let them therefore become a complication over missiles in Cuba was wholly gratuitous.[38]

Were they also upset about the message that Robert Kennedy gave to Dobrynin on the same subject?

BLIGHT: I think so. Paul Nitze said that he wasn't party to that. He didn't know about that until a long time afterward. But Dick Neustadt has said that he once talked to a former member of Nitze's staff who came back after he had found out about the whole arrangement, and said that it was the sorriest day of his professional life, or something like that.[39] Again, it had to do with this perception that we would like to talk with you about, that the strategic balance made all the difference in the world. This is what these people believe. The Russians have got their handcuffs on; Gilpatric has made his speech; they know what the situation is, they know they have no options. As General Taylor said in the taped interview we showed at the meeting, we had Khrushchev on the run, so why hand him a piece of cake?

RUSK: We didn't know that Khrushchev was on the run, given his own situation in the Politburo.[40]

There's an ancient Chinese military notion found in Sun Tzu's treatise on *The Art of War*, several hundred years before Christ, which we ran into in Burma with the Chinese troops during the war. And that is the notion that you should never completely surround an enemy, because if you do he will fight too hard. You must always leave him a route of escape. Now, in World War II we found that a little frustrating and slightly amusing, but in the nuclear world this ancient Chinese doctrine takes on special significance. We aren't going to have nuclear war because a nuclear government makes a deliberate, calm decision to start one. They all realize that that is mutual suicide. But you could have nuclear war if a group of men and women find themselves driven into a corner from which they see no escape and they elect to play the role of Samson and pull down the temple around themselves and everyone else at the same time.

Now, Kennedy did not relate this to Sun Tzu and Chinese doctrine, but he was very much aware of that syndrome, and he went to extraordinary pains to refrain from driving Khrushchev into that kind of corner, because no one can be sure what the reaction of a human being would be in a given situation.[41] After all, this was something Kennedy had to think about that his advisors did not. On the Friday of the week following the television speech to the nation, we didn't have any sense that Khrushchev was on the run. We thought he might be having terrible problems within his own Politburo, as indeed he probably was.[42]

WELCH: It came up at the Hawk's Cay conference that the Jupiter missiles in Turkey were formally handed over to the Turks only on October 22, right in the middle of the crisis.[43]

RUSK: Well, this is something that puzzled me. I have heard since the event that the missiles were not in position during the Cuban missile crisis. Well, that was not our perception at the time. And I clearly remember President Kennedy ordering the warheads to be taken off the Turkish missiles.[44] This idea that they were late in being emplaced there came as a great surprise to me.

WELCH: Were you not worried about the possibility of a negative allied reaction to a public trade? Wouldn't that have been interpreted as the U.S. trading away Turkish security in order to deal with a local American problem?

RUSK: Well, we weren't trading it away. This is the point that I would insist upon. We weren't giving anything away by informing the Soviet Union that, as a U.S. matter, these missiles were on the way out. You see, we had that very critical Joint Atomic Energy Committee report from Congress when Kennedy took office that criticized the emplacement of those missiles in Turkey and in Italy on the grounds that they were obsolete and vulnerable.[45] I remember we joked about which way those missiles would go if they were fired. They were first-generation intermediate missiles with rather primitive guidance systems, and we were told that tourists driving down a public highway with .22-caliber rifles could pass by these missile sites and put holes in them and put them out of action.

Well, Kennedy decided early in his Administration to take the missiles out, and he asked me to initiate conversations about this with the Turks, which I did, as early as May 1961. And it was in that conversation that the Turkish Foreign Minister said that it would be embarrassing, because they had just gotten from their parliament the appropriations for the Turkish side of the cost of those missiles, and it would be very embarrassing to go right back to them and say that they were being taken out. And then he said that it would be very bad for the morale of Turkey as a member of NATO if they were taken out before a Polaris submarine were in the Mediterranean to take their place. It was in the spring of '63 that Polaris submarines would be available in the Mediterranean. I came back to explain this to President Kennedy, and he accepted the notion of a delay in the removal of the Turkish missiles. And the idea that he was furious to learn during the missile crisis that they had not been removed is a little artificial. He said nothing to me about being furious, because he had had from me an explanation of what the problem was.[46] . . .

Let me point out that my letter to you about the Turkish missiles is not subject to corroboration. That's my statement, there's no other witness living, no other record, so you can accept my statement or not. I didn't keep a copy of the little piece that I dictated to Andrew Cordier in New York.

BLIGHT: When I told Mac Bundy about the letter, I talked to him about it because I didn't feel qualified to interpret what I was being told. He told me then that you had said to him that there might be some people who wouldn't believe it.

RUSK: I personally am wholly indifferent to that point.

. . . . .

BLIGHT: Do you think that is something that would have been activated if, as I gather several of you believed, Khrushchev either could not or would not have been able to persuade his colleagues by whatever time limit Bobby Kennedy had set in his ultimatum or statement to Dobrynin? Did it seem to you that there was a fairly high probability that this would have been used, this channel through Cordier?

RUSK: Khrushchev announced on Sunday that the missiles would be removed. Our Armed Forces were ready to move into Cuba by the following Tuesday. I think this Andrew Cordier ploy would have been used before we landed troops in Cuba, because landing those troops in Cuba with thirty thousand or more Russian troops in there and Russian missiles there would have been a major escalation from the Soviet point of view. So I think it's very likely that the Andrew Cordier ploy would have been attempted on the Monday if it had been necessary. But, you know, when Robert Kennedy gave this information to Dobrynin about the missiles in Turkey, Dobrynin said immediately, "This is a very important piece of information." I think it's possible that, from Khrushchev's point of view, this made a difference to the way he handled this matter in the Politburo. . . .

Now, I don't know to what extent your group got into details of this sort, but I went back to my office at the White House before Robert Kennedy was to meet the Russian Ambassador, and I telephoned Bobby Kennedy to make it clear that he should treat this as a piece of information and that we were not making an agreement on the subject. Bobby Kennedy told me on the phone that he was with the Ambassador and he had already said what he had to say to him on that subject. I don't know exactly what language Bobby Kennedy used. But, following that conversation, Dobrynin came back with a piece of paper in his hand which seemed to register this business of the Turkish missiles as some kind of agreement, and we returned that piece of paper to Dobrynin, and told him that that was inappropriate under the circumstances.[47] And we did not accept this—at least, I never thought that we had accepted this—as an agreement with the Soviet Union, but rather as a piece of information. There were several reasons for that. One was that we did not have time for the negotiation of an agreement. Fundamental to this whole situation was the fact that we never saw a warhead on a missile on a launcher ready to be fired, and we were very anxious to get this matter wound up before these missile sites became operational. And secondly, if we tried to work this out as an agreement, there was the complication that if we did not tell the Soviets about our Polaris submarine in the Mediterranean as a replacement, they would accuse us later of acting in bad faith. So I disagree with McGeorge Bundy on whether this was an agreement. It was an important piece of information we were passing on, but I never treated it as an agreement.

WELCH: Why do you suppose Khrushchev replied so quickly to President Kennedy's terms, using the unorthodox method of broadcasting his acceptance over the radio?

RUSK: Well, you see, Bobby Kennedy—this involves an interesting point that comes up in Khrushchev's book, *Khrushchev Remembers*—Bobby Kennedy told Dobrynin that we had to have fast action on these missiles in Cuba, else the situation might move into another military phase and it would be very hard to keep under control. Now, Bobby Kennedy was referring to the possibility that we might have to take direct military action against Cuba, you see. In his book, Khrushchev represented that comment of Bobby's as a statement of a fear that the military would take over in the United States. . . . Well, that's not what Bobby Kennedy had in mind at all. But the situation was getting pretty harried there on that Sunday following President Kennedy's Monday television address, and time was running out on us. You see, the quarantine was looked upon as a possible first step. We would try out the quarantine, and if it didn't work, we could always fall back on more forceful action. Well, the quarantine did not appear to be completely effective, say, on the Friday, and we were getting ready for some kind of strike against Cuba. That would have involved an attack on the missile sites with all sorts of Russians around, and that would have lifted the crisis into a much more heated situation. . . .

Now, we were aware of the high cost of an invasion of Cuba. Some of the Latin American countries who most opposed Castro were nevertheless strongly against an invasion of Cuba on the grounds that a large number of casualties would be inflicted there, particularly among Cubans, and that would leave scars on the hemisphere that would take generations to heal. And then there's always the enormous escalation if we started shooting Russians in Cuba. And so there was no appetite among several of us for an attack on Cuba.

Now, that division in the ExComm [between hawks and doves] was there from the beginning. And people like Dean Acheson, Douglas Dillon, Paul Nitze, and one or two others, felt that we ought to open the crisis with a strike on Cuba of some sort. The quarantine solution was looked upon by that group as too soft a reply. Well, I had no doubt myself that the quarantine was a strong measure that would precipitate a crisis of the greatest danger. And in the handwritten note on a little piece of paper on which I had written down the essence of my opening remarks at the meeting of the ExComm on Saturday, where I was asked to lead off as the Secretary of State, I had written that it should not be assumed that the quarantine would be a weak response, since this would create a crisis of first-class importance. But the crucial thing was that unless we got the crisis settled within a day or two—that is, the Sunday or the Monday—then the prospect that these missile sites would become fully operational was a thing that would put the heat on Kennedy much more than the attitude of Douglas Dillon and these others, because he had already taken their views into account and had discounted them somewhat in applying the quarantine.

WELCH: On that Saturday the 27th, what was your sense of the balance of opinion in the ExComm? Was it swinging toward a majority in favor of the air strike?

RUSK: Well, it doesn't appear on the record anywhere. I myself did not join any one of the working groups that was looking into the various possibilities, because I felt that as Secretary of State I should withhold my judgment and take a look at the work of each of the working groups and then make a recommendation to the President as Secretary of State.[48] Well now, I kept in touch with the various working groups during that week, and then I had several private talks with members of the working groups on a one-on-one basis: Llewellyn Thompson, Robert McNamara, and Robert Kennedy particularly, and in those discussions we built a consensus among those in favor of the quarantine. So, on the Saturday when we all made our recommendations to the President, I knew there was a consensus among Robert McNamara, Bobby Kennedy, and myself that we should go the route of the quarantine. But we could not be certain, one can never be certain about what a President will do at the moment of decision.[49]

WELCH: Was that consensus still intact the following Saturday, the 27th?

RUSK: Oh, yes, but we realized that the quarantine was running out of time.

WELCH: Bromley Smith's minutes of the 27th record Bobby Kennedy as saying that he would prefer an air attack on the missile sites to a confrontation with Soviet ships on the quarantine line, and for that reason he was now advocating the air strike.[50]

RUSK: Well, the trouble with an air strike, if the missile sites were operational, was that there was no guarantee that you'd get them all. There's a possibility you'll have some strikes against the United States. You see, the Air Force was asked about this and they could not guarantee that they would get all the sites. They might get 85 to 90 percent of them, but they wouldn't get them all. And this was an important point to President Kennedy.

BLIGHT: You mentioned something that was discussed at great length at our meeting—and Robert McNamara was in the middle of it—which was the operational status of these missiles, what that meant, when that would happen, and how that would really constrict the options. . . . . . He said there that to him—and I never heard him say this before—but he said to him that didn't make all that much difference, because he felt at the time that he would have and could have maintained that quarantine for days or weeks or months. Now, there was a great deal of disagreement about whether that was true among the people both who were there at the time and from scholars who have their own opinions on that. But I gather that you really did think that time was short and that what Robert Kennedy told the Ambassador was basically factual—that we didn't have much time?

RUSK: Yes, that's right. I don't think I remember McNamara expressing his view of the situation that we would really confront if the missile sites became operational before we got them withdrawn. But I felt that this would throw the crisis into a new level of escalation, much more dangerous than the one we were already in, and that we ought to do our best to get the missiles out of Cuba before they became operational.

BLIGHT: Was that because, if you had to undertake an air strike, you couldn't be sure that there wouldn't be a launch—an accidental or unauthorized launch—that sort of thing?

RUSK: Yes, and if we saw those missile sites become operational, the chance of getting Khrushchev to take them out voluntarily would be greatly reduced. Now this ramifies in all sorts of directions. I have some reason to believe that the missiles in Cuba were a part of Khrushchev's policy on Berlin. As a matter of fact, one senior Russian told one American after the crisis—I forget the details now—that they were planning to make the missiles in Cuba known to us by returning to the Berlin question in the fall of '62, and, at that point, pointing to the missiles in Cuba as additional make-way in the argument over Berlin. . . .

. . . . .

BLIGHT: That's one aspect of the crisis on which you definitely agree with Paul Nitze, because he expressed the view two weeks ago that Berlin was deeply involved in this whole question. . . .

I'd like to ask you a question that I've thought a lot about, though I don't have any real good answers to it. . . . Do you think that the feeling of having some personal responsibility in the outcome was related to why those of you who eventually carried the day, who maintained the quarantine and so forth, felt as if you really had to be cautious?

RUSK: Well, there's no doubt about my feeling on that. I had the feeling that as Kennedy's Secretary of State I shared with him full responsibility for this situation. And this is one of the points where the contrast between the Bay of Pigs and the handling of the Cuban missile crisis came into sharp focus, because over the Bay of Pigs we acted merely as a group of advisors, not as though we were President. . . . I had been a colonel of infantry, Chief of War Plans for General Stilwell, in World War II. As a colonel of infantry, I knew that this Cuban brigade didn't have a chance in hell in the Bay of Pigs. But in the spring of '61 I was not a colonel of infantry, I was the Secretary of State. And I did not throw myself into the military aspects of that problem in the way that the President should have.

No, I was very much involved, and had to be as a principal, sharing the President's responsibility. For example, after the President's television speech, I stayed behind and met with a group of Ambassadors from the non-aligned countries. I got home at two o'clock, woke up next morning at six o'clock and thought to myself, "Well, I'm still here. This is very interesting." I was one of those who felt the degree of responsibility almost as much as the President himself, and I think that injected an element of caution into my approach to the matter.

WELCH: Was it the risk of an inadvertent launch of a missile from Cuba that worried you most?

RUSK: No, it was the possibility that Khrushchev might respond with a full nuclear strike; that he might be in such a situation that he could not control his own Politburo, whatever his own personal views were, because he had a major problem on his hands in dealing with his Politburo.

WELCH: And you didn't think that the strategic balance would have prevented that?

RUSK: Well, rationally, you might think so. But when a man is in that situation and he can't carry his own colleagues with him, what would he do? You had no ability to predict with certainty what a man would do in the circumstances in which he would find himself. I think we always have to leave open the unpredictability of what an actual living, breathing human being would do in a situation in which he finds himself. People who try to predict that with certainty make a great mistake.

WELCH: But it's hard to imagine that the whole Politburo would have opted for a nuclear strike on the United States.

RUSK: Well, you might have had at some point there a real problem with the Politburo. He might not have had their full blessing in putting the missiles in, and therefore this took on the characteristics of a major retreat by Khrushchev. As a matter of fact, President Kennedy told us at the end of the missile crisis that he didn't want anyone in his Administration to gloat over a diplomatic victory. He said that if Khrushchev wants to play the role of peacemaker in this situation, let him do so, because he had that problem to deal with.

BLIGHT: Khrushchev's situation raises the question of the role that almost everybody emphasizes of Llewellyn Thompson. Almost everyone said at the meeting that he was the unsung hero of the crisis.

RUSK: Yes, that's right.

BLIGHT: But it's somewhat difficult for some of the people, anyway, to actually be explicit about what he said or what his role was, why he was so heroic or significant.

RUSK: Well, we used Tommy Thompson as our in-house Russian. From the very beginning of the crisis we talked to Tommy Thompson about what Khrushchev's response to this or that or the other would be, what was moving Khrushchev during that period. We were constantly talking to Tommy Thompson. For example, there was one point that I would get a squawk from some people about. Remember that the decision was made to respond to Khrushchev's first letter and to ignore the second letter because, despite its emotion, Khrushchev's first letter had in it a clue which could lead to a settlement of the thing. Well, the conventional wisdom is that it was Bobby Kennedy who made that suggestion at the meeting of the ExComm. Well, in fact it was Tommy Thompson who originally suggested that. And in private conversation with me and possibly with Bobby Kennedy and others, he had mentioned that possibility. It was indeed Bobby who first brought it out at the table. But the actual idea, I'm convinced, came from Tommy Thompson.[51]

BLIGHT: That was very significant, then. This is what Mac Bundy later called the Trollope Ploy.
You and I have written back and forth about this, but just for the record here, I'd like your thoughts on it. My question was: Was the Cuban missile crisis something special? And I think that many people who came down where you did in the Cuban missile crisis—and I've just talked recently with George Ball, so he's on my mind—thought it was very different and special. He'd never been through anything that intense either before or after. Now, there's the other group, of course, which I think feels that it was special partly because a certain group felt it was. But is that your view?

RUSK: I believe that the Cuban missile crisis was the most dangerous crisis the world has ever seen, because the two nuclear superpowers were at each other's jugular veins and it was not easy to see a way out. With fumbling on either side, this could have resulted in nuclear war.

BLIGHT: So Bobby Kennedy's reconstruction of the acute peril surrounding the crisis was appropriate?

RUSK: When one reads Bobby Kennedy's posthumous book, *Thirteen Days*, most of the details of the book are fairly accurate. But there was an emotional overtone to that book which was I think special to Bobby Kennedy. This was the first major crisis he had ever lived through.

Fortunately, that emotional aspect was not the controlling mood of President Kennedy. He was as calm as an iceberg throughout this situation. The difference in the emotional overtone between Bobby and John was very important to me.

WELCH: It's curious that Bobby was the one who was selected to meet with Dobrynin, partly for that reason.

RUSK: We chose Bobby as a key channel to Dobrynin again somewhat on the advice of Llewellyn Thompson, because we thought that since Bobby Kennedy was the President's brother and this was an unusual channel, it would cause the Russians to pay it special attention as distinct from something which came to them through a diplomatic channel. The Russians having a conspiratorial turn of mind, we thought they would pay more attention to what Bobby was saying more than anyone else short of the President himself. And so we deliberately used Bobby as a key messenger for that reason.

BLIGHT: . . . We've been thinking about trying to draw lessons, and we wonder if there are any you feel particularly strongly about?

RUSK: A major lesson both for us and for the Russians is that we have to do what we can to prevent such crises from arising, because they're just too damn dangerous. That impression is not automatically passed along from one generation to the next, and that bothers me a little.

BLIGHT: Mac Bundy said at the meeting, "For those of you who don't think that the Cuban missile crisis has much import, let's put it in the negative. The governments of both the United States and the U.S.S.R. contain very few people who remember the crisis, and the next generation may not have absorbed the fear."

RUSK: There is that saving thought that when people look down the cannon's mouth of nuclear war, they cannot like what they see. We've now put behind us forty-one years since a nuclear weapon has been fired in anger, and those who really understand nuclear weapons understand that nuclear war is simply that war which must not be fought, because it not only eliminates all the answers, it eliminates all the questions. Unfortunately, people with brains have injected a lot of complications into what is utterly simple. The idea of a limited nuclear war is nonsense. The idea of a prolonged nuclear war from which one side can emerge with some sort of advantage is nonsense. And some of this nonsense is drawn into official discussion. For example, the counterforce strategy: the idea of that is that you aim your own nuclear weapons at their military targets, and that will send a message to their leaders to leave your cities alone. Well, the best way to send a message is to pick up the phone and talk to somebody. Try to construct the telephone conversation between the President of the United States and the General Secretary of the Soviet Union:

"Mr. Secretary, this is the President. I thought I needed to tell you that we launched our missiles a few minutes ago; but I want to assure you that we are aiming them only at military targets, and so we hope that you will leave our cities alone."

"How many, Mr. President?"

"Well, we launched a thousand, but there will be a few misfires, so let's say 950."

"What military targets?"

"Missile sites, of course, the submarine bases at Murmansk and Vladivostok, and by the way, Mr. Secretary, we ought to keep this conversation short, because since Moscow is your central command and control center, I want to give you time to get down into your shelter."

You're immediately in the world of the bizarre when you try to construct the message that you pretend to want to send in a counterforce strike. And so the truth is that if these weapons begin to fly, that's the end. And that simple fact has prevented the firing of these weapons so far.

WELCH: Do you think that Khrushchev's uniqueness as a person makes it dangerous to draw lessons from the Cuban missile crisis about dealing with the Soviets?

RUSK: Well, you have to take that fully into account. Khrushchev probably lost his job partly as a result of the Cuban missile crisis,[52] but one has to be careful about restricting the choices open to an opponent in the nuclear field. I think the present man is probably intelligent enough and savvy enough not to let himself be drawn into this kind of position, and I hope that the American President will do the same. But you're dealing with human beings, and as a Presbyterian, I think that all human beings have feet of clay, and that one can't play games with this sort of thing.

BLIGHT: You mentioned something in a letter to me that I found quite poignant. I wasn't raised a Presbyterian, but I was actually raised by my mother to be a Lutheran minister—that went awry at some point, so I don't know the Westminster Catechism—but I believe you said something like the first article or the first petition is: "What is the fate of man?"

RUSK: The first question of the Westminster Shorter Catechism is: "What is the chief end of man?" And during the Cuban missile crisis, although I hadn't thought of the Westminster Shorter Catechism since I had memorized and recited it as a small boy, driving through the streets of Washington I suddenly realized that this first of these questions, "What is the chief end of man?" had become an operational question before the governments of the world. And that was a sobering thought.

BLIGHT: That comment and some of the comments Robert Kennedy makes in *Thirteen Days* raise the issue of some of the moral questions of the event. I find it encouraging in a way that some of the people who faced up to the possibility of nuclear war felt that somewhere in the hard-boiled business of government, ethical and moral questions came up to the front. I don't know how general that was, but I find it interesting that a Georgia Presbyterian and a New England Catholic could come to somewhat similar views and go through a similar process in thinking about it.

RUSK: Well, at the end of the day, moral and ethical considerations play a very important part, even though people don't wear these things on their shirtsleeves or put these things into official memoranda. They play an important part. People act in reference to their basic moral commitments, and they are likely to come to the fore when situations become critical. And quite apart from one principle, as a practical matter when you are trying to influence the conduct of others, you have to take into account their ethical commitments. So I've always disagreed with Hans Morgenthau and some others who try to rule out the role such ideas play in policy, because at the end of the day you find that you're dealing with human beings, and human beings act in relation to their basic moral concepts.[53]

BLIGHT: I'm sure you know this, thought I hadn't until recently, that the volume of Harold Macmillan's memoirs dealing with the Cuban missile crisis is entitled *At the End of the Day*, and it also contains for me one of the most alive examples of a person trying to explain in relatively cold print how fearful he was at certain points waiting for the President's phone calls, trying to find out what was going on.[54] And he had the same conclusion. I don't know if the use of the phrase has a common etiology, or I don't know enough about Macmillan, but he certainly felt the same way.

RUSK: Well, you know, I've met and worked with a good many people whose names are in the history books or in the headlines. I have never met a demigod or a superman. I have only seen relatively ordinary men and women groping to deal with the problems with which they are faced. One must always remember that element of human fallibility. Now, that is also underlined by the fact that in a crisis of this sort, you can never know all that you need to know. And that's true of both sides. And it's particularly true about how human beings will react to the situations in which they find themselves.

BLIGHT: I take it you would agree then with something Bob McNamara enunciated with his typical vivacity at the meeting, which he called McNamara's Law, which he said should be inscribed over every doorway in the State Department and the Pentagon—which is that in every crisis you will never know what you need to know, and therefore you should behave cautiously. . . .

RUSK: Well, one thing happened early in the Kennedy Administration that ought to happen with every new leader of a nuclear power. President Kennedy assembled a group of about six senior colleagues—McNamara was one of them, I was one of them—and we spent an afternoon going through an examination of the total effects of a nuclear war, both direct and indirect. . . . We had the help of an expert staff that spent all its time studying this thing. And they went through it with charts and things like that, and it was quite an experience. And when we got through with it, President Kennedy asked me to come back to the Oval Office with him, and as we got to the door he looked at me with a strange little look on his face, and he said, "And we call ourselves the human race."

Now, I think there ought to be a committee of scientists drawn from the United States, Great Britain, France, the Soviet Union, and China who would be available to spend at least a day with every new leader of any of these countries to be sure that that leader understands what people are talking about when they talk about nuclear war.

. . . . .

BLIGHT: A seminar like that might prevent the kind of ignorance behind Ronald Reagan's remark about recalling his ICBMs after firing them.

RUSK: As opposed as I am to any consideration of nuclear war, I am almost fanatic about our need to bring this nuclear-arms race to a conclusion and to prevent it from spreading any further than it has. It's a waste of resources, and it leads some people to place false hopes in these weapons. I'm strongly opposed to moving the arms race into outer space, for example.

BLIGHT: Could I ask you a question about that? We have a number of people who say that, even though nuclear weapons are overly destructive, it's good to have some around to prevent an increasingly destructive conventional war.

RUSK: I don't accept the notion that their existence means that sooner or later somebody is going to use them. While you might make the case that this is true for all other weapons, it's not true for nuclear weapons.

Now, I agree with some of the proposals by people like Sam Nunn,* who thinks that we should tighten up the ability of the two sides to communicate with each other about these things—a Joint General Staff, a branch in Washington, a branch in Moscow, with the most modern communications possible to keep in touch with everybody. We've shared some of the technology of safeguards about nuclear weapons with the Russians. We have an interest in their not having an accident. The Russians, too, are human beings and they're not idiots, and I'm relatively encouraged about the prospects of avoiding nuclear war, and I greatly regret the amount of doomsday talk that our young people are being battered with from both sides. . . . . . I think I learned something during the Cuban missile crisis that has to do with the emergency plan for moving the top government to the hills in West Virginia. I'm sure that those plans are psychologically impossible. One has to have an alternative government in place made up of people who had nothing to do with the events which unfold. In the first place, people in the government are not going to abandon all their colleagues and their families to get in a helicopter and go charging out to West Virginia. They just aren't going to do it. In the second place, the first band of shivering survivors who get their hands on the President and the Secretary of State following such a situation will hang them to the nearest tree. It's just a psychologically misbegotten idea.

Well, let me know if there's anything I can add. I suppose I came away from that party down in Florida as a skunk at the tea party.

WELCH: Oh, not at all, on the contrary. . . .

RUSK: Well, the important thing about it is that it was a contingency that never happened.

BLIGHT: No, you were far from the skunk at the tea party. . . . The first thing we did was to see fifteen minutes of General Taylor saying we had Khrushchev over a barrel and we could have done more, and

---

* Senator Sam Nunn (D–Ga.).

then immediately after came the Dean Rusk letter saying that the President was thinking in this direction, and it created a marvelous tension and people could get into it however they wanted. Much of the discussion during the rest of the meeting had to do with this tension introduced by your letter and by General Taylor.

RUSK: You know, Dean Acheson spoke soon after the Cuban missile crisis to the American Society for International Law, and he said that the outcome of the Cuban missile crisis was just dumb luck.[55] Well, my response to him would be that you can give yourself a chance to be lucky, and you can plan to give yourself a chance to be lucky. If we had taken Dean Acheson's advice—and Dean Acheson had never been Secretary of State at a time when a full nuclear exchange was possible—if we had taken his advice and led off with a strike, the crisis would have been infinitely more dangerous. We'd have struck their missiles or struck a large number of Soviet troops. . . .

BLIGHT: . . . Once you decided on the quarantine, did it seem like the logical thing for him to do would be to seize Berlin? He had the same kind of strengths there that you guys had in Cuba.

RUSK: That's right, he had an overwhelming military position around Berlin. . . .

WELCH: Maybe he looked at the strategic balance and thought, "They have five thousand warheads and I only have 340."

RUSK: Well—I think that our reaction caught him with his scenario down. I don't think he had prepared a scenario for a strong U.S. reaction.

BLIGHT: That must have had something to do with the fact that right after the President's speech, immediately following that, there was nothing coming out of Moscow for a while. Bobby Kennedy says in his book that immediately after he saw the photos of those missiles, there was "stunned surprise" in Washington, and the reaction in the Kremlin must have been the same after the speech. They must have needed a little time to get their act together.

RUSK: I met with Dobrynin an hour before President Kennedy's television speech and gave him a copy and went over it with him, and I saw him age ten years right in front of my eyes.

BLIGHT: Is that right.

RUSK: It was really an extraordinary experience.

BLIGHT: I forget sometimes that Dobrynin was very new then, that this fellow had only been in the post less than a year. To be faced with a situation like that was as tough on him as it was on you all.

RUSK: I'm inclined to think that Dobrynin was not cut in on the details of the missiles in Cuba, although Gromyko was.[56] . . .

Interview with Robert S. McNamara, May 21, 1987, Washington, D.C.

BLIGHT: I'd like to begin by asking you about how you recall feeling on the last weekend of the Cuban missile crisis. From some of your statements, I gather that things looked very bleak—that you thought some sort of inadvertent nuclear war had become a live possibility. . . .

. . . . .

ROBERT MCNAMARA: . . . I really did think the missile crisis was dangerous. Very dangerous, in fact. Let me try to explain. I never thought a military action was highly probable, but it seemed sufficiently possible that I had to worry about the potential escalation to some serious conventional conflict and possibly the use of nuclear weapons. So, while I don't want to indicate that I thought there was a high probability of massive conventional warfare, I do want to indicate that when one is pursuing a new and in fact unprecedented course of action, one should recognize the uncertainty, the fallibility, the risk of an error of judgment, and where that risk takes you. To me, while the risk might have been small—I think it was small—an error in judgment could have been disastrous, and that's why I thought we had to act with extreme caution.

BLIGHT: I get the impression that, in your own thinking during and about the missile crisis, you began in a different place than Dillon, Taylor, or Nitze.

MCNAMARA: I did entirely. And Paul Nitze to this day thinks I was nuts.

BLIGHT: Well, he didn't say that to us, but he said you and he had some rather strong differences of opinion, which he laid out. I'd put the difference, as I see it, this way. On October 16, the President calls all of you into the first meeting of what would become the ExComm. People like Dillon, Nitze, Taylor, and Acheson say, in effect: "We've got to take the missiles out and, if we do, the *probability* of a drastic response from the Soviets is very tiny. So let's do it. Let's bomb them." But you seem to have said: "Wait a minute! A drastic response is *possible*. So let's be very careful about how we proceed." Is that about right?

McNAMARA: Yes, exactly. In my mind I attached a very low probability to the ultimate escalation to nuclear war, but a higher probability to the escalation to a conventional confrontation somewhere. And that would be very very dangerous, both in and of itself and also because it might escalate further, leading possibly to nuclear war. So, right from the start, right from that first morning, I felt we should reduce the risks as much as we could to achieve our necessary objective. And that was to get the missiles out of there, for political reasons.

BLIGHT: Did discussion come up about whether the Soviet missiles in Cuba changed the strategic nuclear balance?

McNAMARA: Oh, yes.

BLIGHT: The reason I ask is that Douglas Dillon told us in an interview that it was so obvious to him that the balance had shifted that he could never really appreciate, or even understand, your own view. In Dillon's view, the whole point of the Soviet missiles in Cuba was to provide them with the ability to strike at a far higher proportion of our SAC bomber force than was ever possible before. That was why Dillon thought the missiles had to come out.

McNAMARA: But, you see, to this day I believe it didn't change the strategic balance one bit.

BLIGHT: And you believed that at the time?

McNAMARA: Yes, I did. I believed it at the time. That was obviously one of the major differences of view between myself and some of the others, as you suggest. . . .

Look, in my judgment, in fundamental terms, the so-called strategic balance hasn't shifted since 1962. The significant question isn't: How many weapons did we have then and now, relative to the Soviets? The question you should ask is: What did each side have in its arsenal then and now that was, or is, militarily useful? Let me put it another way: What is the likelihood then and now that either side might initiate the use of nuclear weapons and come away with a net gain? The answer to both questions is: Zero! Then and now, for both the U.S. and the Soviets, there are no militarily useful nuclear weapons in their arsenals and thus there is no advantage in using them. None! Same then as now. The situation hasn't changed one bit.

BLIGHT: You once told me a story about having dinner in Moscow and shocking your Soviet hosts by saying that you believed strategic nuclear parity existed during the missile crisis even though, in terms of sheer numbers, the U.S. had something like a seventeen-to-one advantage.

McNAMARA: Yes. I believe I did surprise them. But they got the point, which is more than I can say for a lot of our American colleagues. The point is this: If you go to nuclear war, and the other side retaliates, and only a few—maybe even only *one*—bomb gets through to destroy an American city, you—the one who just initiated the nuclear war—will have had to shoulder the responsibility for the worst catastrophe in the history of this country. So you won't do it. But this means that all those fancy nuclear weapons are militarily useless. You can't *use* them.

BLIGHT: As you know, your critics say that it is all fine and dandy for Robert McNamara to believe that nuclear weapons are militarily useless, but the Soviets believe otherwise. They use this assumption as justification for developing elaborate counterforce capabilities and strategies.

McNAMARA: Sure, sure. I know that. But look at Khrushchev in the missile crisis. I mean, if he thought—or knew, as we knew by that time—that he was numerically behind by seventeen to one or thereabouts, do you think an extra forty-three missiles in Cuba, each carrying one warhead, would have led him to think he could use his nuclear weapons? No way! Khrushchev had created a *political* problem, not a military problem.

. . . . .

WELCH: Why, then, did *you* believe the missiles had to come out?

McNAMARA: . . . For all kinds of political reasons, especially to preserve unity in the alliance, we had to indicate to the Soviets that we weren't going to accept the presence of offensive missiles in Cuba. However, I believed it was essential to express their unacceptability in ways that did not lead to escalation. I thought the quarantine would accomplish this. And I want to add that even on that last weekend of the crisis I still thought it probable that the quarantine would work. In other words, I did not believe that we had reached a point on that Sunday, October 28, at which our only option was that we should go to war.

Now, I know it says in Bromley Smith's minutes of the ExComm meeting of October 27 that McNamara said war is inevitable, or some such thing.[57] Bromley Smith's minutes, while they may be technically correct, do not convey the proper impression. This is an extremely important point and it relates to whatever lessons are to be drawn from the missile crisis. The lesson is this: the risk of inadvertent nuclear war should lead to extreme caution in determining actions that affect that risk or may increase it. Now, if you believe that, as I strongly do, then on the following Sunday night, had Khrushchev's message not come in, we should not have thought that it was absolutely essential to launch the air strike and invasion Monday morning. And I believe the President and Dobby Kennedy believed as I did. That is why I do not believe that Bobby Kennedy meant to convey, or ever did convey, to Dobrynin any so-called fact: that if the missiles didn't come out immediately we would initiate military action to remove them. I've forgotten exactly what he says in his book, but I know he says something like that. Bobby says the missiles must come out. He implied that if the Soviets failed to do so, we would take them out, and quickly. I just do not believe that he stated it in the way that his book indicates. And if he did state it that way, I don't believe that his brother intended him to communicate the message in that way. The other messages that were sent out did not convey the message in that unequivocal fashion. For example, the cable that went out on Saturday did not imply any high probability of military action Monday if the Soviets didn't immediately indicate they'd take them out.[58]

WELCH: Well, whatever Robert Kennedy said must have really hit the Kremlin hard, because Khrushchev went on the *radio* early the next morning and accepted Kennedy's terms.

McNAMARA: Sure, the crisis was rising, there's no question about that. But the point I want to make, and this is an important point—and it would appear to be inconsistent with what Bobby said—is that I believe there was no way we were going to war on Monday or Tuesday. No way! As I argued at our meeting last March in Hawk's Cay, if Khrushchev had not sent his cable of withdrawal on Sunday, I would not have been in favor of deciding to launch a military attack on Monday, or as soon as we could. As I said, I would have been in favor of turning the screw on the quarantine. And somebody else, I think it was Mac Bundy, indicated that he also would have been in favor of turning the screw on Monday, rather than launching an attack. But more importantly, both Mac and Ted Sorensen agreed with me that President Kennedy would not have authorized the launch of the attack on Monday, but rather would have supported turning the screw on the quarantine.

Now, that's the important point. Let us assume for the moment that I am correct. I *know* I'm correct in what *I* would have done. I'm absolutely positive of that. But assuming that I'm also correct in believing that President Kennedy would have moved in that direction, then I think it's damned unlikely that he intended for Bobby to say what Bobby alleges that he said. That's really my point. And I think this is very, very important: that it is much less important what Bobby said than what President Kennedy and McNamara would have done on Monday,

had the Sunday message from Khrushchev not come in. No way were
we going to war on Monday. We would have tightened the quarantine.

BLIGHT: As I'm sure you recall, one of the most startling revelations
coming out of the Hawk's Cay meeting was that on the evening of October 27, 1962, the President authorized Dean Rusk to open a channel to
the UN along which movement may have occurred toward a public trade
of U.S. Jupiter missiles in Turkey for Soviet SS-4s and SS-5s in Cuba. Do
you think the President would have gone for some such public trade?

McNAMARA: No, I don't think so.

BLIGHT: But Mac Bundy recalls, as do others, that the President expressed in no uncertain terms on October 27 his determination not to
let those obsolete Turkish missiles stand in the way of a resolution to
the crisis. I think the President may have said something like: "I'm not
going to war over any damned useless missiles in Turkey."[59] So why
not trade useless missiles for Soviet missiles which, you must have assumed, could be used effectively against the American homeland?

McNAMARA: I would be very careful about jumping to the conclusion
that the President would have gone to the public trade. What I would
be very certain of, in my mind, is that he would not have authorized
the launch of an attack on Cuba. We had several alternatives to an
attack. One was turning the screw on the quarantine. And another was
a trade. Frankly, what I think we would have done was turn the screw
on the quarantine and wrap into the package something on the trade.
But I do not believe we would have come out with a clear public trade.

WELCH: Is that because you believe the trade—or some deal that
would have been interpreted as a trade—was just politically unfeasible?

McNAMARA: Yes. You have to remember that, right from the beginning, it was President Kennedy who said that it was *politically* unacceptable for us to leave those [Cuban] missile sites alone. He didn't say
militarily, he said *politically*. Now, with that in mind, he would have
had to package any trade in a way that was politically acceptable. The
President is reported to have said that he would have been impeached
if he'd left the missiles alone.[60] Just assume for the moment that he said
it and believed it. The public trade is not much different. People would
have interpreted this as caving in—rightly or wrongly, but this is the
way a lot of people, including a lot of congressmen and our allies, would
have interpreted such a trade. I think it would have required that the
trade be packaged in a way that avoided impeachment, and that might
have been tricky.

Frankly, I don't think he would have been impeached if he'd left the [Cuban] missiles in there. And I really doubt that he believed it either. What he conveyed by that statement about being impeached was his recognition of the political consequences of not appearing to be firm—consequences not so much to him personally but rather to the nation, to the alliance, to the risks of future conflict with the Soviets. All that was in his mind.

Now, if these were real risks and they were on his mind, then he would have been very careful about a trade. Some people say, well, we *did* trade, only privately, when we informed the Soviets, via Bobby, that we were going to remove the Turkish missiles anyway. This is absolutely false.* I was in the room when the discussion occurred as to what Bobby should tell Dobrynin on October 27. And I know exactly what the President intended and how the deal was to have been expressed. I'm absolutely certain Bobby expressed it the way the President wanted him to because this was, in the President's mind, very, very important. The President could not risk anything resembling a public trade because of the risk of a great national controversy and adverse political consequences for him, for the country, and for the NATO alliance. A trade, even a private trade, would also set a bad precedent in dealing with the Soviets. If they could get away with that, what else would they do? We saw in Berlin the previous year that they would go just as far as they thought they could. There was a slicing of the salami; slice by slice they were moving ahead, or trying to. That is why it was absolutely essential, Kennedy believed, and others believed, that we not convey to the Soviets the impression that we either were weak or would behave in a weak fashion. All these things added up to one unequivocal conclusion: We had to get the missiles out of Cuba, but we had to do so in a way that avoided both the political consequences of appearing weak—as we would appear if we publicly traded missiles—and also avoided unacceptable risk of military escalation. In other words, we had to force the missiles out of Cuba, without forcing the Soviets to respond in a way that could have led us all into disaster. And let me tell you, that was no easy task.

. . . . .

WELCH: Do you recall which concerned you more—the danger of possible Soviet responses elsewhere in the world to an American attack on Cuba, or the danger that, say, some Soviet second lieutenant might choose to use the nuclear weapon under his command rather than have it destroyed?

---

* Cf. Afterword, pp. 337–38, 341.

McNAMARA: Both possibilities were very troubling. I was concerned about, and I guess more affected by, the risk presented by the second lieutenant, as far as nuclear war is concerned. But I also believed that there was a fairly high—I would say at least a fifty-fifty—probability of a Soviet military response outside Cuba to a U.S. attack on Cuba.

WELCH: In Berlin or Turkey?

McNAMARA: Those were the two prime candidates.

WELCH: Did you attach any probability to the possibility that Kremlin decisionmakers might think: "My God, nuclear war is now likely or imminent, let's launch the nuclear weapons we have before the Americans destroy them all"?

BLIGHT: That's what Dean Rusk said he was worried about: backing the Soviets into a corner where they might do something irrational like that. . . .

McNAMARA: Well, I didn't think anything like that was probable, but it goes back to my point. I'm not interested only in probable risks. I'm interested in less than probable risks, if they may lead to disastrous consequences. That was what motivated me. I think it is easy to be too analytical about all this after the fact. I mean, was I worried more about conventional war or nuclear war, or a Soviet second lieutenant or a Soviet response in Berlin or Turkey, or about Khrushchev's irrationality? That's putting too fine a point on it. I just don't know the answer to such questions because that's not the way it was. The point you had to keep coming back to was that *any* of these routes could lead you into disaster. All were possible. We should not accept even a small risk of any of them, therefore, if we could avoid it.

WELCH: General Taylor and Paul Nitze seem to have come away from the crisis with the lesson that the crisis really showed the fundamental importance of strategic nuclear superiority.

McNAMARA: I think that's absolute hogwash. Frankly, I don't think Max came away with that. I'm not sure about Paul Nitze.

BLIGHT: Why do you think anyone would believe this? Have you any idea? Is it perhaps that they never felt there was any risk at all in the crisis? That those of you who felt the fear were mistaken? That you just didn't understand how the balance worked? Douglas Dillon mentioned this briefly in Hawk's Cay. And both he and Paul Nitze amplified this view in recent interviews with us.

McNAMARA: I don't know why other people in the ExComm held those views. Perhaps some of the individuals were willing to accept the possible catastrophic consequences of the actions they favored. I wasn't willing to accept that risk. And I know the President wasn't willing to accept it. And I'm talking about one nuclear bomb on one American city. That's all.

· · · · ·

BLIGHT: I wonder if you agree with something Abe Chayes kept saying at the meeting in Hawk's Cay. He said, "You know, the more I listen to all you people talk about the missile crisis for two or three days, I'm convinced more than ever that a little deterrence goes a hell of a long way. Why, this little ragtail three-hundred-weapon arsenal of the Soviets' thoroughly deterred us."

McNAMARA: Abe is right. And that goes back to my point, that when there's even a small risk of total disaster, I'm significantly deterred and very anxious to avoid any risk in that direction if I can.

WELCH: But if you wanted to avoid *any* risk of nuclear war over the missiles in Cuba, wouldn't you have had to simply leave them in—to accept them?

McNAMARA: No, because that risk did not exist in isolation. There were other risks. Most significantly, there was the risk that if we did not respond forcefully in Cuba, the Soviets would continue to poke and prod us elsewhere. And what if the next prod came around Berlin, which had been driving Khrushchev nuts for years? If that happened, then the risk of disaster would go way up, relative to Cuba. I know some people say this is some kind of paranoid delusion. Well, let me tell you something: People who believe that forget what the world was like in the early sixties. Khrushchev wasn't kidding. Neither were we. You just could not passively accept a move like putting Soviet nuclear missiles practically in Florida. But I want to emphasize the reason: because we couldn't accept a higher risk of nuclear disaster somewhere else down the road.

· · · · ·

BLIGHT: Was your concern over low-risk, highly adverse situations unique to the missile crisis? Or were there other times when you were Secretary of Defense that this came into play?

McNAMARA: It was very influential in my decisions relating to Vietnam. Now, I never discuss Vietnam publicly but, on this general point about low-probability, highly adverse consequences, it is relevant. You know the standard criticism, everybody does: McNamara was afraid to use all the force at his command and that is why we failed to win the war in Vietnam. Well, that's a correct statement as far as it goes. What you need to understand is that the rationale was exactly the same rationale as for preferring the quarantine during the Cuban missile crisis. I mean, if you just say the hell with it, let's go all out, bomb them— Cubans or Vietnamese—into oblivion, look what you are doing. You are practically requiring the Soviets, or in certain circumstances the Chinese, to retaliate militarily. And then what happens? I'll tell you what: we're in a major war between nuclear powers. Anything might happen. My view in October 1962—and it was my view all the way through the 1960s, and it is my view today—is that we must maintain some kind of firebreak between conventional conflict and that situation of low-probability but highly adverse consequences you and I have been discussing: a nuclear war, maybe even a little one, but one that kills millions of people. Today, Paul Nitze and Doug Dillon say there was no risk of nuclear war in 1962; none at all. How do they know that? They are both my friends—I admire them immensely and have deep affection for them—but on this point I believe they're wrong. There was *some* risk; not much, but some. And the consequences were so awful that, in my judgment, we had to do everything we could to avoid blundering into it by inadvertence. And people are still saying: McNamara was wrong to believe the Soviets or Chinese would have gone to war over Vietnam. How do they know *that*? (And, by the way, how do they know that if we had gone all out, the North Vietnamese would have surrendered?) They don't. I may have been wrong to be so cautious. But what I'm trying to do is explain that the missile crisis isn't unique. Wherever the U.S. and Soviets have strong interests, these things come into play.

BLIGHT: In fact, Bob, that critique is precisely what Doug Dillon related to us when we discussed the missile crisis with him. He said, roughly: "I cut my teeth on the Eisenhower Doctrine, which stated that you never use military force unless you're willing to use all that you have at your command. *All* of it." That is one of the reasons he said he was for the immediate air strike on Cuba. We had the capability; we should have gone in. We were too cautious.

McNAMARA: *All* of it? Wait a minute. That is a very simplistic statement, and Doug Dillon is not a simplistic person. He must have been overstating his case.[61] I mean, *all* the force at our command in 1962? We could have destroyed the whole world, ourselves included, if we'd used all of it. I think Doug, and Paul Nitze, too, really believed we'd never have to use our forces, certainly not our nuclear forces, because the balance was, in their view, tipped so heavily in our favor. I think they just figured the Soviets would back down. But—and this is my point—there is no way they could *know* that. And—here we are again—with such adverse consequences, who wants to test it? Not I.

. . . . .

WELCH: What would you have done if you had gotten into a war with the U.S.S.R.?

McNAMARA: That is a very important question. Important mainly because I have no idea what the answer is. I'd thought about it and I had discussed it with the President. If we had been attacked with nuclear weapons I am certain that the President would have responded with one, or two, or maybe ten—something like that. Neither he nor I thought we should respond at all, though, until we could determine what had happened. Now I know the SIOP called for a massive response and I also recall that the President said in his speech announcing the quarantine that we'd respond massively.[62] No way would we have done that. But—and this goes to my main point—during the missile crisis we never even talked about it. Sure, it was a low probability, as I've said. But if some damn Soviet second lieutenant had launched a missile and it destroyed, say, Atlanta, would we then have gone to an all-out nuclear war? I hope not. But we never discussed it. We should have, but we didn't.

. . . . .

BLIGHT: You said something at the Hawk's Cay conference that both surprised and impressed me. It's about the importance of experience, or lack of experience, in handling foreign policy, especially during crises. On the very first night at dinner, as we were all musing about the lessons of Cuba, you said one of the most important lessons of the Cuban missile crisis is this (in so many words): Don't hire a president of the Ford Motor Company who is untrained, unschooled in national defense policy, to try and run the United States defense security apparatus.

McNAMARA: That's right.

BLIGHT: Do you recall what it was like when you first came into office? What was it like to face for the first time a whole set of problems with which you had no experience and which you were, by necessity, forced to learn pretty much on the job?

McNAMARA: Let me illustrate the problem with a sort of retrospective example. The Public Broadcasting Station in Atlanta is doing a series of interviews with Secretaries of State and Defense. In order to prepare for the interview, they asked me to name three issues that I wanted to discuss. Now, one of the three I listed was: Under what conditions should the U.S. government consider the application of military force? I don't have to tell you that this is a damned important issue. When should we resort to force—in the Persian Gulf, or Grenada, or Lebanon, or in the Cuban missile crisis? As a former Secretary of Defense, one with a lot of experience in these matters, I have some pretty well-formed opinions on this issue. But—and this goes straight to my point—what in the hell does the president of the Ford Motor Company, which I was, know about the issue? I'll tell you what *this* automobile executive knew: *Zero! Nothing!* I knew it, too. I felt in my heart that my appointment as Secretary of Defense was wrong. I told President-elect Kennedy this, and we worked out a deal. It was based on the following propositions: (a) I would accept the job. It was a tremendous opportunity to serve the country. (b) I wasn't qualified for the job. And, therefore, (c) if I took the job, I could appoint all of my senior people—my advisors— myself, and these choices would be made solely on the basis of ability and experience. Of course, the President would have to endorse my own choices formally. But the emphasis was to be on talent, not politics. To the extent that we succeeded, in the Cuban missile crisis, it was because I had surrounded myself with people who knew a hell of a lot more than the president of the Ford Motor Company knew about national-security issues. *They* taught *me*, make no mistake about it. And so, in the thirty days or so before I assumed office, I learned a lot about nuclear strategy, a subject I had never even thought of before, and that I scarcely knew existed. And I can tell you this: by the time of the Cuban missile crisis my views were pretty well fixed and they haven't changed a lot from that day to this. But I would add that this is not because— or not primarily because, I should say—McNamara has stopped learning. The simple fact is that the reality then is the reality now: the nuclear weapons we have, and the Soviets have, are useless militarily. Everything flows from this simple enduring truth.

WELCH: I'm not so sure I agree with you that it's a bad idea to have the president of the Ford Motor Company step into the role of Secretary of Defense. Look at the makeup of the ExComm. The doves, those who were particularly cautious like yourself, were almost all relatively inexperienced in defense and foreign policy, while the hawks all had a great deal of experience. Don't you think that your own inexperience, and those of your colleagues like Robert Kennedy, Mac Bundy, Ted Sorensen, and maybe even the President, may have insulated you from a misplaced confidence in nuclear diplomacy? Let me put it this way: You inexperienced people were greatly concerned with the problem of inadvertent war. People like Taylor, McCone, Acheson, Nitze, and Dillon were not, or, at least, nowhere near to the same degree. Maybe their years of experience with the defense and foreign-policy establishments systematically desensitized them to certain risks. If you now believe that you were right and they were wrong about what the main risks were at the time, doesn't this argue for, rather than against, the appointment of outsiders to positions of authority who have managed to avoid the common belief in the strategic community that, well, nuclear weapons are just big weapons?

MCNAMARA: I think I see what you are driving at. But you can't mean that, in security matters, ignorance is bliss, because it isn't. Look at the Bay of Pigs fiasco the year before the missile crisis. A little experience and better-developed judgment would have come in handy there. I often wish our American political system were a bit more like that of the British or the West Germans. There, you can't come into office as a know-nothing. It's just not possible. Look at people like Roy Jenkins, Denis Healey, Ted Heath, or Helmut Schmidt.* These people were well seasoned and experienced when they came into office, and they didn't seem hawkish to me.

WELCH: But they were never in a position where they might be tempted into thinking that nuclear superiority can be translated into diplomatic leverage. They never had it.

MCNAMARA: You may be right.

WELCH: . . . I'm not trying to argue for ignorance. I'm only saying that you had a real advantage, as well as a disadvantage. You may have been ignorant, as you say, but this also meant that you could see immediately that nuclear warheads are not nuclear weapons.

MCNAMARA: Well, sure. That's right. But we've got to look for something between the extremes of some experienced war fighter and an ignorant automobile executive. I don't think we want people in office who either think they know everything or who in fact don't know anything. And I agree with you on—quote, unquote—security experts. Now I don't want to demean them as a group. Not all. But there is no question in my mind that many of them do regard nuclear strategy as—I'll say—a kind of regular nine-to-five job. You find some targets; build weapons to hit the targets; then you devise strategies to fight wars in which those targets might be of interest. It's all very abstract and unreal.

---

* Roy Jenkins was a former leader of the British Labour Party; Edward Heath was Prime Minister of Great Britain in the early 1970s.

. . . . .

BLIGHT: I want to return for a moment to the relation between what I'll call the psychology of the missile crisis and the policy conclusions we ought to derive from it. The relation seems to me deeply puzzling and, I admit, also a little disagreeable to me. The problem is this, as Ted Sorensen stated it in Hawk's Cay: "If those missiles had been howitzers, it would have made a hell of a difference." Now, what difference would it have made? On the one hand, maybe the difference is that no one would have cared at all about the hypothetical howitzers. So: no crisis. No risk of much of anything. But Ted could also have meant that because those weapons were nuclear-capable ballistic missiles, not howitzers, the fear of their use, and the fear that their use would lead to, or result in, an unprecedented nuclear catastrophe, led the leaders of the superpowers to act cautiously and ended the crisis peacefully. So, it might mean that, as the theoreticians like to say, a robust nuclear balance is desirable—lots of weapons and, importantly, lots and lots of fear of the consequences of using those weapons. They call this crisis stability, as you know. My question is: Why is it wrong to say that the Cuban missile crisis proves the value of something like the status quo? Why doesn't it prove that, just as a whole generation of deterrence theorists have argued, we ought to want a world with lots of nuclear weapons and lots of nuclear fear? Why take a chance? Why not go for maximum fear?

MCNAMARA: Now we're really getting down to an absolutely fundamental point. There was just too damned much fear in the missile crisis. If you just keep piling it on, well, people may crack. You do not want to reduce your leaders to quivering, panicky, irrational people, do you? Look, we've been piling it on ever since the missile crisis, and even before. That's my point: piling up weapons, reducing flight times, creeping toward a functional launch-on-warning posture—all of these were much less troubling in the missile crisis than now and there was, I assure you, plenty of fear to go around in October 1962.

BLIGHT: So, you are saying we now have a huge surplus of nuclear fear, a surplus that will come back to haunt us in another crisis?

MCNAMARA: That's it exactly. You see, this point is directly related to my enthusiasm for the non-nuclear—or almost non-nuclear—world. I want to get rid of almost all our nuclear weapons so that the ultimate catastrophe will become impossible. It just can't happen, because the weapons aren't available. This is one way to reduce the surplus fear of nuclear holocaust, and it is very important. But there are a lot of other things we need to do too, especially along the lines of lengthening the fuse—of giving ourselves more time to make decisions in a crisis. You see, if a President doesn't believe he's got much time, he may—I don't think he will, but the risk goes up that he may—act impulsively, thinking that by striking first he will limit damage. And this is precisely why huge arsenals and short fuses are both destabilizing—they both lead to surplus fear, which may lead people to act irrationally in a crisis. I think the missile crisis proves beyond a shadow of a doubt that there was enough fear of the consequences of a nuclear war in the American Administration to be deterred. We *were* deterred, plain and simple. So, what you want is enough fear to maintain deterrence in a crisis, and no more. How much is that? Look at the missile crisis. I'll bet the Soviets didn't have more than a few dozen nuclear warheads they could deliver on our forces and cities. That was enough. Conclusion? A few dozen is enough, in principle, because—and it is very frustrating to me when people do not pay sufficient attention to this—because of the facts I (and all of us around the President) discovered in the Cuban missile crisis. That is why I say nuclear deterrence is simple, and the lessons of the missile crisis are simple: Nuclear weapons are useful only for deterrence and it takes very, very few to perform this function.

BLIGHT: What you seem to me to be driving at is the psychological analogue to that classic question asked by those whose job it is to think about deterrence: How much is enough? You and your colleagues, especially Alain Enthoven and Charles Hitch, began giving this question your sustained attention back in the early sixties.[63] But what you seem to be saying now is that enough is really whatever it takes to create enough nuclear fear in the Soviets to cause them to act cautiously.

MCNAMARA: That's right, but only half right. Enough also implies: Do not exceed a force level, and other aspects of nuclear policy and strategy, that lead to fear of adverse consequences, and to caution. If you move across that line—and I'm not saying I know exactly where that line is, only that it exists—what you think you're doing for deterrence starts to look to the Soviets like aggressive tendencies. And this is what makes the situation destabilizing; because, in a crisis, people may act impulsively and they may preempt. And I'd have to say, for example, that in the missile crisis we did think about preemption. But—and this goes straight to my point—not about us preempting the Soviets. No way was that *ever* going to happen, and I want that to be absolutely clear. No. We worried about a *Soviet* preemptive strike. Now, I know that to some people this sounds nonsensical, because, rationally, a Soviet first strike, and our retaliation, would have resulted—or could have—in their complete obliteration. But if I put myself in the Soviets' shoes in those days, and in that crisis, and if I look around and see the U.S.

forces on alert, and if for some reason I become convinced that the U.S. is going to strike, well then, what do I do? Maybe I strike first in an attempt to use my few forces before they are destroyed. I don't know. My point is that you don't want a situation to arise in which there is the slightest chance of this happening. You don't want to make the Soviets that fearful. And the Soviets shouldn't want to make us that fearful. But this means that one lesson—maybe the main lesson—of the Cuban missile crisis is that we must go beyond it. By that I mean there is no doubt that the crisis was resolved because of fear of the adverse consequences of pushing it any further. Read Khrushchev. He was scared. Read Bobby's book. The President was scared, too. And the whole damn thing started because the Soviets were scared that they were so far behind in the nuclear arms race that they'd never catch up if they didn't try something as foolhardy as putting missiles in Cuba. You see: from beginning to end, fear ruled. Do we want that kind of world again, that kind of atmosphere, that kind of risk? No. So, the question posed by the missile crisis for today is: How do we create conditions where fear is not so dominating? How do we prevent crises, not how do we manage them? That's the issue now: How do we keep the peace, just as we kept the peace in October 1962, but with less reliance on fear?

CHAPTER

4

Incommensurable Crises: Hawks and Doves on Power, Perception, and Policy

In a book published the same year as the Cuban missile crisis, Thomas Kuhn retold the stories of several scientific revolutions, describing the ways in which the scientific community responded to anomalies and challenges, which resulted in crises leading, in the cases Kuhn considered, to "paradigm shifts."[1] What astonished readers a quarter of a century ago still evokes controversy today: Kuhn's contention that, in a genuinely revolutionary situation, competing paradigms are incommensurable; "proponents of competing paradigms," according to Kuhn, "practice their trades in different worlds."[2] When Copernicus argued that the earth orbited the sun, he challenged more than the claim that the sun orbited the earth; he challenged an entire understanding of the universe and humanity's place within it. Copernicus's world was fundamentally different from the world of his forebears. Likewise, Einstein's was fundamentally different from Newton's.

In the Cuban missile crisis, the hawks' world was fundamentally different from the doves'.[3] The hawks' Cuban missile crisis was relatively understandable, predictable, controllable, and safe. The doves', on the other hand, was inexplicable, unpredictable, uncontrollable, and, above all, dangerous. Hawks and doves disagreed on their understandings of the relative U.S. and Soviet positions in the crisis; on their perceptions of the risks; and on their policy prescriptions. They differed, in short, on power, perception, and policy. They also differed in their subjective reactions to the crisis. The doves felt enormous anxiety throughout, while the hawks felt virtually none. In what follows, we explore these differences, and suggest some of their implications.

Power: The Importance of the Strategic Balance

One of the most obvious areas of disagreement between hawks and doves concerns the role and importance of the strategic nuclear balance in 1962, which all agree was grossly in the United States' favor.[4] Three questions about the balance stand out: How much of an effect did the Soviet deployment of missiles to Cuba have on the balance? How big a role did the balance play in the resolution of the crisis? What degree of latitude did American nuclear superiority afford the President? The hawks answer all three questions with one voice: a lot. The doves: none.

Paul Nitze and Douglas Dillon agree completely that the Soviet deployment drastically altered the strategic nuclear balance. "Militarily it would be a major step toward nuclear parity—effective nuclear parity, not in numbers but in military effectiveness," Nitze asserts.[5] "[I]f left unchallenged," says Dillon, the deployment "would change the nuclear balance in their favor all over the world and would therefore give the Soviets leverage everywhere."[6] While they agree with McNamara that the deployment of forty-two missiles represented an insignificant numerical change in the balance, they note that it vastly improved the Soviets' capacity to strike targets in the United States. Moreover, the missiles based in Cuba had much shorter flight times to the U.S. than did missiles based in Siberia, complicating coordination of an American first strike.[7] These missiles also short-circuited the United States' elaborate early-warning system, which faced north, not south. Considerations such as these lead the hawks to believe that the deployment in Cuba greatly improved the Soviets' nuclear capability, and therefore dramatically altered the strategic nuclear balance.[8]

McNamara strongly disagrees. He argues that the Soviet deployment did not significantly alter the strategic balance because it did not alter the number of militarily effective weapons each side had, which he asserts was the "same then as now"—zero.[9] By "militarily effective," he means weapons whose use will result in a "net gain" for the initiator.[10] McNamara acknowledges that the SS-4s and SS-5s in Cuba dramatically increased the number of American targets the Soviets could hit, but he denies that there would have been any military utility in hitting them anyway. Presumably, he would also acknowledge that, theoretically, the missiles in Cuba would have complicated American first-strike plans, but he argues that, in any event, there was "no way" the United States was going to attempt a first strike, because the losses that could have resulted from Soviet retaliation would have been unacceptable.[11]

Since McNamara did not perceive any military utility in the United States' vast nuclear arsenal, he did not believe the strategic imbalance gave the Americans any leverage over the Soviets.[12] It was therefore irrelevant to the successful resolution of the crisis, in his view. Because this huge arsenal could not have been used to the net gain of the United States, McNamara reasoned, then the Soviets would have had no reason to fear that it would deliberately be used against them. The implication is that they must have agreed to American terms for ending the crisis for reasons unrelated to American nuclear superiority. Nitze and Dillon are evidently flabbergasted by this interpretation. "I agree totally with Nitze and think the McNamara thesis that our nuclear superiority made little or no difference is dead wrong," says Dillon. "Our nuclear preponderance was essential. That's what made the Russians back off, plus the fact of our total conventional superiority in the region."[13]

Of course, if it were true that the Soviets deployed the missiles in Cuba largely to redress the strategic imbalance, then it follows that the strategic balance mattered to them. And if the strategic balance mattered, it must have been because they believed it posed unacceptable risks of American belligerence, or because it constrained the Soviets from realizing their foreign-policy goals. If the strategic imbalance mattered greatly to the Soviets in their decision to deploy the missiles, the hawks believe, then it had to matter for the same reason in their decision to withdraw them.[14] Consequently, in their view, American nuclear superiority gave the United States tremendous leverage in the missile crisis, whether or not the doves realized it then or believe it now.

It would seem that whether the strategic balance really mattered in the conduct and resolution of the missile crisis turns ultimately not on what the hawks, the doves, or the American leadership as a whole thought of it, but rather on what the Soviets thought of it. If the Soviets saw the balance in McNamara's terms, then McNamara would presumably be correct. If they saw it in Dillon's terms, then Dillon would presumably be correct. How did the Soviets see the nuclear balance?

Dillon is certainly correct when he asserts that "their books and their military theory . . . emphasized that nuclear weapons were a valid weapon and war could be won with them." It would seem to follow, as Dillon notes, that when the Soviets saw the United States with "six or eight times their number of nuclear weapons—or ten times, or whatever it was," then "they would behave accordingly."[15] But Soviet military doctrine and the writings of Soviet military theorists may not shed much light on what Nikita Khrushchev, the man whose opinion mattered most on the issue, thought of the military utility of nuclear weapons, especially in the heat and fog of the crisis itself. At the conclusion of the crisis, for example, a senior Soviet diplomat is reported to have recalled a conversation in which Khrushchev told him "that the United States was ready on October 27 to invade Cuba, and that he decided to pull the missiles out of Cuba because a communist Cuba without missiles was better for Soviet interests than a U.S.–occupied Cuba."[16] This is fully consistent with McNamara's view that nuclear weapons have no military utility, and thus that the outcome of the crisis was not, on either side, driven by considerations of nuclear superiority or inferiority. Khrushchev might have been worried primarily about losing Cuba; this fact may explain both his decision to deploy the missiles and his decision to withdraw them.

For now, we must suspend judgment on the importance of the strategic balance in the Cuban missile crisis. We do not yet have adequate information to address the issue satisfactorily, though we shall return to it in Chapter 6.[17] For now, it should simply be noted that, as with so many crucial issues, the information needed to determine the truth of the matter lies where the light has heretofore been very dim: in the mysterious and obscure world of Soviet decisionmaking in general, and in the thought of Nikita Khrushchev in particular.

Perception: What Were the Risks?

Neither hawks nor doves in the ExComm relished the thought of a major war between the superpowers in 1962, particularly the thought of a catastrophic nuclear war. But they seem to have disagreed sharply on the risk they ran of a nuclear war in the Cuban missile crisis. What risks did hawks and doves perceive? How did they estimate the magnitude of those risks? How great were the real risks?

Hawks and doves alike make frequent references to the probability of various hypothetical chains of events leading to nuclear war, and the first step is to clarify the sense in which "probability" is being used in this context. It is clear that neither the hawks nor the doves believe there was some highly specifiable random chance that nuclear war would occur, because nuclear war is not a random event. They were therefore making probability judgments that were different from those of the gambler, who knows that when two dice are rolled repeatedly, a pair of sixes will show on average once in every thirty-six rolls.

The statement "It is extremely unlikely that the Soviets would have retaliated after an American air strike on the missiles in Cuba" should be interpreted roughly in the same way as the meteorologist's statement that there is an 80 percent chance of rain. Statements of probability in meteorology and in crisis management do not describe statistical patterns of random events, but the level of confidence of the people making the forecasts, which in turn depends upon what people take as relevant information, and what they believe about the power of the causal models with which they are working.[18] In either case, if relevant information is plentiful and of good quality, and if causal mechanisms are well understood, policymakers' and meteorologists' probability judgments can approach certainty, and they can be very reliable guides. But if relevant information is scarce, conflicting, or of poor quality, or if causal mechanisms are poorly understood, their forecasts may be little better than guesses.

In weather forecasting, there is comparatively little disagreement on what counts as relevant information, and causal models are widely shared (though they are constantly being improved). But there is evidently a great deal of disagreement between hawks and doves both on the question of what counts as relevant information for forecasting events in a crisis and on the question of how that information should be processed. This should not be surprising; the weather is subject solely to natural causes, while human beings have minds of their own. Their actions depend not only on their capabilities but also on their intentions, desires, needs, fears, and hopes. The actions of national governments also depend upon such factors as the outcomes of debates within national leaderships, and the integrity of chains of command.

Let us consider the ExComm's assessments of Soviet actions, which were clearly fundamental to their assessments of the risk of nuclear war (for neither hawks nor doves in the ExComm suggested that it would have been wise or necessary for the United States to initiate nuclear war, though there was, of course, some possibility that a breakdown of command and control or an accident of some kind might have resulted in an inadvertent use of an American nuclear weapon). In making these assessments, hawks and doves first had to identify the actions the Soviets could have taken, and then assess the likelihood that they would have taken an action of which they were capable. Hawks and doves tend to agree on the actions the Soviets could have taken, but disagree on the actions they would have taken.

The ExComm believed that the Soviets could have initiated nuclear war in a variety of ways: by means of a "bolt-out-of-the-blue"; by means of a preemptive strike; by means of an inadvertent action, such as the unauthorized launch of a Soviet missile in Cuba during an American air strike, or an unauthorized reprisal elsewhere; by means of a desperate action after a process of escalation, presumably beginning with a response to an attack on the Cuban missiles or a clash on the quarantine line; or as the result of a victory of hard-liners over compromisers in the Kremlin, who might then undertake desperate action without a calm and careful evaluation of the consequences and the alternatives. One can imagine a possible scenario in which a nuclear war was the result of any of these in 1962. What was the magnitude of the risk associated with each path to nuclear war, and how successful were the hawks and doves in gauging it? What information and reasoning processes did they use to reach their judgments on these matters?

Neither hawks nor doves believed that the Soviet Union would deliberately decide to launch a nuclear war out of the blue, even though they were clearly capable of it. The hawks dismissed this possibility on the grounds that the Soviets were vastly overmatched at the nuclear level; the doves, led by Robert McNamara, rejected it on the grounds that there would have been no advantage in it, presumably even if they were not overmatched. No one suggested that the Soviets had a first-strike capability in 1962; the United States could easily have obliterated the Soviet Union under any circumstances.

But McNamara nevertheless voices concern that the Soviets might have launched a surprise attack anyway, precisely because they might not have had the time or the means to think rationally about the suicidal consequences of such an act. According to McNamara:

> [I]n a crisis, people may act impulsively and they may preempt. And I'd have to say, for example, that in the missile crisis we did think about preemption. But—and this goes straight to my point—not about us preempting the Soviets. No way was that *ever* going to happen, and I want that to be absolutely clear. No. We worried about a *Soviet* preemptive strike. Now, I know that to some people this sounds nonsensical, because, rationally, a Soviet first strike, and our retaliation, would have resulted—or could have—in their complete obliteration. But if I put myself in the Soviets' shoes in those days, and in that crisis, and if I look around and see the U.S. forces on alert, and if for some reason I become convinced that the U.S. is going to strike, well then, what do I do? Maybe I strike first in an attempt to use my few forces before they are destroyed.[19]

Presumably, the Soviet leadership was aware of the United States' massive nuclear capability, and of the meagerness of its own. No rational calculation would have led them to attempt a preemptive strike. But McNamara, showing his well-developed sensitivity to the pressures and perversity of the situation, argues that the overriding fear of instantaneous annihilation might have led the Soviets to behave irrationally. So does Dean Rusk, recalling the teachings of Sun Tzu.[20]

Paul Nitze concedes that irrational or desperate action could possibly have resulted in a nuclear war in 1962, but he evidently assigned it a much lower probability than did Rusk or McNamara. Nitze recalls feeling that there was not much risk of the Soviets doing something which would "bring into action our undoubted strategic superiority." This risk was "[n]ot infinitesimal," however, "because you can never tell what people like the Soviets will do, and therefore you could well imagine that some irrational act could take place."[21] But Douglas Dillon recalls feeling certain on this point. "I was convinced," he says, "that the Russians were not crazy and that they would not do anything as crazy as provoke a nuclear war that would surely destroy them."[22]

While McNamara, Rusk, and Nitze all recognize a risk associated with desperate, irrational Soviet action, Nitze evidently believes the risk was very small in October 1962, and like his fellow hawks, he appears to have been willing to run it. McNamara and Rusk do not indicate precisely how great the risk of desperate Soviet preemption appeared to be to them, but it clearly had a profound effect on their view of the crisis and on the caution they exhibited in their choice of actions for dealing with it. What was the real risk that the Soviets might have launched a nuclear war out of desperation?

While most observers would probably agree that this risk was really quite small, most would also agree that the danger would have risen greatly if the Soviets had actually become convinced that a massive American nuclear first strike was imminent. Several developments might have given them this impression. First, the Strategic Air Command (SAC), as was noted at Hawk's Cay, raised the nuclear alert level to DefCon 2 in the clear, surely communicating to the Soviets that the Americans were very confident in their nuclear capability. Second, Soviet intelligence would have noticed the massive American preparations for an air strike and invasion of the island of Cuba, communicating an apparent willingness to use force directly against Soviet troops and their allies. Third, according to Khrushchev's recollections, someone in Washington, possibly Robert Kennedy, succeeded in communicating a profound sense of urgency about the need to resolve the crisis peacefully.[23] And fourth, the stray U-2 over Siberia earlier that day might conceivably have been interpreted as pre-SIOP reconnaissance, as Scott Sagan suggested at Hawk's Cay, and as Khrushchev seems to have feared at the time.[24] If the Soviets were looking for information to confirm their greatest worry, on that most dangerous day of the nuclear age—that the United States would soon resort to military action, and possibly even a first strike—they would have had little trouble finding it. After all, many in the United States and the Soviet Union believed that the U.S. was capable of what the Air Force called a "splendid first strike"; the Kremlin might well have wondered whether the American political leadership, perhaps under pressure from an only partially controllable military establishment, might also have intended to try one.[25] If the Soviets actually believed this, then, like trapped animals, they might have lashed out in a first strike of their own.

One of Raymond Garthoff's recent revelations suggests that this danger may have been greater than the ExComm realized. Colonel Oleg Penkovsky, an officer in Soviet Military Intelligence, had been working for British and American intelligence for some time prior to the missile crisis. Soviet agents, aware of his activities, had been shadowing him in an attempt to identify his contacts, but arrested him immediately after President Kennedy announced the discovery of Soviet missiles in Cuba on October 22. According to Garthoff:

> Penkovsky was given a few standard coded telephonic signals for use in emergencies, including one to be used if he was about to be arrested, and also one to be used in the ultimate contingency: imminent war. When he was being arrested, at his apartment, he had time to send a telephonic signal—but chose to use the signal for an imminent Soviet attack! This seemingly bizarre act rings true. Penkovsky had always been a man with unusual self-importance (for example, he had asked his SIS [British Secret Intelligence Service] handlers, while in London on an official trip in 1961, to be introduced to Queen Elizabeth, and to be whisked to Washington to meet President Kennedy; and he liked to wear British and American colonels' uniforms at his clandestine debriefing sessions when he was traveling in the West). He had tried to egg the Western powers on to more aggressive actions against the Soviet Union during the Berlin crisis in 1961. So when he was about to go down, he evidently decided to play Samson and bring the temple down on everyone else as well. Normally, such an attempt would have been feckless. But October 22, 1962, was not a normal day. Fortunately, his Western intelligence handlers, at the operational level, after weighing a dilemma of great responsibility, decided not to credit Penkovsky's final signal and suppressed it. Not even the higher reaches of the CIA were informed of Penkovsky's provocative farewell.[26]

Of course, it is possible that in his moment of great personal crisis Penkovsky simply mixed up his signals, intending merely to communicate that he was under arrest. We will never know. But had the President and the ExComm heard the signal from Penkovsky and scrambled SAC's ground alert force "just in case," the Soviets might have convinced themselves that an American first strike was imminent. In such a case, their doctrine called for immediate preemption. This does not, of course, mean that they would have preempted; plans and doctrines, especially in moments of extreme crisis, may be poor predictors of political decisions. But there can be no doubt that if Penkovsky's signal had led to further American alert measures, the danger would have increased dramatically.

Clearly, the risk of nuclear war may be profoundly affected by events far beyond the control, or even the awareness, of the most rational and well-intentioned national leaders. Uncontrollable, inadvertent, and accidental actions may figure heavily in the risk—the DefCon 2 alert and the stray U-2 are graphic illustrations of this—as may psychological factors such as the "Samson mentality," a situation-induced irrationality to which both Rusk and Garthoff explicitly refer. But it is precisely the fact that these are unforeseeable and unpredictable that makes it impossible to assess their likelihood with any degree of certainty. We cannot, therefore, reliably quantify the risk of desperate or irrational Soviet action, even with the benefit of hindsight, because it is inseparable from the risk of inadvertent action. We can, however, note that it was undoubtedly possible. Kennedy and Khrushchev both seem to have appreciated this, though Khrushchev was presumably also worried about desperate, irrational, and inadvertent action on the *American* side.[27] It is curious that Nitze and Dillon recall so little fear of inadvertent nuclear war, and so much perplexity and irritation at the presence of this fear in the ExComm's doves.

What of the specific risk of inadvertent war which McNamara says was prominent in his thinking; namely, the possibility that a Soviet second lieutenant might, under attack, fire the nuclear missile under his charge in Cuba rather than see it destroyed in an American air strike?[28] McNamara judged that it was possible both that a second lieutenant could do such a thing and that he would do such a thing. Two considerations seem to have brought this worry to the forefront of McNamara's mind. First, McNamara was greatly impressed by the 1961 Congressional Joint Atomic Energy Committee report which argued that NATO troops in a similar situation could launch their weapons without authorization. By projection, McNamara supposed the Soviets capable of it also.[29] Second, McNamara was impressed by Tactical Air Command (TAC) Chief General Walter C. Sweeney's admission that he could not guarantee that an American air strike would destroy all the Soviet missiles in Cuba.[30] McNamara believed, largely on the basis of considerations such as these, that a Soviet missile from Cuba could have been launched under attack, possibly destroying a major American city and killing millions of American citizens. While he claims in his interview that he believed the probability of such an event was not very high, he was clearly concerned by the possibility.

What was the probability that a Soviet missile in Cuba might have been launched under attack? We can say with a high degree of confidence, if not absolute certainty, that it would not have happened. Moreover, the information was available which would have enabled the ExComm to reach this conclusion themselves, although its key members, in the stress of the crisis, do not appear to have done so.

Photoreconnaissance had enabled the CIA to pinpoint the locations of the Soviet MRBM and IRBM sites and at least twenty-three of the twenty-four surface-to-air missile (SAM) sites on the island of Cuba by the time of the President's initial television speech on October 22.[31] By October 27, it was well known that only the SS-4 MRBM sites had attained or were approaching operational readiness, and that the SS-5 IRBM sites were at least a month or more away from completion.[32] There were four MRBM sites in western Cuba near San Cristóbal, and two in north-central Cuba near Sagua la Grande; there were four launchers at each site, and it was known that, normally, there would be two missiles for each launcher.[33] Therefore, TAC had twenty-four targets of real interest (the SS-4 launchers), which could have been equipped with a maximum of forty-eight missiles.

Guarding the missile sites were five SAM sites and three airfields at which thirty-nine Soviet MiG-21 interceptors were based.[34] General Sweeney's original attack plan called for eight aircraft to attack each SAM site, and twelve aircraft to cover each of the three MiG airfields. The plan itself called for the U.S. planes to attack the MiGs as they became airborne, though Sweeney recommended attacks on the airfields themselves. The "total defense suppression requirement" was one hundred American aircraft.[35]

While the defenses were being attacked, each of the known launchers would be attacked by six aircraft. As the original plan also called for attacks on the IRBM sites that were in earlier stages of construction, Sweeney envisioned attacks on a total of thirty-two to thirty-six launchers, requiring a total of approximately 250 sorties.[36] Allowing 150 extra aircraft for attacking the MiGs and the Il-28 bombers, the overall requirement as Sweeney saw it came to five hundred aircraft. If the IRBM sites had been left alone for the time being, as would have been perfectly reasonable given that they were more than a month away from completion, the number of aircraft required for the air strike would have been significantly lower—approximately four hundred.

The October 27 Cuba Fact Sheet prepared for the President stated: "The infiltration of TAC airplanes into the Florida bases has ended. This infiltration accomplished over the last few days has brought 850 airplanes into these bases. The greater majority of the planes are primarily for the tactical air role [i.e., the air strike] but many (62) will augment CONAD [Continental Air Defense] forces in the air defense role."[37] The United States, therefore, had more than half again as many aircraft available in Florida as were required by Sweeney's original plan, and more than twice as many as were required if the IRBM sites had been left alone for the time being. Assuming that the Cuban air defenses downed 30 percent of the incoming American aircraft—an extremely unlikely success rate, at least an order of magnitude higher than the most probable rate of attrition[38]—well over 160 aircraft would still have reached the MRBM and IRBM sites in the initial attack, an average of over four aircraft per launcher.

At a cruising speed of 450 miles per hour, aircraft from Homestead Air Force Base would have covered the 180 miles to Sagua la Grande in twenty-four minutes; aircraft from Key West would have covered the 150 miles to San Cristóbal in twenty minutes. If the Cubans had prompt warning of the approaching attack from Florida—that is, if they were in radio contact with observers watching the planes scramble and assemble in formation—then they might have had nearly an hour's notice before bombs were dropped. (Sweeney's briefing suggested that the Cubans would have ten minutes' warning of the first wave, forty minutes' warning of the second, and proportionately greater warning of the third.)[39] The CIA knew that the SS-4 missiles were liquid-fueled, and that because of the instability of the fuel, the missiles could only be held on alert a maximum of five hours before the fuel had to be unloaded.[40] When the order for the air strike came down, the missiles would have been empty. Because of the fueling process, the warhead mating process, the targeting process, and the necessary countdown, it was estimated that the fastest the missiles could have been launched after a decision to fire them was eight hours, and it may have taken as long as twenty hours.[41] Thus, on the extremely unlikely chance that Cuban air defenses could destroy all six aircraft destined for one missile launcher, or if all the aircraft attacking a launcher failed to damage it, there would have been ample time and plenty of aircraft available for TAC to send in a second mission, and possibly a third, before the first missile could be fueled, armed, targeted, and fired.[42]

Fueling, arming, targeting, and firing an SS-4 are all processes that require coordinated action by a large number of skilled people.[43] Even if warheads were present for the missiles in Cuba, if the crews manning the sites had not panicked and run for cover, if they had not waited for orders from superiors, and if they escaped death or bodily injury in the attack (all major assumptions), it still would have been virtually impossible to accomplish this extraordinarily complex coordinated activity safely and effectively while American high-explosive and incendiary bombs were falling in the area. Indeed, near-misses would very likely have been more than adequate to disrupt the fueling process; fires would have been widespread. Furthermore, direct hits on the warhead storage bunkers might have rendered entire sites inoperable even if the missiles and launchers themselves escaped injury.

Finally, if a missile, against all the odds, was successfully fired by a local commander, there was some probability that it would malfunction in flight, stray off course, or fail to detonate. Assessments of the reliability of the American first-generation ballistic missiles should have seriously called into question the reliability of Soviet first-generation missiles, especially when they are fueled, armed, aimed, and fired under duress.[44]

The conclusion which follows from this is that something like divine intervention on the side of the Soviets would have been necessary to permit a Soviet second lieutenant to fire the missile under his command successfully during an American air strike. Such a launch would not have been absolutely impossible, but the information available at the time clearly indicated that it was wildly improbable. Though General Sweeney was technically correct in refusing to guarantee that he could destroy all the known missiles, he evidently failed to communicate to McNamara how unlikely a launch-under-attack would be.[45] It would not have been necessary to destroy all the missiles to prevent a launch-under-attack; it would have been sufficient to disrupt the preparatory procedures.[46]

Of course, the possibility of a launch-under-attack was not the only thing the ExComm had to worry about when it considered the air strike. An air attack on Cuba would have jeopardized the carefully crafted international political consensus in favor of the quarantine, especially in Latin America; many believed that it would inevitably have to be followed by an invasion of the island, resulting in an extended, possibly costly military campaign; and perhaps most important, it meant killing Russians and Cubans. Many American decisionmakers doubted that the Soviets would absorb an air strike and an invasion of Cuba, in the face of such a direct affront to its reputation and prestige, without a military response of some kind elsewhere.[47]

Paul Nitze disagrees. The Soviets, according to Nitze, would have had no choice in the matter. The strategic nuclear balance would have dissuaded them from just those retaliatory measures that most concerned the doves—a blockade of Berlin or an air attack on the NATO Jupiter missiles in Turkey. Nitze recalls:

> We thought about all those possibilities. I, in particular, was worrying about that; I think I was given the task of worrying about it by Mr. Kennedy. So you try to put yourself in Mr. Khrushchev's shoes and try to decide what might be the West's most vulnerable

positions, and how you could exploit them. Certainly the reinstitution of the blockade or in fact the invasion of Berlin was within the military capability of the Soviet Union. But, you know, you look at whether you would do that in light of the very great imbalance between our strategic nuclear capability and theirs. And, frankly, I thought it would be wholly unlikely that they would respond in that way because of our strategic nuclear capability— because of our undoubted superior nuclear capability.[48]

It is clear that Nitze was worrying about these contingencies only perfunctorily. He clearly did not believe that they were going to happen. In contrast, McNamara believed that "there was a fairly high—I would say at least a fifty-fifty—probability of a Soviet military response outside Cuba to a U.S. attack on Cuba."[49]

Who is right—Nitze, who believed the risk of what we now call horizontal escalation was minimal, or McNamara, who believed it was as high as fifty percent? Citing an intelligence report received about six months after the crisis from a reliable, well-placed source, Raymond Garthoff has suggested "the Soviet leadership had decided not to go to war over Cuba even if America invaded, and formalized that decision in a signed top-secret Central Committee directive."[50] If this is so, then there may have been virtually no probability of a Soviet military response as the result of a deliberate policy choice in the Kremlin. Moreover, this may have been the direct result of the Soviets' tremendous strategic nuclear inferiority, just as Nitze maintains. However, McNamara and his fellow doves point out that the risk of a military response involved more than just the Kremlin's choice in the matter. A Soviet officer apparently shot down Major Anderson's U-2 on October 27 without orders from Moscow;[51] would another Soviet officer order his planes to bomb Jupiter sites in Turkey without authorization? Would a Soviet or Cuban pilot, if any planes survived an American attack, attempt a reprisal against southern Florida? Would an incensed Soviet brigade commander order his tanks into West Berlin?[52] All these might have been unlikely, but how would one have gone about gathering the information to determine how unlikely they might be? Inadvertent events are unforeseeable; there is simply no way of accurately gauging the risks associated with these possibilities.

Finally, the American leadership faced the specter of political upheaval within the Kremlin and the possibility that the Soviets might have initiated or provoked a major war as a result of it. This was evidently Dean Rusk's main fear. How significant was the risk that a struggle for power within the Presidium might have resulted in a Soviet decision to fire nuclear weapons? The circumstantial evidence at the time seemed to suggest the possibility that Khrushchev's position within the Soviet leadership was tenuous, and that hard-liners were ascendant. The most compelling evidence for this came toward the end of the crisis in the form of Khrushchev's two quite contradictory letters of October 26 and 27. Even the ExComm's Soviet expert, Llewellyn Thompson, said that a revolt within the Kremlin was consistent with the tone of the two letters, though he himself thought such a revolt unlikely.[53] Subsequent disclosures suggest that Thompson was right to be skeptical and that at no time during the crisis was Khrushchev's authority seriously threatened.[54] But the ExComm did not have the information necessary to gauge this with any real degree of accuracy. Unpredictability is sometimes a sign of confusion or of struggle within a nation's leadership, and it is perfectly reasonable for Rusk to have made the connection and to have worried about its ominous possible implications. The fears, it should be emphasized, were a function of Rusk's uncertainty, not his certainty.

Soviet thinking was highly opaque during the Cuban missile crisis. The Soviets were almost entirely inscrutable throughout, and their most significant actions—from their decision to deploy the missiles to the way in which they deployed them, from their conduct during the public phase of the crisis to their sudden and unexpected acceptance of Kennedy's terms—surprised the Kennedy Administration.[55] While hawks and doves tended to agree on the *possible* actions the Soviets could have taken leading ultimately to nuclear war, they were manifestly unable to attach probabilities to them with any significant degree of confidence. Only in one case—the risk of a Soviet missile launched under attack from Cuba—did the information exist which, if processed and appreciated, would have enabled the ExComm to assign a meaningful probability. Why, in this case, did the doves worry about a launch-under-attack at all? Why, in the other cases, did hawks estimate the risks lower than did the doves? How did the hawks and the doves deal with the uncertainties they faced? How did their approaches to risk assessment affect their choice of policies? These are the questions to which we turn next.

Policy: Dealing with Uncertainty and Responsibility

The hawks were daring and confident; the doves were cautious and uncertain. Why were their approaches to the crisis so different? First, hawks and doves clearly employed different methods for dealing with uncertainty. In general, when decisions were to be made among available alternatives, the hawks advocated whichever course of action seemed to have the highest probability of success, whether or not it ran a small risk of disaster. If we were to employ the game theorist's lexicon, we would presumably classify the hawks as "expected-utility maximizers." In contrast, the doves advocated courses of action which minimized the risk of nuclear catastrophe, whether or not those actions were the most effective ones available for removing Soviet missiles from Cuba. Some of the doves may have operated on the "Disaster Avoidance Principle"—"Choose the action with the lowest chance of disaster"—and others may have operated on the "Minimax Principle"—"Choose the action whose worst possible outcome is better than all of the alternative actions' worst possible outcomes."[56] In any case, it is clear that the hawks advocated policies based on their inclination to seek what was probable, while the doves tried to avoid what was possible.

These differences crystallized around the air-strike option. Paul Nitze recalls having no significant discomfort with it, though he is careful to say that he thought it should properly have been used only after the quarantine had demonstrably failed, as he thought it had by October 27.[57] If Kennedy had ordered the air strike, Nitze would have had very few qualms. "It seemed to me that we had both tactical superiority in the area of Cuba and we had overall strategic superiority; under those circumstances, we really were not running that great a risk. It was, as I say, not infinitesimal, but it wasn't that great a risk."[58]

A central objection Douglas Dillon had to the air strike was moral: "I finally agreed with Bobby Kennedy that a surprise attack on Cuba at that time was unacceptable because it was too much like the Japanese attack on Pearl Harbor. If we attacked like that, we would be forsaking the ideals for which I believed we had fought World War II."[59] Demonstrating that there was, and is, something less than total agreement among the hawks, Nitze does not hesitate to label Dillon's moral concern "nonsense."[60] Dillon's objection to the invasion, which seemed a necessary follow-up to the air strike, was political: "I didn't like the idea of Americans fighting Latin Americans. That would have been very bad—maybe not for the first two days, but if you didn't get it done very quickly, you would be in a mess. . . . Latin Americans would turn on us and say, 'There's your Yankee imperialism again.' I didn't want that at all."[61] But Dillon agrees completely with Nitze's claim that the air strike and invasion carried little risk of escalation. "What it really came down to was this: one side—mine—wanted to do something forceful and decisive about the situation, while the other wanted to put off making a decision. That's because we weren't nervous about the consequences, while they were."[62]

But even though the doves did estimate the risks somewhat higher than did the hawks, their probability judgments do not appear to have played much of a role in their deliberations. How can this be? Why would the Secretary of Defense, for instance—a man renowned then, as now, for his enthusiasm for quantification and for calculating and playing the odds—toss probability logic out the window? McNamara explains his approach as follows: "If . . . only a few—maybe even only *one* bomb—gets through to destroy an American city . . . you . . . will have had to shoulder the responsibility for the worst catastrophe in the history of this country. So you won't do it."[63] In place of the probability logic in which he had been trained and which normally guided his thinking, McNamara was in this extraordinary circumstance guided by possibility logic.[64] He fixed his mind on the unthinkable catastrophe that was possible. McNamara clearly knew the facts as well as anyone else on the ExComm; he would have understood, for example—as his deputy Paul Nitze understood—that the risk of the Soviets launching a nuclear missile at the United States during an American air strike on Cuba was extremely small. But it was nonetheless possible, and perhaps even more importantly, it was not an isolated risk. An American air strike would have raised the crisis to a new level of confrontation, and the already palpable uncertainty which made the crisis appear so dangerous and so difficult to control would have increased greatly.

The hawks, it seems, were much more certain of their probability judgments, not because they had any hard information about Soviet actions and intentions that the doves did not have, but because they had a high degree of confidence in the Soviets' rationality. As General Maxwell Taylor put it, Khrushchev would inevitably have backed down, "unless he was crazy and full of vodka," in which case "his colleagues in Moscow would take care of him."[65] McNamara's rejoinder to this view is very straightforward; the hawks "just figured the Soviets would back down. But—and this is my point—there is no way they could *know* that."[66] The doves were clearly more sensitive to the problems of inadvertent, unintended, or desperate action, and they were less confident in the Soviets' rationality. Why?

One reason is that they saw plenty to justify their concerns. Thomas Schelling notes that

> rationality is a collection of attributes, and departures from complete rationality may be in many different directions. Irrationality can imply a disorderly and inconsistent value system, faulty calculation, an inability to receive messages or to communicate efficiently; it can imply random or haphazard influences in the reaching of decisions or the transmission of them, or in the receipt or conveyance of information; and it sometimes merely reflects the collective nature of a decision among individuals who do not have

identical value systems and whose organizational arrangements and communication systems do not cause them to act like a single entity.[67]

The doves clearly recognized that the Soviets were handicapped on all these scores. The Soviet deployment of missiles to Cuba indicated confusion and faulty calculation; their diplomacy prior to and during the crisis indicated that they were unable to receive messages or to communicate efficiently; the bewilderment the ExComm felt at Khrushchev's contradictory letters of October 26 and 27 seemed to indicate haphazard influences in the transmission of decisions, and perhaps also unresolved tensions in the bodies making them. The experience of trying to deal with the Soviets and bring the crisis to a conclusion was frustrating to the ExComm largely because it seemed to confirm time after time that the Soviets were not completely rational in Schelling's sense of the word. Moreover, the ExComm had reason to wonder—and many of its members presumably did wonder—whether they appeared to be exhibiting perfectly rational behavior themselves.

The doves' greater sensitivity to the apparent irrationality of Soviet behavior and to the dangers of inadvertent and uncontrollable events may have something to do with the fact that they seem to have felt the burden of responsibility far more heavily than the hawks. This opinion was expressed by Douglas Dillon. If the doves as a group felt the burden of responsibility more heavily than the hawks—and it is worth noting that all of President Kennedy's closest advisors were doves—then it would stand to reason that they were more finely attuned both to the limitations of rational actor analysis and to the possible, if improbable, catastrophic consequences of their actions.[68]

Nevertheless, the hawks maintain that the doves were simply wrong to approach the crisis the way they did. Douglas Dillon argues that the hawks were more experienced in government and in dealing with the Soviets, and consequently were better informed and better positioned to predict Soviet behavior in the missile crisis:

I think most of the differences between the hawks and doves had something to do with [the difference in experience]. I think simple inexperience led to an inordinate fear of nuclear damage, the fear of what *might* happen.[69]

. . . . .

I didn't understand then, and I don't understand now, why people worried so much about one limited, conventional action leading to nuclear war. The idea is preposterous! The only explanation I can think of is that Ball's (and McNamara's) relative inexperience in these matters caused them to draw unwarranted conclusions.[70]

Clearly, Dillon is absolutely correct to note that the different experiences hawks and doves brought to the missile crisis shaped their approaches to it. But we do not agree that the hawks are thereby vindicated by their obviously greater experience in U.S.–Soviet relations and in government generally. In order for that to be the case, it would have to be true that their experience was relevant to the situation the Kennedy Administration faced in the Cuban missile crisis.[71] And that is precisely what the doves call into question.

A moment's reflection reveals the considerable prima facie validity of Dillon's thesis that the hawks were far more experienced than the doves in matters of national security. Dean Acheson had been Truman's Secretary of State and had guided U.S. foreign policy during such pivotal episodes as the Berlin blockade and airlift and the Korean War. Acheson's protégé, Paul Nitze, had been principal author of that seminal defense of the postwar American policy of Containment, NSC-68. Maxwell Taylor had wide experience in World War II and in Korea and in peacetime also, both as a field commander and a staff officer. John McCone was a long-standing national-security specialist with broad experience in government. Dillon himself had been Eisenhower's Ambassador to France in 1954, when he handled the French request (refused by Eisenhower) to use American nuclear weapons in Southeast Asia to liberate the besieged garrison at Dien Bien Phu. And just before becoming Kennedy's Secretary of the Treasury, Dillon had been Eisenhower's Under Secretary of State and had, on several occasions, engaged Khrushchev personally in what the Soviet leader recalled years later as some of the fiercest debates he had ever had with an American official.[72] The ExComm's hawks were clearly men with considerable experience.

Who were the doves? Dean Rusk was the oldest (at fifty-three) and had risen to Assistant Secretary of State under the tutelage of his idol, General George Marshall, early in the Truman Administration. But in the eight intervening years he had been out of government, as president of the Rockefeller Foundation. McNamara, as he points out in his interview, had no government experience at all beyond serving in the military during World War II. George Ball, the number-two man in the State Department, had also served in the war, but had been a lawyer in private practice ever since. McGeorge Bundy, the National Security Advisor, had been a Harvard dean. Robert Kennedy, the Attorney General, had held a series of relatively insignificant clerkships in the House and Senate. Theodore Sorensen, President Kennedy's Special

Counsel, had been Kennedy's political advisor since 1952. The President himself had arrived in the White House without much experience in foreign affairs; he had for fourteen years been a congressman and senator and had never set foot in the Soviet Union (nor had any of the doves). Relative to the hawks, the doves were very young and quite inexperienced. Dillon obviously believes that it is therefore understandable that they should have been nervous and uncertain during the Cuban missile crisis.

For the most part, the hawks had come to maturity and office in the immediate postwar era, in the depths of the Cold War, and all were fervent anti-Communists who were deeply offended by the Soviet missile deployment. They believed that the United States had successfully forced the Soviets to back down in Berlin in 1948–49, 1958, and 1961, and they believed American nuclear might had restrained the Chinese in the Korean War. They had developed a powerful faith in nuclear coercion during the forties and fifties, the era of American dominance in nuclear weapons. This experience seems to have taught them two lessons: that nuclear superiority and inferiority ought to be judged in the same relative terms as those for non-nuclear weapons; and that the Soviets, vastly behind in deliverable nuclear weapons, could and should have been coerced into behaving themselves.[73] To Dillon and Nitze, it was absolutely, unarguably obvious that the nuclear superiority of the United States rendered the Soviets as helpless in the Cuban missile crisis as they were in Berlin—even more so, perhaps, because the United States also enjoyed conventional superiority in the Caribbean. In their view, the United States could and should have moved with impunity. But, because a young President and his close advisors lacked this experience and this "knowledge," the United States settled for less than it should have, and only muddled through the Cuban missile crisis by means of what Acheson called "dumb luck."[74]

According to Dean Rusk, however: "If we had taken Dean Acheson's advice—and Dean Acheson had never been Secretary of State at a time when a full nuclear exchange was possible—if we had taken his advice and led off with a strike, the crisis would have been infinitely more dangerous."[75] Embedded in Rusk's response to the hawks is the radical and controversial claim that all of their vast experience, all that they had learned in international crises and, most important, all their implicit theories of Soviet behavior that apparently gave them such confidence in their probabilistic predictions—all of this was irrelevant to the reality faced by American and Soviet leaders in the missile crisis. Why? Because "a full nuclear exchange was *possible*."[76] This was not true when Acheson held office. In fact, Kennedy was the first President to enter office when the United States and the Soviet Union were mutually vulnerable to a devastating nuclear strike. Rusk seems to imply that the hawks had simply failed to assimilate the importance of this change. An American air strike might have provided a quick success in an era of American invulnerability, but in 1962 those in positions of significant responsibility could not afford to run the risk that it might not. That responsibility, coupled with the realization that a single misstep could be fatal, focused the doves' minds on the very risks the hawks discounted, and heightened their awareness of the uncertainties surrounding them. Looking down what fellow dove Theodore Sorensen called "the gun barrel of nuclear war,"[77] Rusk was powerfully affected by the realization that "you had no ability to predict with certainty what a man would do in the circumstances in which he would find himself."[78] That was the main source of anxiety in the Cuban missile crisis. "Whoever is educated by anxiety is educated by possibility," said Kierkegaard, and anxiety "is the pivot upon which everything turns"[79]—including, it seems, one's identity as a hawk or a dove.

In our opinion, the doves exhibited the more prudent and realistic approach to coping with uncertainty, and thereby advocated wiser courses of action. Their approach was more prudent because it took into account the fact that there was, for the most part, insufficient information to predict Soviet behavior.[80] Where it is impossible to make reliable probability judgments, all one is left with is a stark appreciation of the possible.[81] And the possible in the Cuban missile crisis was an awesome sight to behold, a sight not mitigated by American nuclear might.[82] The doves' approach was more realistic because it recognized that crisis management had undergone a recent paradigm shift with the novelty of American nuclear vulnerability, and because it was firmly rooted in the psychological experience of shouldering the burden of responsibility attending that recognition. This was a shift that the hawks seem not to have noticed in 1962, precisely because of their vast experience in an earlier era. And because they did not notice the shift, they did not focus on the possible catastrophe; nor, therefore, did they feel a share of the burden of potential responsibility for it.

In the twenty-five years since the Cuban missile crisis, of course, hawks and doves alike have clearly come to recognize the reality of mutual vulnerability. And, to an extent, that realization has affected their views. Douglas Dillon was emphatic on this point at Hawk's Cay: "I want to note that everything I've said about what we should have done at that time doesn't apply today, mostly because of the changes in the military situation. If the Cuban missile crisis happened today, I'd react in much the same way as Bob McNamara, and I would like to make that absolutely clear."[83] But what the hawks may not yet have assimilated is the difference this makes to the psychological experience of shouldering the burden of responsibility, and the way in which that experience powerfully, and usefully, focuses the human mind on the possible catastrophic consequences of their policies, and on the dangers of desperate, irrational, and inadvertent action.[84] The gap between the hawks' and the doves' approaches to and understandings of the Cuban missile crisis, therefore, parallels and can be traced to the same cause as the gap between the scholars' and the policymakers' understandings discussed in Chapter 2. The difference, in both cases, is a difference of responsibility; not merely responsibility per se, but responsibility in the frightening new world of ineradicable, and mutual, nuclear vulnerability.

The world of mutual vulnerability was a new world, and it was incommensurable with the old. When the two worlds clashed in the Cuban missile crisis, the meaning of Great Power crisis management was forever changed, because its aim had shifted from attaining victory to avoiding a catastrophe. Kennedy and the doves understood this, but none expressed it more poignantly than Khrushchev. "What good would it have done me in the last hour of my life," he asked, "to know that though our great nation and the United States were in complete ruins, the national honor of the Soviet Union was intact?"[85]

PART THREE

Soviets
and Americans

Certain historians, sometimes whole generations of historians, find in certain periods of history nothing intelligible, and call them dark ages; but such phrases tell us nothing about those ages themselves, though they tell us a great deal about the persons who use them. . . .

R. G. COLLINGWOOD
The Idea of History

The Cambridge Conference

The Cuban missile crisis is one of the most widely studied events of the nuclear age, but our understanding of it, as the previous chapter indicates, is grossly one-sided. To read the major Western accounts of the event, one would almost conclude that the Soviet Union was, if not wholly irrelevant to the successful management of the crisis, at least entirely secondary. Our understanding of the event is that it was an American problem, solved by President Kennedy and his supremely talented group of advisors, whose "combination of toughness and restraint, of will, nerve and wisdom, so brilliantly controlled, so matchlessly calibrated . . . dazzled the world."[1] The mythos of the Cuban missile crisis has its share of heroic and tragic figures, but they are overwhelmingly American. The Soviet players, even Nikita Khrushchev, hover in the background as ghostly presences, altogether lacking the flesh-and-blood reality of their American counterparts.

To a certain extent, the one-sidedness of our understanding is entirely natural, for every nation and culture is inclined to take more interest in its own heroes and tragic figures than in others', especially their mortal enemies'. Furthermore, in this case at least, the one-sidedness has been unavoidable. The Soviet Union has closely guarded its diplomatic history for seventy years, and it has carefully preserved the shroud of secrecy surrounding the deliberations of its top leaders. All too easily, however, we forget that significant progress in our understanding of the event cannot occur until this imbalance in knowledge is redressed. The answers to most of the important remaining questions depend upon access to Soviet sources. In response to our inability to obtain this access, Western scholars have tended instead to look for the answers in an ever-finer-grained understanding of American decisionmaking, thereby exaggerating the imbalance all the more. Like the proverbial fool who loses his wallet in a dark alley, we have spent our time looking under the lamppost down the street, where the light is much brighter.

But recently, Soviet General Secretary Mikhail Gorbachev's policy of *glasnost* has dramatically altered the climate of Soviet scholarship and has made it possible for Americans and Soviets to conduct unprecedentedly candid and useful dialogues on previously taboo subjects. In the summer of 1987, we began to explore the possibility of starting to redress the imbalance in our understanding of the Cuban missile crisis by organizing a meeting of Soviets and Americans to discuss the many unanswered questions about the Soviet view of the event. The result was the Cambridge conference of October 1987, coinciding with the twenty-fifth anniversary of the missile crisis itself.

We were very fortunate to have three knowledgeable Soviets join us. Fyodor Burlatsky, then a political commentator for *Literaturnaya gazeta* and head of the Philosophy Department of the Social Sciences Institute in Moscow, had been Khrushchev's speechwriter and Political Advisor for Socialist Countries of Eastern Europe. His most recent play, *Burden of Decision*, dramatizing American decisionmaking in the Cuban missile crisis, has been enthusiastically received in Moscow, despite—or perhaps even possibly because of—its sympathetic and very human portrayal of President Kennedy and the ExComm. Sergo Mikoyan, the editor of *Latinskaya amerika*, had accompanied his father, Soviet First Deputy Premier Anastas I. Mikoyan, on his delicate mission to Cuba at the conclusion of the Cuban missile crisis to smooth over relations with an enraged Fidel Castro. The younger Mikoyan was privy to many details of Soviet decisionmaking before and during the crisis, because of his father's closeness to Nikita Khrushchev. Finally, Georgy Shakhnazarov, currently one of a small group of personal aides to General Secretary Gorbachev, has participated in previous U.S.–Soviet dialogues, and is closely connected to several of the Soviet principals during the missile crisis who continue to hold positions of high office. Joining them were a like number of former members of the ExComm—McGeorge Bundy, Robert McNamara, and Theodore Sorensen—as well as a small group of American scholars, most of whom had attended the meeting at Hawk's Cay.

The conference ran in closed session from Sunday evening, October 11, to Monday evening, October 12. Several public events were held on Tuesday, October 13, at which many topics covered in the private sessions were discussed. Although the public events received national media attention, the transcript of the private sessions, which we present here, has not been made public previously.[2]

The conference began with dinner and welcoming remarks by Graham

Allison, dean of the Kennedy School of Government. Allison recalled Mikhail Gorbachev's exhortation to "call things by their real names," and noted that the assembled group stood uniquely poised to shed light on the many lingering misunderstandings, misperceptions, and mysteries of the Cuban missile crisis, "both for historical purposes—the need to set the record straight—and to determine their effect on policy choices in subsequent situations."[3]

Georgy Shakhnazarov followed by unexpectedly announcing that, immediately prior to the conference, he had had a two-hour conversation with Soviet Central Committee Secretary Anatoly Dobrynin, Ambassador to Washington in 1962, about the causes and conduct of the Cuban missile crisis. Shakhnazarov teased the participants, however, by refusing to divulge information from their conversation until the following day. Fyodor Burlatsky introduced himself by noting that it had been his dream for some time "to have the chance to meet with Kennedy Administration figures such as McNamara, Sorensen, and Bundy."[4] He also expressed the opinion that the Cuban missile crisis "was a bad thing with a very good result. It was the first step toward new thinking about each other." It was tragic, Burlatsky said, "that John Kennedy and Khrushchev did not have a longer time in power." He added:

> I am convinced that together they would have had a chance to make real progress in arms control. Since Kennedy and Khrushchev, there has been political asymmetry. When we have had a leader who was ready to reduce tensions, you have not. And when you have had a leader who was ready to reduce tensions, we have not. The two leaders—Kennedy and Khrushchev—were both great reformers who could make some new decisions. And I may be an optimist, but I believe we will have the same opportunity in the future.[5]

While McNamara immediately and enthusiastically professed his agreement, Theodore Sorensen sounded the same cautionary note he had sounded at Hawk's Cay. "[This meeting] is potentially—and I emphasize, potentially—one of the most important meetings of its kind. It could also be an enormous waste of time and money if all we do is exchange old lines. But I hope to trade hard questions here in the next two days; I have some hard questions for you [the Soviet participants], and I hope you have some hard questions for us. The climate is ripe for a candid discussion."[6]

When Sergo Mikoyan had an opportunity to speak, he recalled Albert Einstein's statement, "With the invention of the atomic weapon, everything has changed except our way of thinking." He said:

I agree with Fyodor Burlatsky, who said this was a very important point in our history, the first time the leaders of our countries understood the importance of peace in the nuclear age. Unfortunately, both leaders went out so quickly. I hope this meeting will be a beginning and help us understand what Einstein thought it absolutely important to understand. I believe that the elements of the new political thinking began twenty-five years ago.[7]

With the introductions completed, the participants turned their attention to the video monitor, to view excerpts from two dramatic reconstructions of the Cuban missile crisis: Burlatsky's play, *Burden of Decision*, the Soviet portrayal of American decisionmaking; and *The Missiles of October*, an American film portraying Soviet decisionmaking.

Burlatsky's play had been researched assiduously, drawing heavily upon the same memoirs of the crisis that have powerfully affected our own understanding of the event for so long. But it had an unmistakable Dostoyevskian air of melodrama that the former ExComm members present found highly entertaining. Literary license had also been used extensively to make room for frequent commentary on various aspects of contemporary U.S.–Soviet relations, detracting somewhat from the realism of the presentation; but on the whole Burlatsky had succeeded admirably in capturing the burden of responsibility and presenting to his Russian audience a vivid portrait of attractive and understandable human beings—not capitalist enemies—laboring under it.[8]

The Missiles of October, similarly based on memoirs and secondary accounts, painted a very human picture of Nikita Khrushchev, magnificently played by Howard Da Silva. Da Silva's Khrushchev was painfully aware of the dangers of an accident or a misstep, and was acutely aware of President Kennedy's own political predicament. Desperately seeking a cooperative, mutually face-saving way out of the crisis, Khrushchev in *The Missiles of October* waged a pitched battle against hard-liners in the Presidium who pressed for tougher action. "There was a man in a field between a swarm of bees and a herd of bulls," Da Silva nervously intoned while awaiting Kennedy's response to his October 26 letter. "He knew if he took a false step, he'd be stung to death or trampled to death. Or both."[9]

Burlatsky was the first to comment on the two presentations. "Let me say, the portrayal of Khrushchev was very good. But the portrayal of relations between members of Presidium was not so good. It was not possible to have such open opposition to Khrushchev in the Presidium at that time," he contended.[10] Mikoyan agreed. "I think that the picture of our leadership is fantastic, understandably. The information was not available."[11] But, notably, none of the Soviet participants challenged the portrayal of Khrushchev's caution, or his sensitivity to the cooperative dimensions of resolving the crisis—just as none of the American participants challenged Burlatsky's portrayal of President Kennedy's awesome sense of responsibility, and his painful sense of uncertainty and danger.

Auspiciously, as the opening dinner discussion drew to a close, the participants could not restrain themselves from launching into discussion of topics reserved for Monday's meetings, and an extremely illuminating difference of opinion immediately arose among the Soviet participants. Burlatsky took the lead:

> We had no parity then—the balance was one to eighteen in warheads—and the buildup since then has destroyed security. We have destroyed security together. Our military men and our politicians had no real strategy. Everything was copying: you got the atomic bomb, we got the atomic bomb; you had a buildup, we had a buildup. Perhaps Khrushchev's main idea when he emplaced rockets in Cuba was not only to defend Castro but to take the first step to strategic parity. . . . . When he was in Crimea, it was explained to him that there was an American base across the sea in Turkey, but we had no such thing near the United States. He thought maybe it should be the same for us. Maybe this was part of the reason for Cuba. Castro did not ask for bases, but after the Bay of Pigs, Castro needed some defenses. But the main reason was the first step to strategic parity.[12]

"It would be dull if all participants of our conference were of the same opinion," Mikoyan noted, "so I disagree with Fyodor. I think Khrushchev thought first of the safety of Fidel's regime, though his advisors might have thought of warheads."[13] Many times in the course of the conference this difference of opinion, as well as others, would arise—shocking American scholars accustomed to the homogeneity of old-style Soviet orthodoxy. The Soviets' remarks on other issues were equally portentous:

> SHAKHNAZAROV: . . . It is very strange and a case for meditation why both our countries have quite different political systems but in both cases rarely get good political leaders. Since the October Revolution, we have had a great leader (Lenin), an outstanding leader (Khrushchev), a very good leader for a short time (Andropov), and now Gorbachev. We believe you had one great leader (Franklin Roosevelt), and two outstanding leaders (Kennedy and Woodrow Wilson).

MAY: That's a bit of a surprise.

BUNDY: Isn't it?

SHAKHNAZAROV: Three of yours, four of ours. Why?[14]

"The Cuban missile crisis showed that numerical superiority is nothing,"
Burlatsky added, moving from topic to topic, eager to make the most
of this unique opportunity. "You had *so* much, and yet Kennedy and
Khrushchev understood this."[15] In a matter of minutes, the Soviet participants had touched on the causes of the crisis, the importance of the
strategic balance, the politics of the Kremlin, the effect of the crisis on
later relations, and the importance of leadership. Though time quickly
ran out on the opening discussion, its range and candor clearly startled
and delighted those who had come with guarded expectations, and it
served as a fitting prelude to the next day's conversation, which proved
more exciting and illuminating than even the most optimistic present
would have dared to hope.[16]

October 12, 1987—9 a.m.

JOSEPH NYE: . . . We had what I thought was a very good start last
night, and now it is time to ask: Can historians do as well as playwrights?
[Laughter.] The answer may be no, but we will have to wait and see.
   We will break the discussion into parts, though necessarily there will
be a certain amount of overlap between topics. This morning we are
going to look at the background and causes of the crisis. Just after lunch
we will examine the conduct and resolution of the crisis. Shortly after
three o'clock this afternoon we will turn to the issues associated with
the actual feel of managing a crisis, what the agenda refers to as "The
Look and Feel of Nuclear Danger." Then over dinner—we will have a
working dinner—we will wrap things up with a discussion in which we
try to draw lessons from the event. . . .
   Let's keep discussion informal, but I think it would help if we started
off with a brief introduction. I have asked Ernie May if he would help
start us off, and then when he has finished speaking, I will ask Bill
Taubman and Fyodor Burlatsky to comment briefly before we throw
the floor open. Ernie?

ERNEST MAY: Joe asked me a day or two ago to make some remarks
about causes. It might be useful to think of it first as an event which is far
away in time, and then ask: What questions ought we to ask about it?
Are there any analogies we can make use of to help us understand the

causes of the event? There are probably no really good ones, since the post-Hiroshima world is significantly different in certain ways from the pre-Hiroshima world. But it struck me that the Fashoda crisis of 1898 was similar in certain respects, and so I thought I would begin by drawing a few parallels between the two events.

At the end of the nineteenth century, Britain claimed all of East Africa, and indeed largely controlled that side of the continent. It was a claim that the French did not fully recognize, and they had interests of their own in establishing a presence in the region. Captain Marchand marched up the Nile to a small town named Fashoda, where he promptly planted the French flag and waited. Lord Kitchener, hearing of the French expedition, likewise marched and put up his flag right next to the French flag, without shooting, sat down with Marchand, drank some whiskey with him, and waited for instructions from the two governments. After some weeks, there was a peaceful resolution to the potential conflict.

What were the causes of this event? First, the British had a certain perception of their place in Africa and in the world. They thought of themselves as the strongest world power, preeminent outside of Europe (especially in Africa). They had particular aspirations in the region (for example, people were talking about a railroad from the Cape of Good Hope to Cairo). East Africa had strategic value to Britain, as a land link to the Indian Ocean and the all-important colonies on the Indian subcontinent. In 1895 the Liberal government had made a public commitment to the Upper Nile. There was a good deal of domestic pressure as well; the public was enthusiastic over a British role in East Africa, and there was a certain amount of outrage over France's attempts to expand into the region. There was also pressure from the military: Kitchener had just won the Sudan, and there was a great deal of enthusiasm for maintaining control over the area.

What about using these same categories to look at the French side of the affair? First, there was a perception in France that Britain was overbearing. There was a historical antipathy dating all the way back to the Hundred Years' War. There was a strategic rationale for challenging Britain in the region as well: control over portions of East Africa could be used as powerful leverage against Britain. There was a commitment: Marchand had carried a disassembled steamboat all the way from Senegal to the Nile to challenge the British and was not about to give up his project lightly. There was a lot of domestic pressure; you remember that this was the time of the Dreyfus Affair, and there were deep divisions within French society, a public commitment to Africa, and a bureaucracy and an army both interested in leverage against the British.

Why, then, was there no war? Because cooler heads prevailed—and there were cool heads on both sides: Salisbury and Delcassé.* Both had concerns elsewhere, especially the longer-run German problem in which they would have a common interest to defend. Both perceived a greater interest in avoiding this particular conflict despite the various factors pushing for it.

If these are the categories we use to analyze causes, it seems that some questions arise from them which are relevant to the Cuban missile crisis. Let me ask them with respect to the Soviet side of the crisis. First, on perceptions. What were the perceptions of the leaders, of the relationship with the United States, and of each other's respective roles in the world? Second, on aspirations. Whose matter? What were they? Were they shared? What were the thoughts in the Kremlin at the time about the future Soviet role in Cuba and in Latin America? Third, on strategic questions. What was the importance of the balance? Was the local or the global balance more important, and in what way? What was the relationship of the Cuban missile crisis to Berlin? Is there anything to Adam Ulam's argument that the central Soviet concern in this affair was the relationship with the Chinese?[17] What arguments in favor of deploying missiles to Cuba were advanced? Fourth, how did the commitment develop? How did the Soviet government work back then, and how did that bear on the policy choices? Who thought about relations with Cuba? Who dealt with them? Who dealt with the question of the strategic balance? Fifth, if public division or public opinion was important in Fashoda, what domestic pressures, if any, were working on Khrushchev and the Soviet leadership? What were the effects, if any, of the economy? How did Khrushchev know about these things? I was talking with Bill Taubman last night about Stalin's sources of domestic and international information, and it appears that he had a separate Secretariat for Foreign Affairs. Did Khrushchev also have that Secretariat? What were *his* sources? . . .

NYE: Thank you, Ernie. That is a useful and provocative list. Bill, do you have any comment for us?

WILLIAM TAUBMAN: Let me just further sharpen one or two of Ernie's questions. Last night, our Soviet guests talked about the first step to strategic parity and the defense of Cuba as the two main motivations behind Khrushchev's decision to deploy the missiles. What about Berlin? We in the West have wondered about the role of Berlin in this event

---

* The Marquis of Salisbury was Prime Minister of Britain (Conservative) from 1885 to 1892 (briefly leader of the opposition in 1886), and again from 1895 to 1902. Théophile Delcassé was French Foreign Minister, 1898–1905, and was the architect of the Anglo-French Entente Cordiale.

for quite a while. For four years Khrushchev had tried to force a resolution; he'd given two Berlin ultimatums and had had to back down twice. Was there a Berlin dimension to the deployment in Cuba? If so, what was it? Was he thinking of some kind of trade? Did he want to force the German issue back open again? Was he trying to force a summit on the issue?

On Khrushchev's perceptions of the United States, I wonder if Cuba fits a pattern: an attempt to force a détente, to force a relaxation of tensions. I know that sounds contradictory, but he may have thought both Eisenhower and Kennedy slow to respond to his desire for an improvement of relations. Perhaps he thought he might shock them into some more general relaxation.

American nuclear superiority seemed to pose a challenge. We rubbed it in in 1961, when Roswell Gilpatric gave the speech in which we acknowledged a missile gap very much in *our* favor. How did this bear on Khrushchev's decisionmaking with respect to Cuba? Did the United States pose a temptation as well as a challenge? Khrushchev seriously thought he could get away with placing missiles in Cuba; why? What was his view of American domestic politics? What was his view of Kennedy? What bearing did the Bay of Pigs have on his decisionmaking?

Two other quick points. First, with respect to domestic pressure. Let's face it, in 1962 Khrushchev was facing a series of failures in domestic policy as well as in foreign policy, especially in agriculture and a sluggish economy. Was he facing opposition in the Presidium, open or not? Were there any rumblings in society that he was aware of or responsive to? Did he need a foreign-policy success to bolster his position in the party?

Finally, on this issue of personality, which I have always thought particularly important in this case; it looks to me as though Khrushchev was a unique Soviet leader. He was a gambler; he was willing to take big risks to achieve big results; he was used to employing bluster and bluff; he had made veiled nuclear threats in the Middle East and in Berlin.[18] Was Cuba the result of a very unique personality?

NYE: Thanks, Bill. Fyodor, do you want to be the first to respond?

FYODOR BURLATSKY: Well—that's a lot of questions. [Laughter.]

NYE: You don't have to answer them all at once. [Laughter.]

BURLATSKY: I wonder about them myself. Let me say that there is a first mistake: only trying to find *rational* reasons. There are some *irrational* reasons—psychological or emotional reasons. We must research this case from both points of view.

On Khrushchev's psychology, first of all, he was a leader. He was very unusual, but not totally unusual. Very few people realize that our

revolution had two tendencies, not one. Before the Revolution, we had
the Social Democratic Party. After the Revolution, we had the Communist Party. Two tendencies, two different types of leaders—military
path to socialism vs. NEP,* Stalin vs. Bukharin†—two types of leaders.
It is not surprising Khrushchev followed Stalin, even though Stalin killed
leaders of the liberal tendency. We have always had these two tendencies.

Khrushchev's personality was very interesting. He had sharp political
skills, but was very emotional. He did not necessarily think through all
possible . . . permutations. . . . For example, he gave a speech to the
20th Party Congress on Stalin [in February 1956] even though he knew
95 percent or 98 percent of the members were opposed to his view.

TAUBMAN: Though that was after his elevation to First Secretary.

BURLATSKY: Yes, after his election as First Secretary.[19]

From the historical point of view, it is important to discuss the Cold
War and the military contradiction between the United States and the
Soviet Union. Maybe you don't know, we had a long sense of nuclear
inferiority, especially at this time. I am not sure Khrushchev's analysis
of results went far enough—"What will be the U.S. answer?" Many
people thought this was an adventure, but he was willing to try anyway.
As I understand, it was the first step to strategic parity, and he tested
what would be.

On some other questions: What do Soviet leaders think of the United
States? At that time, we took only one step to understand the United
States. At the 20th Congress, Khrushchev declared peaceful coexistence
between East and West, between United States and Soviet Union. During the Cold War, the majority of Soviet leaders and people believed
the United States was our enemy and wanted to destroy our system.
Many believed the United States could do a first strike. I am sure
Khrushchev did not believe in it. If so, he would not have placed missiles
in Cuba, which could provoke a U.S. first strike.

On China, maybe you don't know, I wrote on China, did a biography
of Mao Zedong, and know their position. Chinese policy was to provoke
Soviet–American conflict. Khrushchev knew this very well, and criticized this very emotionally. When Khrushchev visited the U.S. in 1959,
he went back to Beijing to explain his position to Mao Zedong: a conflict

---

* New Economic Policy, Lenin's economic program, 1921–28. NEP made extensive use
of free enterprise and market mechanisms.
† Nikolai Bukharin's caution and pragmatism stood in marked contrast to Stalin's ruth-
lessness and rigidity. Bukharin advocated extending NEP, opposed promoting violent
revolution abroad, and emphasized the importance of slow, deliberate internal reform.
He was ousted as chairman of the Executive Committee of the Comintern in July 1929
and executed in 1938. Bukharin has been rehabilitated under Gorbachev.

between the United States and the Soviet Union would be very bad for China. China criticized us over the Cuban crisis, and Khrushchev's speech to the Supreme Soviet first dealt with Chinese criticisms.

Who decided to place rockets in Cuba? I am not sure; my opinion is that it was not discussed with full Presidium. Some, maybe—Malinovsky, Mikoyan—but it was a top secret. Khrushchev once joked that it was very strange that Voice of America informed us of our Presidium meetings after one half hour. [Laughter.] It was impossible to discuss it openly and maintain secrecy. Khrushchev may have thought about it first in Bulgaria,[20] I don't know—I was there—

MCGEORGE BUNDY: His memoirs mention Bulgaria.

BURLATSKY: But I read his secret letter,[21] and it mentions conversations in Crimea. . . . . . I don't know for sure. Maybe it was in Bulgaria, maybe it was in Crimea.

I had to laugh at the film last evening, especially the idea that someone in Presidium might struggle directly with Khrushchev after 1957. Maybe some members of Presidium asked questions in a very polite style, as we usually do with our wives [Laughter]—which is more dangerous than Politburo* [Laughter]—but, as I mentioned, direct struggle was not possible. There is a word in Russian, *azartnyi*†—[Discussion in Russian.]

[SEVERAL VOICES]:   "Adventurer," "risky man"—

BURLATSKY: Yes; Khrushchev was this. He was a "risky man."

As for the relation between Cuba and Berlin, during the Cold War, both sides tested the forces—like children, maybe. We tested this in Berlin: if we press the United States, what happens? But the Cuban story is not connected with Berlin, from my point of view. It is connected with Khrushchev feeling: Now we have become a superpower! We have enough rockets and warheads to compare our forces with American forces. We also had responsibilities to the Cubans, especially after the Bay of Pigs—maybe not so connected. I also believe Khrushchev's aim was to begin détente with the U.S.—this was his general aim. But it is very difficult to imagine how placing rockets in Cuba can support this! . . . . . I'm not sure Khrushchev thought out the aims. From my point of view, it was more an emotional than rational decision. He talked a lot about United States bases around the Soviet Union.

. . . . .

NYE: Were the Turkish bases particularly important to him?

---

* In 1962, the Soviet Politburo was known as the Presidium. Throughout these discussions, the Soviets use the terms interchangeably.
† Literally, "One who is venturesome in a game of chance."

BURLATSKY: Yes, but he was concerned about the many bases around us.

Then about meeting with John Kennedy. I didn't like the conversation between the two leaders in Vienna. They did not compare concrete political problems. They discussed ideological and philosophical questions about the contradiction between capitalism and socialism. This was a mistake, in my opinion, since many problems in U.S.–Soviet relations are not ideological; they are problems in the relations of superpowers. The bad thing during this meeting was that Khrushchev and Kennedy did not understand each other. They only understood each other after the missile crisis. They left Vienna without understanding or sympathy. Khrushchev said John Kennedy was very young, too intellectual, not strong enough to handle—

BUNDY: He did say that?

BURLATSKY: Yes, I know this; Khrushchev thought Kennedy too young, intellectual, not prepared well for decisionmaking in crisis situations. Maybe John Kennedy had a wrong feeling about Khrushchev, too.

WILLIAM URY: Too weak, or too ineffective?

BURLATSKY: Too intelligent and too weak.

GEORGY SHAKHNAZAROV: They are the same. [Laughter.]

BURLATSKY: Now, there is a question about Khrushchev's opposition. I have said already that it was not usual to have open opposition in Politburo, or—excuse me—in Presidium. Only during Lenin. Stalin had his opposition killed, and everybody remembered that.

SHAKHNAZAROV: For a short time when Khrushchev was out there was open opposition.

SERGO MIKOYAN: And in the middle of the fifties.

BURLATSKY: Yes, but I don't believe in 1962.

SHAKHNAZAROV: They had disagreements on policy—

BURLATSKY: Sure, but not open opposition. These are two different things. You can have different options discussed, different policies, for example, debate about sending warheads to Cuba—but nobody would step over Khrushchev's authority. After the Cuban missile crisis, Khrushchev took a big blow in prestige.

TAUBMAN: What about Suslov and Kozlov?*

. . . . .

BURLATSKY: Suslov had a bad time during Khrushchev's time. Khrushchev criticized him frequently and openly. The Western press would usually write that Suslov is an old Stalinist. Suslov had a bad position and was silent at that time. He had to wait to destroy Khrushchev's position.

TAUBMAN: But the point was that, though perhaps there was no open opposition, there was unhappiness, and perhaps Khrushchev felt he needed some sort of foreign-policy success.

BURLATSKY: I don't believe there is such a close connection between domestic questions and foreign policy in this case. Khrushchev wanted American help, especially with agricultural problems. When he was in the United States, he visited U.S. farms and told our farmers to do things the same way. The Cuban action was not consistent with this. In '62, Khrushchev had the *biggest* authority during all his time in power. He had a Presidium in which a majority supported him. It was not necessary to have an international success to show public opinion. You must understand, our public opinion was very afraid of the dangers of war. They were not well informed of the Cuban crisis—only some members of the political elite. Only very few knew everything that happened. The public only knew of the letters between Kennedy and Khrushchev; they were very afraid something terrible might happen. Society did not support in their hearts adventurous actions. [There followed a discussion in Russian between Shakhnazarov and Burlatsky.]

BRUCE ALLYN: Shakhnazarov and Burlatsky are clarifying the question of the role of domestic politics. Fyodor doesn't think it played a role in the resolution of the crisis, but Georgy is not so sure.

NYE: All right, we'll give Georgy and Sergei† a chance to speak before the Americans.

SHAKHNAZAROV: In Buckley's novel, if Fidel was to speak for one minute, he would speak for one hour.[22] [Laughter.]

BURLATSKY: Now you have destroyed my speech. [Laughter.]

I had some feeling then and I have the same feeling today that Khrushchev was a great political leader because he ignored the national

---

* Mikhail A. Suslov, a full member of the Presidium, was the regime's senior ideologist. Frol R. Kozlov, also a full member of the Presidium and a Secretary of the Central Committee, was a conservative. Both were critical of Khrushchev's reforms.
† Throughout the conference, Sergo Mikoyan was referred to by his Russified first name.

prestige and his personal problem—the danger to him personally—when he took the rockets from Cuba because he was afraid of war and wanted to avoid it at any length.

NYE:　Thank you, Fyodor. . . . . . Sergei?

MIKOYAN:　I want to add some facts, and perhaps Georgy Shakhna-zarov will make some political analysis later.

The idea to send missiles to Cuba was first expressed at the end of April by Khrushchev to Mikoyan. The main idea was the defense of Fidel's regime. Khrushchev had some reasons to think the United States would repeat the Bay of Pigs, but not make mistakes anymore. He also thought Kennedy was not a strong politician and would submit to CIA preference, led by Allen Dulles.* In 1962, at Punta del Este, Cuba was excluded from the Organization of American States.[23] Khrushchev regarded this exclusion as a diplomatic isolation and a preparation for an invasion. And then the propagandistic preparation was the accusation of exporting revolution. So he thought an invasion was inevitable, that it would be massive, and that it would use all American force.

At the end of April, before his visit to Bulgaria, Khrushchev talked with my father in the garden of his house in Moscow. The members of Presidium used to live in the Kremlin before it was opened to the public, but at that time they lived outside the city at the Lenin Hills. Khrushchev's and Mikoyan's houses were adjacent, and Khrushchev used to walk a lot with my father. They had a curious relationship. They were friends, but Khrushchev was envious of my father's background and education. Khrushchev did not think of himself as my father's superior.

My father was thought of as an expert on Cuba, and when Khrushchev discussed the idea of sending missiles to Cuba, my father opposed the idea. He did not think it could be done without the United States knowing. The intention was to do it very speedily, in September and October, but not to reveal it before the American elections in November. Khrushchev planned to announce it in a letter to be delivered by Dobrynin to the President, and he expected it would be received in the United States as the Turkish missiles were received in the Soviet Union. My father was skeptical that this could be done without American discovery. He felt also we had first to ask Fidel, and he thought that Fidel would strongly object because of the risk that it might cause an American invasion.

BURLATSKY:　So he was a specialist on Cuba? [Laughter.]

---

* Allen W. Dulles, brother of John Foster Dulles, was director of the Central Intelligence Agency, 1953–61.

MIKOYAN: He was a specialist, but he was mistaken on this, as specialists always are. [Laughter.]

After the talk in the garden, discussions were held without note-takers among a small group. There were only six: Khrushchev, Kozlov, Mikoyan, Malinovsky, Gromyko, and Biryuzov.* When Mikoyan posed his objections, Khrushchev said, "Let's send Marshal Biryuzov to Cuba to find out the possibility of installing missiles without American discovery and take with him my letter to Fidel in which I shall ask Fidel's opinion." My father was satisfied, but told me he was amazed Fidel agreed. And he was amazed that Biryuzov thought there were places in the mountains where the Americans would not discover the missiles. I should say, Mikoyan's opinion of this marshal was not very good; he said he was a fool. . . . . .

It was also decided that Alekseev† should be named Ambassador to Havana because he was a friend of Fidel, and under the conditions of that time, it was felt it would be best to have him in Havana in this capacity. It was proposed by Mikoyan, who knew Alekseev rather well.

RAYMOND GARTHOFF: He had been there as a press representative first, isn't that right?

MIKOYAN: Yes, but at the beginning of May he was informed that he would be the new Ambassador, and he was returned to Havana from a short visit to Moscow as the Ambassador while the old Ambassador was still there (who, by the way, had almost no access to Fidel).[24]

So, the main reason for sending missiles to Cuba was the defense of Cuba, though, of course, Malinovsky and others talked of the strategic balance. But this was the second idea. I agree with Fyodor, by the way, that Khrushchev did not think through the U.S. reaction. He thought that, after they were informed of the missiles, U.S. Soviet relations would improve.

BUNDY: Was anybody who was considered an expert on the United States present at all in the discussion sessions at the time?

MIKOYAN: Well, it is not modest of me to mention too much my father's role; but he was skeptical.

BUNDY: What about Gromyko?

MIKOYAN: I didn't ask him, of course, but maybe at that time he could not express his opinion very much. Not until he became a Politburo member.

---

* Marshal S. S. Biryuzov, Deputy Defense Minister and commander of the Strategic Rocket Forces.
† Aleksandr I. Alekseev, Ambassador to Cuba, 1962–68.

BURLATSKY: Sergei, was I right that it was not discussed in the full Presidium?

MIKOYAN: At first, yes, only three of them.[25] For absolute secrecy, it was decided in the beginning to send all messages hand-to-hand. There was no use of radio. By Raúl Castro's visit in July, some members of the Politburo were discussing it, but without any writing down.

URY: What did your father expect the American reaction to be?

MIKOYAN: I am not sure, but he did not think they would tolerate it. But Malinovsky was sure it could be done speedily and that if it was camouflaged it would not be discovered.

THEODORE SORENSEN: Was there any thought or discussion of deploying those missiles openly, by announcing beforehand that they would be installed?

MIKOYAN: Khrushchev's letter to Castro expressed the certainty that there would be an American invasion sometime. It was inevitable. So the only defense against this could be nuclear missiles, and they would have to be installed quickly and secretly.*

SORENSEN: But all of our missiles in Europe were deployed openly. You recall no thought of this at all?

MIKOYAN: No, it was not even discussed. It was decided to inform the American Administration *after* the missiles were installed, and Khrushchev expected the Administration only to discuss the matter with Dobrynin.

ROBERT MCNAMARA: Was Dobrynin asked about the likely U.S. response?

MIKOYAN: No. He didn't even know.

GRAHAM ALLISON: And all of the messages were delivered hand-to-hand for fear of leaks?

MIKOYAN: Yes. It was felt that it was very important to maintain secrecy, and so it was necessary to avoid any risk of word getting out.

RICHARD NED LEBOW: Do you know if there was any discussion of merely using conventional forces in Cuba as a trip wire to deter an American invasion without deploying nuclear weapons, just as we had done in Berlin?

---

* [Mikoyan adds:] Otherwise, if the U.S.S.R. acted like Ted Sorensen thinks would have been better, we could risk being confronted by the same kind of U.S. response: blockade, etc.

MIKOYAN: There was some talk of it, but also concern about retaliation—a buildup—at the American base at Guantánamo.

McNAMARA: I would like to know if Khrushchev ever thought it would be in his interest ever to launch these missiles?

MIKOYAN: Well, the idea was that their very existence would deter an American invasion. It would not be necessary to launch them.

. . . . .

LEBOW: Was the conventional deterrence option discussed at the initial meeting?

MIKOYAN: No, it was discussed in September only, but in connection with the question of conventional protection for the missiles.

NYE: But you said Malinovsky said that they could be deployed quickly and that they could be effectively camouflaged. Yet the workers were *not* working day and night, and the camouflage was done very badly—in fact, not at all.

MIKOYAN: I will get to that. At the beginning of discussions in early May, Khrushchev asked Malinovsky how long it would have taken the Soviet Union to invade such an island from just ninety miles away and to win. He answered, "Three or four days, a week maybe." So Khrushchev told to everybody present that the same time would be needed for a U.S. invasion. That was not long enough to defend against it, even by retaliating somewhere else. So it was thought we must deter an invasion *beforehand*. The forty-two thousand people sent there by ships did not know where or why they were going.[26] So they brought with them everything the detachments are supposed to have at their disposal. They had winter clothes, and skis—

McNAMARA: If we'd known that, it would *really* have upset us! We would have thought they were planning to invade Vermont. [Laughter.]

MIKOYAN: Only the high commanders knew. Others were told only when they passed Gibraltar. The mistake with the camouflage was absolutely Russian: we had to do it speedily, so too many ships were used, and the Americans noticed. We worked as we were used to, and we never asked Fidel about camouflage. Fidel said, "If you had asked us, we could have disguised the missile bases as agricultural projects." Even if we had done that, the roads would have been a real problem. We could not disguise the roads. But it was very Russian not to ask for additional expertise.

The only thing, by the way, that delayed American discovery was very bad weather. The American planes could not see the bases because of it.

Well—this is the story of the preparation, not of the October events.

BUNDY: This is fundamentally your father's story to you?

MIKOYAN: Yes.

URY: Why did your father think Fidel wouldn't agree to take the missiles?

MIKOYAN: I believe he underestimated Fidel's capacity to take risks. He is a very brave man, a very bold man. He is not scared of a challenge.

BUNDY: But did Fidel also perceive the risk of U.S. invasion as being high?

MIKOYAN: Fidel believed that he could take the risk. He was always ready to fight to the last soldier, but he knew if the United States used all of its force, he would fail.

. . . . .

ALLISON: Sergei, how conscious was your father of the details of the nuclear balance?

MIKOYAN: Yes, of course, he took it into account. But this was a second thought.

ALLISON: Was it important or not?

MIKOYAN: It was important, because there were only two thoughts: defend Cuba and repair the imbalance. But defending Cuba was the first thought.

ALLISON: Did you ever discuss the prospect of the United States using nuclear weapons against the U.S.S.R.?

MIKOYAN: Yes, we always lived under conditions of U.S. superiority. We were prepared for war, and we argued about a possible American attack. Khrushchev, I am sure, was very concerned about an American attack.

ALLISON: Did he believe that the danger of an American first strike was real?

MIKOYAN: He worried about the possibility that somebody in the United States might think that a seventeen-to-one superiority would mean that a first strike was possible.

ALLISON: Did people actually use those figures? Did people say the imbalance was seventeen to one?

MIKOYAN: It was known. I cannot guarantee that people were thinking just about seventeen to one, but U.S. superiority was well known.

. . . . .

LEBOW: Sergei, there is a general consensus in the Western literature that the strategic discrepancy was not the only factor, and it is also widely held that the American purpose in informing the Soviet Union of our strategic superiority was to moderate Khrushchev's behavior with respect to Berlin. Now, some think that the perception in Moscow was that the United States was trying to exploit Soviet weakness, and that the American announcement of the gap in strategic nuclear weapons was really intended to be used as a coercive instrument. Khrushchev thus became desperate to shore up that imbalance as quickly as possible even if this entailed significant risks. According to this view, the American attempt to communicate a deterrent threat backfired, with the result that the United States was faced with the kind of challenge it was hoping to forestall. Does that sound at all accurate to you?[27]

MIKOYAN: Yes. Since 1945 we were faced with American strategic superiority. We had always tried to redress it. And in 1962 we were perhaps also trying to redress the strategic imbalance. But still, the main reason for the political decision to send missiles to Cuba was the defense of Fidel's regime.

NYE: But just on that, was Roswell Gilpatric's 1961 speech important at all in that decision, or was the general feeling of nuclear imbalance more important to the decision to deploy?

MIKOYAN: The general feeling. You had such a thing as a position of strength, and our inferior position was impossible for us.

BUNDY: But in the late 1950s, especially after Sputnik, we in the United States seriously believed that you might be well ahead in long-range missiles.[28] Now, when Gilpatric gave that speech, we knew that in fact this was not the case. Probably your top people knew all along that things were moving much more slowly than that, but it must have been a shock when you learned that we had found out what the balance was really like. Did your people see medium-range missiles in Cuba as a way of adjusting for that?

MIKOYAN: Yes, of course. In August 1945, you had only three bombs, and two were used. When we launched Sputnik, we could count our missiles by the fingers on our hands. We understood that they were not enough.

. . . . .

MCNAMARA: Well, this is absolutely fascinating to me, and I'm *very* grateful to you for your candor. I, for one, have never heard anyone speak of these matters so openly, and I think it's tremendous. But I have just one question: Is the story as you relate it to us here known in your top leadership today?

SHAKHNAZAROV: Absolutely.

MCNAMARA: Very good, I'm reassured to hear that.

. . . . .

NYE: . . . We still have a very long list of questions, but before we get to them, I'd like to turn things over to Georgy Shakhnazarov for his comments.

SHAKHNAZAROV: Thank you very much. I would like to ask a question to our American colleagues. I want to ask: During the dramatic days of October, did anyone in the discussions with President Kennedy ever say that the Soviet Union had rights according to international law to deploy missiles in Cuba? Was anything said in defense of our position?

BURLATSKY: I also have a question . . . to Mac Bundy. Why did John Kennedy begin with an open declaration but not secret negotiation with Khrushchev? Was it because of domestic politics? Did he wish to press Khrushchev? Why begin with this?

NYE: Mac, do you want to try to answer those?

BUNDY: Well, those are two extremely searching questions. Let me see if I can try to answer them to your satisfaction.
    Not very many people were saying that Khrushchev had the same right to deploy missiles in Cuba as we had in Turkey, though of course it is perfectly possible to make the international legal case. The basic problem for us was that we had repeatedly taken the public position that the presence of offensive missiles in Cuba was unacceptable. Ever since the Monroe Doctrine, the United States has perceived a special interest in excluding European military power from the Western hemisphere. This was a powerful fact of our political consciousness, regardless of the international legal question. Soviet nuclear missiles in Cuba posed a particularly difficult problem, because our public simply would not tolerate them so close to us. So the first premise of our discussion

was that a policy must be found which leads to the removal of those missiles. This was a premise.

Now, that leads to Fyodor's question: What happens if we go quietly to Khrushchev and tell him we know what he's doing, and that we cannot tolerate it? Why didn't we try that first? *We* believed that if we did that, he would be tempted to go public *first*, and make the international legal case that Georgy referred to, thereby digging himself in and making it all the harder to find a way to get those missiles out. We didn't think it would help us get the missiles out if we approached Khrushchev with our knowledge of the deployment before we knew what we wanted to do about it. Once we decided on the quarantine, we thought the best thing to do was merely to announce it. Now, we informed your government an hour or so before Kennedy went on television, but that didn't do you much good, so that is really beside the point. But let me just say, Fyodor, that many of us that first week thought it a very good idea to write Khrushchev a letter and try the secret negotiation first, and we tried several times to sit down and write that letter. But we could never find a way to do it that didn't seem to make it harder to reach our objective, which was to have those missiles removed. We just couldn't figure out how to do that.

BURLATSKY: Who thought this was a good idea?

BUNDY: Well, I did; Ted Sorensen did—there were others who were inclined to try that route at one point or another.

SORENSEN: In fact, Joe, if I may jump in here, I tried to write a letter that would precede our taking any action. But we never could find a formula that didn't appear to be an ultimatum or that didn't allow Khrushchev to delay responding while the missiles became operational or while he took some other kind of action. It proved impossible to do, and so we gave it up.

McNAMARA: We were also very concerned about leaks and the pressure to act that would be put on the Administration if word got out before we knew what it was that we wanted to do. That argued against the private diplomacy. Had we been engaged in private diplomacy, we would have had less room to maneuver because of the public pressure.

BURLATSKY: Was it a mistake, do you think, to begin with a dramatic public announcement?

BUNDY: I think the October 22 speech was excellent, though in retrospect it seems a little overstated and overemotional—no offense intended, Ted.[29] But still, we did believe that we had to have a clear public position. It was a good speech and it did the job.

NYE: Ted, did you want to comment on the two questions?

SORENSEN: I think the two are directly related. The reason the speech was overemotional was that the President was worried about *your* question [Shakhnazarov's]. He was indeed worried that the world would say, "What's the difference between Soviet missiles ninety miles away from Florida and American missiles right next door to the Soviet Union in Turkey?" It was precisely for that reason that there was so much emphasis on the *sudden* and *deceptive* deployment. Look at that speech very carefully; we relied very heavily on words such as those to make sure the world didn't focus on the question of symmetry. We felt that helped justify the American response.

BURLATSKY: But I am convinced that if John Kennedy said when he met Gromyko, "We know everything about rockets in Cuba," maybe there would be no crisis; because Khrushchev must understand he was discovered and that he would need now to negotiate about a *new* situation. But Kennedy did not say anything to Gromyko.

SORENSEN: We also discussed that option beforehand, but would the missiles have been withdrawn?

BUNDY: You see, we couldn't imagine your obviously adventurous leader backing off from a move of this seriousness if we merely confronted him privately. We imagined him going to the UN and seizing the diplomatic initiative before we had decided what we were going to do. We were still thinking about the various options: the air strike, the quarantine, and so on. We couldn't believe Gromyko could be trusted to handle a private negotiation without going public on us because he had been assuring us in no uncertain terms for a long time that there were no offensive missiles in Cuba.

NYE: Let me note that there are still a number of questions on the table with respect to causes, and let me draw your attention to a comment Ted Sorensen made down at Hawk's Cay, which was that if President Kennedy had had any idea that Khrushchev intended to deploy offensive missiles to Cuba, he would have drawn the line in a different place than he had. In other words, Kennedy drew the line at zero and stated that the U.S. would not tolerate the presence of any offensive weapons because he did not believe that Khrushchev was going to deploy any there anyway—

SORENSEN: Well, that's not exactly what I said. . . . . . What I suggested was that it is conceivable President Kennedy might have taken a different public position if he had been able to anticipate the Soviet deployment.

NYE: That's right, you put it hypothetically. That raises some interesting questions about the failure of the two powers to clearly define their interests beforehand. In other words, if the two powers had successfully communicated their interests to each other, there might not have been a crisis at all. . . . . .

MIKOYAN: If we declared officially in September in the UN that we intended to defend Cuba with missiles, what would have been the American reaction?

. . . . .

BUNDY: Well, it would have been a totally different situation. It's very hard to say.

MIKOYAN: Might it have made it harder for you and easier for us?

BUNDY: That may very well be.

SORENSEN: I think it certainly would have made it more difficult for us.

. . . . .

SHAKHNAZAROV: All of you believed yourselves in both a military and a *moral* position of superiority. You speak of deception, and so on. But, according to international law, we had *no reason* to inform you beforehand. You did not inform us of your intention to put missiles in Turkey.[30] It seems to me Kennedy should have understood in his speech that there was no reason to be insulted. There was no indignity. There is a possible element of hypocrisy here. The conflict was political, and the moral case was unclear.

I still wish to know: Were you all united that the United States was right and the Soviet Union was wrong?

. . . . .

BUNDY: There were people who thought there should be no crisis, but they weren't very many and they weren't very loud. You see, we had already staked out a public position on the issue: if the Soviet Union does anything to threaten the safety of the United States or Latin America, we cannot tolerate it. We said it in September twice. Congress had passed a resolution to that effect. Now, I realize that this is not terribly relevant to international law, but it was how we perceived our national interest—consistently with the Monroe Doctrine. We felt the same way you would feel if we put missiles in Finland. We felt a major violation of our national interest, and we had a vote in Congress and a number of public statements to that effect. These were the things that were of primary concern to us.

. . . . .

SORENSEN: Morality in international affairs essentially boils down to what is generally acceptable. At the time when Soviet ships were moving to Cuba in increasingly large numbers, there were people in Congress who demanded that the President take action, but he recognized the right of the Soviets to send defensive arms to Cuba because this was generally acceptable. In this sense, he drew the line differently than did the hawks. What I said at Hawk's Cay was that, when the line was drawn at no offensive weapons, I believe President Kennedy drew that line there confident that the Soviet Union had no intention of going beyond it.

Let us not forget the subsequent events, which were important as well. Not only did the Soviets fail to notify us of the deployment of missiles, we received repeated messages saying that there were no offensive missiles being installed at all. President Kennedy had come to rely on the Bolshakov channel for direct private information from Khrushchev, and he felt personally deceived.[31] He *was* personally deceived. And this was not considered generally acceptable.

. . . . .

ALLISON: Let me come back and see if Georgy or Sergei want to comment on Khrushchev's perceptions of the objective factors, especially the strategic nuclear balance, the changes in the balance or the trends he saw at the time, and of the situation in Cuba. In particular, did Mikoyan agree that the United States seemed about to take action against Castro? Was the American strategic advantage perceived as changing or getting more decisive in an important way? Would other people have agreed that the United States was likely to take military action? Did Dobrynin say anything about these issues?

SHAKHNAZAROV: No, Mr. Dobrynin did not speak of this.

MIKOYAN: We spoke a bit about your first question already.

SHAKHNAZAROV: Yes, but it is a special and interesting question. McNamara was quite right yesterday: the situation was already partly parity—but only if the Cuban missiles were successfully deployed. It is the ability to deliver a missile that is important for parity, not the quantity of missiles. We had no missiles near the United States. The United States had bases encircling the Soviet Union. It was an attempt by Khrushchev to get parity without spending resources we did not have.

BURLATSKY: I have a little different opinion about this matter. During the 22nd Party Congress [in 1961] we tested nuclear weapons. . . . . . Khrushchev during the Congress remarked that we were testing weapons bigger than the Americans had. I think he was a little bit intoxicated with such possibilities, and he felt he could use or test his strength, to demonstrate it to the Americans. But maybe I am wrong.

BUNDY: He was a great man for nuclear bluster.

ALLISON: Sergei, did your father agree that an American invasion was imminent?

MIKOYAN: I think all the participants in the discussion agreed that the United States was preparing for the liquidation of the Castro regime.

SORENSEN: But I remember that your father referred to Richard Nixon's threats to Cuba at the time, even though Nixon wasn't then part of the government.* I recall that President Kennedy thought this showed a remarkable misunderstanding of the American government.

MIKOYAN: But there were invasion plans.

NYE: There was also a covert operation at the time code-named "Mongoose," whose aim was to destabilize or overthrow the Castro regime. I don't believe the public knew about it, but the Soviets certainly would have. Mac?

BUNDY: I remember that in the fall of '62 there was great frustration about Cuba and considerable confusion about what we should do. In my opinion, covert action is a psychological salve for inaction. We had no intention to invade Cuba, but it seems from what you say that there was a very solid picture in Moscow that we were going to do something more than we were.

McNAMARA: Let me say that we had *no* plan to invade Cuba, and I would have opposed the idea strongly if it ever came up.

SORENSEN: Well, that's the wrong word.

McNAMARA: Okay, we had no *intent*.

SHAKHNAZAROV: But there were subversive actions.

McNAMARA: That's my point. We thought those covert operations were terribly ineffective, and you thought they were ominous. We saw them very differently.[32]

---

* In September 1962, Richard Nixon called for a "quarantine" of Cuba to stem the flow of Soviet arms. At that time, Nixon did not know of the presence of MRBMs in Cuba.

NYE: That's an important point for our discussion of lessons. Small actions can be misperceived in important ways, with disproportionate consequences.

McNAMARA: That's absolutely right. I can assure you that there was no intent in the White House or in the Pentagon—or at least in my Pentagon—to overthrow Castro by force. But if I were on your side, I'd have thought otherwise. I can very easily imagine estimating that an invasion was imminent.

SHAKHNAZAROV: I did not wish to turn the meeting into reciprocal accusation. I am inclined to believe you had no plan. But surely this is very important for lessons.

. . . . .

GARTHOFF: I wish to reemphasize that there was no intention to invade Cuba, although in addition to covert operations there were military contingency plans prepared before the crisis, which were dusted off and available once the Soviet missiles came in. There were three operational plans, in fact, prepared in 1961—an air-strike plan, an invasion plan, and an invasion plan calling for the use of tactical nuclear weapons. And there were contingent military preparations taken after the large military buildup in Cuba in the summer of 1962. But before the October crisis these were nothing more than plans, and they did not reflect national political decisions. If the Soviet Union had a source of information to know these plans were there, they might have thought otherwise. But, even without knowing about these, there were good reasons for leaders in Moscow and Havana to think the United States was a threat to Castro's regime.

ALLISON: Just a footnote to that: the U.S. let it be known that there was going to be a military exercise in the Caribbean in the fall of '62 called "PHIBRIGLEX," in which the Marines were going to invade the mythical Republic of Vieques and liquidate a mythical dictator called Ortsac, which was Castro spelled backwards.

. . . . .

DAVID WELCH: I wonder if one of our Soviet colleagues could say something about relations with China and the role they played in the decision to deploy the missiles in Cuba? [A brief discussion in Russian followed between Allyn, Burlatsky, Mikoyan, and Shakhnazarov.]

. . . . .

MIKOYAN: Our common opinion is that there was absolutely no connection between the missiles and relations with Peking.

BURLATSKY: First of all, we did not inform the Chinese. As you know, Castro sometimes balanced between the Soviet Union and China. Maybe our action had some aspects which might bring him closer to the Soviet Union, but this was not the main reason. As you know, China criticized us during and after the crisis. Their view was that we made two mistakes: a strategic mistake and a tactical mistake. The strategic mistake was that we were wrong in placing missiles in Cuba. You remember that in his speech to Supreme Soviet, first of all, Khrushchev responded to Chinese accusations.[33]

NYE: . . . How could the Soviets believe they could keep this secret from the Americans, given the satellites and the reconnaissance planes? The construction of the missile sites was clumsy; they looked exactly like the missile sites we knew very well in the Soviet Union. You failed to camouflage them. It's hard to reconcile all of this with a desire to maintain secrecy. Some Americans have thought as a result that Khrushchev wanted us to discover the missiles in order to open up the bargaining. Why was this all so clumsy?

BURLATSKY: It is very simple. You know, we are a planned society, but not a real planning society. [Laughter.] It is very typical. We did nothing in the first hours of World War II, despite lots of information about an imminent German invasion.

McNAMARA: Sounds like another confirmation of McNamara's Law to me.

NYE: Were the organizations involved merely following their standard operating procedures?

MIKOYAN: Yes, the organizations involved were simply following their routines. It was not thought through.[34]

. . . . .

GARTHOFF: . . . Did [Khrushchev's message to Castro] include any exhortation that Cuban acceptance of the missiles would bolster socialism on the world scale, or that this sort of assistance was incumbent upon Cuba in return for the aid it had received from the socialist countries?

MIKOYAN: This was not mentioned in the letter from Khrushchev to Castro, but in November Mikoyan asked Castro why he had agreed, and he said he thought the Soviet Union had this in mind.[35]

. . . . .

MAY: . . . Where did Khrushchev go to get special information and evaluations of the United States? For example, Senator Keating had been warning of Soviet missiles in Cuba for a long time before they were photographed. Would Khrushchev have asked about Keating, and if so, who would he have gone to?

. . . . .

BURLATSKY: Dobrynin and Troyanovsky* were the two people he would probably have asked.

MIKOYAN: There are daily communications from the Embassy in Washington, and experts in Moscow who analyze statements in Congress, in the press, everything important in the States.

MAY: Yes, but were they getting it right?

MIKOYAN: The information from Dobrynin and the Embassy in Washington was compared with information in Moscow. But it was difficult for Moscow to get information on how the United States would react to the missiles in Cuba, because Dobrynin and the Embassy did not know about the plan and could not say anything about it.

NYE: That's another important lesson: the more secret the plan, the more you cut yourself off from your expertise. That's very interesting. Bill, you have the absolutely last question for this morning, and please make it brief.

URY: Fyodor, you mentioned earlier the importance of Khrushchev's personality. Imagine if Stalin or Brezhnev had been in charge at the time. First, would the missiles have been deployed in Cuba? Secondly, would they have been withdrawn?

BURLATSKY: Stalin was, let me say, a more rational man. More cruel—

MIKOYAN: *Much* more cruel. [Laughter.]

BURLATSKY: More cruel, but more rational. Stalin remembered Yalta, and I don't think it was likely he would have taken such an adventurous step. As for Brezhnev, he preferred to do nothing. Khrushchev preferred to do something. [Laughter.]

. . . . .

---

* Oleg Troyanovsky, present Soviet Ambassador to the People's Republic of China (and son of the first Soviet Ambassador to the United States), was in 1962 a foreign policy aide to Khrushchev. Having grown up in the U.S., Troyanovsky is fluent in English and was considered an expert on American affairs.

October 12, 1987—1 p.m.

NYE: All right, back to business. This afternoon, we are going to turn our attention to the conduct and resolution of the crisis. Mac, would you like to start us off by making a few remarks about these issues from the American side, and by posing some questions about things you would like to know about the conduct of the crisis on the Soviet side?

BUNDY: I'd be happy to. . . . The crucial moment, it seems to me, came on October 26, when we received that long but encouraging telegram—which we all assumed at the time had been written by Khrushchev himself—essentially proposing the terms on which we finally settled. Of all the communications in the crisis, this one seems to me to have been the most important. But there are a number of mysteries that surround it. First, why was it so long in coming? Apart from the time taken to translate it, there was some six to eight hours' delay between the time it was delivered to the Soviet telegraph office and its delivery in Washington. This seemed to raise a number of technical and political questions. It raised questions about the possibility that this personal communication and the proposal it contained were strongly opposed in the Soviet Union. This leads to the second question: What was the depth, meaning, and importance on the Soviet side of the second message, the one proposing the trade for the Jupiter missiles in Turkey?

The 27th was the crucial day on our side, without any doubt, and the timing of the letters seemed to us very important then. We were very confused by them. We wondered about the importance of the trade proposal; we wondered how important Dobrynin's message to Bobby Kennedy was on this question; we wondered how to interpret the Scali–Fomin messages in the light of it. What went on? What governed Soviet decisions from this point forward? Why the conflicting signals?

NYE: Would one of our Soviet colleagues care to respond, and would you like to put your own questions about the conduct of the crisis on the table?

BURLATSKY: There were alternative opinions about what to do among our leaders and advisors. Maybe Khrushchev thought for Soviet public opinion that it was important to do something for our defense in the conclusion of the crisis, especially having to do with the bases in Turkey. I believe he had information from Fomin that there was some possibility of concessions from the American side, but that is speculation.

. . . . .

WELCH: I have always presumed, as many people have, that the Foreign Ministry had a lot of input into the second message, but not the first. It would not have been normal practice for the more traditional diplomats in the Ministry to offer concessionary terms so quickly, and acting on the principle that you should always try to get as much out of a bargain as you possibly can, they may have persuaded Khrushchev to up the ante. That would certainly explain the differences between the two letters' terms, their tone, and possibly the timing as well. Does that sound right to any of you?

MIKOYAN: Well, it is speculation, but I think that is right. That was the old-style diplomacy: always save face; never give more than you must; never admit to a retreat.

SORENSEN: But why the second letter? Why after the first?

MIKOYAN: It was a big mistake, because we lost some face, for example, in the eyes of Castro, who was indignant that the second letter had turned Cuba into a bargaining chip.

BUNDY: It was the same with the Turks. [Laughter.]

MIKOYAN: But this was the old-style diplomacy.

BUNDY: But what of the first letter? We thought it was written by Khrushchev himself. Is that accurate?

BURLATSKY: Maybe he got new information between the two letters.

BUNDY: Well, yes, there *was* new information. There was the Lippmann column in *The Washington Post* proposing the trade just the day before.

BURLATSKY: I can tell you a story to explain the atmosphere of the second letter. It was prepared at Khrushchev's dacha thirty kilometers from Moscow. When the letter was finished, a man was dispatched with it to drive very quickly to the radio station. He was told to have it for transmission before three o'clock. They were very nervous.

BUNDY: You mean the letter on Sunday the 28th?

BURLATSKY: Yes, on the 28th of October.

BUNDY: That would be the final message.

MIKOYAN: At Radio Moscow there are six elevators in the building. Someone had telephoned ahead, and they reserved one elevator just for this letter to arrive.

. . . . .

ALLISON: Let me push Mac's question a little bit, and let me put it to Sergei and Fyodor. If you read the two letters, what would you think? Tommy Thompson thought for sure that the first letter was written by Khrushchev himself and that the second had been written by a committee. Is that correct? Do we know who was involved in the two letters?

. . . . .

BURLATSKY: I think they were done personally.

BUNDY: Who was working with him in the dacha at the time?

BURLATSKY: I believe it was Gromyko, Ilychev,* Malinovsky, maybe some others.

ALLISON: But, on Thursday, was Khrushchev alone?

. . . . .

MIKOYAN: We only can speculate. We have no information.

BURLATSKY: It was usual for Khrushchev to dictate all his letters personally, but somebody edited them, and maybe they would make it sound more liberal or not.

. . . . .

GARTHOFF: On the same question, do you have any thoughts on whether Khrushchev himself thought of raising the ante in the second letter, or were others urging him? We tend to think the latter, that a harder-line group was pushing him to demand the Turkish missile trade. I realize that you are unable to tell us exactly how the decision worked, but do you have any information?

BURLATSKY: I have a question in this connection. Maybe Bobby Kennedy or Scali gave some information, maybe not directly, but hinted that there might be some possibilities for trading missiles in Turkey?

BUNDY: We have no information to that effect. We certainly hadn't authorized anybody to do it. Scali was acting as an independent, but even then, he was pretty hard-line, so it's difficult to imagine him doing anything like that. The President himself decided not to make a public trade, but undertook to get them out, which was hard work. It involved a lot of secret, delicate negotiations. We needed to be very careful about our own public opinion.

. . . . .

---

* Leonid F. Ilychev, a member of the Communist Party Secretariat, was Khrushchev's ideological ally against Suslov but was never a Presidium member.

SORENSEN: Why Scali? Is there any information on why he was chosen?

BURLATSKY: *You* chose Scali.

BUNDY:*   No no, *Fomin* chose Scali.

BURLATSKY: I don't know, maybe Fomin had some information on Scali.

. . . . .

MAY: I want to back up a bit to the question of whether in the "private" week anyone had a sense that the Americans had caught on and something was happening? If not, then what was the reaction to the President's speech?

NYE: Sergei, do you want to field that one?

MIKOYAN: Nobody knew.

MAY: But a lot of people in Washington knew before the President's speech. I'm surprised that nobody knew in Moscow.

MIKOYAN: I doubt that Anatoly Dobrynin knew; otherwise, he would have informed Moscow.

. . . . .

NYE: Georgy, did you want to speak to this?

SHAKHNAZAROV: Well, I would later like to make some remarks.

NYE: Why don't you go ahead and make them now? Please, say whatever it was that you were going to say, and take as much time as you like.

SHAKHNAZAROV: Thank you very much.

First, let me say that in my conversation with Anatoly Dobrynin he expressed his desire to be with you all, though it was not possible. But we talked for a long time, and he said some things for your information. First, he told me that he did not know anything about the decision to send rockets to Cuba. To him, this was a surprise. He did not believe it when the State Department told it to him; he said, "It cannot be!" He was very surprised.

He also told me that the Turkish idea was born here in the Soviet Embassy, in a conversation, maybe with Robert Kennedy. It was suggested to Moscow, and then it came back—

---

* Shortly after this exchange, Bundy had to leave the conference for pressing business in New York. He returned the next day to attend the public events.

URY: Excuse me, did you say born in the Embassy, or born in a conversation with Americans?

SHAKHNAZAROV: I believe in conversation, maybe with Robert Kennedy or Dean Rusk. Anatoly Dobrynin got the impression from this conversation that this could serve as a basis for agreement. But this is for your own use, here in a secret meeting in a way like the Last Supper.[36] [Laughter.] . . . . .

Many of you can divide your careers into two parts—before and after the Cuban missile crisis—and it seems to me that we have to recall the words of Balzac: "History is falsified at the moment it is made." That is why I believe we shall never know all details. Everyone has his own image of the events—we believe this was so or this was not so—but there are certain objective conclusions which are important.

First, on causes. We talked very much of the surface causes. But the deep cause was American policy toward the U.S.S.R., socialist Cuba, and other socialist countries. The United States did not want to recognize others' rights to equal security. It desired to keep its superiority. I have already asked Bundy and others why the U.S. thought it was okay to surround the U.S.S.R. with bases, and why the U.S.S.R. had no such right. I have had no good answer, and according to international law, both sides have equal rights to make arrangements with third parties to protect their security.

Let me speak of the motives of the Soviet leadership. The main idea was to publicly attain military parity. At the time, the Soviet Union had no real parity with the United States. Even after the Cuban missile crisis there were lots of calculations on the American side, that the Soviet Union could destroy only up to 25 percent of the United States' population, and a reciprocal blow could destroy all of the Soviet Union. I believe there are certain plans based on such calculations, and I believe I could support it with facts.

McNAMARA: Excuse me, I didn't understand that point.

SHAKHNAZAROV: There was no real parity because there were circles in the United States who believed that war with the Soviet Union was possible and could be won. The damage to the United States would not be . . . unacceptable. . . . Therefore, there were plans for attacking the Soviet Union—such plans existed up to Geneva, where Ronald Reagan agreed with Gorbachev that it is impossible to wage and win a nuclear war.[37] Up to then, some Americans thought it possible. Even Secretary of State Alexander Haig thought there were things more awful than nuclear war.

McNamara: May I interrupt just for a second here? At the time of the Cuban missile crisis, did your leaders actually believe that some of us thought it would be in our interest to launch a first strike?

Shakhnazarov: Yes. That is why it seems to me Khrushchev decided to put missiles in Cuba. At some point, as Sergei Mikoyan said, we had no doubt the United States would repeat the attack on Cuba after the Bay of Pigs. I believe also that it is very important that one of Khrushchev's motives was in Tucker's new book on political leadership; that Khrushchev wanted to increase living standards by getting away from military expenditures.[38] He was trying for cheap parity. The crisis between the United States and the Soviet Union on parity was inevitable. If not here, there; if not now, then—but inevitable, because it dealt with the correlation of forces, which was basic to superpower relations. It was very appropriate that it happened in this time and place, because at that time in the Soviet Union there was an opinion that we were strong enough to assert parity. It was a mistake, but our leadership believed it was so.

Burlatsky: First step.

Shakhnazarov: Yes. The first step to strategic parity must be declared and also demonstrated.

Well, what are the arguments against this? One is that real parity and the real start to relaxation of tensions was ten years after the Cuban missile crisis. One explanation is that one leader was killed, one was ousted, and therefore there was a lack of leadership. But objective conditions also help explain this. Through great intensification of our efforts, the Soviet Union got real parity with the United States. This was one of the two most decisive factors, along with the . . . . . stagnation of the economy. We paid too high a price for parity.

Now I want to express that I do not want a unilateral position. We should speak as openly and internationally as possible. We cannot say Khrushchev's actions were . . . . . irreproachable. . . . He should have declared his intention and been prepared to negotiate with the United States. That is why I insist on a moral approach. In terms of political games, there was nothing wrong with it. But one of the most important lessons is that in the nuclear age it is impossible not to be honest and moral, because both sides are interested in survival.

One more question about the role of great people in crisis. We have reasons to give both Khrushchev and Kennedy credit for wisdom, but we have also reasons to give Castro credit for his wisdom, because Fidel understood, even though he was really insulted by certain developments and the lack of consultation.

MIKOYAN: He felt a little bit offended by lack of consultation before-hand, but of course, there was a lack of time.

SHAKHNAZAROV: He is a proud man, and emotional, but he put his prudence above his pride.

Another conclusion: after the Cuban missile crisis, it became much more important for us to consult with our allies. I don't know if it was the same with you, but in Eastern Europe it was feared that the Soviet Union might involve them in a nuclear war. Therefore, it was important to consult with our allies. I work now in the department responsible for consultation with friendly socialist parties, and when Gorbachev became General Secretary it became standard practice to discuss all arms issues with our allies. Now that an [INF] agreement is on the horizon, both the Soviet Union and the United States are sending representatives to each other's allies to negotiate.[39] Why did this discussion come only twenty-five years after the Cuban missile crisis? Because only just now is there parity.

My next point is connected with political leadership. I have just come from a meeting with American colleagues where we discussed this question. The final decision to use or not to use nuclear weapons, despite our different systems and consultations, relies with one man alone—one man alone with God, or Marx and Lenin, or his wife and children, and so on. One of my friend Burlatsky's successes is that for the first time for our political leadership he expressed in his play how Kennedy behaved at this time in his life. I have read Robert Kennedy's book, and I know others helped the President, but I know also the decision rested with him. Of course, it is very important for the President to have the proper man to advise him. I am quite sure if Franklin Roosevelt lived two or three years more, he would not have dropped atomic bombs on Hiroshima and Nagasaki. I have reason to think he might have done no more than demonstrate the power of the atomic weapon on a deserted island. But Truman did drop this bomb. He did not have enough experience, perhaps.

We have to ask if our political systems are well suited to survival in the nuclear era. In an interdependent world, we are interested that you choose a reliable leader, and you are interested that we choose a reliable leader. You have a certain part of our right, and we have a certain part of your right. I prefer experienced men. I believe, for example, that McNamara would be a good judge in such a situation. Let me say that I am disappointed that, in American election campaigns, candidates are not pressed on how they would behave in a nuclear crisis. This is very low on the list. They say much on the economy, on housing, and so on—all of these things are treated as much more important than how they would behave in a nuclear crisis. It is important to learn more about this.[40]

Now my next point. It is about the time needed to make the proper decision in a crisis. Kennedy and Khrushchev had time to think things over, to consult. Theoretically, they could have gone months, not just thirteen days. Today this would be impossible. This is very important. Maybe today they would have thirty minutes—

MIKOYAN: Six minutes.

SHAKHNAZAROV: —Maybe six minutes. It seems to me not people but machines will be making decisions. So we cannot rely on . . . nuclear deterrence. [Margaret] Thatcher still believes it is necessary, as do some people in the United States. But I don't believe anyone thinks the Soviet Union will invade Western Europe. We have enough problems. [Laughter.] On the contrary, we are in need of help from developed countries to improve our economies. This is one reason why we are strongly opposed to Strategic Defense Initiative. It will increase the danger of nuclear confrontation; it forces us down the path of military expenses.

My last point: I think we can conclude from the Cuban missile crisis that we have to establish more general levels of contacts. After the crisis, we established the hot line. Recently, there have been meetings between [George] Shultz and [Eduard] Shevardnadze, and there is now an agreement on crisis-prevention centers.[41] There is an invitation from our Defense Ministry to meet Caspar Weinberger,* and we hope there will be reciprocal meetings. But why not have meetings between advisors at high levels? Perhaps if Bundy, McNamara, and Sorensen had met with Mikoyan, Malinovsky, and Troyanovsky, maybe we would have avoided confrontation.

Mass media also have a very important role, because the Cuban missile crisis was not only a political conflict but also an ideological conflict. Maybe, I hope, it was the last conflict based on pre-nuclear political thinking. After it, we cannot allow ourselves to behave in this way. Now we must have a new way of thinking. There is too much risk in pre-nuclear political thinking in a nuclear era. Thank you very much.

NYE: Thank you, you've given us an awful lot to think about. Bob, you wanted to speak to those points?

MCNAMARA: Yes, let me comment on your very interesting remarks. I think you're right that the underlying cause of the crisis wasn't the deployment of missiles in Cuba but the basic tension—partly ideological—between the two blocs. Today, neither one of us understands this

---

* In 1987, Caspar Weinberger was U.S. Secretary of Defense.

tension very well. There is an immense amount of mistrust between our peoples and between our leaders—and I'm speaking of Democrats as well as Republicans. And this is not limited to the United States; many of our allies feel this mistrust as well. It's a fact, and it's caused us all an awful lot of trouble over the years.

You said at one point in your remarks, Georgy, that "surely no one believes the Soviet Union will invade Western Europe," or words to that effect. I don't believe it, and *you* don't believe it, but . . . it's just not the case that no one believes the Soviet Union will invade Western Europe. . . . How else can Americans view the Warsaw Pact–NATO conventional balance other than as a sign of aggression? Why do you need three times as many tanks, or whatever it is? Quite frankly, I know the answer: you're just as stupid as we are. [Laughter.]

BURLATSKY: Before, more than you; now, less than you. [Laughter.]

MCNAMARA: You've got people sitting over in your Defense Ministry, just as we do in the Pentagon, who buy all kinds of things you just don't need! And we perceive it over here as a clear sign of aggressive intent.

Now, I know all the millions of people you lost in World War II had a powerful effect on your policy. I realize that you aren't willing to suffer that again, and that you're determined to be prepared, so you never have to. But, nevertheless, people over here interpret your conventional strength differently, and it causes many of us to worry about you.

Now, let me say that at the time of Cuba the risks of inadvertence were very high. I can understand your worries about a first strike, given the balance at the time, though I can say with certainty that none of the seven Presidents I knew of ever thought of a first strike. But things such as our own strategic buildup, LeMay's remarks, the imbalance of five thousand warheads on our side to three hundred on yours—all of these influenced your behavior. But yours influenced ours as well, and to this day there is deep mistrust. . . .

To· the details: I have a couple of questions. First, I would like to ask, did the Soviets believe on Saturday the 27th that Bobby Kennedy had delivered an ultimatum?

. . . . .

BURLATSKY: It looked like an ultimatum, because Khrushchev was in a hurry with his answer. . . . . . At the same time, Robert told Dobrynin about the secret agreement on Jupiters.

MCNAMARA: That was on specific instructions from the President. Four or five of us were there in the room and we all agreed that Bobby should inform Dobrynin that the Jupiters would be withdrawn, though he shouldn't conclude a public deal to that effect. And by the way, right away I went back to the Pentagon and ordered them withdrawn, cut up, and photographed, so that I could personally see that those missiles had been destroyed.

LEBOW: When did you do that, Bob?

McNAMARA: I guess that was probably not until the 29th. But it was clear that Bobby was told to communicate that we had unilaterally agreed to withdraw the Turkish missiles, though not as part of a public deal.

BURLATSKY: And we understood this was your last concession. Therefore, Khrushchev was in a hurry on Sunday to reply. He was worried there might be something new—not necessarily an air strike, but perhaps some action.

MIKOYAN: There was a special leak of information to impress us with an imminent invasion. Was that correct, or was that disinformation?[42]

McNAMARA: It wasn't necessarily disinformation. Bobby was told to impress Dobrynin, there's no doubt about that, but I can guarantee that Kennedy had neither decided to invade Cuba nor decided *not* to invade Cuba. He hadn't made up his mind at that point what he would do next.

MIKOYAN: How is that possible?

McNAMARA: The advisors were divided, and he kept his options open. Many of the advisors who recommended the air strike believed that it would be so imperfect that it would have to be followed up by a land invasion. The alternatives were an air strike and invasion, or some other kind of action. By Saturday, the tension had really increased and there was a tremendous sense of urgency. I don't know if we've ever had a military man as wise and as able as Maxwell Taylor—he always displayed terrific judgment and professionalism to me—but Taylor was *absolutely convinced* that we had to attack Cuba. The pressure was on. . . .

NYE: . . . Uncertainty has two dimensions. First, there is the uncertainty from a split in opinion over what to do. This is the uncertainty that is associated with a rational process of deliberation that is not yet complete. Second, there is an uncertainty that is captured by Khrushchev's rope analogy;[43] that things are getting out of control, that if another plane is shot down it may no longer be possible to avoid a series of events that lead to unintended and unwanted escalation. Which type of uncertainty was important to Khrushchev on Sunday when he was in a hurry to settle? In other words, was he more worried that Kennedy would make a rational decision to escalate or that things were spinning out of control?

MIKOYAN: I think he had a definite impression that invasion would follow. I don't know exactly why.

. . . . .

SHAKHNAZAROV: What would have been the next step if we had not withdrawn the missiles?

. . . . .

MCNAMARA: It's a big question, and it's a good one. As I see it, we had three options. First, we could have gone ahead with the air strike and the invasion. To my mind, this was not terribly likely, but it was still an option which was on the table. Second, we could have opted for a negotiated solution that was closer to the open trade of the Jupiters proposed in Khrushchev's second letter. I say "closer to," because I'm convinced that if the President had opted for the trade, it would have been packaged in such a way as to allow each side to represent it whichever way was necessary for its own political purposes. On our side, it would probably have been represented roughly in the way Bobby represented it to Dobrynin: something we were going to do anyway, and not something the Soviets forced us to do to get their missiles out of Cuba. Third—and this was the most likely option, to my mind—we could have tightened the quarantine, what I call "turning the screw," by adding a number of other items to the prohibited materials list, such as oil and petroleum products. That option was still open as well.

SHAKHNAZAROV: But how is that an alternative? Still Kennedy would have to choose another action sometime.

GARTHOFF: The point was that adding POL to the quarantine was just another step that could have been taken to try to get the missiles out through further negotiations rather than attack—

SHAKHNAZAROV: So invasion was still inevitable?

MCNAMARA: Well, not necessarily. It's possible that a turning of the screw might have done the trick. It's also possible that the President would have settled on something like the missile trade. Invasion was not inevitable, though it was a possibility. To my mind, it was highly unlikely.

. . . . .

BURLATSKY: From my own point of view, the question in Khrushchev's mind was not: What is the next concrete action of John Kennedy? Rather, he felt from the beginning, once the Americans discovered the missiles, that we must end this crisis peacefully with the maximum possible result for us. There are two different things: the maximum possible result for Cuba, and the maximum possible result for us. Therefore, maybe he was not so afraid about the next American action, since he used these possibilities to end the crisis, especially because there was a very nervous atmosphere in the Politburo and he worried about his authority. And therefore, from my personal point of view, when Robert Kennedy told Dobrynin that there will be this decision soon, it was quite enough for Khrushchev. He wasn't worried about Americans bombing Cuba, and because our soldiers were there he would have to do something, and there would be a war. He had decided that it was enough. Therefore, he used these possibilities as a reason to end the crisis. He wasn't afraid of concrete action.

. . . . .

ALLISON: I'd be very interested in hearing what you say about what Khrushchev says in his memoirs about Robert Kennedy's meeting with Dobrynin—and I'm also interested in hearing what Dobrynin might think about this. Khrushchev wrote: "Robert Kennedy looked exhausted. One could see from his eyes that he had not slept for days. He himself said that he had not been home for six days and nights. 'The President is in a grave situation,' Robert Kennedy said, 'and he does not know how to get out of it. We are under very severe stress. In fact, we are under pressure from our military to use force against Cuba. . . . Even though the President himself is very much against starting a war over Cuba, an irreversible chain of events could occur against his will. That is why the President is appealing directly to Chairman Khrushchev for his help in liquidating the conflict. If the situation continues much longer, the President is not sure that the military will not overthrow him and seize power. The American Army could get out of control.' "[44]

MIKOYAN: This is not Dobrynin; it is Khrushchev's fantasy.

. . . . .

BURLATSKY: It is not fantasy. I did not know this was in Khrushchev's memoirs, but it is the same in my play.

McNAMARA: But where did you get it from?

BURLATSKY: I got it from your books, from Robert Kennedy's book—[There followed a twenty-second discussion in Russian, as well as a simultaneous discussion in English in which several participants registered their disagreement, noting that no references to a possible coup or a loss of civilian control over the military may be found in the standard American accounts of the meeting.] But I used the very same sentence in my play.

MIKOYAN: It was your imagination, Fyodor. [Laughter.]

BURLATSKY: Maybe Andropov* said something to me from Khrushchev's memoirs, I am not sure. But I believe that Robert Kennedy said something like this to Dobrynin.

SORENSEN: Is it correct, in your view, that there was a danger of a coup by the American military?

BURLATSKY: No, but—

MIKOYAN: But perhaps this was used by Robert Kennedy to impress Dobrynin. That is possible.

SORENSEN: Exactly. Here we are twenty-five years later, talking about two conversations—one between Robert Kennedy and Dobrynin, and one between Dobrynin and Khrushchev—conversations involving three men who aren't here. All three of them were anxious to end the crisis. All three of them had motives to exaggerate and paint a dire picture—not that it had to be painted much more dire than it actually was.

My recollection differs somewhat from Bob McNamara's when he states that by the 27th there was a preponderance of opinion in the ExComm in favor of the air strike and invasion.[45] I would agree that those voices were on the rise, but I do not believe that the President would have gone the air-strike route within two days, as Robert reportedly told Dobrynin he would. If Robert had said the following, he would not have been exaggerating at all: "The situation is extremely serious. It is difficult for the President to keep the situation from getting out of control, and his advisors are increasingly inclined toward military action against Cuba. The ExComm will meet tomorrow morning to discuss a series of important issues: what to do about our surveillance, and what to do if any more of our reconnaissance planes are shot down; what to do about the [Soviet ship] *Grozny*, which was moving toward the quarantine line; what to do about further military preparations for different contingencies. Therefore, we need an answer from your government, and we need it before we meet at nine tomorrow morning, which just so happens to be 3:00 p.m., Moscow time." That, to my

---

* Yuri Andropov, Soviet General Secretary, November 1982 to February 1984.

mind, would give Khrushchev plenty of reason to rush an answer by that deadline.

. . . . .

GARTHOFF: I would like to ask our Soviet colleagues whether they had any other sources of information than Robert Kennedy? In his speech to the Supreme Soviet, Khrushchev refers to very precise warnings of air strikes in forty-eight hours—one from Cuba, one from the United States, and possibly a third. Can you illuminate the basis on which Khrushchev might have decided he had only a matter of hours? It has always been unclear what additional reinforcing warnings there were.

. . . . .

BURLATSKY: I, too, have a question on details. I don't remember exactly, but it may be that Dobrynin informed Khrushchev that Robert told him John Kennedy was going to pray before he made his decision, and this had a big effect on Khrushchev. Is this possible, or not?

WELCH: It's certainly possible.

ALLISON: I don't recollect any reference to that, though.

URY: Why is that important?

MIKOYAN: Because it shows that Kennedy's decision might be his last.

. . . . .

SORENSEN: I'd like to go back and look at the days between President Kennedy's speech and the resolution of the crisis, and I'd like to ask Fyodor, Sergei, and Georgy what outside influences were brought to bear on the Kremlin's decisionmaking during this period of time. For example, did the UN's pleas make any difference to the way Khrushchev handled things? Did the fact that the OAS had unanimously backed the American blockade make any difference? In the record of our own decisions, it's clear that world opinion more generally figured heavily in President Kennedy's evaluation of his options. Did this make any difference in the Kremlin at all?

. . . . .

BURLATSKY: The first influence was from Castro. We had to research his view and accept something of his advice. The second was from the Eastern European countries—not at the beginning, but during the crisis there were contacts between Khrushchev and the leaders of these countries, necessarily. The third influence was China, and this was not a good influence, but Khrushchev had to react to Chinese criticism. Next was the United Nations. Khrushchev tried to use U Thant as a mediator, but we lost that possibility during the crisis. What about world opinion? Maybe it was not so important at that time for Khrushchev because there was an escalating situation and he was more worried about the fate of our two countries.

SORENSEN: But Castro always complained that no one listened to him.

MIKOYAN: That is not correct.

BURLATSKY: We did not *agree*— [Laughter.]

MIKOYAN: On some points we did not agree, on some we did.

BURLATSKY: —But we had close contacts with Castro throughout.

MIKOYAN: Without his approval, for example, we could not get those missiles physically out of Cuba.

SORENSEN: But, during that week, was Castro worried about an American invasion or not?

MIKOYAN: He was in close contact with Alekseev, and he was not ignored. His opinion was always sought. Castro said to U Thant, to Alekseev, to Mikoyan—he said to them all, "You don't know the Americans. We know them better. Any agreement with them is just paper. When they agree not to invade, then they will start to pile on conditions, one by one. So you must be hard with the Americans. They only understand the language of force."

SORENSEN: Some here said that of *you*. [Laughter.]

MIKOYAN: Well, you must decide if that is correct or not. [Laughter.]

BURLATSKY: Castro was concerned only with the language of force.

SHAKHNAZAROV: Yes, Castro thought that after the withdrawal there would be an invasion. He only agreed after he got assurances.

MIKOYAN: And one condition was that one Soviet brigade would remain on the island as a guarantee.

GARTHOFF: That was the brigade that caused all the embarrassment in the Carter Administration, which didn't realize it had been in Cuba all along.[46]

SHAKHNAZAROV: But, you know, Castro thought well of Kennedy personally afterward.

SORENSEN: What about the OAS? Did that make any difference?

MIKOYAN: No, I don't think so. We saw it as a machine in American hands. So it was not, from our point of view, very important.

. . . . .

MAY: Could you speak a little bit more about consultations with the East Europeans, and especially with the Germans, who I imagine felt they had more at stake here than most of the others?

BURLATSKY: During the Cuban missile crisis, I am not sure when, our Ambassadors informed the leaders of Eastern European countries about our communications with the United States. Many were very worried about escalation, especially Kádár;* and their opinion had influence on Khrushchev.

MIKOYAN: U Thant was very important also. He came to Havana and spoke with Castro. He persuaded Fidel that the agreement would be met. Fidel liked him and believed him, though he did not believe you. He thought that U Thant had good intentions.

BURLATSKY: Many years later, you know, Castro told one of our leaders that Khrushchev was right.

MIKOYAN: Castro's prediction that the Americans would pile on conditions was also right. First, the agreement was that we would remove the missiles only; then [Adlai] Stevenson wrote a letter to my father demanding that we remove the [Il-28] bombers also, and the torpedo boats, and so on. Castro was correct, and it looked to him like the Americans were trying to get out of the agreement.

SORENSEN: Well, that's a question we'll get back to. Our agreement referred to "offensive weapons." We never said missiles only.

MIKOYAN: But the torpedo boats were there before, and the bombers were not the reason for the crisis. The missiles were the reason for the crisis. The bombers and the torpedo boats were added later. My father had to persuade Fidel in parts. First, he had to persuade Fidel to let the missiles go; then he had to persuade him to let the bombers go. Castro was furious! He said to my father, "I told you so!"

NYE: Sergei, last night at dinner we talked about the sense in which the crisis wasn't over on Sunday, and you were in Havana then, isn't that right? Do you want to talk about your experience?

---

* János Kádár, Hungarian Premier, 1956–65; Party First Secretary, 1956–88.

MIKOYAN: The day before we arrived, Castro had laid out his five conditions.* At the airport, without consulting with Moscow, Mikoyan hailed those five conditions, though he knew not all of them would hold. Castro was still angry. He did not want to meet my father at the airport. Alekseev had to persuade Castro to meet my father at the airport, not as a representative of the U.S.S.R., but as his old friend. The talks were very difficult. I still maintain that Sunday was not the very end of the conflict, because Fidel had to be convinced of the necessity to take out other armaments as well as missiles. Some of them were part of *his* army. We had given them to him, and now we had to take them back.

[Seymour Hersh's] article in *The Washington Post*, I should say, is very foolish. I absolutely exclude the possibility of any military confrontation between Castro's army and Soviet troops. It is an impossibility. But the talks were very difficult. Some days, Fidel refused to talk. One day, Mikoyan was to talk with Fidel, and he found out that Fidel went to an agrarian project rather than negotiate, and he would not come back. My father once met with Antonio Núñez Jiménez† and said to him, "Maybe I should go home and get someone else to talk with Fidel. I am not succeeding." But when he heard this, Fidel came right back and continued the talks.

The question of inspection was very important. Where and how would the removal of the missiles be inspected? Fidel refused any inspection on his land, but this was an American condition in the agreement. It was necessary to find a way out. By the way, in 1983, Ronald Reagan declared that since inspection was not carried out, therefore the agreement was not in force.[47] But this was not correct. There was inspection of our ships as they left Cuba, and this inspection was proposed to my father by McCloy‡ in New York, because Fidel's refusal was well known. So there was a kind of blind alley; but still the agreement is valid, because there was a form of inspection proposed by McCloy presumably with the Administration's agreement.

NYE: Bob, did you want to comment on that?

---

* Castro's five conditions for complying with the U.S.–Soviet agreement were: (1) that the U.S. lift the naval quarantine; (2) that the U.S. lift its economic blockade of Cuba; (3) that the U.S. discontinue "subversive activities and piratical attacks"; (4) that the U.S. cease violating Cuban airspace and territorial waters; and (5) that the U.S. shut down its naval base at Guantánamo.
† Antonio Núñez Jiménez was head of the Cuban Agrarian Reform Institute, and was also a close confidant of Fidel Castro. A long-standing member of the Cuban Communist Party, he served for many years as a bridge between Cuba and the U.S.S.R.
‡ John Jay McCloy, chairman of the President's General Advisory Committee on Arms Control and Disarmament.

McNAMARA: First, let me say that I don't think any Administration can just walk away from the basic terms of the agreement. The crisis was settled on terms satisfactory to both sides, and we were satisfied that the missiles had been taken out. But, having said that, I don't think the inspection as it was carried out was thought of as a substitute for the original inspection; isn't that right, Ted?

SORENSEN: That's right, I agree.

McNAMARA: We told McCloy to find a way with Mikoyan to inspect as best we could under the circumstances. But you know, since we didn't have ground inspection, there were people like Keating who were insisting as late as in December that the missiles were still there! That part of the agreement had not been fulfilled—

MIKOYAN: But that is dangerous.

McNAMARA: I agree it's dangerous to say there's no agreement not to invade, but it's interesting to my mind that Ronald Reagan put out feelers to test the agreement.

MIKOYAN: Wayne Smith tells in his last book, *The Closest of Enemies*, that William Clements from Texas insisted in 1983 and 1984 that there was no agreement.[48]

SORENSEN: But in the Nixon Administration, in 1970, I believe, it *was* decided that there was a de facto agreement.

GARTHOFF: That's right, it was in connection with Cienfuegos. It was the first affirmation of the agreement. This question is dealt with in detail in my book.[49]

MIKOYAN: Not the first. In 1963, just after the funeral of John Kennedy, Mikoyan talked with President Johnson, who reaffirmed the agreement to him. Each new Administration repeated this. So it is very strange that this Administration made an attempt to repudiate it, but it is good that after 1984 there was no further attempt.

NYE: Do you have any other reflections on the *Post* article, Sergei?

MIKOYAN: Do you mean about the U-2?

NYE: Yes, for example, or anything else.

MIKOYAN: This is, I believe, an instance of how a misunderstanding of one or another commander can lead to conflict, or to a perception of conflict. Fidel ordered his antiaircraft forces and his antiaircraft missile units to shoot at everything, but his missiles could only reach to a height of about eleven thousand meters.* They could not reach the U-2s. But our missiles in Cuba could reach them, and our troops did not know what to do. There is an impression that one of our commanders saw the U-2 on radar, and he had only two minutes' warning and had to decide quickly what to do. But the story in the *Post* is absolutely false.

URY: But if there were no orders for the Soviet forces to shoot down the U-2, then why was there a predicament at the SAM site?

BURLATSKY: I don't believe there was a direct order from Moscow—

MIKOYAN: No, there was no order.

BURLATSKY: —But I don't believe our soldiers shot down the plane unauthorized. Khrushchev was *so* concerned to be careful.

MIKOYAN: But there is no guarantee a commander in the field cannot do something without orders.

NYE: Let's stick just on this question for a minute, because it's central to the questions of lessons and the risks of the unexpected. Let's see if we can nail it down, because it's a very important episode. It relates very directly to theories of how crises escalate and how conflicts begin.
    A question for Fyodor: Can commanders do things without orders? You say that's not likely. But how did the plane come down?

MIKOYAN: Under conditions where Moscow and Washington were very anxious not to do anything, and when commanders don't know what to do, *anything* can happen.

BURLATSKY: But why then was there only one shot down? There were so many flying over Cuba

McNAMARA: There were very few U-2s, at most an average of one flight per day.

GARTHOFF: Though there were four to eight low-level reconnaissance flights each day.

NYE: But was this plane shot down by Cubans, or by Soviets? Sergei says the Cubans didn't have missiles capable of doing it.

MIKOYAN: Fidel said that his missiles could only reach eleven thousand meters, and he said he could not shoot it down.

---

* [Raymond Garthoff notes:] Mikoyan's reference to SAMs owned and wholly controlled by Cubans is puzzling. It was thought at the time, and is thought today, that Cuba had only antiaircraft artillery, which would not have been capable of hitting aircraft at an altitude of eleven thousand meters. [See Afterword.]

BURLATSKY: But I researched this for my play. The Soviet commanders in Cuba had orders *not* to shoot, and did not shoot. Khrushchev was shocked when he found out about it. Why was only one plane shot down?

SHAKHNAZAROV: Let me tell you a story about my experience in the war with big guns. We had some 152-mm guns, and one day we were attacked by German tanks. I ordered my battery to fire, but we were by a garden, and there were branches in front of us, so our soldiers loaded blank shells. But a real shell was loaded by accident, and when it hit the branches, the shrapnel scattered and injured several men. Nobody knows what a soldier will do under stress.

NYE: But there is a third possibility here: the Cubans could have gotten control of a missile that could go high enough to hit a U-2. That is what this Hersh article suggests may have happened. It is based on an intercepted transmission from a Soviet base at Banes indicating fighting and casualties at the Los Angeles SAM site. Now, if the Cubans had taken control of that SAM site and had shot down the U-2, it would be perfectly consistent with the claim that Soviet troops had orders not to shoot.

ALLISON: Sergei, your father was in Havana immediately after this alleged event. Did he hear nothing about it?

MIKOYAN: Absolutely never. I don't believe there was any conflict between our troops and Cuban troops.

. . . . .

SHAKHNAZAROV: It does not matter who shot it down. Khrushchev chose to end the crisis right away—

MIKOYAN: I believe it was shot down by Soviet troops, but the man who did it would not confess, and he was never found.

McNAMARA: . . . I have no difficulty at all believing that the officers at that Soviet SAM site in Cuba had been instructed not to shoot down the U-2 on that particular day. But it could have been just like the KAL 007 incident four years ago; no one ordered that Soviet pilot to shoot down a civilian airliner over Kamchatka.[50] Almost certainly the pilot didn't know at the time that he was killing civilians. These mistakes happen. The likelihood of accident and error is *very* high in a crisis situation, and we must take account of that fact. It could happen as easily with a nuclear weapon as it did with that U-2, and we've got to keep these things in mind.

ALLISON: But, Bob, the guy who shot down 007 was identified and punished. We know which SAM site shot the U-2 down—

MIKOYAN: But we did not know who did it.

ALLISON: But we know the site, so presumably we could find out who did it.

MIKOYAN: I only found out much later from a conversation—not necessarily a reliable conversation—that it was a Soviet acting without orders. He had never confessed it, because he was afraid of punishment. [Several voices at once asked for details of the conversation.] I should not talk about the conversation any more than that, because it is not necessarily reliable, and the person is still alive.

NYE: Yes, I think we can leave it at that and respect Sergei's judgment on that point. It's very interesting and helpful as is, and it reaffirms the theory that accidents can happen and that they can have momentous consequences.*

Bob, you said before the break that you had a couple of questions, and you only got one of them in. Would you like to ask your second question now?

McNAMARA: Yes, I suppose so, because my second question deals with this tangentially. Did the Soviets ever worry about a nuclear exchange in the event of an American air strike and invasion?

BURLATSKY: Excuse me, do you mean a strike on the Soviet homeland?

McNAMARA: Well, initially, a launch from Cuba. And if there was a launch of a Soviet missile from Cuba, how did Moscow think we would respond?

BURLATSKY: In my opinion, Cuba was not a casus belli for a nuclear war between the Soviet Union and the United States.

MIKOYAN: But there were Russian troops and missiles in Cuba. How could there not be a response to an American attack?

BURLATSKY: A response, perhaps, but not an atomic blow.

SHAKHNAZAROV: I'm not so sure.

McNAMARA: The reason I ask is that I don't believe at the time your warheads were fitted with permissive action links, and I believe it was physically possible for your people in Cuba to arm and launch a missile with or without orders from Moscow.

Early in the Kennedy Administration, we set out to reduce the risks of inadvertent nuclear war, and we introduced PALs on most of our

---

* For further information on the shoot-down, see Afterword, pp. 338–40.

nuclear weapons. These were mechanical or electronic locks that only opened after the proper code was inserted, and so only the President, who kept the code, could order the warheads armed. The reason for this was that it was the conventional wisdom among our military that, even though our forces were highly disciplined, it was not unlikely that, in the event of war, some troops would use the nuclear weapons under their control rather than allow them to be overrun. During the Cuban missile crisis, I was concerned that your troops or Cuban troops would feel the same way, and if you didn't have PALs on your warheads down there, some second lieutenant could start a nuclear war. Didn't this concern you at all?

MIKOYAN: I agree that such a possibility existed.

NYE: Wait a minute: were there nuclear warheads in Cuba? We had a lengthy debate about this in March at Hawk's Cay. American intelligence never confirmed the presence of Soviet warheads in Cuba, and there were several people there who said they were absolutely convinced Khrushchev would not have sent any warheads in. Were they there, or were they not?

MIKOYAN: Warheads were in Cuba, surely.

BURLATSKY: I'm not so sure. Who told you?

MIKOYAN: Well, it would be senseless to have the missiles there but no warheads.

TAUBMAN: No, it wouldn't. It could have been a bluff.

MIKOYAN: But look at the logic. There would be no point—

LEBOW: Not necessarily; if we believed there were warheads there, then you would have had the deterrent value of the missiles.

MIKOYAN: I am sure there were warheads there.

BURLATSKY: But why? This is your subjective opinion. This is your view of what is logical only. I am sure we did *not* have warheads in Cuba.

McNAMARA: If you didn't have warheads there, you'd suffer all the same costs and run all the same risks.

NYE: There's one risk they wouldn't run, though, Bob, and that is the risk of an inadvertent nuclear launch.

McNAMARA: That's true, yes.

NYE: And besides, sending missiles without warheads would be perfectly sensible if you were really interested in trying to get a trade.

BURLATSKY: I am sure we had no warheads. The reasons are very simple. Nobody knew when the missiles would be operational, and there were risks that the Americans would discover them and that there would be an invasion. If the missiles were not ready to use, it would be very bad to have warheads there. You must look at Khrushchev's psychology. He did not put all his cards on the table. He took risks, but not more than he had to take. It would be a big risk to send both missiles and warheads. I had some conversations at that time, and I was told that warheads were *not* there. This was to be the *second* step. If the Americans agreed to the presence of our missiles, *then* warheads would go there. I don't know where Sergei gets his information that warheads were there.*

MIKOYAN: Well, it was just my logic. It is in very good company—with McNamara's. [Laughter.]

NYE: Georgy?

SHAKHNAZAROV: Let me comment on the interesting hypothetical by McNamara. I don't agree with my friend Burlatsky that Cuba was not a *casus belli* between the Soviet Union and the United States. His approach is too logical, and there is no precise answer. Sometimes it was recognized that the United States would defend only some countries with nuclear forces. If the Soviet Union attacked Brazil, would you think of using nuclear forces? Why do you suppose if the United States attacked Cuba with nuclear forces we would not have to respond? If the United States attacked Cuba with conventional forces only, then maybe there would not necessarily be a Soviet nuclear response.

McNAMARA: I don't think we're discussing the same point, but I agree that if the United States attacked conventionally, the Politburo probably would not have authorized a nuclear response. So that's not the danger. But what about the second lieutenant? What about the risk of inadvertent nuclear strikes?

BURLATSKY: It would not be possible. There is military control, and elaborate protections against this.

SHAKHNAZAROV: In general, is your question: Can a commander start a nuclear war?

McNAMARA: The question is not can this happen today, but could this have happened then? Our commanders in the field could have started a nuclear war if they wanted to, because we didn't have PALs.

_____
* See Afterword, pp. 335–36.

. . . . .

GARTHOFF: Back to the question of warheads in Cuba, for a minute—
there is an important lesson in it. We had no hard information that
there were warheads in Cuba, though by the third day we saw the
construction of warhead storage facilities. On the other hand, we
couldn't be certain we would detect the arrival of warheads and we had
to assume that they were there already, for the sake of prudence. There
was intelligence, however, that there were warheads en route, and that
they were on a ship a couple of days out of Cuba, but the ship, the
Poltava, stopped and turned back. That didn't make any difference to
American actions in Washington, but it would be virtually certain that
on the 23rd or 24th the Soviet leadership would find out exactly what
was on the island: forty-two of forty-eight SS-4s, at least half the SS-5s
en route, and warheads en route though not yet in Cuba. This would
look to them like an awful lot more than a coincidence. The timing of
the quarantine would look as though it were designed directly to interdict
the shipment of the warheads. So it may be nothing more than speculation, but Khrushchev may have thought we intended to interdict the
warheads and that we had done so in time. Our perception was the
opposite. We had no direct evidence of nuclear weapons yet in Cuba,
but prudence required that we had to assume the missile warheads were
there. This may have been a clear case of how differences in information
lead to differences in perceptions and interpretations of events. And,
by the way, this all supports the view that Khrushchev had intended to
arm the missiles eventually, though it is also consistent with the judgment
that the warheads were not there when the quarantine went up.

. . . . .

LEBOW: Just on that, there is a very interesting report of this in the
Cuba history prepared for McGeorge Bundy after the crisis. It discusses
a difference of opinion within the intelligence community with respect
to this question of whether the warheads were on the way. There was
information suggesting that warheads had been loaded on the *Poltava*
in Odessa. The ship left for Cuba with a false manifest and having
declared for a false destination, Algeria. Out in the Atlantic, it made a
rendezvous with three submarines from the Soviet Northern Fleet, and
then proceeded on toward Cuba. On October 24, when the quarantine
was declared, it stopped and headed back to the Soviet Union.[51]

GARTHOFF: By the way, to the best of our knowledge, this was the
only ship to rendezvous with Soviet submarines on the high seas.

LEBOW: I have some follow-up questions, and these are relevant to a number of current debates in the United States today. First, in the ExComm during the crisis, and more generally afterward, there was a debate about what the Soviet reaction would have been to an American air strike on the missiles in Cuba. Now, you've suggested that there would have been no nuclear response to an American conventional strike, but there were groups in the United States who believed it very likely that there would be a response in kind against the Jupiter missiles in Turkey, or some other reaction in Europe, possibly in Berlin, and that this would lead to an escalation eventually resulting in a nuclear war. On the other hand, there were people like Maxwell Taylor and Paul Nitze who thought that the Soviet Union would have done nothing precisely because of the strategic imbalance. What's your sense of the likely Soviet response?

Second, on the Soviet strategic buildup in the years after the crisis: did this indicate a decision following the Cuban missile crisis to augment the balance? Was there a direct link between this decision and the events of the crisis itself?

. . . . .

BURLATSKY: First, let me comment on *Poltava*. If you had such excellent spies, why did you not know about the warheads in Cuba? This supports my conclusion that there were no warheads there. Of course, I do not know anything in particular about *Poltava*.

Second, to answer your question of what would have happened if the Americans had made an air strike on Cuba, let me say that, in my opinion, it would be a very difficult question in the Soviet Union. What would be the answer? I don't know exactly the alternatives, but there are many possibilities, and probably many advisors would argue for each of them—blockade Berlin, bomb Turkey, and so on—but in my opinion, one of the reasons why Khrushchev was in such a hurry to answer is that there was no *effective* alternative.

LEBOW: Why is that? Because of the consequences of escalation?

BURLATSKY: Cuba is so far away; we would have to open up a new theater elsewhere. Escalation might get out of control. It was a real risk. That is why there was no effective answer. It is one reason why, in my opinion, Khrushchev was in a hurry to compromise.

Why, after this terrible shock for both sides, did we continue the arms race? It is a very important question. I believe it was not Khrushchev's decision. I believe it was done by the next leadership as an answer to American activities. We lost a good chance to stop the arms race after the Cuban missile crisis together. These are military games—nobody knows why we are doing it. If you ask the physicists, they will tell you that it is not possible to stop modernizing technology. But I am not so sure; I believe that, after Kennedy's death and Khrushchev's ouster, our two countries lost a good chance to reduce arms.

NYE: This technical detail is an interesting one. Some American analysts think that the decision to build up the Soviet arsenal was taken after Cuba, whereas others, such as Michael MccGwire, argue that it was taken before Cuba, in response to the American buildup.[52] Do you have any idea which is right?

BURLATSKY: It was all action and reaction. When you build up, we build up. Only once were we original; that was with the SS-20, without big success. [Laughter.] But, you know, we had a very deep complex after our war with the Germans. For us it was like your Pearl Harbor. Our politicians and a majority of our people think we have to be prepared, so we react to every American move. Maybe with Gorbachev we begin with our own military and political strategy.

. . . . .

MIKOYAN: My own response to the question about the reaction to an American air strike is different from Burlatsky's. In my own opinion, it would be impossible not to respond somehow. I knew Khrushchev very well, and I met him at home many times, and I think I understand his nature and his perception of the prestige of our country. For both reasons, in my opinion, we could not swallow an air strike without a very strong reply. I do not know where or how; but I do not think we would do nothing.

McNAMARA: As a clarification, I didn't hear Burlatsky say you would do *nothing*. Both of you, I think, are suggesting that in your opinion *some* military action was likely.

MIKOYAN: Maybe I am wrong, but his last statement was that there was no effective answer—

BURLATSKY: *Effective* answer, yes.

McNAMARA: There might very well have been no effective answer, but that doesn't mean there would be no answer at all. I understand you to be saying two things, Fyodor: first, if we'd killed Soviet soldiers, you'd have to respond; second, since there was no very good response, that's why Khrushchev hurried to compromise—to avoid an attack, so that no Soviet soldiers would be killed.

BURLATSKY: That is right, in my opinion. All options were very bad for us, you understand.

McNAMARA: They were all bad for us, too. [Laughter.]

NYE: You might say there are two dangers here, or that two things might cause you a good deal of worry: first, the possibility that the opponent has a winning move; and second, that you have no good options. It seems that the second was felt on both sides. Bill?

TAUBMAN: We talked a bit about the hurry on the 28th; but what about the hurry on the 26th? Khrushchev's response to Kennedy's speech on the 22nd was initially very strong; why did he offer such a conciliatory deal so soon afterwards?

NYE: Sergei, do you have an answer to that?

MIKOYAN: On the 25th, there was rapid construction on the medium-range missiles with camouflage.*

TAUBMAN: That just adds to my point. What's the answer to the question?

BURLATSKY: The rope was being pulled back and forth. The knot was being pulled tighter and tighter. We looked for a good compromise, and if we found one, it's enough. It's usual in a conversation.

TAUBMAN: But why not go on for a couple of days?

BURLATSKY: We do not know everything Khrushchev was hearing from the United States. Maybe communications were not working well; maybe there were distortions through the links in the chain of communication. We did not know the relations between John Kennedy's advisors; we did not know what Kennedy was thinking. Also, of course, we do not know what Khrushchev was thinking, and therefore we can only imagine. We do not have full information. Maybe we will know during Gorbachev's time.

. . . . .

October 12, 1987—6 p.m.

NYE: I think we should start . . . because Georgy Shakhnazarov has to leave soon, and we want to make sure he has an opportunity to give us his final reflections. What we want to talk about in this last segment are

* [Mikoyan adds:] But when Khrushchev learned about the U.S. preparations for an invasion against the island, he and all his colleagues decided to act in a different way.

the lessons of the Cuban missile crisis, and we also want to make sure we say anything that we'd intended to say earlier but didn't get the chance to mention. Georgy, if you'd like to make some remarks from the Soviet side, I'll ask Bob McNamara to do the same from the American side before we have a more general discussion.

SHAKHNAZAROV: Thank you very much. Earlier, I tried to say something about this unsystematically, and I will try to say something better in an article for you. But I believe we should do this for all contemporary issues, because it is very important and very useful.

This discussion was very important not only because so many scholars are trying to understand the Cuban missile crisis. It is also important because so many things are related to the contemporary situation. If I were here tomorrow and had time to speak, I would try to relate some of the lessons of the Caribbean crisis for today in detail, especially about the steps toward an all-encompassing system of world security on the scale discussed by Mr. Gorbachev. But since time is short, my comments will be brief.

. . . I believe it is very important for Americans to understand *perestroika* and the new political thinking—not only liberal Democrats, but also conservative Republicans. It seems to me that liberal Democrats must do a very large part of the work of educating the public to understand the new political thinking in the nuclear age.

In my department, we will do our utmost to lay the new foundation for the Soviet Union and the United States not to be in constant danger of confrontation, but to lead to greater cooperation and understanding in order to meet the new coming age and secure a good future for our civilization and our children. Thank you very much for the chance to be with you all and to discuss these important events.

NYE: I'm delighted you could come. Let me just add that when I read your article on foreign policy in the nuclear age, I saw an example of new political thinking before I'd even heard the term. So thank you very much, Georgy, and have a safe trip back to the Soviet Union. [Applause.]

Bob, why don't we turn things over to you?

McNAMARA: Joe, the thing I want to emphasize now is that we've got a unique opportunity here to take advantage of the changes in the Soviet Union and open up U.S.–Soviet relations, start reducing tensions, and work to eliminate this mistrust I've been talking about. I just hope the next Administration can take advantage of it, even if this one can't.

There's a lot that you could say about the lessons of the Cuban missile crisis, and I won't go through them all, but the most important lesson has got to be the importance of avoiding crises of this kind. Crisis management is a very uncertain and very difficult thing to do, and, therefore, you've just got to avoid the crises in the first place. How do you do that? Three things. First, be clear on what your interests are and state them clearly. I'm not sure we did this at all well in 1962, and it's obvious to me now that the Soviets miscalculated largely because we didn't. Second, never leave your adversary in any uncertainty about these interests. Now, I realize that people like Henry Kissinger might disagree with me about that; I realize some people see some value in keeping your opponent guessing about the nature of your commitments—but it seems to me that that's just too dangerous in the nuclear age. You can't afford to take the chance that your adversary is going to guess wrong. Third, over time, we must attack the basic source of friction between our two countries: mistrust. As I've said before, there's a lot more mistrust out there than is warranted, but we cannot just dismiss it out of hand. We've got to work to reduce it. I believe Gorbachev has helped a great deal already, and we've got to take him up on his challenge to reduce East–West tensions.

Now, the second main lesson is that we have to recognize that even very small risks of nuclear war must be avoided. We in the West must recognize the need to raise the nuclear threshold by improving the conventional balance, either by negotiation—Gorbachev is now indicating he's willing to negotiate—or by building up if we have to. But we must reduce the risk of a nuclear confrontation if we're going to maintain a nuclear deterrent at all.

The third main lesson is that we have to recognize that the width of the band of nuclear parity is very, very great. Maybe it's not seventeen to one, but it's certainly quite wide. Once we recognize this, it opens up all sorts of possibilities for verification, for arms control, and for military strategy. Until we recognize the width of the band of parity, we will constantly be dickering over small differences in forces at the margins and we'll never get anywhere.

To improve crisis management, we should first recognize that human beings are fallible, and that we are prone to misjudgment, misinformation, miscalculation, and emotion. It's for this reason that I've formulated McNamara's Law: "In this nuclear age, it is not possible to predict with a high degree of certainty what the effects of the use of military force will be because of the risks of accident, misperception, miscalculation, and inadvertence." Nothing I've heard in the last day or two has led me to change my mind about this; in fact, I feel it all the more strongly. We are *so* affected by our shortcomings, and we just can't afford to let them get us into a situation we can't get out of.

Second, you've got to be concerned about the experience of the people who are going to deal with crises when they arise. The responsible officials must think in advance of how to deal with crises, especially when they involve even a remote possibility of a nuclear response. Georgy asked me a few minutes ago if our Administration had been adequately briefed by the prior Administration on superpower relations and crisis management—and the answer is absolutely no! We have no institutional memory. Each new Administration starts all over again. I've said this before, and I know some of you laugh at it, but we've got to do better than to have the president of Ford Motor Company step directly into the job of Secretary of Defense! [Laughter.] This is very dangerous! Look at what happened in the Bay of Pigs. The Administration had no experience—we didn't know what we were doing. Some of us learned very quickly, but it's very dangerous to bring into positions of authority individuals who are totally illiterate with respect to handling superpower relations and managing international crises. It's a big problem.

Some specific lessons seem to me to follow pretty easily from the handling of the Cuban missile crisis. First, take time to plan. Thank God we did. I don't know what we would have done if we'd had to rush a decision. Second, provide the President with knowledgeable associates. Draw on the experience of informed people. Look at the mess our nation got into in the Iran–Contra affair, and in Vietnam. The present Administration had absolutely no understanding of Iran, and we had little more of Indochina because we had eliminated all of the Chinese specialists during the McCarthy era of the 1950s. The real unsung heroes of the Cuban missile crisis, people such as George Kennan,* Chip Bohlen, and Tommy Thompson—especially Tommy Thompson, who was there twenty-four hours a day—were the people who were real students of the Soviet Union. Third, maintain communication. Dobrynin did play a crucial role, not only in the Cuban missile crisis, but during the whole time he was in Washington. He was an extraordinarily sophisticated diplomatic conduit, and he played a very important role for both governments. Fourth, look at the problem from the adversary's point of view. There are lots of good examples of our failing to do this and suffering the consequences in our arms decisions. Look at the decision to MIRV† our missiles, for instance. The U.S. decision to MIRV led to a quadrupling of the number of warheads in the inventories of the two superpowers. Obviously, the Soviets would follow suit. But when

---

* George F. Kennan, Ambassador to Yugoslavia in 1962 (and a former Ambassador to the Soviet Union). Although McNamara implies here that Kennan's opinions were sought during the Cuban missile crisis, there is no indication that he was involved.
† Multiple independently-targetable reentry vehicles; i.e., multiple nuclear warheads on a single missile.

that decision was made, the U.S. failed to anticipate the situation that would develop, because the U.S. government did not put itself in the Soviets' shoes. In 1962, we tried to do this during the missile crisis, and this was one reason for the successful outcome. Our two leaders rapidly became more sensitive to each other's positions. And, finally, for God's sake, don't force the adversary into a corner—don't force him into taking some kind of desperate action. Always leave him a way out. Those are among the main lessons I think we can take away from this event, though of course there are many, many others.

NYE: Thanks, Bob. That was quite a list, and I think those are all terribly important. Sergei or Fyodor, does either one of you want to comment on that, or do you want to draw some other lessons from the Soviet point of view? Is there something else you'd like to bring up— some information you'd like to add, or some questions you'd like to ask that you didn't get a chance to ask earlier?

BURLATSKY: First of all, let me say that I agree with McNamara's analysis and his view that the Cuban missile crisis was maybe the only case where there was a real danger of nuclear conflict. Therefore, it is very useful for drawing lessons today.

First, from my point of view, is that both sides understood at that time that neither side wants atomic war. It is impossible to win a nuclear war, and both sides realized that, maybe for the first time. This is very important for lessons today, because it is as valid now as twenty-five years ago.

About the question of superiority: you had an advantage that was sixteen or seventeen to one, and despite this fact, you could not use it. This is a very good lesson for both sides.

I want to mention what John Kennedy said: that the first step, called the problem of escalation, is a very dangerous problem in a nuclear crisis—especially today, because time is shorter than before. Now we have perhaps six or seven minutes, where before maybe we had one hour. And then—maybe you will disagree—but I believe that during a crisis we need secret personal negotiations between our leaders; because if they communicate openly, then the propagandistic elements and public opinion must play a role. Perhaps we succeeded in the Cuban missile crisis because we had secret private communications: between Robert Kennedy and Dobrynin, between Scali and Fomin, and so on. Direct interaction between leaders is also very important. I had the same feeling at Geneva and at Reykjavik.[53] It was very important that both leaders had the chance to touch each other and to know each other.

Next, both sides must be prepared for compromise and negotiation, and they must be prepared to ignore such things as national prestige and superpower status. The main interest both sides have is preventing nuclear war.

I like very much McNamara's idea of coming back to a lower level of armaments. You mentioned in your last articles 120 or 150 warheads; it's quite enough. It's quite enough, and it could be an excellent step toward Gorbachev's idea of eliminating nuclear weapons. I realize this looks now unrealistic—what about the British, what about the French, what about the Chinese, what about some other new nuclear powers?— but this idea would be a very important step, an excellent idea we can both support.

Now, about the leaders. Our age requires world leaders who understand not national interests but global interests. I believe that Kennedy and Khrushchev, especially at the end of the Cuban missile crisis, managed to emerge as real world leaders. The main problem for humanity today is leaders who are not world leaders. Maybe the next election will destroy the political asymmetry—when we have a bad leader, you have a good leader; when we have a good leader, you have a bad leader—

MIKOYAN: Or no leader at all. [Laughter.]

SORENSEN: That may be better than two bad leaders. [Laughter.]

BURLATSKY: I wrote an article recently in which I said that, in East and West, our main enemy is conservatism. We are fighting conservative views on our economy, and conservative views on relations with the West. You need to fight conservative views on relations with us and on arms control. Perhaps this conference helped a little bit.

NYE: We all hope so. Sergei?

MIKOYAN: Perhaps I can give you some thoughts, though not very profound ones. But I would draw your attention to the fact that the missile crisis was a result of our adventurism. We may now confess it. But, happily, it did not result in war. Paradoxically, it has helped us lower the risks of war. If there had been no Cuban missile crisis, we should perhaps have organized it. [Laughter.]

Adventurism is a dangerous thing. It is difficult to get away with it without drastic results. I believe the main lesson is for big countries not to be adventurist. I think it is on the way to being excluded. We have had leaders who make unwise decisions, such as Afghanistan, and we are now aware of the dangers of adventurism. We are in the process of major improvements now for two years and a half.

I agree with Fyodor that the two countries must have adequate leadership. My only wish is for officials as well as experts to draw lessons from the Cuban missile crisis and to be able either not to take adventurist steps or to find the easiest way to reverse them. These must be the main lessons for us and for those who take decisions.

NYE: Thank you, Sergei. Ted?

SORENSEN: I think the major lessons have already been extremely well summarized. But I would like to warn against the danger of two unjustified moods. Today we had an extraordinarily candid exchange. It is evident that we are all sensible men; but let us not assume that this will now be typical of all such exchanges between our countries. Unfortunately, the people in this room are not representative of our two peoples and governments. Getting the right men at the top of our governments is key, and in our country it has clearly been proven that getting the right man is extremely difficult. So let's beware of premature elation.

Secondly, in this room and over the past twenty-five years there has been a great deal of self-congratulation that a serious crisis was successfully resolved. But let us not forget that what we did in the first place was to bring the world closer to the brink of nuclear destruction than it has ever been. That is nothing to be proud of. And, for that reason, Bob McNamara is absolutely right that the first lesson of the Cuban missile crisis is the importance of avoiding crises in the first place.

NYE: That's a very sobering set of thoughts, and you're right to put things in that perspective. One of the key questions we have to answer is: How do we get these lessons understood in our two countries? After Hawk's Cay, we wrote a *Foreign Affairs* article on the subject, but that only reaches a very small segment of society, and it appeals to a certain kind of elite. How do you get these lessons to the broadest possible audience? In the Soviet Union, what has been written on the Cuban missile crisis to date has been almost totally misleading in teaching the lessons of the event to the Soviet public. Can *glasnost* increase the amount of information available to the Soviet public so that these lessons may be learned? What is the situation concerning what you can say or publish? Can you say or publish things like you have said today?

BURLATSKY: I wrote an article recently about a new style of information and the possibilities of analysis and criticism. Now, we are beginning with this, but this is not so easy to do in foreign policy as it is with domestic policy. It is not so difficult to write about the economy and the need to make changes, but for seventy years we have always said we were right about what we were doing in foreign policy. But now I am preparing a television film about our conference, and possibly I will also prepare a film about Khrushchev during the Cuban missile crisis. I will have one hour for discussion about our conference. I will explain not only Soviet views but your views also. Before, there were very few publications on the Cuban missile crisis. But now we start.

MIKOYAN: I can add that I am going to publish an article in my journal by Raymond Garthoff, along with an article by a professor from Havana and an article by me. We will have the whole triangle represented in this issue.[54]

BURLATSKY: And, by the way, if Mac Bundy, or Sorensen, or McNamara want to publish in my journal, that's okay—

SORENSEN: I'll take you up on that.

. . . . .

MIKOYAN: . . . I would like to underline Fyodor's note on the importance of looking again at foreign policy and at history. It is as he says; it is very important. I think this conference is a very good beginning.

NYE: When I was in Moscow in June with Graham, we found that Khrushchev was not a popular figure of discussion. But if you're going to write on the Cuban missile crisis, surely you must talk about Khrushchev? Is it possible to do so now?

MIKOYAN: When were you there?

NYE: In June.

MIKOYAN: Four months is a very long time in the Soviet Union nowadays. [Laughter.]

ALLISON: Sergei, do you think the debate about foreign policy will ever be as open as the debate about domestic policy?

MIKOYAN: Maybe not as open, but it will begin.

BURLATSKY: It is important to be an open and informed society in order to develop our economy and our culture. Our officials recognize this. But it is still more difficult to discuss foreign policy than domestic policy. . . .

. . . . .

TAUBMAN: . . . [Has] Gorbachev . . . drawn lessons from Khrushchev and from the Cuban missile crisis[?] I think one of the lessons he may have drawn is the importance of avoiding adventures, but could either of you reflect on any other lessons the current leadership has learned from the Khrushchev era?

. . . . .

BURLATSKY: New thinking. The new thinking began after the Cuban missile crisis. Before it, the majority of our party members and our leadership believed the Americans wanted to destroy our system with an atomic war. You know, Gorbachev has said that the interests of humanity are more important than the interests of classes and nations. He wants to open our country for human and cultural and economic relations with other countries. Already he has taken some steps.

What about the crisis? The new leadership knows about the importance of avoiding adventures. But this is not only from the Cuban missile crisis. Afghanistan is very difficult. As you know from Vietnam, it is very easy to get in, and very difficult to get out. But I believe in a short time our forces will be out of Afghanistan.

Changes in international relations are coming. A military buildup needs money, but new thinking and new relations do not need money. But remember: it cannot come only from our side—it must come also from the West. I have a feeling the West is waiting. It is waiting to see what happens in the Soviet Union, and it is not stepping forward to us. The West is not using the opportunities before them. I am very happy to hear that McNamara is very optimistic; maybe in thirty or forty years, we will live in a new world.

NYE: Graham?

ALLISON: Bill has a good question, but the question prior to it is: How did Khrushchev and the Politburo learn the lessons of the Cuban missile crisis? If you read Khrushchev's comments at the time and then his memoirs, you realize that his image of how a nuclear war might come about looks really quite modern. He talked a lot about uncontrollable or inadvertent causes leading to an outcome no sane man would possibly choose. He uses a number of truly striking metaphors—

TAUBMAN: He was a great one for that.

ALLISON: —He talks about the United States and the Soviet Union as "two blind moles," and they're pulling on the "rope of war" and the knot is getting tighter and tighter—

SORENSEN: He also uses the metaphor of "two goats on a bridge"—

ALLISON: —So the question is, while sane people wouldn't choose nuclear war, there's this other problem; is this an important idea in, say, Gorbachev's or Yakovlev's* heads?

* Aleksandr Yakovlev, full member of the Politburo and Secretary of the Central Committee of the Communist Party.

BURLATSKY: Yes, of course. As you know, Mr. Ury has had a big success on the communications question, and in spite of the political atmosphere now, direct relations between the leaders of our countries, and our Ministers of Foreign Affairs, and between others, would support the psychological climate that would help in avoiding crises.[55] Then the disarmament process—the double-zero option, the 50 percent reduction in strategic weapons—this is also in our leaders' minds.

I am sure Gorbachev personally is quite informed of the Cuba crisis.

MIKOYAN: He even asked Ambassador Alekseev to write an account of all events he knew happened in Havana and Moscow, and I think he also asked Dobrynin to do so. He pays very close attention.

. . . . .

NYE: That's fascinating. I'm afraid we are running out of time, and it would be terrific if we could talk forever, but I think we ought to focus now on the question of the puzzles that are left. Perhaps this could be the focus of an agenda for a follow-up meeting in Moscow. But let's hear what you have to say about it now before we go meet the press.

I'll start by saying that I'm still puzzled by the relationship between Berlin and Cuba. After Cuba we learned an awful lot about avoiding crises, but as Georgi remarked, before Cuba we were still operating on what he called "pre-nuclear thinking." I was very surprised that you all didn't have more to say about Berlin. After all, we still hadn't solved World War II; but after Cuba, we finally get a stable status quo on Berlin. I would have thought the two were very closely connected. Am I wrong about this? Fyodor?

BURLATSKY: First, let me say about the next meeting, I spoke with Tolkunov* about the possibility of inviting Americans to Moscow to discuss the Cuban missile crisis, and he was very interested—very interested. I can't promise it, but I had the opinion it could be possible. . . . . . We are simple advisors. But some of you were members of the government, and perhaps in Moscow we could have some of our members of the government explain their views.

But now, on Berlin and Cuba; I don't know. We had no such feeling that it was a dramatic story with Berlin. It was one more step in the Cold War, but we did not think it was that dangerous. We pressed you, you pressed us, but it was not that dangerous. Only games—political games. That is all.

MIKOYAN: I agree with Fyodor on this.

_____
* Lev Tolkunov, chairman of one of the two houses of the Supreme Soviet.

BURLATSKY: For the first time we felt real danger only with the Cuban missile crisis.

MIKOYAN: I remember one phrase Khrushchev used at home; he said Berlin is the tail of imperialism, and we can yank it when they do something wrong to us. I think this was his idea, but I do not believe it was that important for us.

. . . . .

NYE: That's another interesting point about the perception of crises. Bob, if I'm not mistaken, I think you reported thinking of Berlin as very serious—

McNAMARA: Yes indeed, very serious; though not as serious as Cuba. . . .

BURLATSKY: It was a different case, however, because we could manage it. We could stop at any time.

McNAMARA: *Maybe.*

. . . . .

MIKOYAN: It was less serious—it was only a diplomatic game. You were thinking of using nuclear weapons?

McNAMARA: Absolutely not, but some people thought it might come to that.

NYE: This all hearkens back to the clarity of interest definition and its importance. Obviously, neither the United States nor the Soviet Union had clearly defined its interests in Berlin prior to the crisis. In contrast, look at the Persian Gulf. We've had a major war there for six or seven years involving what the United States has defined as key interests for a long time, but our communications with the Soviets have been very good and there's been no significant escalation.

SORENSEN: Let's give credit where credit is due on that, too. The Reagan Administration has been very good about communications with the Soviets on the Gulf, especially in the last three months.

NYE: But, in Cuba, we had a formula for disaster. When you mix unclear communication of interests with a gambling man, you're asking for a major unintended confrontation. . . . . . Ernie May?

MAY: I have two quick comments to make. First, this has been an extraordinarily impressive event. I felt for the first time after this morning's session that I understood Soviet decisionmaking in the Cuban missile crisis better than in any other event since 1941. Now, this is in part a tribute to the candor of the commentary, but it is also an indication of how little we really know about Soviet decisionmaking in general. There is so much important detail to know that we've never even dreamed about. I hope this meeting is symptomatic of a real opportunity not only to learn about the Cuban missile crisis, but about other important Cold War events as well. I noted this morning how Fashoda shocked Britain and France into an understanding which helped lay the groundwork for a later alliance; I hope we can learn a lot more about this and other important events—especially about the German issue, by the way, which I think has been central to U.S.–Soviet conflict through most of the postwar period—so that we can reduce misunderstandings and ease international tensions. The more we know about the history of our relationship, the better off we are all going to be.

. . . . .

NYE: . . . [This] has been an extraordinarily useful and exciting day. If this is what *glasnost* means, then I think it bodes very well not only for the better understanding of history but also for the future of U.S.–Soviet relations. . . . Let me congratulate you all for a job exceedingly well done. Thank you all for coming. [Applause.]

CHAPTER
6

Another
October Revolution

The poet Dylan Thomas remembered October as the month in Wales when "the weather turned around."[1] On the eve of the seventieth anniversary of the revolution that brought the Bolsheviks to power in Russia, and almost exactly on the twenty-fifth anniversary of the Cuban missile crisis, another October revolution took place in a small conference room in Cambridge, Massachusetts—this time, a revolution in U.S.–Soviet scholarly relations, and in our understanding of the Cuban missile crisis. The meeting shed a great deal of light on such perplexing issues as the Soviet decision to deploy missiles in Cuba, the conduct of the crisis from the Soviet perspective, and the scope and implications of U.S. and Soviet misunderstandings about one another's motives and intentions. It also represented a serious, honest, cooperative investigation of issues central to the key interests of the superpowers, and to the problems of war and peace in the nuclear age. In October 1987, "the weather turned around"—unexpectedly, as usual—with a heady blast of *glasnost*.

Fyodor Burlatsky set the tone for the rest of the conference in his frank response to Ernest May's long list of questions on Monday morning. Burlatsky took the position that Khrushchev may have put the missiles in Cuba for what he called "irrational reasons," that Khrushchev did not think through the implications of what he was doing, that he had a very poor understanding of the likely American response, that in fact Khrushchev took unnecessary risks, and that many in the Soviet Union regarded the emplacement of missiles in Cuba as what the Soviets disparagingly call an "adventurist" act.[2] Sergo Mikoyan then methodically described the Soviet decisionmaking process that led to the emplacement of missiles in Cuba, as told to him by his father, Soviet First

Deputy Premier Anastas I. Mikoyan. He revealed for the first time the
names of those in Khrushchev's inner circle who helped plan and implement the deployment; he related the conversations his father had
had with Khrushchev during their private walks in the Lenin Hills; he
frankly told the story of the delicate negotiations between the Soviet
and Cuban governments before, during, and after the crisis; and with
the help of Burlatsky and Shakhnazarov, he shed light on many lingering
puzzles about the Soviet side of the crisis that have perplexed American
scholars and policymakers for a quarter of a century.[3] For the members
of the ExComm present, this was heady enough; it was all the more
shocking to the scholars in the room who were familiar with the traditional Soviet analyses of the crisis, the best known of which—Anatoly
Gromyko's *The Caribbean Crisis*—is vague and defensive in tone.
Though it discusses decisionmaking in the ExComm at some length,
using American sources, it never once discusses decisionmaking in the
Kremlin. In fact, it never even mentions Khrushchev by name.[4]

That the Soviets divulged hard information and offered candid, informed opinion was only one aspect of the Cambridge conference that
was revolutionary. A second was that the participants acknowledged
that the United States and the Soviet Union shared responsibility for
the confrontation. In the stock Soviet treatments of the crisis, including
Khrushchev's important speech to the Supreme Soviet on December 12,
1962, his two volumes of memoirs, and the "official" account by Anatoly
Gromyko, the United States is excoriated for interfering with the Cuban
revolution, for relentlessly seeking to overthrow Castro, forcing the
Soviet Union to take strong measures to protect its new ally, deliberately
instigating a crisis by announcing an unexpected blockade of the island
when it had several opportunities to negotiate peacefully and quietly,
and—not insignificantly—for violating international law and denying the
Soviet Union the same rights and privileges to ship arms and establish
bases in Cuba that the United States openly enjoyed in countries such
as Turkey, Italy, and Great Britain.[5] Similarly, the best-known American accounts of the crisis, including the memoirs of Robert Kennedy,
Theodore Sorensen, and Arthur Schlesinger, Jr., blame the Soviets for
deceitfully, cynically, and aggressively attempting to establish an offensive base in America's back yard, in flagrant defiance of the interests
and wishes of the inter-American system, the Monroe Doctrine, and
the repeated warnings of both the executive and legislative branches of
the American government.[6]

Kennedy and Khrushchev set the beat to which subsequent historiography has marched. In his radio and television address of October
22, 1962, the President claimed that the Cuban missile crisis had been
caused by "the secret, swift and extraordinary buildup of Communist

missiles in an area well known to have a special and historical relationship to the United States and the nations of the Western Hemisphere." "This sudden, clandestine decision to station strategic weapons for the first time outside the Soviet Union," Kennedy went on, represented "a deliberately provocative and unjustified change in the status quo."[7] In forceful, indignant tones, the President called upon Khrushchev "to halt and eliminate this clandestine, reckless and provocative threat to world peace and to stable relations between our two nations."[8] Khrushchev replied "that the armaments which are in Cuba, regardless of the classification to which they may belong, are intended solely for defensive purposes in order to secure the Republic of Cuba against the attack of an aggressor."[9] When Khrushchev spoke of the missiles as "defensive," he meant they were to serve as a deterrent. His point, however, could not be missed: that the ultimate cause of the crisis was the abortive Bay of Pigs invasion and subsequent American attempts to isolate and liquidate the Castro regime. Kennedy was not persuaded. "I think you will recognize," he said in his message to Khrushchev of October 23, "that the step which started the current chain of events was the action of your government secretly furnishing offensive weapons to Cuba."[10]

At the Cambridge meeting, for the first time on record, knowledgeable Soviets accepted a share in the responsibility for causing the crisis. They also listened with some astonishment as former close associates of President Kennedy acknowledged their own share. Equally astounding to both Soviets and Americans were the many revelations of misunderstandings and miscalculations that led to the crisis and that nearly led to disaster. A new kind of conversation, a more honest kind of inquiry had begun with the assumption of shared responsibility and with the recognition of a common interest in understanding the event the same way.

The Causes of the Crisis

Needless to say, there would have been no Cuban missile crisis if Nikita Khrushchev had not decided to deploy missiles in Cuba. In that sense, Khrushchev's decision was clearly a necessary cause of the crisis. At the Cambridge conference, Soviets who were in a position to know something about the matter undertook to explain what Khrushchev sought to gain from such a move. In so doing, they shed light on a debate that has preoccupied Western scholars of the crisis since 1962, and which was inconclusively repeated at Hawk's Cay.[11]

In Chapter 2, we briefly discuss eight dominant theories of Khrushchev's motivations. To summarize, he may have intended for missiles in Cuba (1) to deter American aggression (defense of Cuba); (2) to redress the strategic imbalance (missile-gap repair); (3) to help him secure the negotiated withdrawal of American weapons on the Soviet periphery (bargaining chip); (4) to force a favorable settlement in Berlin (Berlin gambit); (5) to restore Soviet preeminence in the socialist world and/or to help his campaign against Chinese nuclear armament (socialist hegemony); (6) to boost the morale and prestige of the Soviet bloc (Cold War politics); (7) to bolster his domestic position against hard-liners and his rivals in the Presidium (Soviet domestic politics I); and (8) to accommodate the pressures of hard-liners (Soviet domestic politics II).[12] Burlatsky, Mikoyan, and Shakhnazarov heavily discounted all but the first two motives. However, they sharply disagreed over whether the defense of Cuba or missile-gap repair was Khrushchev's primary concern.

Most Americans have dismissed the defense-of-Cuba rationale out of hand, in part because it was the only rationale which enabled Khrushchev to claim a measure of success from the ultimate resolution of the crisis. And there is no doubt that Khrushchev squeezed as much as he possibly could from Kennedy's promise not to invade the island, short of declaring that the resolution of the crisis was a victory for the Soviet Union and a defeat for the United States.[13] Adam Ulam called Khrushchev's claim that he was only interested in defending Cuba "laughable," a vain and pitiful post-hoc reconstruction of events designed exclusively to help him save face.[14] Arnold Horelick wrote: "To regard the outcome of the Cuban missile crisis as coinciding in any substantial way with Soviet intentions or interests is to mistake skillful salvage of a shipwreck for brilliant navigation."[15] Michel Tatu declared: "It is safe to ignore the reason consistently adduced by Khrushchev, namely, that he wished to defend Castro and him alone."[16]

Certainly, both Khrushchev's and Anatoly Gromyko's accounts read more like polemics than analyses, and American (and Soviet) audiences can be forgiven for being skeptical as a result. But Sergo Mikoyan told the tale in a way which made the defense-of-Cuba hypothesis appear both plausible and persuasive. The United States had already tried to topple Castro by supporting the Bay of Pigs invasion, and next time, Khrushchev surmised, it would certainly do the job correctly. Khrushchev also thought Kennedy weak and easily pressured into action by hard-liners in the CIA and the Pentagon, who no doubt were maneuvering him closer to an invasion every day. The OAS meeting at Punta del Este, at which Cuba was formally expelled, seemed to Khrushchev to be the diplomatic prelude to the liquidation of the Castro regime.[17] As if to confirm Khrushchev's worst fears, as summer turned to fall, Kennedy began calling up reservists, the Marines prepared to exercise amphibious landings in the Caribbean, to liberate an imprisoned island from a mythical dictator whose name was "Castro" spelled backwards, and Congress passed a resolution authorizing the President to take military action against Cuba, if necessary, to protect American interests.

If Khrushchev had been convinced that an American invasion of Cuba was inevitable—and as McNamara noted at the Cambridge meeting, this would have been an entirely understandable if mistaken conviction[18]—he could hardly afford to sit on the sidelines and watch it unfold. The political costs of "losing Cuba" must have seemed every bit as unpalatable to the Soviets as the political costs of "losing Korea" or "losing Vietnam" seemed to one earlier and one later American Administration. No doubt, equally bold action would have seemed justified to prevent it.[19] But even though all three Soviets at the Cambridge conference agreed that Khrushchev was concerned with deterring an American invasion, they could not agree that this was his primary motivation. Both Burlatsky and Shakhnazarov believed his main intent was to redress the strategic nuclear imbalance, which had been successfully hidden until Roswell Gilpatric's speech of October 1961. Khrushchev himself let down his guard—once—and admitted that this was indeed on his mind. "In addition to protecting Cuba," he wrote in his memoirs, "our missiles would have equalized what the West likes to call 'the balance of power.' "[20] Burlatsky's statement that the missile deployment was undertaken mainly to repair the strategic imbalance is ironic; for Burlatsky played a major role in drafting the December 12, 1962, speech in which Khrushchev proclaimed that the one and only reason for the missile deployment was to defend Cuba against American aggression. His revised account, of course, requires him to acknowledge now that the principal goal, as he saw it, was not achieved: the missiles had to be withdrawn, leaving the Soviets no closer to parity than before.

The speeches Khrushchev gave in Bulgaria in May, which Burlatsky helped to write, reveal a preoccupation with nuclear issues. In particular, these speeches concerned the presence of American Jupiter missiles in Turkey, Bulgaria's neighbor on the Black Sea. In Varna on May 16, 1962, Khrushchev asked, "Would it not be better if the shores on which are located NATO's military bases and the launching sites for their armed rockets were converted into areas of peaceful labor and prosperity?"[21] The U.S., he said, "is pulling Turkey deeper and deeper into the coils of the NATO military alliance."[22] Later, on May 19 in Sofia, Khrushchev responded angrily to President Kennedy's comment that he might "take the initiative in a nuclear conflict with the Soviet Union," replying, "Anyone who dared unleash a military conflict of that kind would receive a shattering retaliatory blow using all the very latest weapons of war. The Socialist camp, the Soviet Union, possesses these

weapons in ample quantity."[23] Khrushchev was evidently deeply concerned with the NATO threat and by the possibility that Soviet nuclear
inferiority might under certain circumstances put the Soviet Union at
risk of an American first strike.

Burlatsky is convinced, however, that Khrushchev's motives cannot
be understood in purely rational-actor terms, and though it might have
been reasonable for Khrushchev to want to repair his missile gap in a
bold, economical stroke, more than simple calculations of costs and
benefits went into his decision; more than one motivation was at work;
and the decision Khrushchev made was probably at least as visceral as
cerebral. What Burlatsky called "irrational reasons"—"psychological or
emotional reasons"—featured heavily in Khrushchev's decision. He was
a "risky man," eager to flex his nuclear muscles, and intoxicated with
superpower status. "I am not sure Khrushchev thought out the aims,"
Burlatsky noted. "From my point of view, it was more an emotional
than rational decision."[24]

Even though "irrational reasons" probably played a major role in
Khrushchev's decision to deploy the missiles, he may have had a dominant motivation in mind. For that matter, he may have had two dominant motivations. It seems unlikely that we will ever be able to decide
whether he was more concerned with defending Castro or with repairing
the missile gap, in part because it is unlikely that Khrushchev asked the
question of himself; one does not need to decide which of two birds is
the more important target when both can be killed with one stone. But
the discussion at the Cambridge meeting should satisfy us that both
motivations were very much at work in the Soviet deployment.[25] Mikoyan, Burlatsky, and Shakhnazarov can all be forgiven for emphasizing
the motivation which falls closest to their areas of interest and expertise.
We should simply be instructed by the fact that there is legitimate room
for a debate of this kind, even among prominent and knowledgeable
Soviets, because it powerfully suggests that Khrushchev's own motives
were mixed.[26]

We should be surprised, however, at their unanimous view that China,
Berlin, and Soviet domestic politics were irrelevant to the deployment.
Adam Ulam's argument that the missiles were intended primarily to
impress the Chinese was one view given some credence at an earlier
time,[27] but Mikoyan spoke for all three in unequivocally pronouncing
"that there was absolutely no connection between the missiles and relations with Peking."[28] Likewise, though the President, many members
of the ExComm, many prominent American scholars, and much of the
American public interpreted the Cuban move as part of a larger scheme
involving the status of Berlin[29]—understandably, in view of the prom-

inence of the Berlin issue in the latter part of Eisenhower's Presidency and the earlier part of Kennedy's—Burlatsky and Mikoyan dismissed the Berlin connection out of hand. The diplomatic skirmishing over Berlin was merely "one more step in the Cold War," Burlatsky maintained, which the Soviets did not believe was very dangerous. "We pressed you, you pressed us, but it was not that dangerous. Only games— political games. That is all."[30] Mikoyan agreed: "I remember one phrase Khrushchev used at home; he said Berlin is the tail of imperialism, and we can yank it when they do something wrong to us. I think this was his idea, but I do not believe it was that important for us."[31] Finally, Burlatsky flatly denied that Khrushchev felt compelled to act for domestic political reasons. In 1962, Burlatsky maintained, "Khrushchev had the *biggest* authority during all his time in power. He had a Presidium in which a majority supported him. It was not necessary to have an international success to show public opinion."[32]

The Cambridge meeting not only shed a good deal of light on why Khrushchev decided to deploy missiles in Cuba, it also proved useful (if less than wholly conclusive) in explaining why he thought he could get away with it. The standard Western view of the matter is that Khrushchev grossly miscalculated; that he made an enormous error in judgment in believing that his fait accompli would succeed and that the United States would tolerate the presence of Soviet missiles in Cuba once their presence was revealed.[33] The implication of these views is that Khrushchev should have known better; and, to an extent, the Soviets at the Cambridge meeting would agree.[34]

It is useful to reconstruct, inferentially and speculatively, the considerations which may have led Khrushchev to believe his gamble would succeed. Arnold Horelick, in a penetrating study written shortly after the crisis, had no difficulty imagining plausible reasons:

1. The Bay of Pigs showed that the Americans were reluctant to use U.S. forces against Cuba.[35]

2. American attempts to subvert Castro legitimized Soviet assistance to Cuba. Khrushchev therefore expected worldwide political support in his attempt to support the Castro regime.

3. The midterm congressional elections were coming up; it would be bad for the Democrats if Soviet missiles were exposed but still on the island of Cuba, and it would be unreasonable to expect the Americans to secure their withdrawal quickly. Consequently, Kennedy would probably sit on any information he had about the

construction of missiles in Cuba long enough to enable at least the MRBMs to become operational.

4. Khrushchev may not have believed the U.S. capable of a rapid response because of its need to consult its NATO allies—a cumbersome, divisive, and time-consuming process.

5. The Soviets may have expected the OAS to oppose a forceful American response.

6. Khrushchev may have hoped that American fear of a response in Berlin might deter American action against Cuba.[36]

For all these reasons, Horelick surmised, the Soviets may have thought prompt unilateral American action extremely unlikely; but, as Horelick notes, "events proved them to be wrong on almost every point."[37]

Several other considerations may have bolstered Khrushchev's confidence that his gamble was a reasonable one. First, the MRBMs could be deployed more rapidly than Moscow may have thought the U.S. was aware.[38] Second, Khrushchev may have felt that the United States had been deterred by Soviet nuclear power in the past, and he may have seen the deployment of missiles in Cuba merely as an augmentation and consolidation of an established position.[39] Third, he may sincerely have believed that he could make a plausible argument before the world that the deployment was fully equivalent to similar American deployments in Turkey, Italy, and Britain.[40] And, fourth, he may have thought Kennedy personally incapable of a firm and prompt response, largely because of his unimpressive performance at the Vienna summit. According to Burlatsky, based on a debriefing just after the summit, Kennedy then seemed to the Soviet leader too young, too weak, and too intellectual to stand up to a bold challenge.[41]

If Khrushchev believed he could get away with a missile deployment at the time he made the decision, he probably believed all the more strongly that his gamble would pay off even as the crisis approached.[42] He may have discounted Kennedy's warnings of September 4 and 13 as attempts to calm an American public that was being whipped into a frenzy of anti-Castro fervor by opportunistic Republicans;[43] but even if he had read them as intended for his benefit, he may not have taken them seriously. Kennedy's September 4 statement warned that if the United States had firm evidence of the presence of "offensive ground-to-ground missiles," then "the gravest issues would arise."[44] Khrushchev, however, may not have understood this as an unambiguous warning. The warnings Moscow was issuing at the same time against an

American attack on Cuba were much harsher, much clearer, and much more threatening: an attack on Cuba would mean nuclear war.[45] Kennedy's September 13 statement was no less impressive and no less ambiguous: its strongest threat was that if the Soviets established "an offensive military base of significant capacity then this country will do whatever must be done to protect its own security and that of its allies"; but, almost in the same breath, Kennedy pledged neither to "initiate nor permit aggression in this Hemisphere."[46] Was Kennedy not publicly pledging never to attack Cuba with American armed forces, unless the United States was attacked first? Khrushchev may well have wondered. Why, unless he was timid and uncertain, was Kennedy talking about "the gravest issues" and "doing whatever must be done" when the Soviets were talking about nuclear war?[47]

On October 14, the Soviets were given what could have been read as the clearest sign yet that their gambit was going to work. McGeorge Bundy appeared on ABC's *Issues and Answers* and stated: "I *know* there is no present evidence, and I think there is no present likelihood that the Cubans and the Soviet government would, in combination, attempt to install a major offensive capability. . . . So far, everything that has been delivered in Cuba falls within the categories of aid which the Soviet Union has provided, for example, to neutral states like Egypt or Indonesia, and I should not be surprised to see additional military assistance of that sort."[48] Among the systems already delivered to Cuba were Il-28 bombers, which could have been construed as offensive weapons. Khrushchev might therefore have believed either that the deployment of missiles had still gone undetected (in fact, it was discovered on the evidence of photographs taken that very day) or that the Administration was going to tolerate it. Four days later, when Foreign Minister Andrei Gromyko met with President Kennedy for two hours,[49] the President was given a clear opportunity to reveal his knowledge of the deployment and to voice his objections; his silence may have been taken as a sign of ignorance or acquiescence.[50]

With the benefit of hindsight, it seems easy to say that Khrushchev's move was destined to provoke a crisis and was guaranteed to fail. But we forget too easily that his fait accompli very nearly worked; only mistakes in the deployment process enabled the Americans to identify the missiles before they became operational. These mistakes, according to Sergo Mikoyan, were "absolutely Russian": too many troops and too many ships were sent to do the job, and no one asked the Cubans for help in camouflaging the installations.[51] Khrushchev presumably thought the missile sites *were* camouflaged, and was, accordingly, hopeful that his deception would succeed.

It is difficult, of course, to say with any certainty what would have happened had Khrushchev's gambit worked.[52] It seems likely that at the very least the President would have been even less willing to entertain the idea of military strikes against the missiles than he was when their status was ambiguous. His uncertainty about their "operability" strongly inclined him toward a negotiated solution, and if that uncertainty had been resolved, he may have felt that he had very little leverage.[53] If so, Khrushchev stood a good chance of realizing a considerable gain from whatever settlement the two nations came to. Khrushchev probably saw the Cuban deployment as the mirror image of American deployments in Turkey, Italy, and Britain, where the U.S.S.R. protested but did nothing in the face of American intransigence. A successful fait accompli, with the roles reversed, would have meant that it was the United States' turn to holler and back down.[54]

Though all these considerations, when taken together, plausibly account for Khrushchev's belief that he could get away with his bold move, they nevertheless leave many crucial questions unanswered. Most puzzling is the fact that some of the considerations that probably inclined Khrushchev to believe that he could get away with the deployment—his impression that Kennedy was weak, timid, and unwilling to use American forces against Cuba—are at odds with one of his apparent motivations for the deployment in the first place: the need to deter an inevitable American invasion. It is tempting to resolve this perplexity by concluding either that Khrushchev did not fear an American invasion or that he did not believe Kennedy weak; but the weight of evidence suggests that neither conclusion would be correct. To fit the seemingly square peg into the evidently round hole, we have to put a great deal of weight on Khrushchev's confidence that secrecy could be preserved until the missiles were operational, and a great deal of weight on Sergo Mikoyan's claim that Khrushchev feared a weak President could easily be pushed into action by hard-liners. Only by giving these considerations prominence is it possible to assert that Khrushchev expected an American invasion *and* believed that Kennedy was weak. But if this is what Khrushchev believed, he surely must have recognized all the more strongly the recklessness and dangerousness of his gamble; for he would have had to anticipate uproar and chaos in the American decisionmaking apparatus, once the presence of the missiles was revealed, as hard-liners pushed a weak and vacillating President into taking forceful action. What he sought to avoid would therefore have been all the more likely: a precipitous invasion of Cuba and the liquidation of the Castro regime. The resolution of the first puzzle, therefore, spawns a second.

Mysteries such as these, in the absence of hard information that might clear them up, force us to return to Burlatsky's observation about the central role of "irrational reasons" in Khrushchev's decisionmaking process. He was, as Burlatsky said, *azartnyi*—one who takes great risks in a game of chance.[55] Khrushchev was a bold and reckless gambler, a man who could "dream great dreams" but who often did not think through the consequences of his acts.[56] We should look therefore to psychological explanations of Khrushchev's misjudgments.[57] He may have been unduly influenced by his wants and needs, and insufficiently informed by considerations that would have led an ideal observer to be more sensitive to the dangers of the deployment and more pessimistic about its chances of success. Unfortunately, there is a limit to how far we can go with a psychological analysis of this kind. Khrushchev is no longer available for cross-examination, and the record he left behind is too scanty to permit more than a speculative reconstruction of the filters through which he processed his information.

It would be easy to stop the inquiry at this point and conclude that the explanations we seek are locked forever in the secrets of Khrushchev's psyche. It would also be comfortable to do so: if we rest our case on the undeniable claim that Khrushchev was less than fully rational, we may lay the blame for causing the crisis squarely at the feet of his incapacities. But this is a temptation we should resist, even though many have succumbed to it in the past;[58] for if Khrushchev miscalculated and misjudged, the United States was an accomplice to the crime. President Kennedy failed to appreciate that his activities throughout 1961 and 1962 could reasonably persuade the Soviet Union that an invasion of Cuba was inevitable, even though he intended no such thing. By making known the extent of the strategic imbalance in a public and demonstrative way in October 1961—even if for the understandable and laudable purpose of bolstering the credibility of the American nuclear guarantee of Berlin—he failed to appreciate the awkwardness and instability of the position in which it put Khrushchev.[59] Further, he failed to communicate in a timely and unambiguous way that the deployment of Soviet nuclear missiles in Cuba would be unacceptable and would precipitate a crisis of the most dangerous kind. If communication could have prevented the Cuban missile crisis, the United States must shoulder some of the blame for failing to communicate clearly. Most of Washington's signals to Moscow—intended or unintended—were garbled in transmission.

We can safely say that Khrushchev misperceived American interests and misjudged American intentions.[60] That he did so was partly his own fault; he was profoundly ignorant of the United States, and the secrecy in which the operation was shrouded had the effect of cutting him off from his experts, who may well have had a more accurate sense of his prospects for success (though it is possible that they might have been as wrong about the American reaction to missiles in Cuba as American "experts" were about the likelihood that Khrushchev would deploy them).[61] But perceptions are only as accurate as the information on which they are based, and the United States was not giving Khrushchev much useful raw material to work with. To blame Khrushchev alone for misperceiving American interests and misjudging American intentions is to hold him to an unreasonable standard: it is to require him to read minds and to foretell the future.

At the Cambridge meeting, the former ExComm members were forthcoming in their acknowledgment that insufficient attention was paid to the ways in which the Soviets would read American actions, insufficient thought was given to the pressures American actions put on Khrushchev, and communications with the Soviets were quite poor.[62] President Kennedy himself acknowledged as much after the crisis was brought to a conclusion. "I think," he said, "looking back on Cuba, what is of concern is that both governments were so far out of contact, really."[63] It is, of course, an open question whether clearer communication alone could have prevented a confrontation.[64] And, to be fair, not all the blame for the miscommunication and misunderstanding can be laid at Kennedy's and Khrushchev's feet. The Soviets, for example, were listening to sources over which President Kennedy had no control, such as Congress and the American press. No doubt they also overestimated the President's control over the CIA's activities in Florida and Cuba, which appeared so ominously to foreshadow an American invasion.[65] Likewise, statements in the Soviet press and the pronouncements of many Soviet officials (including Dobrynin and Zorin) disavowing any intention of deploying missiles to Cuba were universally understood in the West as parts of an elaborate and deliberate deception, even though TASS, *Pravda, Izvestia,* and officials below the Presidium level simply did not realize that the statements they were making were false.[66] Many Soviet sources were simply repeating orthodoxy as they understood it.

Nevertheless, Kennedy and Khrushchev were doing a poor job of crisis avoidance. "Of Khrushchev's dream," Arthur Schlesinger has written, "the Americans knew nothing."[67] How could they? The President and his closest advisors believed that their conclusion from the Bay of Pigs fiasco would also be the Soviets' conclusion; they mistakenly believed that the Soviet Union could feel secure despite their massive nuclear inferiority; they assumed that the Soviet leaders would understand that the United States had no interest in launching a first strike against the Soviet Union; and they assumed that the Soviets would read their various warnings in exactly the way they were intended. The Soviets, for their part, failed to appreciate the damage their deployment would do to Kennedy's prestige;[68] they were out of touch with the realities of American domestic and alliance politics; they naïvely assumed that Americans would understand that the missiles in Cuba were, from their point of view, legitimately "defensive" weapons; and they equally naïvely assumed that the Americans, and the rest of the world, would appreciate the force of their conviction that what they were doing in Cuba was no different from, and no less sinister than, what the United States had already done elsewhere.

At the Cambridge conference, these misunderstandings surfaced early and often. Georgy Shakhnazarov, his voice ringing with emotion, asked, "Did anyone in the discussions with President Kennedy ever say that the Soviet Union had rights, according to international law, to deploy missiles in Cuba? Was anything said in defense of our position?"[69] McGeorge Bundy replied that "not very many people were saying Khrushchev had the same right to deploy missiles in Cuba as we had in Turkey"[70]—not because the right did not exist, but because, in the domestic and international climate of 1962, it carried very little political weight.[71] Shakhnazarov's evident perplexity at Bundy's response indicated how difficult it is for Soviets even twenty-five years later to grasp the importance of this fact; in 1962, it must have eluded them completely. But Shakhnazarov saw the point when Bundy suggested that the Soviets probably would have responded the same way if the U.S. had deployed nuclear missiles in Finland, even though doing so certainly would have been consistent with international law.[72]

Fyodor Burlatsky wanted to know why the President began with "an open declaration but not secret negotiation with Khrushchev," claiming that "if John Kennedy said when he met Gromyko, 'We know everything about rockets in Cuba,' maybe there would be no crisis."[73] If the Americans were deeply offended by Soviet secrecy, the Soviets, it seems, were equally offended by American publicity. But the former ExComm members at the Cambridge conference could not imagine Khrushchev backing down under those circumstances. Nor could they imagine that the Soviets could have been trusted to negotiate privately without going public with the information in order to seize the diplomatic initiative. Mikoyan then asked, "If we declared officially in September in the UN that we intended to defend Cuba with missiles, what would have been the American reaction. . . . . . Might it have made it harder for you and easier for us?"[74] Bundy and Sorensen strongly agreed that it would. It is striking that Khrushchev and his colleagues seem never even to have considered the possibility. The absolute secrecy which the Soviets regarded as essential to the success of their operation actually worked against them, because it gave the Americans the best weapon they had: the surreptitiousness and mendacity of the Soviet deployment.

Nowhere was the failure to communicate so apparent as in the Kennedy–Gromyko meeting of October 18; and if Burlatsky is correct in his implication that the Soviets might have backed down had Kennedy quietly revealed his knowledge of the deployment, nowhere was the cost of miscommunication so great.[75] It was, the Soviets believe, the last chance for Kennedy to pursue the course of quiet diplomacy, thus avoiding the public, military confrontation that plunged the world into crisis for six days.

The official Soviet account of the meeting is that given by Anatoly Gromyko:

> Kennedy did not once directly raise the presence of Soviet medium-range missiles in Cuba. Consequently, he could not have been given the answer that such weapons were or were not in Cuba. Further, it may be concluded that President Kennedy consciously misled the Soviet party to the conversation by concealing the real intentions of the U.S. government with regard to Cuba and by emphasizing the rejection by the U.S. government of plans for aggression against Cuba at the same time as a group of persons close to him [the ExComm] were, in the strictest secrecy, considering a number of variants of attack upon the island by U.S. Armed Forces.[76]

The former ExComm members are quick to acknowledge that the President declined to tell Gromyko what he knew about the missiles, but not for the reasons given in the official Soviet account. They also acknowledge that the Soviet Foreign Minister reemphasized the defensive nature of arms shipments to Cuba.[77]

Kennedy apparently remained impassive throughout Gromyko's statement. He gave no sign of tension or anger. But to *avoid* misleading his adversary he sent for and read aloud his September 4 warning. Gromyko "must have wondered why I was reading it," he said later, "but he did not respond."[78] The President offered Gromyko every opportunity to come forward and tell what he knew about the missiles in Cuba, but Gromyko did not take the bait.

According to Sorensen, the President was obviously relieved that Gromyko had not confronted him about the missiles in Cuba. The President must have also been very grateful that Gromyko did not, as some feared he might, proceed from the meeting to the White House steps and, before the entire nation and the world, announce that "defensive"

Soviet missiles were now deployed in Cuba. One wonders indeed what the President would have said or done in the face of a brutally honest, private presentation from Gromyko at that meeting. Kennedy wanted the advantage of surprise and he used deceit to retain it; he believed he could not afford in this instance to speak what was really on his mind.

The same was true for Gromyko. By October 18, many of the missile sites were nearly completed. All the MRBM sites were scheduled for completion within two weeks, and shortly afterwards, their presence would be triumphantly, but quietly, revealed to President Kennedy. This would be the culmination of Khrushchev's dream. To call the whole thing off on October 18, relinquishing what at that point Gromyko may still have felt was the necessary advantage of surprise, was unthinkable. Gromyko scarcely felt he could justify tipping the Soviet hand. He was, therefore, as relieved as Kennedy that he had not been confronted directly on the matter of missiles in Cuba. In his account of the crisis, Elie Abel reports Gromyko "leaving the White House that evening in a mood of unwonted joviality. The Soviet Foreign Minister described his talk with the President as 'useful, very useful.' "[79]

Despite over two hours of talking on a few subjects of intense mutual interest, there seems to have been almost no accurate or meaningful communication between the President of the United States and the Soviet Foreign Minister.[80] Real communication, perhaps, was impossible. Each man was too bound up with his schemes, his prejudices, his misjudgments, and his mistrust of the other, to understand what the dalliance meant, and to recognize in it an opportunity to head off a confrontation. It was the perfect metaphor for the previous year and a half of U.S.–Soviet diplomacy.

The Conduct and Resolution of the Crisis

If Kennedy and Khrushchev performed poorly at crisis avoidance, it must be said that they fared much better at crisis management. That they did so despite their evident inability to communicate and to understand each other prior to the crisis is nothing less than astounding.

We have every reason to believe that Khrushchev was as shocked at Kennedy's October 22 address as Kennedy was at the discovery of Soviet missiles in Cuba. For several hours, there was no response from Moscow; Soviet diplomacy was thrown into complete disarray. Dobrynin in Washington and Zorin at the UN were caught completely unprepared to respond, because they themselves had not been aware of the deployment.[81] Khrushchev, believing either that the secrecy surrounding the deployment would hold or that the United States would use quiet diplomacy to voice its objections if the missiles were discovered prematurely, seems indeed to have been caught, as Dean Rusk put it in his interview, with his scenario down.[82]

When Khrushchev finally responded, he was clearly outraged. The first salvo of his October 23 barrage was the charge that "the United States has openly taken the path of grossly violating the United Nations Charter, the path of violating international norms of freedom of navigation on the high seas, the path of aggressive actions both against Cuba and against the Soviet Union."[83] Wednesday's *Pravda* headlines screamed: "The unleashed American aggressors must be stopped!" and "Hands off Cuba!"[84] Of course, the ExComm expected a clamor of this kind; what they did not know was that Khrushchev's reaction to Kennedy's speech of October 22 was every bit as violent, irrational, and dangerous as the doves had feared it might be.

According to dissident Soviet historian Roy Medvedev, Khrushchev immediately issued an order to speed up work on the missile sites so as to make them operational as soon as possible. Though Kennedy intended the quarantine to persuade Khrushchev to halt construction of the missile sites and defuse the crisis through negotiation, Khrushchev's fury inclined him to do just the opposite.[85] But even more ominously, according to Medvedev's account, Khrushchev began "denouncing the naval blockade as banditry, the folly of degenerate imperialism . . . [and] issued orders to the captains of Soviet ships as they were approaching the blockade zone to ignore it and to hold course for the Cuban ports."[86] If this order had held, war between the superpowers would probably have commenced at sea, shortly after ten o'clock on Wednesday morning, October 24, 1962, several hundred miles off the coast of Cuba.[87]

According to Medvedev, it was Anastas Mikoyan who, as Soviet ships approached the quarantine line, preempted Khrushchev's order to run the blockade, and ordered Soviet ships to stop just short of the quarantine line—prompting Dean Rusk to utter his famous line: "We were eyeball to eyeball and the other fella just blinked."[88] Medvedev's account has attracted surprisingly little attention in the West, perhaps in part because it appears in an unlikely place for scholars of the missile crisis to look: in a book on Stalin's associates. And, until recently, there has been no independent confirmation of Medvedev's account, so we have been unable to gauge its accuracy.[89] But, shortly after the Cambridge conference, Sergo Mikoyan confirmed to us that Medvedev's account is factual.[90] Khrushchev's blink may have come just in the nick of time.[91]

Khrushchev's reaction to the announcement of the quarantine was similar in many respects to President Kennedy's (and most of his advisors') initial reaction to the discovery of Soviet missiles in Cuba. On both sides, outrage and anger were clearly the dominant emotions.[92] Not surprisingly, then, the initial inclination on both sides was to respond belligerently. There can be no mistaking the hawkish tone of the discussions in the White House on October 16: the President, for example, seemed at one point to have decided at a minimum to order a surgical air strike against the Soviet missiles;[93] his brother Robert—who in *Thirteen Days* portrayed himself as a leader of the doves—proposed to engineer an incident to use as a pretext for an attack, suggesting that it might be a good idea to "sink the *Maine* again or something."[94] But by October 22 the President and his advisors had had time to consider their options, reevaluate the chain of events that had led to the crisis, ponder Soviet motives and intentions, and absorb the awesome implications of irreversible actions and mistakes. In those six days, they seem to have become aware of the monumental misjudgments both they and the Soviets had made, and they came to appreciate some of the dangers associated with that fact.[95] It is therefore with a slight tone of injured innocence that the President, in his message to Khrushchev on October 22, took pains to point out that "it was in order to avoid any incorrect assessment on the part of your Government with respect to Cuba that I publicly stated that if certain developments in Cuba took place, the United States would do whatever must be done to protect its own security and that of its allies," and that "this minimum response should not be taken as a basis . . . for any misjudgment on your part"[96]—as though the accuracy and prudence of Khrushchev's judgments could be improved by urging him not to misjudge.

Khrushchev's opening salvo clearly disheartened Kennedy; in his fury, Khrushchev was not getting the point. He was not seeing that misjudgments had gotten them both into the predicament in the first place, and he certainly had not yet appreciated the potential for the confrontation to take on an uncontrollable momentum of its own. Kennedy should not have been surprised; he had had more than a week to learn his lessons, and Khrushchev had had but a few hours. But the President could not afford to wait very long; he had to try to speed Khrushchev's learning process. In reply to Khrushchev's October 23 statement, therefore, Kennedy poignantly urged "that we both show prudence and do nothing to allow events to make the situation more difficult to control than it already is."[97] By urging that they *both* show prudence, Kennedy sought to communicate the mutuality of their predicament, and the cooperative dimension of the requirements for its resolution.

Khrushchev very nearly did not get the point in time. But by October 26 Khrushchev and Kennedy had "clicked," as Khrushchev's letter of that date clearly indicates. The two leaders had finally come to see their predicament in approximately the same light: they recognized at last that they were symmetrically placed; that they faced common dangers; and that, more than anything else, they shared a common interest in resolving the confrontation on mutually satisfactory terms. They did so by virtue of being, as Khrushchev put it, "invested with authority, trust and responsibility" to secure the peace.[98]

> I have received your letter of October 25. From your letter I got the feeling that you have some understanding of the situation which has developed and a sense of responsibility. I appreciate this. . . . I can see, Mr. President, that you also are not without a sense of anxiety for the fate of the world. . . . Should war indeed break out, it would not be in our power to contain or stop it, for such is the logic of war. I have taken part in two wars, and I know that war ends only when it has rolled through cities and villages, sowing death and destruction everywhere. . . . You and I should not now pull on the ends of the rope in which you have tied a knot of war, because the harder you and I pull, the tighter this knot will become. And a time may come when this knot is tied so tight that the person who tied it is no longer capable of untying it, and then the knot will have to be cut.[99]

Khrushchev's more conciliatory and cooperative tone was echoed in the headlines of *Pravda*, which underwent a remarkable transformation between October 25 ("The aggressive designs of the United States imperialists must be foiled. Peace on earth must be defended and strengthened!") and October 26 ("Everything to prevent war," with an editorial entitled "Reason must prevail").[100]

In his letter of October 26, Khrushchev vaguely offered to settle on terms that Kennedy and the ExComm could accept: the missiles in Cuba would be withdrawn in return for an American pledge not to invade the island. Khrushchev, it seems, had made up his mind that securing one of his goals—the defense of Cuba—was all that he could reasonably hope for under the present circumstances, and that redressing the strategic imbalance was obviously going to have to wait. But then something unexpected happened, according to Shakhnazarov at the Cambridge meeting; Dobrynin informed Moscow that the United States might be willing to trade Jupiter missiles in Turkey for SS-4s and SS-5s in Cuba.[101]

The circumstances surrounding the missile-trade proposal have always been rather puzzling, and the Cambridge conference only added to the mystery. "Anatoly Dobrynin," said Shakhnazarov, "told me that the Turkish idea was born here, in the Soviet embassy, in a conversation, maybe with Robert Kennedy. It was suggested to Moscow and then it came back."[102] Originally, we thought perhaps Dobrynin had interpreted a cryptic remark made by Robert Kennedy in their meeting on October 23 to suggest that a trade was possible. According to Arthur Schlesinger, "the Attorney General noted that the American President had met Khrushchev's request for the withdrawal of American troops from Thailand."[103] This remark, obviously intended by Robert Kennedy to remind Dobrynin of the President's reasonableness and willingness to compromise, could have provided Dobrynin with what he took to be a clue to mutually acceptable terms of settlement. Dobrynin could also have been paying attention to other sources. It is possible, for example, that he mistakenly concluded that journalist Walter Lippmann was speaking for the American government when he proposed a Cuban–Turkish missile swap on October 25.[104] Confirmation that the Soviet Embassy had picked up on Lippmann's proposal came when John Scali was sent to ask Aleksandr Fomin why the (acceptable) proposal of October 26 had been superseded by the missile-trade proposal before the President had even had a chance to reply; Fomin is reported to have mentioned that Lippmann himself had proposed it.[105] It was not until the Moscow conference, however, that Dobrynin's cryptic remarks became clearer, if no less startling. Speaking to the issue at length, Dobrynin insisted in Moscow that Robert Kennedy himself had raised the possibility of a missile trade explicitly in a secret meeting on October 26.*

The genesis of the missile-trade idea may be puzzling, but Khrushchev's decision to propose it—publicly, no less—is downright mystifying. At the Cambridge conference, Mikoyan suggested that the Foreign Ministry—and by implication Andrei Gromyko—may have convinced Khrushchev that an American non invasion pledge was an insufficient quid pro quo, or that it would be both possible and desirable to demand more.[106] It is conceivable, perhaps, that Khrushchev merely intended to use it as a lever for securing Kennedy's agreement on his previous offer by trying to make it look more attractive against the background of toughening terms. Whatever his thinking, the missile-swap proposal of October 27 was, as Tatu notes, "the most important Soviet blunder during the entire crisis."[107] It threw a wrench into the delicate negotiations by forcing Kennedy and the ExComm to waste time and energy trying to ascertain which of Khrushchev's proposals was operative, and debating the merits and implications of the new one, even as events began to look as if they were spinning out of control. The missile-trade proposal also enraged both Cuba and Turkey, who had no intention of being treated as bargaining chips.[108] It may be that

---

* For full details, see the Afterword, pp. 337–38.

Khrushchev simply had not thought through the implications of the proposal; "irrational reasons" may have been at work here as well as in his decision to deploy missiles to Cuba in the first place. But, whatever the explanation, he committed a serious gaffe at the climax of the confrontation.

As the ExComm agonized over Khrushchev's new initiative on October 27, word reached Washington that a U-2 reconnaissance plane had been shot down by a surface-to-air missile fired from Cuba. The crisis seemed to have moved into a new, more dangerous phase.[109] The circumstances surrounding the shoot-down of the U-2 have always been unclear. Many members of the ExComm appear to have believed that it signaled a deliberate escalation of the crisis.[110] Jorge Domínguez suggests, based on his reading of Cuban sources, that Cubans had gained control of the SAMs as a matter of course some months earlier, and thus that Cubans were responsible, though Soviets probably executed the order to shoot, because only they at that point had the technical competence to operate the batteries.[111] Former Castro associate and former editor of *Revolución*, Carlos Franqui, reported in his memoir that Castro had told him he had personally pushed the button that downed the U-2.[112] Castro himself has recently returned to espousing a view he has held from time to time, that the Soviets controlled the SAMs and that he has no idea whether Moscow ordered it or not.[113]

Fortuitously, on the day the Cambridge meeting convened for its opening dinner, a long and detailed article on the U-2 shoot-down appeared in *The Washington Post*.[114] Drawn partly from an interview conducted with former Defense Department analyst Daniel Ellsberg, who was himself citing classified material from a post-crisis study of the event he had carried out for Robert McNamara, the article claimed that on October 26, 1962, a unit from the Cuban army attacked and overran the Soviet-controlled SAM site at Los Angeles, in Cuba, killing many Soviets and seizing control of the site. According to Ellsberg, the Cubans held the site until Soviets retook it the next day, but not before Cubans had fired the SAM that brought down the American U-2. Thus, Ellsberg implied, on the most dangerous day of the nuclear age, "a Cuban finger was on the button."[115] Cubans had nearly provoked a superpower war.

Sergo Mikoyan unequivocally denies that Cuban and Soviet troops fought for control of the Los Angeles SAM site, though he has suggested in conversation that the cable on which Ellsberg rests his case may indicate that a Cuban exile group—or perhaps even a roving "Mongoose" team—may have been active in the area at that time. But it is inconceivable to him that a conflict between Cubans and Soviets could have escaped his notice, since he was with his father in Cuba at the conclusion of the crisis. At the Cambridge conference, Mikoyan seemed to have other reasons for rejecting Ellsberg's thesis, too, though he was evidently reticent to discuss them.[116]

Shortly after the Cambridge meeting, CBS News made public the fact that a prominent Cuban defector, General Rafael del Piño, had told the CIA in his debriefing that a Soviet officer shot down Major Anderson's U-2.[117] General del Piño was close to Castro throughout the missile crisis and is probably better informed about Cuban military affairs during that period than anyone else. His account, therefore, is prima facie credible. In attempting to confirm del Piño's claim, we discussed the question again privately with Sergo Mikoyan, whose reticence quickly vanished. He identified the Soviet officer responsible for the U-2 shootdown as General Igor D. Statsenko, then a senior Soviet officer in Cuba.[118] According to his own account, his reluctance to discuss the matter in detail at the Cambridge conference stemmed from a promise he had made to Statsenko not to divulge his identity while he was alive. Ironically, Statsenko died shortly after the conference itself.

Although Statsenko claimed responsibility for the shoot-down, subsequent information suggests that he was not involved and that he deliberately misled Mikoyan; in the Afterword, we identify the responsible officers and discuss the incident in greater detail. It seems that the standing orders of Soviet air-defense forces in Cuba were ambiguous, allowing local commanders some discretion in deciding whether or not to open fire. With little advance warning and no opportunity to consult Moscow, the officers in question decided to fire on their own initiative. Their decision may have been decisively affected by the psychological climate in which it was made: Castro's antiaircraft batteries were already shooting at everything in sight; Soviet forces were thousands of miles from home, exposed on an island just ninety miles from Florida, surrounded by the U.S. Navy, and daily buzzed by American planes. Indeed, the United States was doing its best to flex its muscles in the area as visibly as possible.[119]

Whatever the exact details of the event, it is fortunate that both the ExComm and Nikita Khrushchev had by that time already tuned in to the dangers of accidents, inadvertencies, and breakdowns in command and control. The ExComm was therefore able to take the shoot-down surprisingly in stride,[120] and Khrushchev, we may surmise, was able to appreciate that he could not afford to prolong the crisis indefinitely without risking—or inviting—a clash between Soviet and American forces, or another unauthorized attack on an American plane. Robert Kennedy was very clear in telling Dobrynin on October 27 that the United States could not accept the loss of another aircraft without retaliation; Khrushchev was not inclined to test him.

Khrushchev must have realized that his position was no longer tenable and that further delays were unwarranted. It was time to settle. As Burlatsky said at the Cambridge meeting, he had no "effective alternative" for responding to an American attack on Cuba.[121] While it may or may not have been a *casus belli* between the superpowers—the Soviets at the Cambridge conference debated this point, and no doubt there would have been some debate also in Moscow[122]—Khrushchev and his colleagues could not risk having to resolve the ambiguity one way or another. It is hardly surprising, then, that near-panic seized the small group working with Khrushchev at his dacha outside Moscow, as they feverishly composed a brief reply to President Kennedy's October 27 letter, rushed it to Radio Moscow, and took a specially secured elevator to the sixth floor in order to meet what they took to be the President's deadline for a decision.[123] It was time to cash in the chips and go home.

The Educations of John Fitzgerald Kennedy and Nikita Sergeievich Khrushchev

Why were Kennedy and Khrushchev so poor at crisis avoidance, yet so capable of effective crisis management, even when events conspired to defeat them? The answer, it seems, is that they never appreciated the symmetry of their position until they were forced to "stare down the gun barrel of nuclear war" together.[124] Khrushchev's letter of October 26 had hit the nail squarely on the head: he and Kennedy shared an awesome responsibility in the Cuban missile crisis, a responsibility no two men had ever had to share before. The weight of their misunderstandings and their different cultures, ideologies, faiths, backgrounds, and national interests—which had proven to be such impediments to meaningful and successful communication before the crisis—was nothing compared to the weight of the responsibility they shared during the crisis. Their joint responsibility for the survival of their nations and the peace of the world, and the powerful anxiety that accompanied it, overcame their ignorance, their prejudice, their bluster, and their blindness, when it really mattered.[125]

It is instructive to recognize that they each experienced the crisis in much the same way, though on different timetables. Their initial reactions to their respective shocks—the discovery of Soviet missiles in Cuba for Kennedy, and the announcement of the quarantine for Khrushchev—were the same: outrage and anger. Both of them were initially inclined to react belligerently. After a period of reflection, however, in which righteous indignation gave way to introspection, and during which tempers cooled, they both came to see the predicament in approximately the same light. They both came to recognize that their chief enemy was the unpredictability and uncontrollability of events;[126] that they could not afford to drive the other into a corner; and that their crucial task was to find a safe exit through which they could escape on short notice. With their minds thus focused on the mutuality of their predicament and on the cooperative requirements of its successful resolution, Kennedy and Khrushchev were able to develop an empathy that swept aside their earlier animosity, leaving behind a deep and abiding mutual respect.[127] Of Kennedy, Khrushchev wrote, "his death was a great loss. He was gifted with the ability to resolve international conflicts by negotiation, as the whole world learned during the so-called Cuban crisis. Regardless of his youth, he was a real statesman. . . . He showed great flexibility and, together, we avoided disaster."[128] Kennedy would doubtless have said the same of Khrushchev.[129] Perhaps partly for this reason, neither of them was willing to declare victory at the conclusion of the crisis, even though Khrushchev, in his public statements, rarely shied away from making outrageous claims about other matters, and even though most of the rest of the world thought Kennedy clearly had something to crow about.[130]

If there is such a thing as "nuclear learning," then surely Kennedy and Khrushchev provide the textbook case.[131] But it is important to recognize that, even though they learned their lessons quickly, they very nearly did not learn them quickly enough. Robert Kennedy writes:

> The time that was available to the President and his advisers to work secretly, quietly, privately, developing a course of action and recommendations for the President, was essential. If our deliberations had been publicized, if we had had to make a decision in twenty-four hours, I believe the course that we ultimately would have taken would have been quite different and filled with far greater risks. The fact that we were able to talk, debate, argue, disagree, and then debate some more was essential in choosing our ultimate course.[132]

One might be tempted to think that Robert Kennedy is suggesting here that time was essential because it was necessary for the full exploration of the available options and their implications; but, as we noted in Chapter 2, this was not the way in which the ExComm used its time. The time was needed for the President and his advisors to learn. They needed time for their tempers to cool; they needed time to realize the weight of their responsibility; they needed time to recognize the dangers of the misperceptions and misjudgments that had brought them to the crisis in the first place, and the multidimensionality of the danger which they now faced. Had they not had that time, the President might indeed have found a *Maine* to sink, and the crisis, as Dean Rusk remarked, would have been "infinitely more dangerous."[133]

The delay between the President's October 22 speech and the time when the quarantine went into effect—thirty-nine hours—may have been unavoidable for diplomatic reasons (the OAS still had to vote on the quarantine resolution), but there can be no question that it was vital. If Khrushchev had not had thirty-nine hours in which to settle down, his order to run the blockade might not have been rescinded. Similarly, if the U-2 shoot-down had occurred on October 17, rather than on October 27, the President's mind might not yet have been focused on the dangers it posed, and in his outrage he might not have been able to take it in stride. If the events of the Cuban missile crisis, therefore, had taken place over a three-day period, rather than a thirteen-day period, war between the superpowers might have been all but unavoidable, because Kennedy and Khrushchev would not have had time to learn their lessons.

That Kennedy and Khrushchev had so many lessons to learn—about each other, about the origins of crises, about the risks of war, and about crisis resolution—was a function of the fact that they started from such a low base level. U.S.–Soviet relations were at a low ebb in the early 1960s, and during the first two years of Kennedy's Presidency there had been virtually no meaningful dialogue between the superpowers on issues that divided them, or on issues that united them. Among the most startling revelations of the Cambridge conference, quite apart from the volume of hard data and informed opinion the Soviet participants provided, was the vast extent of the gulf between the view from Washington and the view from Moscow prior to the crisis, and how quickly a gulf of that kind can be narrowed if, in the serious and cooperative atmosphere that permeated the Cambridge conference itself, Americans and Soviets speak candidly and soberly about it.

The extent to which the participants at the Cambridge conference learned from the encounter can be seen clearly in some of their post-conference publications. Mikoyan has now recorded his reflections on the conference in several articles, including one to appear in a joint U.S.–Soviet publication on crisis prevention.[134] He argues—correctly, in our view—that misunderstandings lay at the bottom of the event. According to Mikoyan, Khrushchev believed that the Bay of Pigs had been a humiliating failure for President Kennedy; that Kennedy was inexperienced and weak, and controlled by the CIA and the Pentagon; that Kennedy would be unable to resist the CIA and the Pentagon's call for an invasion; that U.S. forces would be used in the invasion, and Cuba would be overwhelmed; that the invasion would be massive and unexpected, leaving the U.S.S.R. unable to respond; that deploying nuclear missiles in Cuba would deter the Americans from invading; that the U.S. would ultimately accept the presence of Soviet missiles in Cuba; and that the missiles, by partially redressing the nuclear imbalance, would restrain American aggression worldwide.[135] In contrast, according to Mikoyan, Kennedy believed that the CIA and the American military were not to be trusted after the Bay of Pigs; that, prior to the discovery of the missiles, an invasion of Cuba was out of the question; that the deployment of Soviet missiles in Cuba indicated that the U.S.S.R. could not be trusted; that the U.S.S.R. would, after the missiles were in place, issue an ultimatum on Berlin; that missiles so close to the American coast could never be accepted by the American people or their government; and that an invasion of Cuba might be necessary to remove them.[136] In this way, Mikoyan tries to explain how Khrushchev almost provoked the event his missiles were deployed to prevent, and how Kennedy, by demanding removal of the missiles, nearly provoked a war that would have carried with it a far higher probability of triggering what he wrongly feared the Soviets were ultimately going to demand. Though Mikoyan's interpretations of events may be disputed, they indicate that he had absorbed what his American colleagues had told him at the Cambridge meeting.

Burlatsky's challenge to former ExComm members to publish their reflections in his newspaper resulted in Theodore Sorensen's "Reflections on a Grim but Hopeful Anniversary," published in the *Miami Herald* and slated to appear in the Moscow *Literaturnaya gazeta*.[137] The piece is a marvel of condensed wisdom derived from his reading of the results of the Cambridge meeting regarding mutual misunderstanding and the common but, in 1962, unacknowledged problems faced by the leaders of both superpowers. Sorensen also reiterated a message he conveyed at the Cambridge meeting and which is particularly significant considering that Sorensen is its source: "The crisis was . . . unwise, unwarranted and unnecessary in the first place. And all management efforts notwithstanding, it came close to spinning out of control before it was ended."[138] The man now characterizing the missile crisis as "unwise, unwarranted and unnecessary" is the same man who wrote the speech that launched it. In that speech, it was Sorensen's pen that labeled the Soviet action deceitful, aggressive, and unprovoked. Sorensen, too, had absorbed what he had heard.

But, for sheer path-breaking evidence of the seriousness and significance of this denouement, an article by Fyodor Burlatsky is foremost. His "The Caribbean Crisis and Its Lessons" is fundamentally at odds with the official Soviet line and is therefore revolutionary in its own right.[139] For the first time in the Soviet press, so far as we are aware, Burlatsky lists the deployment of missiles in Cuba as an important cause of the crisis, for which Khrushchev and his colleagues must be held responsible; and he argues that repairing the nuclear imbalance—not the defense of Cuba—was Khrushchev's main motivation. For seventy years, the Soviets had never admitted to a mistake in foreign policy; Burlatsky decided that the Cuban missile crisis was the appropriate place for them to begin.

Misperceptions die hard in the absence of dialogue, and the Cambridge meeting was only the beginning. For all the hard information and informed opinion the Soviets brought to the conference and shared with us, and despite the speed and ease with which great gaps between the Soviet and American understandings of the event were narrowed, many questions lay unanswered. But now that the weather has turned around, and Moscow is at last upwind, new voices are being carried on the air. Eventually, if the wind holds out, those voices will help us solve the mysteries that remain.

Epilogue

. . . In history, as in all serious matters, no achievement is final. . . .
Every new generation must re-write history in its own way; every new
historian, not content with giving new answers to old questions, must
revise the questions themselves.

R. G. COLLINGWOOD
The Idea of History

It is customary nowadays to end a book with a summary of its conclusions, perhaps out of fear that the body of the work itself is insufficiently
clear, or perhaps as a courtesy to those who only read introductions and
conclusions. But we are hesitant to do so here, for three reasons. First,
the subtleties and complexities of the issues we discuss are, we strongly
believe, the heart and soul of the message we wish to convey. It would
be self-defeating for us to attempt to boil down hundreds of pages of
discussion into a handful of pithy propositions and maxims when we
believe that a useful and accurate view of crisis prevention and management, and a proper understanding of the Cuban missile crisis, militate
against the very possibility. Second, the conclusions we have reached
are not conclusions which can easily be gleaned, as it were, from the
conventional closing chapter; they are conclusions that we ourselves
came to only by undergoing a process of exploration and discovery, a
process that we have tried to re-create in these pages so that the reader,
vicariously, can experience it, and learn from it, in approximately the
same way. Third, our process of exploration and discovery is not, by
any stretch of the imagination, "concluded." We hope that it will continue and that it will progress; we recognize that it is incomplete; and
we self-consciously regard our findings, in many cases, as provisional.

That said, it is worth drawing the reader's attention to several points
about those findings, with the caveat that they should not be taken to
exhaust the usefulness of what we hope has been a broader and richer
exercise. We hope the reader has noticed, for example, that the sequence
of discussions represented in these pages roughly mirrors the typical
sequence of events before and during a crisis: policymakers first engage
their "experts" (Part One), move on to debate policy choices among

themselves (Part Two), and then confront the adversary (Part Three). The differences, of course, between the discussions represented here and the Cuban missile crisis itself are vast. First, our discussions were cooperative exercises, while the missile crisis, at least until October 26, was a conflict of Olympian proportions. Second, no mere conversation in the comfort of a resort in the Florida Keys, in an office in Washington, D.C., or in a conference room in Cambridge, Massachusetts, can fully recapture the psychological reality of a nuclear crisis. Third, the participants in our discussions had the full benefit of hindsight, whereas policymakers in the White House and the Kremlin in 1962 worked through a very thick fog, a fog only penetrated by what Joseph Nye at Hawk's Cay called the "nuclear crystal ball."

But, despite these differences, several implications follow from the parallel, and from our analyses in Chapters 2, 4, and 6. For instance, the fact that our discussions were cooperative exercises, while the missile crisis itself, for the most part, was not, highlights the extent to which communication can be facilitated or impeded by its dynamics. In the cooperative contexts of our conferences and interviews, communication was easy and usually very productive. Even though the parties to our conversations generally failed to arrive at fully compatible understandings of events, in each case there was at least a recognition of contrary views, an ability to explore them on common terms, and, from time to time, some convergence of opinion. But when Americans and Soviets attempted to communicate in the confrontational, competitive climate of 1962, they failed almost completely—second-guessing, mistrust, and misjudgment were endemic, and very nearly disastrous—until Kennedy and Khrushchev came to appreciate that they were in precisely the same predicament and that they could only extract themselves from it safely through cooperation.

It would be ridiculous to claim that the United States and the Soviet Union have fully compatible interests, of course, or that all potential U.S.–Soviet disputes could be forestalled by timely and effective communication. But the superpowers do share one overriding interest: the prevention of catastrophic nuclear war. And as international crises are the events in which the specter of nuclear war looms largest, it follows that they also share an important interest in avoiding such crises—all the more so in view of the evident delicacy and unpredictability of crisis management itself. Thus, the superpowers have a powerful interest in communicating their interests clearly, understanding their respective needs, clarifying the norms and principles governing their behavior in the international arena, and doing their best to ensure that potential conflicts are identified and defused well in advance. Fortunately, the two countries are in a far better position to do this today than they were in 1962, largely because the Cuban missile crisis was useful in driving this lesson home. In 1962, the superpowers had not yet worked out the rules of the road governing such novelties as a Marxist regime in the Western Hemisphere or overseas Soviet military bases. Nor had the two countries yet appreciated the significance of crisis stability; the importance of fast, direct communications between Washington and Moscow; the decreasing utility of force as an instrument of policy; and what we have called the Kuhnian "paradigm shift" of crisis management which accompanied the advent of mutual vulnerability. The superpowers have indeed learned a great deal since—and largely because of—the Cuban missile crisis.

*   *   *

In Chapter 2, we tried to show that those who claim expertise in analyzing and understanding international affairs had great difficulty appreciating the impact of President Kennedy's position on his understanding of the crisis, and on his approach to dealing with it. As a consequence, their own understandings overemphasized the cerebral and the strategic dimensions of crisis management, and underestimated the visceral and reactive elements, degrading (if not vitiating) the relevance of scholarship to policymaking. In Chapter 4, we tried to show that the policymaking community itself divided into camps reflecting a cleavage similar in many ways to the cleavage dividing scholars and policymakers at Hawk's Cay. Those who strongly felt the burden of responsibility were inclined to understand power and risk in a radically different way from those who did not. But, remarkably, as we tried to show in Chapter 6, the common experience of crisis management in 1962 enabled Kennedy and Khrushchev to understand their predicament in the same terms, even though they started with far greater misunderstandings than did American scholars and policymakers, or hawks and doves within the Kennedy Administration itself. The two men most separated by culture, language, ideology, background, and national interests were the two men who ultimately came to share an understanding of the dangers of superpower crises, and the requirements of successful crisis resolution, most fully.

If there is one major theme common to all three parts of our journey, therefore, it is the significance of the burden of responsibility. That the policymakers at Hawk's Cay felt this burden so powerfully, while the scholars there felt it not at all, primarily accounted for the gulf between their understandings of the event. It was also the burden of responsibility, reinforced by the personal histories, professional experiences, and individual world views of the men in question, that primarily accounted for the many differences between the hawks' and the doves' approaches to the crisis. And it was the burden of responsibility, shared by Kennedy and Khrushchev, which more than anything else enabled the two, despite themselves, to bring the most dangerous confrontation of the nuclear age to a successful, peaceful resolution.

We find it surprising that the significance of the burden of responsibility and the psychological experience of shouldering it have been so poorly assimilated in academe, and, seemingly, so easily forgotten in Washington and Moscow. Recall McGeorge Bundy's observation: "Think tank analysts can set levels of 'acceptable' damage well up in the tens of millions of lives. They can assume that the loss of dozens of great cities is somehow a real choice for sane men. They are in an unreal world."[1] The unreality of their world is a function of their not having absorbed the implications of responsibility, the basic frame of reference for any policymaker confronted with the awesome knowledge that he or she is a trustee for the fate of humanity. As we argued in Chapters 4 and 6, the perceptions, propensities for risk-taking, and policy choices of those who feel this responsibility in a crisis are profoundly affected by it in systematic ways—with positive effects on their performance—but only after a significant and extremely dangerous intervening period of time in which rage and belligerence are likely to dominate their responses.

There is by now almost an ingrained tendency among those familiar with the main lines of American writing on the Cuban missile crisis to resist litanies of lessons drawn by its main participants.[2] Now, over twenty-six years after the fact, the resistance seems stronger than ever: for either the lessons must be hopelessly concrete, mired in an epoch long past, or hopelessly vague, applicable in principle to all situations but really relevant to none.[3] But one of the main sources of disdain for the litanies of lessons is that they are like lyrics without the music; they lack the capacity to move the reader by eliciting the sense of what the situation was like from which the lessons are drawn. What is lacking is a sense of the look and feel of nuclear danger.

The experience of nuclear danger, coupled with the responsibility the policymaker must shoulder for dealing with it, does suggest some lessons of its own. First, recognizing the positive role of the burden of responsibility in crisis management underscores Robert Kennedy's observation in *Thirteen Days*—that the wisdom of the President's decisions was vitally dependent upon the amount of time he had to formulate a response to the discovery of Soviet missiles in Cuba—though time may not have been vital in the way most of us have assumed.[4] Similarly vital were the thirty-nine hours Khrushchev had to ponder his response before the quarantine went into effect, and the fact that the quarantine was not an irreversible action that backed him into a corner from which he

could not escape without humiliation or catastrophe. We are tempted
to underscore as well, therefore, the lessons that Dean Rusk and George
Ball drew from the event.[5] Effective crisis management requires taking
time to formulate one's own responses, giving the adversary time to find
the cooperative and peaceful way out, and, as Sun Tzu stressed in *The
Art of War*, building golden bridges behind the enemy. But, alas, though
we may be in a better position today to prevent crises, we are, if anything, in a worse position to manage them. Time it seems, is a com-
modity in increasingly short supply. The pressures of the modern media,
of modern force structures, and of complex, tightly bound command
and control systems, will surely make the next major crisis more difficult
to handle.

*   *   *

The men who led their nations into and through the Cuban missile
crisis—President Kennedy and Chairman Khrushchev—came to understand the significance of responsibility very profoundly, and it forged a
bond between them that enabled them to reverse seventeen years of
steadily eroding relations and enter into a period of productive détente.
We are inclined to agree with Fyodor Burlatsky, therefore, that both
superpower relations and global security suffered a serious setback when
Kennedy was felled by an assassin's bullet and when Khrushchev was
forced from office in the Byzantine politics of the Kremlin; for both
Kennedy and Khrushchev were succeeded by men who appear not to
have felt the acute danger of the Cuban missile crisis, and the brief
détente wilted and died. Instead of engaging in meaningful communication on both their common and their conflicting interests, Johnson,
Brezhnev, and their successors engaged in a spectacular, and extremely
costly, nuclear arms race.

*   *   *

Scholarly conferences, in our experience, seldom change the views of
the participants in fundamental ways. These events are usually regarded
as opportunities to meet people known only in print and to pick up
leads to be explored in subsequent research. Clearly, however, the Cambridge conference was an exception to this, and in our view it was another
vindication of the assumptions underlying critical oral history. The Soviets and Americans present, all of whom came to the conference with
well-defined views on the crisis, began to question some of the assumptions they had held most dearly for twenty-five years. This was evident,
for example, when Sergo Mikoyan admitted at a public colloquium, the
day after discussing the matter with former members of the Kennedy
Administration, that he was just then beginning to believe that an Amer-

ican invasion of Cuba may not have been inevitable, contrary to what Soviets and Cubans strongly believed in 1962.[6] Later that evening, McGeorge Bundy delivered a public lecture in which he expressed his "utter astonishment" at the firmness of the Soviet conviction that Kennedy was keen to invade Cuba.[7] Of course, Bundy had long been aware that the fear of invasion and the concomitant need to deter it had been the official Soviet rationale for the missile deployment. What astonished Bundy and his colleagues was the array of highly detailed, internally coherent, but utterly mistaken arguments provided by the Soviets.

The Cambridge conference and critical oral history were the beneficiaries of what Burlatsky believed had sprouted and died in the early 1960s: what the Soviets today call "new political thinking." The twin pillars of the new political thinking are *perestroika* (economic and social restructuring of the Soviet system) and *glasnost* (openness, honesty, self-criticism, and the search for truth). In a perceptive piece published shortly after the Cambridge conference, Joseph Nye and Kurt Campbell emphasized that the connections between Mikhail Gorbachev's reforms and Khrushchev's own attempts to de-Stalinize the Soviet Union are strong and direct, while other important characteristics of Khrushchev and his era have come in for harsh criticism from Gorbachev and his followers.[8] On the latter, Nye and Campbell note especially Gorbachev's "rejection of the adventurist and aggressive policies followed by Soviet party boss Nikita Khrushchev," his recent, repeated insistence on the importance of the role of misperception, and his personal conviction that crises in the nuclear age are too dangerous to try to manage, so that they must be prevented by the establishment of an international system characterized by "comprehensive security." Yet Gorbachev is not without admiration for Khrushchev. It was Khrushchev, after all, who paved the way for Gorbachev, a generation later, to emphasize the importance of telling history accurately. It was Khrushchev who ridded the Soviet system of the very worst excesses of the Stalinist police state. Perhaps most of all, Gorbachev believes that Khrushchev really tried, in his clumsy, adventurist way, to find a basis for peaceful coexistence with the West. "Khrushchev," says Gorbachev in his book *Perestroika*, "was an emotional man and took it very much to heart that his sincere efforts and specific proposals to improve the international situation came up against a brick wall of incomprehension and resistance."[9]

We were told by the Soviets at the Cambridge meeting that Gorbachev is intensely interested in the Cuban missile crisis and that he has taken important steps to inform himself about it. He has, for example, commissioned a study led by Aleksandr Alekseev, Ambassador to Cuba during the crisis and an experienced journalist, which will draw on both Soviet and Cuban archival material to provide a detailed picture of events as they unfolded. We were also told that Anatoly Dobrynin will participate in the study, indicating that Gorbachev is interested in producing a balanced picture of all phases of the crisis as it evolved in Moscow, Washington, and Havana. Critical oral history of the Cuban missile crisis, it seems, has caught on in the Soviet Union. If so, its greatest successes may yet lie ahead.

Afterword

Update: The Moscow Conference and After[1]

Path-breaking though it was, the Cambridge conference suffered from two main deficiencies. The first was the asymmetry between Soviet and American participants, both in numbers and in seniority. We were fortunate to have three knowledgeable Soviets in Fyodor Burlatsky, Sergo Mikoyan, and Georgy Shakhnazarov; but none of them played a role in the Cuban missile crisis precisely analogous to that played by McGeorge Bundy, Robert McNamara, or Theodore Sorensen on the American side, all of whom were actively engaged in managing the crisis at the highest level. The second deficiency was the absence of Cubans. If, as the Soviets insisted, Khrushchev's concern for the defense of Cuba was an important motivation for the deployment of missiles in the first place, then the representation at the Cambridge conference merely perpetuated the American prejudice that the crisis was a Cold War superpower confrontation to which Cuba was, if not entirely irrelevant, then certainly little more than incidental. We began to appreciate the justice of the question Fidel Castro asked Georgy Shakhnazarov shortly after the conference itself: "Why was I not invited?"[2]

The Moscow conference of January 27–29, 1989, was an attempt to remedy both of those deficiencies. The six principals from the Cambridge conference were joined by (among others) former Soviet Foreign Minister Andrei Gromyko; former Ambassador to the United States Anatoly Dobrynin; former Ambassador to Cuba Aleksandr Alekseev; Sergei Khrushchev, son of former Soviet Premier Nikita Khrushchev; and General Dimitry Volkogonov, head of the Soviet Ministry of Defense Institute of Military History. A high-level Cuban delegation also participated, led by Jorge Risquet, currently a member of the Cuban Politburo and a longtime compatriot of Fidel Castro. Also participating were Sergio del Valle, a member of the Central Committee of the Cuban Communist Party and chief of staff of the Cuban Army in 1962; Emilio Aragonés, secretary of the Cuban Central Committee in 1962 and a former aide to Che Guevara; and José Arbesú, chief of the Cuban Interest Section, Washington, D.C., and former deputy director of the

Americas Department of the Cuban Central Committee.[3] The three delegations engaged in a frank exchange of information, criticism, and opinion, the results of which we summarize here.

As has proven the case at each stage of our inquiry, the answer provided to each question raised in Moscow spawned several new ones. Although the conference brought the details of Soviet and Cuban decisionmaking prior to and during the crisis into sharper focus, we sought to pursue the lingering puzzles, and several new ones, in a subsequent series of interviews both in Moscow and in Havana. The most interesting and useful parts of those interviews are also discussed here.

After the Cambridge conference—and especially in the wake of the Moscow conference—several articles appeared in the Soviet press relating the recollections of those who were involved, either centrally or peripherally, in what the Soviets call the "Caribbean crisis." On a lesser scale, Cubans have begun to publish information and commentary on what they refer to as the "October crisis." We also draw upon these recent writings.[4] For the most efficient use of space, our treatment is organized by topic, in roughly chronological order.

The new testimony from the Soviets and Cubans has enriched the story of the Cuban missile crisis considerably, though it has opened as many questions as it has plausibly answered. All the new evidence assembled here, however, has been testimonial. To date, we have not seen a single Soviet or Cuban document against which to check the recollections of Soviet and Cuban participants and scholars, and for that reason, this phase of our research has yet to satisfy all the requirements of critical oral history. This has been unavoidable: Cuba and the Soviet Union have no history of declassifying diplomatic documents for historical uses, and have no procedures for doing so; and in any case, the relevant diplomatic archives in both Moscow and Havana are reported to be sparse, by American standards. According to Soviet testimony, no written records of Kremlin decisionmaking regarding the missile deployment were kept prior to October 22, 1962, precisely to avoid breaches of secrecy; and according to the director of the Institute of Cuban History, the Cuban government in 1962 was so young and so disorganized that it had not yet established procedures for handling paperwork. Most of the relevant decisions were made in conversations that were simply not recorded.[5]

The next major step forward in the historiography of the Cuban missile crisis will have to await the release of those documents that do exist in Moscow and Havana. In the meantime, we must make what we can of written and verbal testimonies. We believe that the Soviets and Cubans who have spoken out have treated the opportunity to do so with due seriousness; in our opinion, therefore—bearing in mind the inherent limitations of oral history—their testimonies represent significant contributions to the understanding of the causes, conduct, and implications of the Cuban missile crisis.

Motives for the Soviet Deployment

Soviet participants at the Moscow conference endorsed the view that the decision to deploy medium- and intermediate-range ballistic missiles in Cuba was a response to the perceived need to deter an American invasion of Cuba, and to the perceived need to redress the gross imbalance in deliverable strategic nuclear weapons that favored the United States. A third motivation—the desire to counter American deployments of nuclear weapons on the Soviet periphery, largely for reasons of national pride and prestige—was frequently mentioned as a subsidiary but reinforcing factor. Significantly, there was no dissent to Burlatsky's and Mikoyan's conviction that there was no direct connection between the Cuban missile crisis and the unstable situation in Berlin. In Moscow, Andrei Gromyko added his voice to the chorus.[6]

As at the Cambridge conference, there was disagreement on the proper assignments of weight to each of these motivations. Several of the most well-placed Soviets, including Gromyko, Alekseev, and Sergei Khrushchev, agreed with Sergo Mikoyan's conviction that fears of an American invasion were in fact uppermost in Khrushchev's mind, grounded in what appeared to be a consistent and deliberate pattern of American activity designed to subvert and overthrow the regime of Fidel Castro, leading up to and including the use of American military force if necessary.[7] Alekseev recalled that Khrushchev asked Defense Minister Malinovsky to estimate the period of time that Cuba could resist a full-scale American invasion. Malinovsky's estimate was three or four days—not long enough for the Soviets to send reinforcements.[8] According to Alekseev, Khrushchev maintained at meetings with Presidium members that "there was no other path" to save the Cuban revolution than through the deployment of nuclear missiles.[9] If this is so, then Khrushchev may not have believed that deploying conventional forces to the island as a trip wire would have sufficed (possibly because of the marginal credibility of any explicit or implicit strategic nuclear threat undergirding it), nor may he have believed that the Soviet Union could credibly deter an American invasion by threats of retaliation elsewhere.

At the Moscow conference, Cuban participants sharply contradicted Khrushchev's analysis in several interesting ways. Though stopping short of insisting that Cuba could have held off a full-scale American attack, Jorge Risquet contended that Cuba could have resisted far longer than three days, and expressed indignation at Malinovsky's estimate. Sergio del Valle, chief of staff of the Cuban Army in 1962, claimed that Cuba had armed and mobilized 270,000 people—double Secretary of Defense Robert McNamara's 1962 estimate.[10] If this is correct, then the five American divisions slated for the invasion under 316 OPLAN would certainly have faced stiffer resistance than anticipated.[11] Even more striking, the Cuban delegation maintained that Fidel Castro's grounds for approving the deployment differed significantly from Khrushchev's grounds for proposing it. Dismissing the utility of Soviet nuclear missiles in Cuba for deterrence or defense (noting that they served primarily to turn Cuba into a target), Emilio Aragonés, one of the six members of the Cuban Communist Party Secretariat in 1962, claimed that Castro and the Cuban leadership accepted the deployment for two reasons: first, because the missiles would have shifted the global correlation of forces in favor of socialism; and second, because Cuba should accept "its share of the risk," since Cuba owed a debt of gratitude to the Soviet Union for its efforts made on her behalf. Although the deployment posed certain risks for Cuba, the Soviet Union had already taken risks in support of the Cuban revolution.[12] Castro himself has made similar statements in the past.[13] It is clear, however, that Cuba's national pride is better preserved by these claims than by the admission that Cuba required assistance from another nation, in the form of a nuclear deterrent, to protect her own sovereignty and independence. In subsequent interviews, both del Valle and Aragonés acknowledged that, in 1962, they had been attracted to the idea of the deployment largely because of its potential for deterring an American invasion.[14]

The Cubans' argument in Moscow, however, serves to highlight the link between the deployment of missiles to Cuba and the Soviet desire to redress the strategic nuclear imbalance. General Dimitry Volkogonov, who had reviewed the relevant archival materials, stated at the Moscow conference that, in 1962, the Soviet Union had succeeded in deploying only twenty ICBMs capable of reaching the United States, far fewer than the seventy-five hitherto estimated by Western intelligence analysts. Thus, the disparity in strategic nuclear weapons appears to have been even greater than was appreciated at the time. A successful Cuban deployment could have more than quadrupled the number of warheads that Soviet missiles could have delivered on the United States.[15] Most Western analysts have assumed that some such calculation was the primary, though not fully articulated, initial motivation for the deployment of missiles.[16] Even if Khrushchev's chief concern had been the political problem of preserving a socialist Cuba, the strategic value of the deployment probably contributed to the attractiveness of the deployment. Indeed, several Soviets, including Volkogonov himself, maintain that the missiles served a "dual purpose."[17] Malinovsky and Biryuzov may have supported the idea *primarily* for its strategic value.[18] In short, different individuals within the Soviet decisionmaking establishment, and different branches of the Soviet state, may have understood the deployment in different ways, which may have complicated Khrushchev's task of enlisting support for the terms on which the crisis was ultimately resolved.

As at Cambridge, the question arose at the Moscow conference whether the decision was well thought out in advance. Most agreed that Khrushchev's personality was an important factor. Gromyko acknowledged that "Khrushchev was an emotional man. He had enough emotion for ten people—at least." But, not surprisingly, Gromyko argued that the deployment had been decided upon only after a thorough, careful, "cool-headed" evaluation. Jorge Risquet, on the other hand, expressed some doubt, claiming that "Comrade Khrushchev did not think through all the moves in advance." Dobrynin agreed to some extent, stating that there was "improvisation as things unfolded; at least, that is what we felt in the embassy."[19] The discussions at the Moscow conference gave little reason for revising the common wisdom that "irrational reasons" played an important role. The venture was, in important respects, ill-conceived and subject to insufficient critical examination.[20]

The American Threat to Cuba: Perception and Misperception

American intentions toward Cuba in 1962 have long been the subject of debate, and continue to be so. The crucial question is whether or not the Kennedy Administration intended, at some point, to use American military force to oust Fidel Castro and establish a regime more congenial to American interests. Soviet and Cuban fears that this was the case seem to have played an important part in the decision to deploy nuclear missiles; disavowals of any such intention by former Kennedy Administration officials have long been received with skepticism both by Soviets and Cubans and by revisionist historians in the United States. More is at stake in the debate than simply the accuracy of the historical record or the reputation of President Kennedy. The issue sheds important light on the role of perceptions and misperceptions in the genesis of crises.

Former Secretary of Defense Robert McNamara insisted at the Moscow conference, as he had in Cambridge, that, "if I was a Cuban and read the evidence of covert American action against their government, I would be quite ready to believe that the U.S. intended to mount an invasion." His frankness on this point was welcomed by both the Soviet and the Cuban delegations. McNamara insisted, however, that despite the extent of American covert operations against Castro, and despite the preparation of military contingencies in October 1962, the Kennedy Administration did not intend to invade Cuba, by which he meant that no political decision to invade Cuba had been taken, and no serious discussions to consider such an operation had taken place among senior policymakers. The Cuban and Soviet delegations in Moscow expressed skepticism on this point.

Several publications have called into question the veracity of McNamara's disclaimer. Attention has focused on recently declassified documents that show that the Kennedy Administration actively sought to destroy the Castro regime.[21] One memorandum, for example—the "Cuba Project" program review dated February 20, 1962, and signed by Chief of Operations Brigadier General Edward G. Lansdale—specified late October 1962 as the target for Castro's ouster, and suggested that American military force might be required to accomplish that objective.[22] Another document—CINCLANT Admiral Robert L. Dennison's official retrospective history of the crisis—records that on October 1, more than two weeks before the missiles were discovered, orders were given to prepare the air strike option, 312 OPLAN, for "maximum readiness" by October 20.[23]

These documents show clearly that the United States was increasingly harassing the government of Fidel Castro, and that the Kennedy Administration was actively laying the military groundwork for possible contingencies, such as a discovery of offensive nuclear weapons in Cuba. This much, both McNamara and Bundy concede.[24] However, the stronger claim—that such documents show that the Kennedy Administration had actually decided to use American military force against Cuba—is entirely speculative. In our opinion, the evidence strongly suggests otherwise. For example, the tapes of the White House discussions on October 16, immediately following the discovery of the missiles in Cuba, strongly evince a belligerent attitude on the part of the President and his advisors, but nowhere refer to any prior decision to invade Cuba, any established intention to invade Cuba, or even any previous exploration of the desirability of such an invasion.[25] If indeed there had been even serious consideration of the possibility, one would expect it to be reflected in those early, formative discussions, because an invasion would have been a comparatively well-formulated option already on the table. Instead, the process of option-formation began from scratch. President Kennedy's reluctance to use more than a display of force during the crisis itself further reinforces doubt that he had harbored an intention to undertake military action against Cuba prior to the discovery of the missiles.

Despite the fact that there is no evidence of intent on the part of the Kennedy Administration to invade Cuba prior to the deployment of the missiles, it seems clear that Cuba and the Soviet Union quite understandably applied worst-case analyses to the various covert activities of CIA operatives in Cuba and to the activities of the American military in 1961 and 1962. The Cuban participants at the Moscow conference reported that Cuba had well-placed informants in the American defense and intelligence communities who kept them abreast of the various contingencies under consideration. Ambassador Alekseev explicitly claimed that the Cubans had "precise data" about American plans to invade the island.[26] Although operational plans and operational contingencies are not conclusive evidence of political intentions, they are nevertheless strong evidence of the worst possible case, and were apparently interpreted by Cuban and Soviet intelligence as reflecting a policy decision of the Kennedy Administration to invade Cuba and to overthrow Castro. When McNamara explicitly refers to these interpretations as Soviet and Cuban "misperceptions," he correctly points out that mistaken conclusions were drawn from the available evidence. But the United States had provided virtually *no* evidence suggesting otherwise. As current Deputy Foreign Minister Viktor Komplektov argued at the Moscow conference, "everything suggested that there *were* intentions." Indeed, it was the avowed policy of the United States to destabilize the Castro regime, and part of that effort involved convincing Cuba of its vulnerability to American attack. The Kennedy Administration, therefore, actively promoted the very "misperceptions" that led, in part, to the Soviet decision to deploy nuclear missiles to Cuba.

The Genesis, Terms, and Conduct of the Deployment

In his memoirs, Khrushchev claims that the idea to deploy nuclear missiles in Cuba first occurred to him when he was in Bulgaria, between May 14 and 20, 1962.[27] Sergo Mikoyan reported at the Cambridge conference that Khrushchev had already discussed the idea with Mikoyan's father at the end of April.[28] Shortly after the Moscow conference, Andrei Gromyko claimed that Khrushchev first discussed the idea with him on the flight home from Bulgaria.[29]

According to Gromyko, the discussions during the formative phase were candid and exploratory, although Khrushchev was clearly the "dominant" figure.[30] Sergei Khrushchev confirmed Sergo Mikoyan's claim that Anastas Mikoyan expressed strong reservations, cautioning that the proposed deployment was "a very dangerous step."[31] The only other member reported to have expressed doubt in Presidium meetings was Otto Kuusinen.[32] Gromyko, not at that time a member of the Presidium, reported that he told Khrushchev in May that a deployment of nuclear missiles in Cuba could call forth a "political explosion" in the United States, but Khrushchev seemed bent on the plan.[33] Though it was not characteristic of Gromyko to object to an idea proposed by Khrushchev, it is quite plausible that he voiced the pros and cons of the idea. If his testimony is accurate, then Khrushchev ultimately decided to disregard the cautions of two of his advisors who knew American politics best.

On Mikoyan's recommendation, Alekseev was urgently recalled to Moscow at the beginning of May and informed that he would be the new ambassador to Havana, effective May 31, by an order of the Presidium of the Supreme Soviet on May 7. When Khrushchev returned from Bulgaria, Alekseev was informed of the plan to deploy nuclear missiles to Cuba and was included in the decisionmaking circle.[34] When Khrushchev asked him how Castro would react to the proposal, Alekseev reports that he expressed grave doubts that Castro would agree, because accepting the missiles would cause him to be perceived as too tightly bound to the Soviet Union, jeopardizing his support in Latin America. Malinovsky, evidently strongly in favor of the plan, took exception to Alekseev's doubts when they were expressed in a meeting of the Presidium. In retrospect, Alekseev claims that he underestimated Castro's internationalism, and he now believes Castro was sincere when he said he would accept the missiles to bolster socialism on the world scale.[35]

Khrushchev decided to send a special mission to Cuba to test the waters, and to determine whether or not the missiles could be secretly deployed under the prying eyes of the United States. A ten-day "agricultural mission" traveled to Havana at the very end of May.[36] The mission included Alekseev; Sharif Rashidov, an alternate member of the Presidium; Biryuzov, traveling under the pseudonym "engineer Petrov"; and two other rocket specialists, named Ushakov and Ageyev.[37] The group arrived in Havana even before Ambassador Kudryavtsev had been informed of his imminent replacement by Aleksandr Alekseev, a move underscoring the secrecy and urgency surrounding the operation.[38] As soon as the delegation arrived, Alekseev informed Raúl Castro that "engineer Petrov" was actually the commander of the Strategic Rocket Forces, and a meeting was arranged with Fidel for that same evening. According to Alekseev, Fidel expressed immediate interest in the proposal, and left to confer with the other five members of the Cuban secretariat. Aragonés reports that he and the remaining four—Raúl Castro, Che Guevara, President Osvaldo Dorticós, and Blas Roca— were all strongly in favor of the idea.[39]

Much to Mikoyan's surprise, Biryuzov returned to the Soviet Union with Fidel's agreement and with an optimistic assessment of the chances of deploying the missiles secretly.[40] At a meeting of the Presidium on June 10, Biryuzov reported the results of the negotiations. The Presidium officially ordered the Defense Ministry to develop specific plans for the type and size of missile deployment, as well as air and coastal defense forces.[41]

In early July, a Cuban delegation led by Raúl Castro visited Moscow to discuss Soviet arms shipments to Cuba, and to finalize operational details of the missile deployment. Delegations led by Raúl Castro and Marshal Malinovsky met for two weeks, with Khrushchev himself present at meetings on July 3 and 8.[42] The first step would be to install a network of the latest Soviet SA-2 surface-to-air missiles (SAMs) around the perimeter of the island, and especially near the MRBM and IRBM sites at San Cristóbal, Sagua la Grande, Guanajay, and Remedios. The first SAMs and supporting equipment for the MRBMs were shipped at the very end of July.[43]

While in Moscow, Raúl Castro and Malinovsky drafted an agreement covering various details of the deployment, including the rights and obligations of the host country and the Soviet forces building and manning the missile sites. The agreement was a formal treaty with the following terms: (1) the Soviets would at all times have complete custody and control of the nuclear missiles in Cuba, the exact number of which was not specified in the treaty itself; (2) the Soviets would be given temporary use of the sites as rocket bases for a period of five years, though the sites themselves would remain sovereign Cuban territory; (3) after five years, there would be a further decision to annul or continue the arrangement; (4) all costs associated with the deployment were to be borne by the Soviet Union, and (5) some SAMs were to be provided to the Cubans, though the SA-2 SAMs would initially be installed, manned, and operated by the Soviets until Cuban forces could be trained to operate and maintain them. Raúl and Malinovsky individually signed every paragraph of the agreement, and space was provided at the end of the document for the signatures of Fidel and Khrushchev. But the two leaders never signed it, intending to do so at a public ceremony in Havana in November.[44]

When Raúl returned from Moscow with a draft of the document in hand, Fidel elaborated and modified the wording of the preamble. His amended version declared that the purpose of the agreement was "to provide mutual military assistance" rather than "to save the Cuban revolution," and it strongly affirmed the legality of the deployment.[45] Che Guevara and Emilio Aragonés traveled to Moscow at the end of the summer (August 27–September 2) to secure Soviet approval for

Castro's changes.[46] While there, they proposed that the agreement be made public immediately, prior to the deployment itself, to remove any pretext for a hostile American reaction. The Cubans warned the Soviet leadership that the situation in the United States was becoming increasingly volatile; concerned by the prospect that rising suspicions in the United States might eventually lead to war hysteria, they sought to draw international attention to the legality of the deployment.[47] But Khrushchev insisted that making the deployment public would be a terrible mistake; it might precipitate the very invasion the missiles were intended to forestall. Aragonés reported that they told Khrushchev that there might be "a preventive strike with severe consequences for us" if the Americans were not given adequate opportunity to reconcile themselves to the deployment; but Khrushchev was confident that this would not be the case. As Aragonés relates the story, "he said to Che and me, with Malinovsky in the room, 'You don't have to worry; there will be no big reaction from the U.S. And if there is a problem, we will send the Baltic Fleet.' " When asked if he thought Khrushchev was serious or joking, Aragonés replied, "He was totally serious. When he said it, Che and I looked at each other with raised eyebrows. But, you know, we were deferential to the Soviets' judgments, because, after all, they had a great deal of experience with the Americans, and they had superior information than we had. We trusted their judgment."[48] The Cubans therefore let the matter drop. At the Moscow conference, the Cuban delegation identified Khrushchev's judgment as a serious mistake.[49]

The Soviet expedition to Cuba was placed under the overall command of General Issa Pliyev, a former cavalry officer with no experience with nuclear missiles. Why Khrushchev chose Pliyev is unclear, though one plausible explanation is offered by Ambassador Alekseev, who suggests that he did so to throw American intelligence off the scent.[50] As part of the operation, according to General Volkogonov, over forty thousand Soviet troops were sent to Cuba, confirming Sergo Mikoyan's estimate at the Cambridge conference.[51] The deployments appear to have had their share of both gravity and comedy. For example, the commanders of the vessels involved in the operation were reportedly instructed to open sealed orders, at a predetermined point in the voyage, charging them to scuttle their ships if an attempt was made to stop and search them. In a lighter vein, in order to avoid identification, Soviet personnel are reported to have been directed to dance on deck, when American reconnaissance planes flew overhead, in an attempt to look like tourists.[52]

The first SS-4 MRBMs arrived on September 15,[53] eleven days after President Kennedy's first major warning against the deployment of "offensive weapons" to Cuba, two days after his second warning, and just four days after the denial by TASS that any such deployment was in the offing.[54] Once in Cuban ports, the missiles and their related equipment were off-loaded under cover of darkness, with elaborate precautions taken to ensure that the shipments went undetected. One of those who came off a Soviet ship was the thirty-nine-year-old commander of a motorized infantry regiment, Lieutenant Colonel Dimitry Yazov, now Soviet Minister of Defense.[55]

Only Soviets were involved in the unloading, transportation, and installation of the missiles; indeed, the Soviets themselves even chose the locations of the missile sites.[56] Camouflage was a Soviet responsibility. The Cuban Armed Forces' role in the deployment was limited to guiding the preliminary exploration of the terrain, choosing the routes from the ports to the missile sites, and building roads where necessary.[57]

Soviet Missiles in Cuba: Warheads, Targets, and Orders

One of the more persistent puzzles of the Cuban missile crisis concerns whether or not nuclear warheads for the Soviet MRBMs ever reached Cuba. American intelligence never detected nuclear warhead in Cuba, and interpreted the incomplete assembly of likely warhead storage bunkers at the missile sites, as revealed by reconnaissance photographs, as evidence that they had not yet arrived.[58] But the Kennedy Administration, in the face of uncertainty, operated on the assumption that they had.[59]

According to General Volkogonov, twenty nuclear warheads had arrived in Cuba in late September or early October, and twenty others were in transit, aboard the *Poltava*, when the quarantine went into effect.[60] Apparently, the Soviets did not keep the Cubans well informed of the warhead shipments. General del Valle, the Cuban chief of staff, was informed on October 23 or 24 by General Pliyev merely that "everything was ready," which he interpreted to mean that warheads had arrived. Only later did he learn the details of the warhead shipments, and discover that they were incomplete.[61] According to Volkogonov, the warheads that had arrived in Cuba were kept "well away" from the missiles themselves, and at no time were measures taken to mate them, even when alert levels were raised following President Kennedy's speech of October 22. Had the order to prepare the missiles come down, Volkogonov claimed, they could have been targeted in four hours, and would have require a subsequent countdown of fifteen minutes.[62]

Sergei Khrushchev claimed at the Moscow conference that the inaccuracy of the SS-4 missiles restricted their useful targets to large cities and industrial centers, such as Washington or New York. Contrary to newspaper accounts of the conference, however, at no time did Khrushchev suggest that either Washington or New York was actually targeted, because at no time were targeting procedures under way. "My father would not have allowed [the warheads] to be mounted," Sergei Khrushchev insisted. "He felt that would have made it easier for a madman to start a war."[63]

General Volkogonov said that the standing orders given to the three SS-4 and two SS-5 regiments deployed to Cuba were extremely clear. He read from Defense Ministry Archives to the Moscow conferees that "the rocket forces are to be used only in the event of a U.S. attack, unleashing a war, and under the strict condition of receiving a command from Moscow." Both conditions had to be satisfied before the missiles were to be used.[64] While these orders defined the limits of the local commanders' authority to launch nuclear missiles, however, none of the Soviets we have interviewed believed that physical mechanisms preventing unauthorized use (such as modern permissive action links) were built into the warheads.

Diplomatic Miscellany: J.F.K. and Gromyko, Scali and Fomin

Two days after President Kennedy learned of the Soviet deployment, Soviet Foreign Minister Andrei Gromyko paid a visit to the White House which, as we noted in Chapter 6, he described as "the most complex discussion" of his diplomatic career.[65] Kennedy did not ask Gromyko directly about the presence of Soviet missiles in Cuba, nor did Gromyko volunteer any information about them, much to the relief of both. Gromyko has since asserted, however, that he was instructed to be forthcoming if confronted directly. At the Moscow conference, he maintained merely that he would have given a "proper answer" to a direct question from the President; but, in a subsequent article, he claimed that he was instructed by Moscow to say that the Soviets were deploying a "small quantity of missiles of a defensive nature" to Cuba, and to encourage quiet diplomacy if Kennedy's reaction were negative.[66]

The President's speech of October 22 launched the public phase of the crisis; not until October 26 did the White House perceive conciliatory signals from the Soviets. At 1:00 p.m. on October 26, Aleksandr Fomin, an official at the Soviet Embassy in Washington known to be the senior KGB official in Washington, met ABC's State Department correspondent John Scali for lunch, at Fomin's request.[67] Fomin asked Scali to determine whether or not the United States would be interested in resolving the crisis by pledging not to invade Cuba, in return for the withdrawal of the nuclear missiles. It has widely been held that Fomin was acting on instructions from Moscow; it now appears that he was acting on his own initiative.[68] Scali replied at 7:30 p.m. that the Administration was interested in Fomin's suggestion. Dobrynin was uncertain whether this channel reflected the views of the White House, and did not authorize a telegram to Moscow; but Fomin may have cabled a report notwithstanding.[69]

The State Department began to receive a private, conciliatory letter from Khrushchev to Kennedy between 6:00 and 9:00 p.m. on Friday, October 26, vaguely proposing to conclude a deal along the same lines as Fomin had suggested to Scali.[70] Most students of the crisis have assumed that the letter merely formalized Fomin's earlier trial balloon; but it appears now that this assumption is incorrect. The American Embassy in Moscow began receiving the message at 4:43 p.m. Moscow time (early Friday morning in Washington), many hours before Fomin's initiative. The Fomin–Scali communication would have been too late to have influenced the content of the letter.[71]

The Origin of the Turkish Missile Trade

On Saturday, October 27, before President Kennedy could respond to Khrushchev's letter of the day before, a second letter, taking a harder line, was broadcast by Radio Moscow. Khrushchev now insisted that the United States remove its intermediate-range Jupiter missiles in Turkey as a quid pro quo for the removal of Soviet missiles in Cuba.[72] Khrushchev's quick about-face has always puzzled not only Western students of the crisis but members of the ExComm as well, who show considerable surprise and confusion in the transcripts of the October 27 meetings.[73] At the Cambridge conference, Shakhnazarov conveyed a message from Dobrynin suggesting that the idea for the missile trade had been hatched in the Soviet Embassy in Washington.[74] His rather cryptic remark remained unclear until the Moscow conference, where Dobrynin provided further details previously unknown. According to Dobrynin, he and Robert Kennedy met secretly on the night of Friday, October 26, as part of an ongoing series of private, late-night back-channel discussions. Dobrynin remarked to the Attorney General that the Administration's extreme reaction to the deployment of Soviet missiles in Cuba seemed puzzling in view of the fact that the United States had deployed similar missiles in Turkey, next door to the Soviet Union. In raising the issue, Dobrynin says, he was acting entirely on his own initiative, not expecting it to be interpreted as part of a negotiating position. He was merely attempting to make the point that the Soviet side had an equal right to provide for its own security. Dobrynin reports:

> Robert Kennedy said, "You are interested in the missiles in Turkey?" He thought pensively and said, "One minute, I will go and talk to the President." He went out of the room. . . . [He] came back and said, "The President said that we are ready to consider the question of Turkey, to examine favorably the question of Turkey."[75]

Dobrynin immediately reported this conversation to Moscow. Shortly thereafter, Khrushchev demanded the missile trade. Dobrynin hastened to add to his account that he believes his cable to have been the source of the missile-trade proposal, though it is possible that the idea arose simultaneously in Moscow. No one at the Moscow conference, however, offered the latter interpretation, even though some, such as Andrei Gromyko, were presumably in a position to know.

If Dobrynin's story is accurate, then traditional understandings of the climax of the crisis must give way. The tapes of the ExComm meetings of October 27 clearly indicate that the question of the missile trade dominated the discussion, and that the President himself was its strongest advocate. But at no point in those discussions did the President or his brother discuss Robert Kennedy's meeting with Dobrynin of the previous day; nor did they reveal that they had already communicated to the Soviet Union that the Jupiter missiles in Turkey were negotiable. In conjunction with the revelation of the "Cordier maneuver,"[76] and in view of the secrecy surrounding Robert Kennedy's October 27 meeting with Ambassador Dobrynin (several members of the ExComm were unaware even that such a meeting was to take place), the President's reticence in the transcripts of the October 27 meetings strongly suggests that the ExComm had become largely irrelevant to the President's decisionmaking at the height of the crisis. Crucial decisions were being made by the President and a small group of close advisors, well away from—and unbeknownst to—the ExComm as a whole. The group that the President had found so useful in the early option-formation phase of the crisis seems to have been left out of important aspects of decision-making at its climax.[77]

The U-2 Shoot-down of October 27

At the Moscow conference, the Soviet delegation released new information confirming that the U-2 shoot-down of October 27 was indeed the act of Soviet air-defense forces. According to Alekseev, two generals were involved in the decisionmaking when the U-2 was detected on radar at approximately 10:00 a.m. General Volkogonov publicly identified one as Pliyev's deputy for air defense, the late Lieutenant General Stepan N. Grechko. The second general was apparently Leonid S. Garbuz, now retired, then Pliyev's deputy for military training.[78] General Igor Statsenko, who had told Sergo Mikoyan that he personally gave the order to fire on the U-2, was in Cuba with the Strategic Rocket Forces and would not have been in the air-defense decisionmaking loop.[79] In giving false testimony, Statsenko may have sought to make public the fact that the shoot-down was indeed the result of action by Soviet forces; military secrecy would not have allowed him to release the identities of those who actually did make the decision.

Once the U-2 was spotted near Banes, the two generals had twenty minutes to make a decision whether or not to fire. After attempting unsuccessfully to contact General Pliyev, they apparently decided to shoot on their own authority. As recently disclosed by the newspaper of the Cuban armed forces, *Bastión*, the local commander who actually gave the order to fire was apparently General Georgy A. Voronkov, now retired and living in Odessa.[80]

Contrary to previous accounts of the shoot-down, which suggested that Soviet SAM units had standing orders not to fire on American aircraft, Alekseev claims that there was "no direct prohibition"against doing so.[81] Del Valle confirms this, noting that the officer on site was criticized by Khrushchev, but that he defended himself by saying that he had only followed Soviet standing orders "to fire on any aircraft that flies overhead in wartime," an action for which he was later decorated by Fidel Castro personally.[82] From the Cuban point of view, the situation could indeed have been construed as "wartime." Throughout the crisis, Castro had authorized his own antiaircraft (AA) artillery to fire at groups of two or more low-flying American planes; on October 26, he ordered his AA units to fire on any American aircraft within range.[83] That same day, Voronkov received an order to begin operating the radar stations.[84] Cuban Politburo member Jorge Risquet claimed at the Moscow conference that Soviet air-defense forces were willing to fire on American aircraft on October 27 because they had been "inspired by the enthusiasm of the Cubans." Indeed, the downing of the U-2 was a tremendous boost to Cuban morale; news of it spread rapidly throughout the island and was greeted everywhere with wild celebration. As Risquet put it, "our people felt that we were not defenseless."[85] But many Cuban leaders reportedly felt that the shoot-down was "very dangerous" and worried "that it would inflame the situation."[86]

At the Moscow conference, Volkogonov read from Malinovsky's telegram to Pliyev immediately following the shoot-down, rebuking him for "hastily [shooting] down the U.S. plane" because "an agreement for a peaceful way to deter an invasion of Cuba was already taking shape." This contradicts the English version of Khrushchev's memoirs, which indicate that he believed that it was Cubans who had shot down the American plane.[87] Yet Sergei Khrushchev insists that his father knew at the time that Soviets had shot down the plane, and that in the tape recordings on which Khrushchev's memoirs were based, he clearly stated this. Strobe Talbott, editor and translator of Khrushchev's memoirs, reports the discrepancy in the English edition as a "mistake." But the Russian-language version of Khrushchev's memoirs published by Progress Publishers (currently in limited special circulation in the Soviet Union) also states that Cubans shot down the plane, because it is a retranslation of Talbott's English version.

There is some evidence to suggest that there may have been a partial, unsuccessful cover-up attempt by the Soviet military. Ambassador Alekseev reported that he did not find out that the Soviets were responsible for the shoot-down until over a decade later, and he has speculated that Malinovsky himself may have tried to prevent details of the event from spreading in order to prevent embarrassment to the Ministry of Defense and the responsible Soviet officers in Cuba.[88]

The Resolution of the Crisis: R.F.K., Dobrynin, and Turkish Missiles (Again)

At 7:15 p.m. on Saturday, October 27, Robert Kennedy telephoned Dobrynin to request another meeting. The two met at 7:45 in the Department of Justice. The reports of important aspects of the meeting in Robert Kennedy's *Thirteen Days* were starkly contradicted by Ambassador Dobrynin in Moscow. First, Robert Kennedy reported telling Dobrynin that "we had to have a commitment by tomorrow that those bases would be removed. I was not giving them an ultimatum but a statement of fact. He should understand that if they did not remove those bases, we would remove them."[89] Though the Attorney General explicitly denied that this was an ultimatum, it has generally been interpreted by Western historians as a clear compellent threat. However, in Moscow, Dobrynin denied that Robert Kennedy issued any ultimatum or made any threats. He further denied that Robert Kennedy warned of an imminent coup or loss of civilian control of the military, in contradiction to Soviet accounts of the meeting, including Khrushchev's own.[90] In fact, according to Dobrynin, Robert Kennedy soft-pedaled the danger of imminent American action, and Dobrynin claimed that his cable to Moscow reporting the meeting was similarly low-key on that point.[91]

The second respect in which Dobrynin contradicted Robert Kennedy's account of the meeting sheds light on the first, and concerns the status of the missile trade. Robert Kennedy wrote:

> He asked me what offer the United States was making, and I told him of the letter that President Kennedy had just transmitted to Khrushchev. He raised the question of our removing the missiles from Turkey. I said that there could be no quid pro quo or any arrangement made under this kind of threat or pressure, and that in the last analysis this was a decision that would have to be made by NATO. However, I said, the President had been anxious to remove those missiles from Turkey and Italy for a long period of time. He had ordered their removal some time ago, and it was our judgment that, within a short time after this crisis was over, those missiles would be gone.[92]

Dobrynin insists that it was Robert Kennedy who pursued the idea of an explicit "deal" on the Turkish missiles; that he wished to portray it as a significant concession by the United States; and that he never said that the President had already ordered their removal.[93] Dobrynin's version of the meeting was confirmed in an important respect by Theodore Sorensen in Moscow, who edited *Thirteen Days* prior to its publication. Sorensen confessed that the missile trade had been portrayed as an explicit deal in the diaries on which the book was based, and that he had seen fit to revise that account in view of the fact that the trade was still a secret at the time, known to only six members of the ExComm.[94]

Andrei Gromyko stressed at the Moscow conference that the question of the Turkish missiles was "not trivial," and that the Soviet Union had a solid foundation to consider that their removal was part of the terms on which the crisis was resolved.[95] Indeed, Khrushchev sent the President a letter after the conclusion of the crisis, in which he described the withdrawal of Jupiter missiles from Turkey as an integral part of the agreement on which the crisis was resolved. Sorensen admitted in Moscow that this letter had been received, but explained its absence from the complete Kennedy–Khrushchev correspondence by noting that the Administration decided against acknowledging the withdrawal of the Jupiters as a quid pro quo, and returned the letter as if it had never been opened.[96]

It appears, therefore, that the withdrawal of the Jupiter missiles from Turkey in the spring of 1963 was indeed part of a private deal which led to the withdrawal of Soviet missiles from Cuba in November 1962.

However, both the United States and the Soviet Union have subsequently found it expedient not to insist on this point, the United States because of the complications and ill will it would cause among its NATO allies (and because of the domestic political consequences to the President had he publicly traded missiles); and the Soviet Union because of Castro's objection to being treated like a "bargaining chip" on a par with a "minor" NATO ally such as Turkey.[97]

Khrushchev's Sense of Urgency and Castro's Telegram

Between the time Dobrynin took his leave of Robert Kennedy on October 27 and the time the ExComm met again at 9:00 a.m. on Sunday, Khrushchev had decided to bring the confrontation to an end.[98] Western students of the crisis have long wondered what had caused Khrushchev to do so at that particular time. Dobrynin's claim that he did not interpret Robert Kennedy's messages of October 27 as a threat or an ultimatum only adds to the puzzle, since Robert Kennedy's account of the meeting has been widely regarded as the best explanation of Khrushchev's sense of urgency.

If Khrushchev's urgency was a reaction to any verbal message, it may have been that of John Scali, rather than Robert Kennedy. At the Moscow conference, Aleksandr Fomin reported that in his meeting with Scali on Saturday, October 27, at which Scali attempted to ascertain the reason why Khrushchev's Friday letter had been so quickly superseded by a letter demanding a missile trade, Scali angrily threatened that there would be an American attack within hours if the missiles were not removed. After the resolution of the crisis, Fomin communicated a personal message from Khrushchev to Scali that his outburst had been "very valuable."[99]

It seems probable, however, that Khrushchev was paying greater attention to his own intelligence sources than to Scali's extracurricular theatrics, since Scali was not the only one who appeared to be speaking for the Administration. During the night of October 25–26, Soviet intelligence apparently reported hard evidence of an imminent American attack, leading Khrushchev to propose conciliatory terms in his Friday letter. Later in the day on October 26, Soviet intelligence reversed its earlier estimate, possibly encouraging Khrushchev to toughen his terms in his second letter. But some time late on October 26 or on October 27, Soviet and Cuban intelligence appear once again to have concluded that an American attack could be expected momentarily. If this indeed had been their assessment, it may have weighed heavily in Khrushchev's decision to bring the crisis to an end.[100]

Other factors apparently played a significant role, such as the U-2 shoot-down and the inadvertent straying of another American U-2 over Soviet air space on October 27. But perhaps at least as important, it seems, was a communication from Castro to Khrushchev, via Alekseev, on October 27. That message came to light at the Moscow conference, and was reported in the press as Castro's attempt to urge Khrushchev to fire the nuclear missiles in Cuba against the United States.[101]

It remains unclear exactly what Castro communicated to Khrushchev. We have reason to believe that, in an unpublished passage of his memoirs, Khrushchev reported it thus: "Suddenly, we received through our Ambassador a cable from Castro. The Ambassador reported that Castro had given him the report face-to-face. Castro informed him that he had reliable information that an American invasion would take place within a few hours. Therefore, he was proposing to preempt the invasion and inflict a nuclear strike on the U.S."[102] But well-placed Soviets and Cubans deny that this was the content of the message. According to both Ambassador Alekseev (who transmitted the message to Khrushchev) and Emilio Aragonés (who helped draft it, and who had felt on October 26 that Khrushchev's resolve was weakening), the telegram was intended to communicate the Cuban people's willingness to fight to the last man and the last bullet in the event of an American attack, and to urge Khrushchev to show firmness. Both Alekseev and Aragonés believe that Khrushchev misinterpreted the telegram to be urging a preemptive strike—an entirely plausible belief, given Khrushchev's state of mind at the climax of the confrontation.[103] Until the cable itself is made public by the Soviets or Cubans, the issue cannot be resolved conclusively. A great deal depends upon the precise wording of the telegram, and whether it accurately reflects Castro's verbal communication to Alekseev.

An appropriate interpretation of the cable may also turn crucially on an appreciation of the psychological context in which it was written. A confidential source has informed us that, in February 1989, Castro remarked that he believed the missiles should have been fired in the event of an American invasion, though neither preemptively nor in response to an air strike. Del Valle reports that, in 1962, he shared this view.[104] These are entirely understandable sentiments; as del Valle put it, Cuba had "no atomic culture" at the time, meaning that Cubans had not yet developed the understanding of the consequences of nuclear explosions that existed in the United States and the Soviet Union in 1962. But, in any case, the consequences for Cuba of a full-scale American invasion would not have differed in important respects from the consequences of a nuclear war. In either event, the island faced devastation. Castro's apparent willingness to see Soviet nuclear missiles fired from Cuban soil in the event of a full-scale invasion must be understood from this perspective.

What does seem clear is that, in the telegram in question, Alekseev communicated to Khrushchev Castro's conviction, based in part on Cuban intelligence sources, that an American attack was imminent. If indeed Cuba had informants well placed in the American defense and intelligence communities, then the President's instructions on the morning of October 27 to prepare for a possible attack on the morning of October 30 may have been an important factor. Scott Sagan has suggested to us that "pathfinder" teams may have been infiltrated into Cuba as part of the contingency planning, and that the detection or capture of one of these teams would have been interpreted as strong evidence of a forthcoming invasion. It has also been claimed that Soviet military intelligence had tapped into Washington phone lines in 1962, raising the possibility that the Soviets would have overheard discussion of preparations for an attack the following week.[105] But if Khrushchev did misinterpret the telegram from Castro, then it would stand as one more reminder of the significance of major miscommunications during crises. In this case, a misinterpretation may have facilitated a rapid resolution; in other circumstances, it might have complicated one.

Khrushchev was not the only one who felt a powerful sense of urgency at the climax of the confrontation; many members of the ExComm did as well. In his memoir of the crisis, Robert Kennedy noted that one factor contributing to the sense of urgency at the climax of the confrontation was an FBI report that Soviet personnel in New York were preparing to burn their files.[106] At Hawk's Cay, Raymond Garthoff insisted that it was the Soviet Embassy in Washington that began burning its archives on October 27.[107] But at the Moscow conference, Ambassador Dobrynin emphatically dismissed these claims as unfounded, claiming that at no time did Soviet diplomatic personnel prepare to destroy records.

Cuba and the Conclusion of the Crisis

Castro's displeasure at Khrushchev's failure to consult him before agreeing to withdraw the missiles from Cuba is a matter of record. Apparently, Cuba first heard of Khrushchev's decision on the radio. Ambassador Alekseev reports that upon hearing the news, "I felt myself the most unhappy man on earth, as I imagined what Fidel's reaction to this would be." Indeed, Castro refused to see him for several days.[108]

Part of Castro's fury at not having been consulted may have stemmed from his conviction that Khrushchev did not get as much as he could have from the Americans. At the Moscow conference, Jorge Risquet insisted that the "five conditions" Castro proclaimed as the price for his assent to the withdrawal of the missiles were indeed within reach, including American withdrawal from Guantánamo.[109] If indeed Castro was convinced that this was a concession to which the United States would agree, then it would seem that both Kennedy and Khrushchev were very wise indeed to conclude the crisis bilaterally, for it bespeaks an appalling ignorance of American political realities on Castro's part.[110] Aragonés, however, maintains that Castro's five conditions represented merely a statement of principles, not an attempt to stake out a negotiating position, and that they were intended primarily to serve domestic political purposes. Cuba had been badly treated by both superpowers, and its national honor required a public articulation of Cuban dissent.[111]

Raymond Garthoff has reported that Cuban troops surrounded the missile sites on October 28, and only stood down after the arrival in Havana of Soviet First Deputy Premier Anastas Mikoyan, whose task was to persuade Castro to go along with the U.S.–Soviet agreement.[112] The Moscow conference and subsequent discussions have shed light on the issue and raised interesting new questions in the process. Ambassador Alekseev believes, for example, that the troops that took up positions around the missile sites were in fact Soviet soldiers in Cuban uniforms, and insists that there was no danger of a Soviet–Cuban clash at that time.[113] Both Sergio del Valle and Emilio Aragonés insist that the troops were Cuban antiaircraft units deployed to protect the missile sites from low-level attack.[114]

Anastas Mikoyan's success in persuading Castro to accept the November withdrawal of the Il-28 light bombers, in addition to the withdrawal of the missiles, was a remarkable achievement. The American demand that Cuba relinquish weapons intended for the Cuban Air Force wholly independently of the Soviet missile deployment only added insult to injury. Mikoyan's success was aided by one of those curious interventions of fate: Castro's initial attitude toward the Soviet representative was softened by the sudden death of Mikoyan's wife at the very moment he arrived in Havana.[115] But according to Cuban testimony, the published American views of the negotiations involving the bombers are mistaken in a variety of ways. First, American intelligence believed in 1962 that forty-two Il-28s had been delivered to Cuba, only seven of which were assembled;[116] Sergio del Valle, however, maintains that twelve Il-28s had been delivered, only three of which were to be transferred to the Cuban Air Force. None of the three Cuban bombers had been uncrated during the crisis, and the Soviets simply withdrew them at the same time they withdrew their own bombers, an operation facilitated by the fact that the aircraft were all located at the same bases.[117]

It may be, therefore, that none of the bombers had yet been formally transferred to Cuba, and that Mikoyan did not have to persuade Castro to relinquish something he had already been given. Second, some American analysts have believed that Mikoyan's task was abetted by President Kennedy's message to the NATO allies of November 19, warning that if the bombers were not promptly withdrawn, air strikes might be necessary to destroy them. The President reportedly intended the message to leak to the Soviets.[118] However, Emilio Aragonés, who was present throughout the negotiations between Castro and Mikoyan, does not recall any discussion of the American threat and does not believe that it was communicated to Castro. Aragonés recalls that Mikoyan represented the withdrawal of the bombers merely as a request from the Soviet and American negotiators in New York, and persuaded him to go along by appealing to the necessity for a quick solution. Describing the scene with some amusement, Aragonés claimed Mikoyan "related the discussions in New York he had had with Kuznetsov and McCloy; Fidel told him that he had committed the serious mistake of showing weakness to the Americans. Fidel said, 'What will happen if the U.S. wants the bombers out, too?' Mikoyan launched into this long, confusing exposition on Soviet–Cuban friendship, on the overthrow of the Tsars, and all kinds of things that had nothing to do with the problem at hand. It was very confusing and surreal. And then, at the end, he said that the Americans had requested the withdrawal of the Il-28s. Well, Fidel exploded. He leaned back, waved his hand, and shouted, 'Oh, to hell with the airplanes!' "[119]

The fact that the Il-28 bombers were a subject of debate at all, according to Sergo Mikoyan, was largely the fault of the Soviet Union itself. Khrushchev, by his letter to the President of October 28 stating that he had given an order "to dismantle the arms which you described as offensive," was attempting to deny that the nuclear missiles in Cuba were in fact, "offensive," and was indeed attempting to avoid using the word "missiles" publicly.[120] But the effect was to give the United States *carte blanche* to define which weapon systems were to be withdrawn, and the Kennedy Administration chose to insist upon the removal of the Il-28s—obsolete, short-range bombers believed to have a nuclear capability, but for which no nuclear weapons had been supplied. The withdrawal of the Il-28s was a blow to Cuba's national pride, and it further strained Soviet–Cuban relations. As Sergo Mikoyan put it, the Soviets fell victim to their own "propagandistic tendencies."[121]

Meta-lessons

For the most part, the lists of "dos" and "don'ts" that participants at the Moscow conference drew from the event differed little from the lists that emerged from earlier conferences. But those lists do not exhaust the usefulness of discussions of this kind. The lessons participants draw from these discussions yield important lessons of their own. We believe that one of the most important of these "meta-lessons" is that candid mutual exploration of pivotal moments of danger in superpower relations can cultivate and cross-fertilize attitudes which may themselves contribute to the likelihood that similar events may be avoided in the future. The Moscow conference provided two important illustrations of this.

The first concerns perceptions of risks. Those perceptions have changed over time as our understanding of the events of the crisis has improved. As we argue in Chapter 4, significant constituencies in both the United States and the Soviet Union have traditionally understood the confrontation in starkly rational-actor terms, and have discounted the danger that the crisis might have resulted in nuclear war. Their skepticism stems from the evident difficulty of constructing a chain of rational decisions whose end point is a serious nuclear confrontation. From such a vantage point, it is easy to criticize decisionmakers for being overly timid and for not pressing their apparent advantages. Many American scholars of the crisis—and many of those in the ExComm who have come to be known as "hawks"—have faulted President Kennedy for being overly cautious in his handling of the confrontation, for not seizing the opportunity to take decisive action against the Castro regime, and for concluding the crisis on what were perceived as unfavorable terms.[122] Khrushchev himself has reported that he came under considerable criticism, particularly from the military, for not pursuing a harder line.[123] And at the Moscow conference, the Cuban delegation reported that Fidel roundly excoriated Khrushchev for not demanding greater concessions from the Americans.[124] When rational-actor analysis effectively removes nuclear war from the list of viable options, a serious disincentive to taking a harder line is removed as well.

At the Moscow conference, Andrei Gromyko stimulated a productive disagreement by insisting early in the conference that there was "no direct threat of nuclear war" during the crisis, by which he meant, according to his later elaboration, that at no time did he perceive a significant risk of an imminent nuclear clash. In voicing this opinion, he was representing what might be termed the "old thinking" on matters of nuclear risk. His diplomatic career spanned more than four decades; and *realpolitik*, which sees the world as a chessboard, characterized his understanding of international politics. Gromyko maintained that the Soviet side

> . . . weighed all the factors for and against; they were weighed by Khrushchev. Now, looking back, we can say that he correctly evaluated them—the effects of these factors and possible outcomes. Correctly. Was there a risk of a nuclear clash? . . . [T]here was a certain level of risk. But a direct threat of nuclear war did not exist—nuclear war between the Soviet Union and the United States. This can be seen from the line pursued by President Kennedy at the final stage of the crisis. . . . There was a certain level of risk of war. But there was no direct threat of war. Of this I can assure you; I am in a position to know. These are not just conjectures.[125]

Gromyko was virtually alone in his assessment. The "new thinking" on matters of nuclear risk—emphasizing the dangers of accidents, inadvertence, breakdowns of command and control, psychological pressures, and the limits of rationality under stress and uncertainty[126]— dominated the Moscow conference participants' understanding of the real dangers faced in the Cuban missile crisis. "The most dramatic moment of my long experience in America," Dobrynin reported, "was when I was watching television as our tankers approached the imaginary line in the ocean, across which President Kennedy said he would not allow Soviet vessels. There were helicopters flying back and forth. Our tankers did stop . . . But if bombing had begun, or if an invasion had been initiated, there was no guarantee that accidental factors could not have resulted in a nuclear war."[127]

Those who understand the risks in this way are inclined to praise rather than fault Khrushchev and Kennedy for their caution in handling the crisis. The responsibility they shared for avoiding a catastrophe— while protecting their national interests and commitments—focused their minds on the many dimensions of the danger they faced.[128] As we learn more about the details of events on all sides, we can appreciate the propriety of their circumspection. The extent to which all sides misjudged, misperceived, and misunderstood the actions and intentions of the others grows more astonishing with every new discovery. At the Moscow conference, the majority clearly concluded from those discoveries that the risks of nuclear war had not only been greater than was previously thought but lay primarily in dangers that had not been properly understood at the time. The discussion strongly indicated that the equilibrium point in attitudes toward the use of force and the risks of war has shifted considerably since 1962.

The flip side of risk is control. In the light of recent information, it is positively disorienting now to read some of the early evaluations of the Kennedy Administration's handling of the crisis, which lavishly praised its brilliant control and its matchless calibration.[129] What makes such an evaluation disorienting is precisely what the Moscow conferees found difficult to credit in Andrei Gromyko's confident assurances—the supposition that Kennedy and Khrushchev had unfettered mastery of events. If anything, the most important virtue of their handling of the crisis is that they both recognized the very severe limits of their control.

The growing realization that the successful outcome of the crisis was due more to circumspection and restraint than to skillful play on the geopolitical chessboard was reflected in a second striking feature of the lessons drawn at the Moscow conference: the extent to which participants on all sides have largely replaced self-congratulation with humility and self-criticism. Theodore Sorensen spoke to this point most eloquently. He emphasized that the crisis was first and foremost a demonstration of the fallibility—not the wisdom—of national leaders. Noting that there was "enough blame to go around," and reciting a long list of mistaken assumptions on which national leaders were operating in 1962, Sorensen sought to lay to rest the American perception, largely cultivated by earlier writings such as his own, that the Cuban missile crisis was the Kennedy Administration's finest hour, a clear-cut foreign policy victory, and a major Soviet defeat on a scale proportionate to their degree of responsibility for the crisis in the first place. Several Soviet participants voiced similar views. Georgy Arbatov, for example, candidly called the Soviet operation a "humiliation" and "a gross error."[130]

What the Moscow conference has confirmed is that the common wisdom on the Cuban missile crisis has dramatically changed. In the 1960s, when nuclear risk was understood in overwhelmingly rational-actor terms, and when the Kennedy Administration was credited with brilliant control and matchless calibration, the common wisdom both on the missile crisis and on superpower relations more generally was reflected in Coral Bell's quotation of Robert McNamara's apocryphal remark: "There is no longer any such thing as strategy, only crisis management."[131] The new common wisdom is that the term "crisis management" overemphasizes the degree to which national leaders can control both risks and events in a serious confrontation, and that much higher priority must be given to crisis avoidance. A healthy awareness of the dangers and limitations of crisis management is a useful deterrent to carelessness or recklessness in foreign policy. We are inclined to view the circumspection and self-criticism evident in recent discussions of the crisis, therefore, as an important ingredient in successful crisis prevention itself.

Most participants at the Moscow conference, however, were eager to register their conviction that the crisis was, on the whole, a positive development in superpower relations. As Georgy Shakhnazarov put it, the experience of "fear and illumination" in the missile crisis contributed to an atmosphere which helped bring about the Hot Line, the Limited Test Ban Treaty, and a brief but constructive period of détente.[132] But the positive effects of the crisis were merely fortuitous consequences of an event that was very nearly catastrophic. It is this thought that is so humbling today. The more we learn, the more humbling it seems. We regard that as perhaps the most important meta-lesson of the ongoing study of the Cuban missile crisis.

Notes

PROLOGUE

1. See, e.g., Graham T. Allison, *Essence of Decision: Explaining the Cuban Missile Crisis* (Boston: Little, Brown, 1971); Herbert S. Dinerstein, *The Making of a Missile Crisis: October 1962* (Baltimore: Johns Hopkins University Press, 1976); Alexander L. George and Richard Smoke, *Deterrence in American Foreign Policy* (New York: Columbia University Press, 1974), pp. 447–99; Henry M. Pachter, *Collision Course: The Cuban Missile Crisis and Coexistence* (New York: Praeger, 1963); and Albert and Roberta Wohlstetter, "Controlling the Risks in Cuba," Adelphi Paper No. 17 (London: Institute for Strategic Studies, 1965). Two useful collections of resource materials are: Robert A. Divine, ed., *The Cuban Missile Crisis* (Chicago: Quadrangle, 1971); and David A. Larson, ed., *The "Cuban Crisis" of 1962: Selected Documents, Chronology and Bibliography*, 2nd ed. (Lanham, Md.: University Press of America, 1986).

2. For an excellent review of Soviet statements and analyses of the Cuban missile crisis, see Ronald R. Pope, ed., *Soviet Views on the Cuban Missile Crisis: Myth and Reality in Foreign Policy Analysis* (Lanham, Md.: University Press of America, 1982).

3. See, e.g., Elie Abel, *The Missile Crisis* (Philadelphia: J. B. Lippincott, 1966); David Detzer, *The Brink: Cuban Missile Crisis, 1962* (New York: Thomas Y. Crowell, 1979); Roger Hilsman, *To Move a Nation: The Politics of Foreign Policy in the Administration of John F. Kennedy* (New York: Doubleday, 1967), pp. 160–229; Robert F. Kennedy, *Thirteen Days: A Memoir of the Cuban Missile Crisis* (New York: Norton, 1969); Arthur M. Schlesinger, Jr., *A Thousand Days* (New York: Fawcett, 1965), pp. 726–69; and Theodore C. Sorensen, *Kennedy* (New York: Harper & Row, 1965), pp. 667–718.

4. Several illustrations of the apparent unreliability of Robert Kennedy's recollections, for example, may be found in David A. Welch and James G. Blight, "The Eleventh Hour of the Cuban Missile Crisis: An Introduction to the ExComm Transcripts," *International Security*, Vol. 12, No. 3 (Winter 1987/88), pp. 5–29.

5. The two best collections of these materials are at the John F. Kennedy Library in Dorchester, Massachusetts, and at the National Security Archive in Washington, D.C.

6. See, e.g., "White House Tapes and Minutes of the Cuban Missile Crisis," *International Security*, Vol. 10, No. 1 (Summer 1985), pp. 164–203; and "October 27, 1962: Transcripts of the Meetings of the ExComm," *International Security*, Vol. 12, No. 3 (Winter 1987/88), pp. 30–92.

7. The unedited document is available from the Center for Science and International Affairs, Harvard University (David A. Welch, ed., *Proceedings*

of the Hawk's Cay Conference on the Cuban Missile Crisis, March 5–8, 1987, CSIA Working Paper 89-1).
8. The unedited transcript is also available from the Center for Science and International Affairs, Harvard University (David A. Welch, ed., *Proceedings of the Cambridge Conference on the Cuban Missile Crisis, October 11–12, 1987*, CSIA Working Paper 89-2).

CHAPTER I

1. See J. Anthony Lukas, "Class Reunion: Kennedy's Men Relive the Cuban Missile Crisis," *The New York Times Magazine* (August 30, 1987), pp. 22–27, 51, 58, 61.
2. Several lessons which emerged from the conference are discussed in James G. Blight, Joseph S. Nye, Jr., and David A. Welch, "The Cuban Missile Crisis Revisited," *Foreign Affairs*, Vol. 66, No. 1 (Fall 1987), pp. 170–88.
3. McNamara then went on to state, "I think the main puzzle we face in the Cuban episode is this: What in God's name did Khrushchev think he was doing? I'm not sure I have any idea, and I'm not sure we will ever find out. Back then I was thought to be a dove and now I'm thought to have been a hawk—there's no telling what the passage of time will do to interpretations of events. But does any man have the right to put us in the position of facing the possibility of nuclear war?"
4. Schlesinger, *A Thousand Days*, p. 759.
5. Cf. Marc Trachtenberg, "The Influence of Nuclear Weapons in the Cuban Missile Crisis," *International Security*, Vol. 10, No. 1 (Summer 1985), pp. 137–63.
6. Dinerstein, *The Making of a Missile Crisis.*
7. The preliminary discussion on this point is not reproduced here, but may be found in the unedited transcript: David A. Welch, ed., *Proceedings of the Hawk's Cay Conference on the Cuban Missile Crisis*, CSIA Working Paper (hereafter *HCT*, for "Hawk's Cay Transcript"), p. 24. McNamara and Schlesinger noted that the details of Senator Keating's claims proved to be mistaken, casting doubt on the reliability of his sources; Dillon believed that though McCone expressed worries that Soviet deployments of SAMs might conceivably be intended to protect MRBMs, "he had no actual knowledge of the introduction of offensive missiles until October 15th"; and McNamara noted that if either McCone or Anderson knew anything, they had not informed him.
8. Cf. Schlesinger, *A Thousand Days*, p. 742.
9. See Raymond L. Garthoff, *Reflections on the Cuban Missile Crisis* (Washington, D.C.: Brookings Institution, 1987), p. 11; and János Radvanyi, *Hungary and the Superpowers: The 1956 Revolution and Realpolitik* (Stanford: Hoover Institution Press, 1972), p. 137.
10. Scott D. Sagan, "SIOP-62: The Nuclear War Plan Briefing to President Kennedy," *International Security*, Vol. 12, No. 1 (Summer 1987), pp. 22–51.
11. This is a controversial statement. Zbigniew Brzezinski writes, for example: "It has been very roughly estimated that in the event of a war, American losses would have been in the vicinity of 30 million lives, Soviet losses approximately four times higher." Zbigniew Brzezinski, "U.S.–Soviet Relations," in Henry Owen, ed., *The Next Phase in Foreign Policy* (Washington, D.C.: Brookings Institution, 1973), p. 119n.

12. For an analysis, and declassified documents, dealing with the decisions to set high strategic force goals in 1961, hedging against uncertainties in estimates of future Soviet strategic force levels, and in 1962 not to change those American force goals after the estimated Soviet force levels were sharply reduced, see Raymond L. Garthoff, *Intelligence Assessment and Policymaking: A Decision Point in the Kennedy Administration* (Washington, D.C.: Brookings Institution, 1984).

13. See *ibid.*, pp. 27–34; reprinted in Garthoff, *Reflections on the Cuban Missile Crisis*, pp. 138–39.

14. On this issue, see especially Klaus Knorr, "Failures in National Intelligence Estimates: The Case of the Cuban Missiles," *World Politics*, Vol. 16, No. 3 (April 1964), pp. 455–67, which argues that it is an open question whether there were any American intelligence "failures" in view of the fact that the U.S.S.R. may have been the one that incorrectly gauged the situation; and Roberta Wohlstetter, "Cuba and Pearl Harbor: Hindsight and Foresight," *Foreign Affairs*, Vol. 43, No. 4 (July 1965), pp. 691–707.

15. In the unedited transcript, Garthoff states: "I believe that the idea of a trade for missiles in Turkey was purely *ad hoc* and was born during the crisis itself." *HCT*, p. 44. Cf. the discussion on pp. 253–57.

16. We have not been able to find a passage in Khrushchev's memoirs that says explicitly this, but cf. Strobe Talbott, ed., *Khrushchev Remembers* (Boston: Little, Brown, 1970), p. 498.

17. Cf. Fyodor Burlatsky's remarks, p. 236.

18. Cf. the contrary discussion, pp. 236–37.

19. Cf. Edward Crankshaw, *Khrushchev: A Career* (New York: Viking, 1966), pp. 280–81.

20. *The Washington Post*, December 10, 1962; Cf. Arnold L. Horelick, "The Cuban Missile Crisis: An Analysis of Soviet Calculations and Behavior," *World Politics*, Vol. 16, No. 3 (April 1964), p. 363.

21. Cf. *ibid.*, pp. 363–89.

22. See Allison, *Essence of Decision*, pp. 106–12.

23. L. Sedin, "Be on Guard and Keep Your Powder Dry!" *Voyennaya mysl'* (*Military Thought*), No. 12 (December 1961).

24. Anatoly Gromyko, "The Caribbean Crisis," reprinted in Pope, ed., *Soviet Views on the Cuban Missile Crisis*, pp. 161–226.

25. See Igor D. Statsenko, "On Some Military-Political Aspects of the Caribbean Crisis," *Latinskaya amerika*, November–December 1977, pp. 108–17. Statsenko was a senior officer with the Soviet forces in Cuba. His argument is the same as Anatoly Gromyko's, with the exception that he refers explicitly to "strategic rockets" in Cuba. See also Fyodor Burlatsky, "Black Saturday," *Literaturnaya gazeta*, November 23, 1983, pp. 9–10; Anatoly Gromyko and Andrei Kokoshin, *Bratya Kennedi* (*The Kennedy Brothers*) (Moscow: Mysl', 1985); and Andrei Kokoshin and Sergei Rogov, *Serye kardinali belogo domo* (*Grey Cardinals of the White House*) (Moscow: Novosti, 1986).

26. Schlei's memorandum is reprinted in Abram Chayes, *The Cuban Missile Crisis: International Crises and the Role of Law* (New York: Oxford University Press, 1974), pp. 108–16.

27. Refer to the chronology.

28. See George and Smoke, *Deterrence in American Foreign Policy*, pp. 474–75.

29. Sorensen noted that Kennedy believed Bolshakov when he relayed word that there were no missiles in Cuba. But Schlesinger wondered whether Bolshakov would have known. See *HCT*, p. 54.
30. Cf. chapters 5 and 6, and Afterword, p. 331.
31. In his memoirs, Gromyko claims: "In spite of several allegations circulating in the West, not once in the whole course of the conversation did Kennedy raise the question of the presence of Soviet missiles in Cuba. Consequently, I did not have to answer whether or not there were such weapons in Cuba." *The New York Times*, February 22, 1988, p. A6.
32. See the discussion on pp. 274–77, and in the Afterword, p 335.
33. See Alexander L. George, David K. Hall, and William R. Simons, *The Limits of Coercive Diplomacy* (Boston: Little, Brown, 1971), pp. 21–32.
34. See *ibid.*, pp. 27–28.
35. See Welch and Blight, "The Eleventh Hour of the Cuban Missile Crisis," pp. 22–23, especially n. 55; and Sorensen, *Kennedy*, pp. 714–16.
36. See Welch and Blight, "The Eleventh Hour of the Cuban Missile Crisis," pp. 8–9, and the citations therein.
37. "At first [Rusk] was for a strike; later he was silent or absent. He had, Robert Kennedy wrote laconically in *Thirteen Days*, 'duties during this period of time and frequently could not attend our meetings.' Privately, Kennedy was less circumspect. Rusk, he thought in 1965, 'had a virtually complete breakdown mentally and physically.' " Arthur Schlesinger, Jr., *Robert Kennedy and His Times* (New York: Ballantine, 1978), pp. 546–47. We find this extremely dubious. See Welch and Blight, "The Eleventh Hour of the Cuban Missile Crisis," pp. 22–23.
38. A fuller discussion of this point may be found in *HCT*, pp. 78–80. The issue is also discussed in the Dillon interview on pp. 166–68.
39. Robert Kennedy writes: "We had to have a commitment by tomorrow that those bases would be removed. I was not giving them an ultimatum but a statement of fact. He should understand that if they did not remove those bases, we would remove them." *Thirteen Days*, p. 108.

   Khrushchev's account of Dobrynin's report of the meeting is as follows: "Robert Kennedy looked exhausted. One could see from his eyes that he had not slept for days. He himself said that he had not been home for six days and nights. 'The President is in a grave situation,' Robert Kennedy said, 'and he does not know how to get out of it. We are under very severe stress. In fact, we are under pressure from our military to use force against Cuba. . . . Even though the President himself is very much against starting a war over Cuba, an irreversible chain of events could occur against his will. That is why the President is appealing directly to Chairman Khrushchev for his help in liquidating the conflict. If the situation continues much longer, the President is not sure that the military will not overthrow him and seize power. The American army could get out of control.' " *Khrushchev Remembers*, pp. 497–98. Anatoly Gromyko, citing Soviet Foreign Ministry Archives, gives a calmer account of the Dobrynin–R.F.K. meeting on October 27 and never mentions a possible American military coup. See Pope, ed., *Soviet Views on the Cuban Missile Crisis*, pp. 214–16. For the most recent testimony, see Afterword, pp. 340–42.
40. Cf. the contrary discussion on pp. 267–68.
41. Cf. chapters 5 and 6.
42. The 1962 estimate was eight to twenty hours. Cf. the discussion in chapter 4.

43. Central Intelligence Agency memorandum, subject: "The Crisis: USSR/ Cuba," October 27, 1962, p. III-3. (Available in the Cuban Missile Crisis file, National Security Archive, Washington, D.C.)

44. "White House Tapes and Minutes of the Cuban Missile Crisis," pp. 173–74.

45. More precisely, the CIA reported that Khrushchev told Knox that the Soviet missiles in Cuba were "under strict Soviet control." "The Crisis: USSR/Cuba," October 27, 1962, p. III-3.

46. See Carl von Clausewitz, *On War*, tr. and ed. Michael Howard and Peter Paret (Princeton: Princeton University Press, 1976), p. 605.

47. George, Hall, and Simons, *The Limits of Coercive Diplomacy*, p. 124. In support of this assertion, George et al. cite a now controversial account of the shoot-down in Robert Kennedy's *Thirteen Days*. See Welch and Blight, "The Eleventh Hour of the Cuban Missile Crisis," pp. 19–20.

48. Trachtenberg is quoting here from Executive Secretary of the National Security Council Bromley Smith's summary record of the ExComm meetings of October 27 (available in the Cuban Missile Crisis file, National Security Archive, Washington, D.C.). Smith's records seem to be inaccurate on this point, for nowhere in McGeorge Bundy's transcription of the October 27 tapes does McNamara baldly state that an invasion of Cuba had become almost inevitable. The closest he comes to doing so is in the context of an argument he formulates designed to convince the Turks to allow the Jupiter missiles to be defused. That is, McNamara proposes telling the Turks that invasion is almost inevitable—and that a Soviet reprisal in Turkey might be expected to follow—in order to secure Turkish cooperation in reducing a possible distant risk. But this does not mean that McNamara himself believed that an invasion of Cuba was in fact inevitable; his point is a rhetorical one. Cf. the unedited version of McGeorge Bundy's transcription, available at the John F. Kennedy Library, Dorchester, Mass.

49. Adam Yarmolinsky, Department of Defense, Office of the Secretary of Defense, *Department of Defense Operations During the Cuban Missile Crisis*, 1963, p. 12.

50. See Pope, ed., *Soviet Views on the Cuban Missile Crisis*, p. 215.

51. In the unedited transcript, Garthoff makes the following comment: Burlatsky "is quite open about the fact that he used literary license, and when I told him that some of the things he said were simply incorrect, he admitted being selective and imprecise in what he used. He said that he thought there was a lesson to be learned from the article ["Black Saturday," in *Literaturnaya gazeta*] and the play he wrote [*Burden of Decision*] about civilian/military relations *in general*, including in the U.S.S.R., and not just with respect to the Cuban missile crisis. He thought that insufficient attention was being paid to the idea of crisis management in his country, and that's why he felt justified in playing with history. Remember that his account came out right after the KAL 007 incident, which was a very tense time in U.S.–Soviet relations, and he wanted to remind people that it was possible to have effective and constructive relations with the United States even during periods of tension." See *HCT*, pp. 100–1.

52. Here Dillon implies that Robert Kennedy's instructions to Dobrynin were discussed in the ExComm itself. There is no record in the transcripts of that day's ExComm meetings of any such discussion. Moreover, some members of the ExComm, such as Nitze and Taylor, were not informed

of the mission at all. It seems that the President discussed the matter privately with a handful of advisors, and that the ExComm was never even briefed about the encounter the next day. See the interview with Dean Rusk, as well as Welch and Blight, "The Eleventh Hour of the Cuban Missile Crisis," pp. 11, 16.

53. *Khrushchev Remembers*, p. 497. Cf. Afterword, pp. 340–44.
54. December 12, 1962; reprinted in Pope, ed., *Soviet Views on the Cuban Missile Crisis*, pp. 71–106.
55. See the discussion on pp. 271–73, 310–11, and in the Afterword, p. 345.
56. NSAM 160. See Peter Stein and Peter Feaver, *Assuring Control of Nuclear Weapons: The Evolution of Permissive Action Links*, Center for Science and International Affairs Occasional Paper No. 2 (Lanham, Md.: University Press of America, 1987), pp. 36–40.
57. JCS 2311/25, 22 May 1961, Report on Exercise Pine Cone, CCS 3510, Joint and Combined Exercises, 6 Feb 1961, Record Group 218, Joint Chiefs of Staff 1961, National Archives.
58. *Op. cit.*
59. Cf. Garthoff, *Reflections on the Cuban Missile Crisis*, p. 37n.
60. Michel Tatu also claims that "Polaris missile submarines throughout the seven seas were exchanging with their bases uncoded messages about targeting." *Power in the Kremlin: From Khrushchev's Decline to Collective Leadership*, tr. Helen Katel (London: Collins, 1969), p. 264.
61. Cf. Scott Sagan, "Nuclear Alerts and Crisis Management," *International Security*, Vol. 9, No. 4 (Spring 1985), p. 108. At this point, Robert McNamara rolled his eyes, visibly shocked. According to Scott Sagan, however, McNamara had been informed of this incident before. During an interview with Sagan, McNamara reportedly stated that he "was not surprised" that General Power sent the alert out in the clear, and that had he known Power had done so, he might have approved.
62. Cf. the contrary discussion on pp. 266–68.
63. The statements to which Taylor is referring were made on September 4 and 13, 1962. See the chronology.
64. Interestingly, Taylor discounted the effect of the nuclear imbalance in a 1974 article, writing that "the strategic forces of the United States and the U.S.S.R. simply cancelled each other out as effectual instruments for influencing the outcome of the confrontation." Maxwell D. Taylor, "The Legitimate Claims of National Security," *Foreign Affairs*, Vol. 52, No. 3 (April 1974), p. 582. Cited in Trachtenberg, "The Influence of Nuclear Weapons in the Cuban Missile Crisis," p. 138.
65. According to the transcripts of the October 27 meetings, Taylor was present at ·least periodically.
66. See Welch and Blight, "The Eleventh Hour of the Cuban Missile Crisis," pp. 12–18.
67. Trachtenberg argues in a lengthy footnote in the unedited transcript that this initiative can only be understood against the background of the UN's mishandling of Kennedy's standstill proposal. See *HCT*, pp. 129–30.
68. The statement that the Cordier maneuver shows that "the underlying risk was one of loss of control, rather than deliberate choice" seems arguable, though indeed this may have been a large part of President Kennedy's reason for preparing the contingency.
69. See Graham T. Allison, Joseph S. Nye, Jr., and Albert Carnesale, eds.,

Hawks, Doves, & Owls: An Agenda for Avoiding Nuclear War (New York: Norton, 1985), p. 235.

70. Trachtenberg, "Nuclear Weapons and the Cuban Missile Crisis," pp. 137–63.

71. Trachtenberg argues that a "strong" yet "speculative" case be made that the Soviets were powerfully affected by their strategic inferiority, because they did not go to a heightened alert, and because they recognized the value of a first strike. *Ibid.*, pp. 156–61. However, even if the Soviets had attained parity, it would have been in their interest not to go to a heightened alert, so as not to increase the tension and, possibly, provoke an attack.

72. "White House Tapes and Minutes," p. 176. May is not quoting verbatim, but the point is the same.

73. Barbara Tuchman in *The Guns of August* (New York: Macmillan, 1962) traces the outbreak of the First World War to a series of misperceptions, misjudgments, and inadvertent actions. According to Robert Kennedy's memoir, Tuchman's book exerted a profound influence on President Kennedy's thinking. See *Thirteen Days*, pp. 62, 127–28.

74. See *ibid.*, pp. 89–106.

75. Cf. Dean Rusk's discussion in the interview on pp. 171–72.

76. In the unedited transcript, Garthoff proceeds with a detailed discussion of the diplomatic aftermath of the missile crisis. The U.S. did not formalize its commitment not to invade Cuba with the Soviets in an exchange of letters, because the question of inspection was never resolved, until August 7, 1970. This commitment was made public on November 13, 1970. Both sides portrayed it as a reaffirmation of the 1962 agreement, though the American interest in it was to prevent certain Soviet moves in Cuba in the future. The Soviets learned in 1970 that the U.S. would not accept a Soviet submarine base at Cienfuegos, though they learned that the U.S. would accept the presence of Tu-95 Bears (at least in the reconnaissance and ASW versions). The Soviets never sent SSBNs to Cuba, though in May 1972 they brought a G-II diesel-powered ballistic-missile submarine to the port of Nipe, waiting to see if it would be mentioned at the Moscow summit. It was not. At that very time, the Incidents at Sea Agreement was also being concluded. And there was also a last-minute dispute about including the G-class SSBs toward the conclusion of SALT I. When the Soviet sub left Cuba on May 6, American P-3 ASW planes (based at Guantánamo Bay) forced it to surface repeatedly until it was well into the Atlantic, despite the fact that it fired flares to chase them off.

Elsewhere, the U.S. issued several private and ineffective warnings against intervention in Afghanistan in 1979. In June 1979, at Vienna, President Carter warned against an increased Soviet military presence in Cuba. The Soviets did nothing, but the U.S. nevertheless protested the discovery of a brigade which had been there all along. The U.S. warned the Soviets not to move into Cam Ranh Bay, but they did, in 1979. However, in November 1982, a strong private warning to the Soviets not to introduce MiGs into Nicaragua dissuaded them from doing so, despite the fact that Nicaraguan pilots had been training on MiGs in Bulgaria. "The Soviets were willing to accept our constraints on the deployment of MiGs to Nicaragua because the context is different from that of Cam Ranh Bay, which is no longer in our bailiwick."

Garthoff noted that when the Soviets threatened "countermeasures" to the INF missile deployment in Europe, in 1983–84, they made oblique public references to American sensitivities to missiles nearby in Cuba. "But they also found opportunities at the same time to give us private reassurances that they did *not* have in mind Soviet missiles in Cuba or Nicaragua, but only forward patrolling missile submarines to provide a counterpart to the Pershing II's short time to target threat." See *HCT*, pp. 148–50. See also Raymond L. Garthoff, "Handling the Cienfuegos Crisis," *International Security*, Vol. 8, No. 1 (Summer 1983), pp. 46–66.

77. "At a meeting of senior officials, including a number of members of the Executive Committee, the night before the President's speech, Robert McNamara had said we would be lucky to get out of the crisis with only a trade of the Turkish missiles. In response to Robert Kennedy's direct question to every person at the table, there was no disagreement with McNamara's evaluation." Chayes, *The Cuban Missile Crisis*, p. 95.

78. In the unedited transcript, Schelling goes on to make the following points: (1) If the ExComm had taken Maxwell Taylor's view—that the Soviets were over a barrel—the same choices of alternatives would probably have been made, because "we would have wanted to avoid the political costs of forever ruining the possibility of future relations with Cuba; we would have wanted to avoid the drop we would have suffered in world opinion; we wouldn't have wanted to humiliate the Russians in a way that would have made them more dangerous over the long run." (2) Valid lessons can sometimes be drawn from a comparison of two or more cases. At least two emerge: "Don't push your luck"; and "Don't be *too* slow." For an elaboration of these points, see *HCT*, pp. 174–75.

79. Cf. Welch and Blight, "The Eleventh Hour of the Cuban Missile Crisis," pp. 25–27.

80. See McGeorge Bundy, Minutes of ExComm meeting No. 24, November 12, 1962 (National Security Archive, Washington, D.C.). See also "The Air Force Response to the Cuban Crisis" (declassified, 1977, USAF Historical Division Liaison Office), pp. 5–15.

81. See Stephen E. Ambrose, *Eisenhower: The President* (New York: Simon and Schuster, 1984), p. 533.

82. In the unedited transcript, Trachtenberg elaborates this point in a lengthy footnote. See *HCT*, pp. 187–88.

83. John F. Kennedy, Foreword to Theodore C. Sorensen, *Decision-Making in the White House* (New York: Columbia University Press, 1963), p. xi.

CHAPTER 2

1. Søren Kierkegaard, *Journal* entry, 1843. Cited in Richard Wollheim, *The Thread of Life* (Cambridge, Mass.: Harvard University Press, 1984), p. 1.

2. When we speak of "scholars" and "policymakers" we are unavoidably oversimplifying the identities both of the participants at Hawk's Cay and of the members of the larger academic and policy communities to which they belong. Some, such as McGeorge Bundy, Abram Chayes, and Arthur Schlesinger, fit comfortably into both camps. In particular, it should be noted that what we say of policymakers in general in this chapter will be refined in the light of the rift between hawks and doves. We speak in terms of these categories here not because they are watertight but because they are useful in establishing our more general claims.

3. Media coverage was stimulated by the cover story in *The New York Times*

Magazine by J. Anthony Lukas, "Class Reunion: Kennedy's Men Relive the Cuban Missile Crisis," pp. 22–27, 51, 58, 61. But the week before its publication, the staff of the daily *New York Times*, having seen the Lukas manuscript, published its own story, focusing on the "Rusk revelation." See Eric Pace, "Rusk Tells a Kennedy Secret: Fallback Plan in Cuba Crisis," *The New York Times*, August 28, 1987, pp. 1, A9.

4. The tendency of even responsible journalists to emphasize the sensational aspects of Rusk's story, and to draw snap judgments from it, is beautifully illustrated in the titles of the first two stories about the revelation: Pace, "Rusk Tells a Kennedy Secret"; and Richard Harwood, "Kennedy Secretly a 'Dove' in Cuba Crisis, Letter Shows" (*The Washington Post*, August 29, 1987). The author of the latter piece attempted to equate the position of President Kennedy with that of UN Ambassador (and Kennedy rival) Adlai Stevenson, overlooking the fact that Stevenson recommended the missile trade as the initial American response, while Kennedy may have been willing to trade as a very last resort, to avoid a war in Cuba, and perhaps elsewhere. This is significant because it is very unlikely that such a deal, by itself, would have interested Khrushchev at the outset of the crisis, unless (as seems extraordinarily unlikely) the sole or overwhelming purpose of the deployment was to secure such a trade in the first place. And as the results of the final weekend of the crisis demonstrate, Khrushchev did not require the trade as a quid pro quo for resolving it. In short, while it is true that neither Kennedy nor Stevenson wanted a war, their approaches to resolving the crisis were very different and the Rusk revelation does not alter this in the least.

5. Many scholars were quick to recognize that the Rusk revelation was certainly shocking in one respect: President Kennedy's interest in a potential missile trade to end the crisis has been denied, universally and vehemently, by memoirists like Theodore Sorensen, Arthur Schlesinger, and Robert Kennedy, each of whom ought to have been in a position to know the President's state of mind toward the end of the missile crisis. Theodore Sorensen was blunt about his view of President Kennedy's opinion of the public Turkish–Cuban missile swap suggested by Khrushchev. "The President," according to Sorensen, "had no intention of destroying the alliance by backing down. . . . He decided to treat the latest Khrushchev letter as propaganda." *Kennedy*, p. 714. Robert Kennedy says in his memoir that he told Dobrynin on the evening of October 27 that "there could be no quid pro quo" with regard to the Turkish missiles. *Thirteen Days*, p. 108. And in his memoir of the Kennedy Administration, Arthur Schlesinger, Jr., states: "The notion of trading the Cuban and Turkish bases had been much discussed in England; Walter Lippmann and others had urged it in the United States. But Kennedy regarded the idea as unacceptable, and the swap was promptly rejected." *A Thousand Days*, p. 756. Since for many years these three accounts have dominated all discussion of the President's role in the crisis—both laudatory and condemnatory—everyone has assumed that the President, having rejected Stevenson's proposal for a trade on October 20, and having sent his brother to Dobrynin to reinforce his lack of interest in a public trade, considered the trade entirely unacceptable. Indeed, in his later biography of Robert Kennedy, Schlesinger offers several pages of rationale for why a public trade would have been next-to-impossible politically for the President. *Robert Kennedy and His Times*, pp. 560–66. But Rusk revealed a fact that calls all these previous

memoirs into question, the very books which scholars have depended upon
most for their understanding of a President who did not live to write a
memoir of his own. Which books, if any, about President Kennedy are we
now to believe—on this point of the President's interest in the missile
trade, certainly, but perhaps on many other points as well? For an analysis
of the manner and extent to which the "Rusk revelation" in conjunction
with other new information causes us to reconsider the accuracy of these
standard memoirs of the Cuban missile crisis, see Welch and Blight, "The
Eleventh Hour of the Cuban Missile Crisis," pp. 5–29.

6. Dean Rusk, cited in Pace, "Rusk Tells a Kennedy Secret," p. A9.

7. Dean Rusk, in an interview with John Hockenberry on "All Things Considered," National Public Radio, August 28, 1987. It must be borne in
   mind that there is another reason why Rusk believes his information to
   be relatively unimpòrtant: he is convinced that the Jupiter missiles in
   Turkey were scheduled for removal in any event, and that the United
   States was giving up nothing in using them as a lever for the withdrawal
   of Soviet missiles from Cuba. See the interview in chapter 3.

8. When pressed by the scholars at Hawk's Cay, Bundy said that, in his view,
   if Khrushchev had not responded promptly and positively to the American
   offer of October 27, the President would have tightened the quarantine
   rather than agree to a missile trade. See p. 89.

9. Theodore C. Sorensen, draft letter for the President, October 18, 1962.
   (John F. Kennedy Library, National Security File, Box 49.)

10. See Welch and Blight, "The Eleventh Hour of the Cuban Missile Crisis,"
    pp. 12–18.

11. Scholars tend to distinguish readily between deep and proximate causes
    of events. Candidates for the leading "deep causes" of the missile crisis
    include the bipolar distribution of power in the international system; the
    trends in that distribution (Soviet ascendance and relative American de-
    cline); and the ideological incompatibility between capitalism and social-
    ism. These are the features of the world situation which may have made
    some conflict between the Soviet Union and the United States likely some-
    where at some point in time. See, e.g., Kenneth Waltz, *Man, the State,
    and War* (New York: Columbia University Press, 1959) and *Theory of
    International Politics* (Reading, Mass.: Addison-Wesley, 1979); Robert
    Gilpin, *War and Change in World Politics* (Cambridge: Cambridge Uni-
    versity Press, 1981). Proximate causes are the considerations which singly
    or in concert may have been responsible for the fact that there was a U.S.–
    Soviet confrontation in the Caribbean in October 1962.

    It is worth noting that the discussion at Hawk's Cay focused exclusively
    on proximate causes. This had the effect of highlighting the element of
    choice in the origins of the confrontation, and consequently its avoid-
    ability—for the moves which collectively led up to the crisis were policy
    choices. Had the discussion focused instead on the background causes of
    the crisis, no doubt we would have heard more on the "inevitability" of
    a cold-war showdown, if not in Cuba, then somewhere else, and presum-
    ably we would also have heard more discussion of the "inevitability" of
    the outcome. But analyses of "inevitability" must always be taken with a
    grain of salt. "Had that crisis led to war the next generation of historians,
    assuming there was one, would have portrayed the crisis and the war that
    followed as the natural even inevitable result of almost twenty years of
    Cold War between the Soviet Union and the United States. Ideology, the

nuclear arms race, competition for spheres of influence, and domestic payoffs of aggressive foreign policies would all have been described as important underlying causes of the war. In retrospect, World War III would appear as unavoidable as World War I." Richard Ned Lebow, *Between Peace and War: The Nature of International Crisis* (Baltimore: Johns Hopkins University Press, 1981), p. 3.

12. These last two points are discussed more fully in chapter 6.

13. See Allison, *Essence of Decision*, pp. 47–50. Cf. Khrushchev's report to the Supreme Soviet, December 12, 1962; reprinted in Pope, ed., *Soviet Views on the Cuban Missile Crisis*, p. 83: "Our purpose was only the defense of Cuba. Everybody saw how the American imperialists were sharpening the knives and threatening Cuba with a massed attack. In the face of this highwayman's policy that contradicts all standards of relations among states and the U.N. Charter, we could not remain indifferent bystanders. We decided to hold out a helping hand to Cuba."

For an argument that Khrushchev could not have meant the missiles "solely or primarily" to deter an American attack on Cuba, see George and Smoke, *Deterrence in American Foreign Policy*, p. 462n. George and Smoke note that if this was Khrushchev's purpose, he had other options which were less risky, such as making "vigorous deterrent statements," concluding a formal treaty guarantee, supplying conventional military aid, deploying Soviet conventional combat forces as a trip-wire, threatening retaliation elsewhere (e.g. in Berlin), and bringing Cuba into the Warsaw Pact. Furthermore, even if Khrushchev thought missiles would be required to deter a U.S. attack, the Soviet deployment was unnecessarily large. A handful of MRBMs would have been enough; the IRBMs were wholly redundant for the purpose. Thus, George and Smoke conclude that Khrushchev had something else primarily in mind. Khrushchev says as much himself: "In addition to protecting Cuba, our missiles would have equalized what the West likes to call 'the balance of power.' " *Khrushchev Remembers*, pp. 493–94. See also Allison, *Essence of Decision*, pp. 44–45; Arnold Horelick and Myron Rush, *Strategic Power and Soviet Foreign Policy* (Chicago: University of Chicago Press, 1965), p. 127–36; Horelick, "The Cuban Missile Crisis," pp. 363–80; and Hilsman, *To Move a Nation*, pp. 161–65, 201–2.

14. Allison, *Essence of Decision*, pp. 52–56.

15. *Ibid.*, pp. 43–45.

16. Cf. *ibid.*, pp. 45–46.

17. Cf. Dinerstein, *The Making of a Missile Crisis*, p. 187; and Adam B. Ulam, *Expansion and Coexistence: Soviet Foreign Policy, 1917–73*, 2nd ed. (New York: Holt, Rinehart and Winston, 1974), pp. 661–71. Ulam's argument also underscores Moscow's eagerness to secure West Germany's status as a non-nuclear power. Cf. Adam B. Ulam, *The Rivals: America and Russia Since World War II* (New York: Viking, 1971), p. 329. One weakness of Ulam's thesis is that the Soviets never demanded what he believed they might have intended to demand to force Beijing's hand: "that the United States remove its protection of Formosa." *Ibid.*

18. This particular hypothesis is not usually disassociated from the others, though it is analytically useful to distinguish it from them. Cf. the discussion in Allison, *Essence of Decision*, pp. 40–56.

19. William Taubman argues this in chapter 1, pp. 35–36. Cf. Crankshaw, *Khrushchev: A Career*, pp. 280–81.

20. Garthoff reports this as Averell Harriman's view of the deployment, p. 53.
21. See pp. 35–36.
22. Pp. 27–28.
23. Pp. 32–33.
24. P. 33.
25. P. 38.
26. P. 38.
27. P. 28.
28. P. 29.
29. See, e.g., pp. 30–31. In his remarks toward the end of the conference, Richard Ned Lebow makes the following rather puzzling statement: "When we were trying to determine why the Soviets were putting missiles in Cuba, there was a difference of opinion between scholars and the members of the ExComm. The ExComm at the time of the crisis read it as an episode of Soviet expansion encouraged by their perceptions of Kennedy's apparent lack of resolve, while the scholars here have been describing the deployment as a defensive move, something Khrushchev had to do because of his own political needs. It's interesting to me that the ExComm people are coming around to this latter view in this conference" (pp. 105–6). While it is correct that some of the scholars present described the move in defensive terms, we disagree with Lebow's characterization of the ExComm members' views, which we regard as self-consciously uncertain.
30. Pp. 33–34.
31. In his statement, Ball speculated that Khrushchev could have had all of the various motivations in mind, but doubts that he thought them through. The lone scholar who voices sympathy for this point of view is Arnold Horelick (p. 36).
32. Robert Kennedy has described in his memoir of the crisis the mood at the first gathering of what became known as the ExComm. "The dominant feeling at the meeting," he recalled, "was stunned surprise." *Thirteen Days*, p. 24. The transcription of the tapes of that meeting corroborates Robert Kennedy's recollection. In his opening remarks, for example, Dean Rusk says: "Mr. President, this is a . . . serious development. It's one that we, all of us, had not really believed the Soviets could, uh, carry this far." Dean Rusk, cited in "White House Tapes and Minutes," p. 171. The President, too, is shocked and perplexed. He asks: "What is the, uh, advant— . . . must be some major reason for the Russians to, uh, set this up. . . ." (*Ibid.*, p. 176.) Finally, Rusk, echoing Ball's recollection twenty-five years later, has this to say about Khrushchev: "Uhm, for the first time, I'm beginning really to wonder whether maybe Mr. Khrushchev is entirely rational. . . ." (p. 177).
33. Many of the so-called hawks to this day assert that there was no significant risk of a Soviet response to American military action, because of their gross inferiority at the strategic nuclear level. See the discussion in chapters 3 and 4.
34. In *Thirteen Days*, Robert Kennedy reports: "The general feeling in the beginning was that some form of action was required. There were those, although they were a small minority, who felt the missiles did not alter the balance of power and therefore necessitated no action" (p. 31). We can find no record of any of the President's advisors suggesting that the

missiles "necessitated no action." Cf., e.g., "White House Tapes and Minutes," where the issue is first discussed.

35. P. 77.
36. Pp. 30–31. Of course, if this were the only reason why the missiles could not be tolerated, it would seem odd that there was never a serious attempt on the part of the United States to prevent the U.S.S.R. from attaining strategic nuclear parity later.
37. P. 23.
38. The President and McNamara, on October 16, explicitly referred to the problem as a domestic and international "political" problem. See "White House Tapes and Minutes," pp. 186–87, 192.
39. P. 25.
40. On July 13, 1960, Khrushchev stated in a press conference: "We believe that the Monroe Doctrine has had its day, has outlived itself and has, so to speak, died a natural death. Now the remains of that doctrine have to be buried, as any dead body is buried, so as not to foul the air with its putrefaction." Dinerstein, *The Making of a Missile Crisis*, p. 91. Khrushchev might well have wondered about the status of the Monroe Doctrine. According to a letter written by Norbert Schlei to Abram Chayes (reprinted in Chayes's *The Cuban Missile Crisis*, p. 133): "Sometime in early September, there was a meeting in the Cabinet Room at the White House to discuss the proposed Presidential statement. . . . We discussed the statement and the President was critical of our draft because it mentioned the Monroe Doctrine. 'The Monroe Doctrine,' he snapped at me. 'What the hell is that?' "
41. See Garthoff's analysis, p. 31
42. See Trachtenberg's comments, p. 110.
43. Chayes is the one who notes explicitly that there was no international legal objection to the Soviet deployment. At the same time, nowhere does he clearly express the view that the deployment of Soviet missiles in Cuba could or should have been tolerated. His dual identity at Hawk's Cay— as both scholar and former policymaker—seems to heighten his sensitivity to arguments on both sides of the issue. See the discussion on pp. 40–41.
44. Theodore Draper, *The Very Best Men* (New York: Oxford University Press, 1986).
45. The following remark by Theodore Sorensen strikes us as puzzling in this regard: "I believe the President drew the line precisely where he thought the Soviets were not and would not be; that is to say, if we had known that the Soviets were putting forty missiles in Cuba, we might under this hypothesis have drawn the line at one hundred, and said with great fanfare that we would absolutely not tolerate the presence of more than one hundred missiles in Cuba. I say that believing very strongly that that would have been an act of *prudence*, not weakness. But I am suggesting that one reason the line was drawn at zero was because we simply thought the Soviets weren't going to deploy any there anyway" (p. 43). If Sorensen is correct, then the reason the President considered the Soviet deployment unacceptable was that it challenged his public commitments not to tolerate it, which were based on a faulty assessment of Soviet intentions. The implication of this is that, in the absence of those public commitments, the President might have tolerated Soviet missiles in Cuba. Given the public's fears of Soviet encroachment in the Western Hemisphere, and given the

outcry in Congress throughout September and October, we find Sorensen's implication, and therefore his "hypothesis" as well, extremely dubious. But it is worth noting that Sorensen's comment is nonetheless the closest any of the former policymakers at Hawk's Cay comes to conceding the possibility that the Soviet deployment might not have been entirely unacceptable, at least under certain circumstances.

46. See Blight, Nye, and Welch, "The Cuban Missile Crisis Revisited," p. 182.
47. See George, Hall, and Simons, *The Limits of Coercive Diplomacy*, pp. 21–32.
48. *Ibid.*, pp. 26–27.
49. *Ibid.*, p. 27. George notes that these two variants of the strategy are in reality the ends of a continuum.
50. See pp. 46–47.
51. P. 57.
52. P. 52.
53. P. 58.
54. George Ball's remarks at the opening dinner discussion, p. 25.
55. P. 72.
56. P. 89.
57. P. 88.
58. See "October 27, 1962: Transcripts of the Meetings of the ExComm," pp. 30–92; and Welch and Blight, "The Eleventh Hour of the Cuban Missile Crisis," pp. 27–28.
59. In the October 27 transcript, McNamara does repeatedly attempt to discuss a contingency which he believes would reduce the likelihood of Soviet retaliation against the Jupiters in Turkey in response to an American air strike on the Soviet missiles in Cuba. He proposes that the Jupiters be "defused" and that the Soviets be told of this in advance. McNamara's argument is misunderstood in the ExComm, and was clearly inadequately examined. See "October 27, 1962: Transcripts of the Meetings of the ExComm," pp. 52, 56, 75; and Welch and Blight, "The Eleventh Hour of the Cuban Missile Crisis," p. 16n.
60. Cf. chapters 3 and 4.
61. P. 61.
62. Curiously, McNamara and Bundy both assert that the status of Soviet forces and their nuclear alerts were not a source of concern. See p. 70.
63. Pp. 56–57.
64. Douglas Dillon noted that "on the first Friday, the report that the missiles were 'becoming operational' made a big difference to our deliberations." P. 55.
65. David A. Welch interview with Ray Cline, June 2, 1987, Washington, D.C.
66. Cf. CIA memorandum, subject: "The Crisis: USSR/Cuba," 27 October 1962.
67. See, e.g., "October 27, 1962: Transcripts of the Meetings of the ExComm," p. 47.
68. P. 55.
69. P. 62.
70. P. 63.
71. John F. Kennedy, "Radio and Television Report to the American People

on the Soviet Buildup in Cuba," in Larson, ed., *The "Cuban Crisis" of 1962*, p. 63.
72. P. 60.
73. According to General David Burchinal, who was with McNamara when news of the stray U-2 reached the Pentagon, McNamara "turned absolutely white and yelled hysterically, 'This means war with the Soviet Union. The President must get on the hot line to Moscow!' And he ran out of the meeting in a frenzy." Transcript of oral history interview of General David Burchinal, April 11, 1975, pp. 114–15. Office of Air Force History, Bolling Air Force Base, Washington, D.C.; cited in Trachtenberg, "The Influence of Nuclear Weapons in the Cuban Missile Crisis," p. 152. Of course, there was no "hot line" at the time of the Cuban missile crisis; and in conversation McNamara denies Burchinal's story.
74. P. 70. This contradicts McNamara's statement that he did fear a Soviet preemptive strike. See the interview in chapter 3.
75. P. 70.
76. P. 71.
77. This is not to deny the importance of strategy, merely to call into question the relative weight of the two. McNamara himself describes the handling of the missile crisis in explicitly strategic terms in his introduction to Robert Kennedy's *Thirteen Days*, p. 15. But the primacy of McNamara's Law in his own thought clearly indicates that he believes strategy to be less central to crisis management than is circumspection. Or, even more strongly, " 'Managing' crises is the wrong term; you don't 'manage' them because you *can't* 'manage' them" (p. 100).
78. See, e.g., Joseph de Rivera, *The Psychological Dimensions of Foreign Policy* (Columbus, Ohio: Bobbs-Merrill, 1968), pp. 150–51; Ole R. Holsti, *Crisis, Escalation, War* (Montreal: McGill-Queen's University Press, 1972); Ole R. Holsti and Alexander L. George, "The Effects of Stress on the Performance of Foreign Policy-Makers," in C. P. Cotter, ed., *Political Science Annual: An International Review* (Indianapolis: Bobbs-Merrill, 1975), pp. 255–319; and Richard Ned Lebow, *Nuclear Crisis Management: A Dangerous Illusion* (Ithaca, N.Y.: Cornell University Press, 1987), pp. 142–53. For good discussions of important historical breakdowns (Kaiser Wilhelm, Stalin, Nehru, Nasser), see Lebow, *Between Peace and War*, pp. 135–45, 283–85.
79. See Welch and Blight, "The Eleventh Hour of the Cuban Missile Crisis," pp. 22–23.
80. Theoretically, President Kennedy could have stopped the crisis whenever he wanted to. Before October 27, he would have had to pay a heavy political price to back away from the crisis, but at least by doing so he could have prevented a possible nuclear war. By October 27, he knew that at a minimum he could get out of the crisis with a public trade of Jupiter missiles in Turkey for SS-4s and SS-5s in Cuba. If he knew he wanted to avoid the ladder of escalation altogether, and if he knew he could have done so, there would have been no particular reason to dwell on it.
81. P. 74.
82. McGeorge Bundy, *Danger and Survival* (New York: Random House, 1988), especially chapters VIII ("Khrushchev, Berlin and the West") and IX ("The Cuban Missile Crisis").
83. The psychological study of nuclear crises continues to be dominated by

the first important book in the field, Thomas C. Schelling, *The Strategy of Conflict* (Cambridge, Mass.: Harvard University Press, 1960). Schelling applied his microeconomic and game-theory-derived psychology to the Cuban missile crisis in *Arms and Influence* (New Haven: Yale University Press, 1966). Schelling's most significant protégé is Robert Jervis. See especially his *Perception and Misperception in International Politics* (Princeton: Princeton University Press, 1976) and his introductory chapter in Robert Jervis, Richard Ned Lebow, and Janice Gross Stein, *Psychology and Deterrence* (Baltimore: Johns Hopkins University Press, 1985). One may look in vain throughout this (by now) vast literature originating in Schelling's work for any mention of the emotional life, any indication that the experience of managing a nuclear crisis might be worth considering. To get a quantitative index of the hyper-cognitive orientation of this literature, one ought to ponder the implication of the fact that Jervis, in *Perception and Misperception*, can append an enormous bibliography to his book without ever mentioning Freud. Indeed, reading through much of this work, one gets the bizarre and quite inverted impression that the Freudian revolution never occurred. Not that Freud had all the answers; but one would have thought he at least demonstrated the power and ubiquity of the emotional substrata, especially in crisis situations.

84. The leading light in this movement is political scientist Richard Ned Lebow. See *Between Peace and War* and *Nuclear Crisis Management*. For a critique of Lebow's efforts to treat emotion as, essentially, a "nuisance variable," see James G. Blight, *The Shattered Crystal Ball: Fear and Learning in the Cuban Missile Crisis* (Totowa, N.J.: Rowman & Littlefield, 1990), chapter 9.

85. For a detailed consideration of why the psychology of nuclear crises ought to be phenomenological, see *ibid.*, and the references to Blight's more purely psychological articles contained there in footnote 3, chapter 2.

86. Movement in this direction may be achieved by means of what Thomas Nagel calls an "objective phenomenology," which permits the private experiences of one person—or, in this case, of a small group of people—to become at least partially intelligible to individuals who lack those experiences. See Thomas Nagel, "What is it Like to Be a Bat?" in Nagel, *Mortal Questions* (New York: Cambridge University Press, 1979), pp. 165–80. For insight into a method for getting "inside" the experiences of others, the psychology of William James remains unmatched. See his *Principles of Psychology*, Vol. I (New York: Henry Holt, 1890), especially chapter IX, "The Stream of Thought." And for a general orientation to the psychological changes occurring in a crisis, nothing we have seen supersedes the classic: Søren Kierkegaard, *The Concept of Anxiety*, tr. and ed. Reider Thomte (Princeton: Princeton University Press, 1980). For a synthesis as applied to this particular case, see Blight, *The Shattered Crystal Ball*.

87. P. 105.
88. P. 108.
89. Pp. 85–86.
90. Pp. 86–87.
91. Pp. 107–8.
92. P. 108.

CHAPTER 3

1. The terms "hawks" and "doves," as we now use them, originated in an article about the missile crisis written shortly after its conclusion. Stewart Alsop and Charles Bartlett, "In Time of Crisis," *The Saturday Evening Post*, December 8, 1962. An earlier treatment of the differences in the views of the hawks and the doves as they manifested themselves at Hawk's Cay may be found in Blight, Nye, and Welch, "The Cuban Missile Crisis Revisited," pp. 170–88.

2. General Taylor died shortly after the meeting at Hawk's Cay. See *The New York Times*, April 2, 1987, p. 1.

3. Rusk was convalescing in Georgia, and had been forbidden to travel by his doctors; Nitze was unable to attend the meeting because of his duties at the arms control negotiations in Geneva.

4. Other interviews not presented here include Theodore Sorensen (Blight and Welch, April 29, 1987, New York); George Ball (Blight and Janet Lang, May 1, 1987, Princeton, N.J.); Leonard C. Meeker, Deputy Legal Counsel to the State Department in the Kennedy Administration (Blight and Welch, May 6, 1987, Washington, D.C.); and Ray Cline, CIA Deputy Director of Intelligence during the missile crisis (Welch, June 2, 1987, Washington, D.C.).

5. In order to allow the interviewees to express themselves as candidly as possible, and to allow them to indicate which issues they felt were most important, we decided to let them largely determine the course of the discussions, which are consequently rather freewheeling. In general— though we did not feel obliged to adhere strictly to this division of labor— Blight's role was to raise the broad topics we wished to hear their views on, and Welch would ask more specific questions when the discussion turned to particular controversial issues (a task ably performed by Janet Lang in the Dillon interview, which Welch was unable to attend).

6. Cf. "White House Tapes and Minutes of the Cuban Missile Crisis," pp. 164–203; "October 27, 1962: Transcripts of the Meetings of the ExComm," pp. 30–92; Welch and Blight, "The Eleventh Hour of the Cuban Missile Crisis," pp. 20–22.

7. Karl Popper, *Conjectures and Refutations* (New York: Harper & Row, 1963).

8. Gromyko arrived in Washington on October 18, after the discovery of the missiles. Contrary to Nitze's recollection, his visit was not part of any negotiation.

9. The dinner in question was given by Dean Rusk for Gerhard Schroeder, Foreign Minister of the Federal Republic of Germany.

10. Nitze was deeply involved in the Berlin crisis the previous year. Khrushchev had threatened at the Vienna summit in June, and in later speeches, to sign a separate peace treaty with the East German government and "turn over" operation of the access routes to West Berlin to the East Germans. Over the summer of 1961, Kennedy called up American reservists. To stop the huge flow of Germans from East to West, the Berlin Wall was erected in August. Khrushchev and Walter Ulbricht, East German Premier, never signed the threatened peace treaty, and West Berlin remained open.

11. Thor intermediate-range ballistic missiles (IRBMs) were stationed in Great Britain, and were already in the process of being withdrawn during the missile crisis. Jupiters (also IRBMs) were stationed in Italy and Turkey.

12. Here Nitze is implying that the United States would have prepared a nuclear response to a Soviet reprisal. The discussion at Hawk's Cay suggests that this was not the direction of the President's thought.

13. All American commands were placed on DefCon 3 on October 22, and the Strategic Air Command was placed on DefCon 2—its highest level of alert ever—on October 24. See Garthoff, *Reflections on the Cuban Missile Crisis*, p. 37.

14. For a full discussion of what American intelligence in 1962 believed the balance to have been, and what in retrospect it appears the balance actually was, see *ibid.*, pp. 138–46, and the discussion in the Afterword, pp. 328–29, 399–400, n. 15.

15. See n. 11, above.

16. Kennedy, *Thirteen Days*, p. 97. Cf. Welch and Blight, "The Eleventh Hour of the Cuban Missile Crisis," pp. 19–22.

17. It is not altogether clear that Nitze was present in the ExComm meeting when General Taylor arrived with news of the U-2 shoot-down; for although Nitze speaks quite frequently in certain portions of the October 27 transcripts, he does not speak at all during the time the shoot-down is discussed. See "October 27, 1962: Transcripts of the Meetings of the ExComm," pp. 66–72.

18. See Leon Festinger, *A Theory of Cognitive Dissonance* (Stanford: Stanford University Press, 1957), and *Conflict, Decisions, and Dissonance* (Stanford: Stanford University Press, 1964). While Nitze's application of cognitive dissonance theory to Sorensen and Bundy is of course debatable, he has the theory approximately right: one develops a powerful belief involving, perhaps, predictions of certain events. If the events occur, the belief is regarded as confirmed. If they do not, the original beliefs are still regarded as confirmed, for reasons that are inserted into the argument after the fact. The point, as Nitze implies, is that prior beliefs may powerfully color one's interpretations of subsequent events.

19. Reprinted in Garthoff, *Reflections on the Cuban Missile Crisis*, pp. 138– 39. It is not clear why Nitze finds it extraordinary that Garthoff agreed with him on the military significance of the missiles; nor would it be correct to say that Garthoff and Nitze were alone in their assessment. Perhaps Nitze is reacting to Garthoff's "dovishness" (relative to Nitze). In *Reflections on the Cuban Missile Crisis*, Garthoff recalls a meeting at which he was uncomfortable being "the only non-hawk present" (p. 44n).

20. Douglas Dillon also expresses approximately the same view at Hawk's Cay and in his interview. See pp. 23, 165–67.

21. Garthoff at the time was working at the State Department, as a senior staff-level advisor in Soviet affairs, intelligence analysis, and politico-military affairs. He had, however, served as a member of the Office of National Estimates of the Central Intelligence Agency from 1957 to the fall of 1961, responsible for estimating Soviet foreign policy and strategy, and undoubtedly Nitze has this background in mind.

22. Adlai Stevenson, American Ambassador to the United Nations, came down to Washington on October 20, 1962, for a meeting with the President and his advisors. Stevenson argued that he be given authority to advance a UN resolution in which the U.S. promised to withdraw its naval base at Guantánamo on the island of Cuba, and to remove NATO Jupiter missiles in Turkey, if the Soviets would promise to remove their missiles from Cuba. Contrary to what Nitze recollects, Stevenson's proposals were re-

soundingly rejected by the President. Only George Ball spoke in support of them. In fact, Stevenson's repudiation was blown up into a scandal after the crisis in an article by Stewart Alsop and Charles Bartlett in *The Saturday Evening Post*, Vol. 235 (December 8, 1962), pp. 16–20. They quote an unnamed official, presumably a member of the ExComm, as saying that "Adlai wanted a Munich."

23. See Taylor's remarks, p. 81.
24. See the discussion in the McNamara interview, pp. 193–95.
25. Dillon may be referring here to Norman Podhoretz, *Why We Were in Vietnam* (New York: Simon and Schuster, 1982).
26. See McGeorge Bundy, *Danger and Survival*, chapter IX.
27. Cf. Welch and Blight, "The Eleventh Hour of the Cuban Missile Crisis," pp. 20–22.
28. The transcript of the meeting of October 16, 1962, reveals that Dean Rusk was concerned about Berlin and Cuba providing an analogue for the Soviets to what he called "the Suez–Hungarian combination." See "White House Tapes and Minutes," p. 178.
29. Dillon means, of course, that the deployment would improve the Soviets' relative strategic nuclear position, not that it would substitute Soviet superiority for American superiority. Even after a successful deployment in Cuba, the Soviets would still have faced a massively superior American nuclear force.
30. Thor missiles were only deployed in Britain.
31. The idea of responding to Khrushchev's first letter while ignoring his second, contrary to most subsequent memoirs (including *Thirteen Days*), was hardly Robert Kennedy's alone. It was discussed throughout the ExComm meeting of October 27. If anyone can be said to have come up with the idea, McGeorge Bundy and Edwin Martin would seem to be the strongest candidates. Llewellyn Thompson certainly persuaded the President that it might actually work. But the idea entered the discussion gradually, and was embraced by several members. See Welch and Blight, "The Eleventh Hour of the Cuban Missile Crisis," p. 19. We have no information to confirm or refute Dillon's claim that Robert Kennedy came up with the idea of issuing a strong ultimatum; this was not apparently discussed by the ExComm as a whole.
32. George Ball, interview with Blight and Lang, May 1, 1987, Princeton, N.J.; Theodore Sorensen, interview with Blight and Welch, April 29, 1987, New York City.
33. There was, in fact, disagreement on this point. See "White House Tapes and Minutes."
34. Note the different choice of phrase in this second formulation. Dillon initially stated that when one has decided to use force, one should use all force available (p. 156). Here, he states that one should use all force necessary to achieve the immediate military objective. It would appear that Dillon actually intends the second formulation, not the first. The issue arises again in the McNamara interview.
35. See chapter 1, where General Taylor concurs: a quick, decisive strike at the missile bases, according to Taylor, would "have really shaken Khrushchev" (p. 78). Interestingly, doves like Rusk and McNamara agreed with this assessment, but used it as an argument for not bombing Cuba. They reasoned that he would be so shaken that he might act irrationally, perhaps by launching a first strike against the United States.

36. Dillon's account here complicates the issue of the persuasiveness of Robert Kennedy's moral argument. At Hawk's Cay, and earlier in this interview, Dillon implied that the power of the moral argument flowed from the importance of fidelity to America's national ideals. Here, however, he implies that the moral argument was persuasive because of its prudence; that is, an air strike on the missiles would improve the Soviets' public position.

37. Available from the Alfred P. Sloan Foundation, New York.

38. Rusk implies that a decision had already been made to withdraw these missiles. While it is clear that the President and his advisors planned to remove the missiles eventually, no concrete decision had yet been made or even discussed with Turkey, Italy, or NATO. Cf. Welch and Blight, "The Eleventh Hour of the Cuban Missile Crisis," pp. 16–18. See also Donald L. Hafner, "Bureaucratic Politics and 'Those Frigging Missiles': JFK, Cuba and U.S. Missiles in Turkey," *Orbis*, Vol. 21, No. 2 (Summer 1977), pp. 307–33; and Barton J. Bernstein, "The Cuban Missile Crisis: Trading the Jupiters in Turkey?" *Political Science Quarterly*, Vol. 95, No. 1 (Spring 1980), pp. 102–4.

39. Richard E. Neustadt, Sloan Foundation videotaped discussions of the Cuban missile crisis.

40. In 1962, this body was called the Presidium.

41. President Kennedy probably did connect the missile crisis to Sun Tzu in pretty much the same way Rusk did. Kennedy is reported by Arthur Schlesinger to have been much impressed with the following passage in B. H. Liddell-Hart, *Deterrent or Defence* (New York: Praeger, 1960): "Study war and learn from its history. Keep strong if possible. In any case, keep cool. Have unlimited patience. Never corner an opponent, and always assist him to save his face. Put yourself in his shoes—so as to see things through his eyes" (pp. 247–48). This is the passage cited by Schlesinger, *A Thousand Days*, pp. 108–9. But in the paragraph immediately following, Liddell-Hart says: "These points were all made, explicitly or implicitly, in the earliest known book on the problems of war and peace—Sun Tzu's, about 500 B.C." (p. 248).

42. Cf. the contrary discussion, pp. 236–37.

43. Cf. Garthoff, *Reflections on the Cuban Missile Crisis*, p. 37.

44. Kennedy ordered the missiles "defused." It would not have been normal procedure for the warheads to be on the missiles in any case, and consequently the significance of "defusing" the missiles is difficult to understand.

45. See, generally, Stein and Feaver, *Assuring Control of Nuclear Weapons*.

46. In *Thirteen Days*, pp. 94–95, Robert Kennedy notes: "At the President's insistence, Secretary Rusk had raised the question with the representatives of Turkey following a NATO meeting in the spring of 1962. The Turks objected, and the matter was permitted to drop. In the summer of 1962, when Rusk was in Europe, President Kennedy raised the question again. He was told by the State Department that they felt it unwise to press the matter with Turkey. But the President disagreed. He wanted the missiles removed even if it would cause political problems for our government. The State Department representatives discussed it again with the Turks and, finding they still objected, did not pursue the matter. The President believed he was President and that, his wishes having been made clear, they would be followed and the missiles removed. He therefore dismissed the matter from his mind. Now he learned that the failure to follow up on

this matter had permitted the same obsolete Turkish missiles to become hostages to the Soviet Union. He was angry." It seems that Rusk is correct, not Robert Kennedy, whose account is one of a long line of attempts to suggest that the State Department generally, and Rusk in particular, performed poorly before and during the Cuban missile crisis. These suggestions are not borne out by the facts. See Welch and Blight, "The Eleventh Hour of the Cuban Missile Crisis," pp. 12–18.

47. Cf. Schlesinger, *Robert Kennedy and His Times*, p. 523.

48. Rusk obviously misunderstood the question to require him to explain his position regarding the available options during the first week of deliberation, when most ExComm members (though not Rusk) joined one of the working groups.

49. Elie Abel's reconstruction of that "moment of decision" indicates some of the tension and high drama in that situation. According to Abel, "Dean Rusk had prepared a two-page summary in his own handwriting, carefully marked TOP SECRET. He read it to the assembled group, then handed the papers to the President, who handed them back. . . . It recommended that the President choose the blockade track, while warning that this course would be neither safe nor comfortable, carrying with it the risks of rapid escalation. . . . The President paused gravely before speaking his mind. He said he preferred to start with limited action." *The Missile Crisis*, pp. 93–94.

50. Bromley Smith's minutes read: "At the meeting at the State Department, the Attorney General repeated his view that we should keep the focus on the missile bases. He preferred to let the Soviet tankers through the quarantine line in order to avoid a confrontation with the Soviets over one of their ships. He said if we attack a Soviet tanker, the balloon would go up. He urged that we buy time now in order to launch an air attack Monday or Tuesday." "Summary Record of NSC Executive Committee Meeting No. 7, October 27, 1962, 10:00 AM," Bromley Smith, reporting, p. 5. (Available at the National Security Archive, Washington, D.C.) This statement does not appear in McGeorge Bundy's transcript of the tapes of the ExComm meetings on October 27.

51. Cf. n. 31, above.

52. Most specialists now believe that the "Caribbean Crisis," as the Soviets refer to it, played hardly any direct role in Khrushchev's fall from power. Of the fifteen charges brought against him at a special meeting of the Presidium on October 13, 1964, only two involved foreign affairs, and on those counts Khrushchev was criticized for profligacy with regard to aiding Indonesia and with ignoring socialist trading partners. Domestic issues dominated the list of charges. Of the twenty-two members present, only First Deputy Premier Anastas I. Mikoyan spoke for Khrushchev. The next day, Leonid Brezhnev was elected First Secretary of the Central Committee, and Alexei Kosygin was elected Chairman of the Council of Ministers. See Roy Medvedev, *Khrushchev* (New York: Anchor, 1984), pp. 235–45.

53. Hans Morgenthau is widely known for arguing that morality should play no role in foreign policy, but in his most sophisticated statement he argues that prudence and morality coincide in policy. Self-preservation, he writes, is a moral duty for nations as well as for individuals. Thus, "the antithesis between moral principles and the national interest is not only intellectually mistaken but also morally pernicious. A foreign policy derived from the

national interest is in fact morally superior to a foreign policy inspired by universal moral principles." This view is open to at least three objections: (1) It is by no means clear that self-preservation is a moral duty for nations. (2) Even if it were, it is not clear that it would be an overriding moral duty. (3) Self-preservation is rarely at stake in foreign policy. See Hans Morgenthau, "The Mainsprings of American Foreign Policy: The National Interest vs. Moral Abstractions," *American Political Science Review*, Vol. 44, No. 4 (December 1950), p. 854.

54. Harold Macmillan, *At the End of the Day, 1961–1963* (New York: Harper & Row, 1973).

55. Acheson stated his view of the missile crisis in the form of a review essay of Robert Kennedy's *Thirteen Days*. "Dean Acheson's Version of Robert Kennedy's Version of the Cuban Missile Affair," *Esquire*, Vol. 71 (February 1969), pp. 76–77, 44, 46.

56. Cf. p. 256, in which Dobrynin confirmed to us, via Georgy Shakhnazarov, that it was Rusk who had informed him about the missiles in Cuba. Dobrynin had not been informed by his own government.

57. See chapter 1, n. 48.

58. The closest Kennedy's October 27 cable to Khrushchev comes to threatening further action is this: "The continuation of this threat, or a prolonging of this discussion concerning Cuba by linking these problems to the broader questions of European and world security, would surely lead to an intensified situation on the Cuban crisis and a grave risk to the peace of the world." For the full text of the cable, see Kennedy, *Thirteen Days*, pp. 202–3.

59. See "October 27, 1962: Transcripts of the Meetings of the ExComm," passim; and Welch and Blight, "The Eleventh Hour of the Cuban Missile Crisis," p. 15. Throughout that document, there is unmistakable evidence of the President's reluctance to go to war when peace could be preserved by trading away the obsolete Jupiter missiles in Turkey.

60. Kennedy, *Thirteen Days*, p. 67.

61. Recall Dillon's two different formulations. See n. 34, above.

62. The SIOP (Single Integrated Operational Plan) for nuclear war was conceived late in the Eisenhower Administration. Its key feature, in McNamara's view as he assumed office, was its inflexibility. It provided for an American nuclear response to destroy the entire "Sino-Soviet bloc." His favored approach, "flexible response," a term borrowed from Maxwell Taylor, was far from established doctrine at the time of the Cuban missile crisis, however.

63. See Alain Enthoven and K. Wayne Smith, *How Much Is Enough? Shaping the Defense Program, 1961–1969* (New York: Harper & Row, 1969). Within the high-ranking military establishment during the McNamara years, the emphasis on quantification, reorganization, and systems analysis was often called "Hitch-craft," after Pentagon whiz kid Charles Hitch.

CHAPTER 4

1. Thomas S. Kuhn, *The Structure of Scientific Revolutions* (Chicago: Chicago University Press, 1962).

2. *Ibid.*, p. 150.

3. Elsewhere we have used the tripartite distinction between hawks, doves, and owls (Blight, Nye, and Welch, "The Cuban Missile Crisis Revisited,"

pp. 170–88), as developed in Allison, Nye, and Carnesale, eds., *Hawks, Doves, & Owls*, according to which owls are distinguished from doves by their heightened concern for the risks of inadvertent conflict. While not denying the usefulness of that distinction, we have chosen here to use the binary classification that has dominated common parlance.

4. For further details on the nuclear balance, see Raymond L. Garthoff, "The Meaning of the Missiles," *The Washington Quarterly*, (Autumn 1982), pp. 76–82, 78–79, and *Reflections on the Cuban Missile Crisis*, pp. 138–46.

5. P. 141.

6. P. 160.

7. Cf. Horelick, "The Cuban Missile Crisis", p. 375.

8. On October 17, Theodore Sorensen prepared a memo on the options for removing the missiles from Cuba in which he stated: "It is generally agreed that these missiles, even when fully operational, do not significantly alter the balance of power—i.e., they do not significantly increase the potential megatonnage capable of being unleashed on American soil, even after a surprise American nuclear strike" (National Security Archive, Washington, D.C.). Although we cannot know for certain who "generally agreed" with this controversial contention, it is clear that from the outset of the crisis at least some of the doves denied that the hawks' calculations were correct on their own terms.

9. P. 187. Note that at the initial dinner discussion at Hawk's Cay, McNamara seemed to suggest that the reason why he did not believe that the Soviet deployment significantly affected the strategic balance was that it represented only a minor numerical increment (see chapter 1). In his interview, however, he denies this and clarifies his view.

10. P. 187. Cf. Robert S. McNamara, "The Military Role of Nuclear Weapons: Perceptions and Misperceptions," *Foreign Affairs*, Vol. 62, No. 1 (Fall 1983), especially p. 79: "Nuclear weapons serve no military purpose whatsoever. They are totally useless—except only to deter one's opponent from using them."

11. P. 188. After leaving the government, former Special Assistant for National Security McGeorge Bundy tried, on the basis of his experience in crises, to clarify the "real" meaning of that often used strategic phrase, "unacceptable losses." He writes: "There is an enormous gulf between what political leaders really think about nuclear weapons and what is assumed in complex calculations of relative 'advantage' in simulated strategic warfare. Think tank analysts can set levels of 'acceptable' damage well up in the tens of millions of lives. They can assume that the loss of dozens of great cities is somehow a real choice for sane men. They are in an unreal world. In the real world of real political leaders—whether here or in the Soviet Union—a decision that would bring even one hydrogen bomb on one city of one's own country would be recognized in advance as a catastrophic blunder; ten bombs on ten cities would be a disaster beyond history; and a hundred bombs on a hundred cities are unthinkable." McGeorge Bundy, "To Cap the Volcano," *Foreign Affairs*, Vol. 48, No. 1 (October 1969), pp. 9–10.

12. General David Burchinal apparently misunderstands McNamara's position. The value of superiority, he states, "was totally missed by the Kennedy administration, both by the executive leadership and by McNamara. They did not understand what had been created and handed to them, and what it had given them. SAC was about at its peak. We had, not supremacy,

but complete nuclear superiority over the Soviets. . . . We could have written our own book at that time, but our politicians did not understand what happens when you have such a degree of superiority as we had, or they simply didn't know how to use it. They were busily engaged in saving face for the Soviets and making concessions, giving up the IRBMs, the Thors and Jupiters deployed overseas—when all we had to do was write our own ticket." In Richard H. Kohn and Joseph P. Harahan, eds., "U.S. Strategic Air Power, 1948–1962: Excerpts from an Interview with Generals Curtis E. LeMay, Leon W. Johnson, David A. Burchinal, and Jack J. Catton," *International Security*, Vol. 12, No. 4 (Spring 1988), pp. 932–93.

13. Pp. 152–53. Alexander George believes that what finally convinced Khrushchev to retreat was American naval action against the Soviet submarines which were trying to shield the merchant ships approaching the quarantine line. See George, Hall, and Simons, *The Limits of Coercive Diplomacy*, pp. 112–13.

14. Douglas Dillon makes an interesting point when he argues that the Soviet deployment showed Khrushchev's rationality, not, as many worried, his irrationality. He says (pp. 167–70): "Don't you see—they put the missiles in Cuba in order to beef up their strategic position, which was grossly inferior to ours. But this meant that if we caught them in the act, that is, in their inferior position, and we took action to insure that they stayed inferior, they would have withdrawn. I mean, they acted rationally, in a way, by putting them in. If we'd struck at the bases, they'd have acted rationally and stayed put, I think, around Berlin and elsewhere. The Russians are rational. They're not like Khomeini or Qaddafi. I don't think McNamara and the others understood this." This attitude was a controlling influence on the hawks, who felt that Khrushchev was playing with a set of rules that were well understood—or should have been—on both sides.

15. P. 153. Interestingly, the Soviet military newspaper *Red Star* was considerably more militant and intransigent during the crisis than was either *Izvestia* or *Pravda*; one would have expected a Clausewitzian military establishment to have been very conciliatory if Nitze and Dillon are correct. See Garthoff, *Reflections on the Cuban Missile Crisis*, p. 46.

16. *Ibid.*, p. 57.

17. Several recent Soviet revelations indicate that although Soviet military doctrine gives great credence to the nuclear balance, it may have been a secondary consideration to Khrushchev in the Cuban missile crisis. But there is evidently a difference of opinion on this matter within the Soviet Union itself. See the discussion in chapter 5 and in the Afterword.

18. Of course, statistical probabilities may, in some cases and at some levels, bear. on a decisionmaker's estimate of the likelihood of an event in an international crisis. Below, for example, we examine the likelihood that a Soviet officer in Cuba might have launched a nuclear missile during an American air strike. This likelihood was affected by (among other things) the statistical probability that the attacking American planes might have missed their targets.

19. Pp. 199–200.

20. Pp. 171–72. Rusk's recollection of the pertinence of the ancient wisdom of Sun Tzu is consistent with some of the most influential strategic thinking of the modern era. Cf. Schelling, *The Strategy of Conflict*, p. 6: "We have observed that the rationality of the adversary is pertinent to the efficacy of a threat, and that madmen, like small children, can often not be con-

trolled by threats. We have recognized that the efficacy of the threat may depend on what alternatives are available to the potential enemy, who, if he is not to react like a trapped lion, must be left some tolerable recourse."

21. P. 147.
22. P. 153.
23. See n. 39, p. 354; and Afterword, pp. 340–42.
24. In his letter to Kennedy of October 28, Khrushchev asked, "What is this, a provocation?" Letter from Khrushchev to Kennedy, October 28, 1962, reprinted in Larson, ed., *The "Cuban Crisis" of 1962*, p. 192.
25. In 1957, General Curtis LeMay reportedly told Robert Sprague, Co-Chairman of Eisenhower's Gaither Commission (examining American strategic vulnerability): "If I see that the Russians are amassing their planes for an attack . . . I'm going to knock the shit out of them before they take off the ground." When Sprague protested that this was contrary to national policy, LeMay replied: "I don't care. . . . It's my policy. That's what I'm going to do." Fred Kaplan, *The Wizards of Armageddon* (New York: Simon and Schuster, 1983), pp. 133–34. On the Air Force's search for first-strike capability, see Robert C. Aldridge, *First Strike* (Boston: South End Press, 1983).
26. Garthoff, *Reflections on the Cuban Missile Crisis*, p. 41. Garthoff notes that he has been unable to confirm this story, but believes it to be true. He was told at the time by a trusted colleague, a CIA officer directly responsible for handling the Penkovsky case.
27. In his letter of October 26 to the President, Khrushchev pleaded to Kennedy not to escalate the crisis, fearing that they would "come to a clash, like blind moles, and then reciprocal extermination will begin." And in his letter of October 28, Kennedy praised Khrushchev for agreeing to withdraw the missiles from Cuba because "developments were approaching a point where events could have become unmanageable." Larson, ed., *The "Cuban Crisis" of 1962*, pp. 179, 194.
28. The transcripts of the October 16 meetings indicate very clearly that McNamara worried about a launch from Cuba, and that the President did as well. At one point, the President unequivocally states: "If we come and attack, they're going to use them," the editor's notes. The Kennedy Tapes of the Cuban Missile Crisis," pp. 176, 179.
29. See Sagan, "SIOP-62: The Nuclear War Plan Briefing to President Kennedy," and Stein and Feaver, *Assuring Control of Nuclear Weapons*.
30. Cf. Taylor's remarks at Hawk's Cay, pp. 79–80; Stein and Feaver, *Assuring Control of Nuclear Weapons*; and McNamara's (signed) file memo on the October 21, 1962, meeting with President Kennedy, Robert Kennedy, General Taylor, and General Sweeney (Cuban Missile Crisis file, National Security Archive, Washington, D.C.): "General Sweeney stated that he was certain the air strike would be 'successful'; however, even under optimal conditions, it was not likely that all of the known missiles would be destroyed. (. . . The known missiles are probably no more than 60% of the total missiles on the island.) General Taylor stated, 'The best we can offer you is to destroy 90% of the known missiles.' " (p. 2).
31. CIA memorandum on the construction of missile sites in Cuba, October 19, 1962 (National Security Archive, Washington, D.C.); Laurence Chang, Donna Rich, Chris Wallace, *A Chronology of the Cuban Missile Crisis* (National Security Archive, Washington, D.C., October 9, 1987), p. 32.
32. CIA memorandum, subject: "The Crisis: USSR/Cuba," October 27, 1962.

33. CIA memorandum on the construction of missile sites in Cuba, October 19, 1962. There was some ambiguity in this document; on one page it stated that there were three SS-4 sites with four launchers each, but pinpointed the locations of six sites on another. Presumably, the earlier page was from an earlier assessment. There were in fact six MRBM sites under construction. Four of these sites were at San Cristóbal, and two were at Sagua la Grande. These locations were all known by October 19.

34. *A Chronology of the Cuban Missile Crisis*, pp. 38–41. The United States believed Cuba also had twenty-two Il-28 light jet bombers, and sixty-two older jet fighters. *Ibid.*, taken from SNIE 11–19–62, "Major Consequences of Certain US Courses of Action on Cuba." Cf. Afterword, pp. 345–46.

35. *A Chronology of the Cuban Missile Crisis*, pp. 40–41.

36. *Ibid.*

37. October 27, 1962, "Cuba Fact Sheet," National Security Archive, Washington, D.C.

38. For comparison, it is worth noting that in Vietnam the United States lost one aircraft to enemy fire in every 1,176 sorties, for an attrition rate of .085%; the U.S. Army Air Force in the Second World War suffered an attrition rate of 1.04%; and in Korea the American attrition rate was .02%. In the Second World War, some of the heaviest losses were suffered by the Japanese in the air campaign around the island of Rabaul in the South Pacific. From October 1943 to February 1944, the Japanese—outnumbered, flying inferior aircraft, and fielding poorly trained pilots—suffered an attrition rate of 14%. The British, in contrast, suffered an attrition rate of only 3% in the Battle of Britain. "Attrition in Air Combat," a briefing by Trevor Dupuy, Historical Evaluation and Research Organization (HERO), division of Data Memory Systems Ltd., Fairfax, Va. (courtesy of Stephen Biddle, Institute for Defense Analyses). The air defenses in Cuba in 1962 would have been very fortunate to down a handful of American aircraft. The SA-2 missiles providing the main defense were single-shot systems easily saturated by a coordinated attack. Moreover, the shootdown of the U-2 on October 27 was the first indication that any of the radar systems guiding the SA-2s was operational. Presumably, many of the SAM sites were still being wired and tested, and many of the crews manning the sites were still familiarizing themselves with their operation. Cf. "October 27, 1962: Transcripts of the Meetings of the ExComm," pp. 66–67.

39. McNamara's (signed) file memo on the October 21, 1962, meeting with President Kennedy, Robert Kennedy, General Taylor, and General Sweeney, p. 2.

40. CIA memorandum on the construction of missile sites in Cuba, October 19, 1962.

41. *Ibid.*

42. The Administration considered giving advanced warning of an attack in order to make it more politically acceptable. (October 19 NSC memo on the air-strike option, National Security Archive, Washington, D.C.) These time estimates assume that the Administration, in providing such warning, would avoid fixing the time of attack accurately enough to enable the advanced fueling of the MRBMs.

   It is evident from documents recently declassified that the members of the ExComm were intent on minimizing casualties in the event of an air strike. For example, Bromley Smith's minutes of the 10 a.m. ExComm meeting of October 27 report: "Secretary McNamara expressed his view that before we attack Cuba we must notify the Cubans." ("White House Tapes and Minutes," p. 200.) And in the concluding passage to the narrative of a top-secret State Department retrospective prepared in 1963, Frank A. Sieverts wrote: "During the day [October 27] approximately 5 million leaflets for Cuba had been loaded into containers. The order to drop them was never given." John F. Kennedy Library, National Security File, Drawer 49 (declassified 1984).

43. According to *Jane's*, an SS-4 missile crew consists of "some 20 men." Bernard Blake, ed., *Jane's Weapon Systems 1987–88* (London: Jane's, 1987), p. 6.

44. Of the Jupiters in Turkey, for example, Dean Rusk writes: "I remember that we joked about which way these missiles would fly if they were fired." See Welch and Blight, "The Eleventh Hour of the Cuban Missile Crisis," p. 17n.

45. It should be noted that at the time of General Sweeney's briefing, there was some doubt whether American intelligence had identified all the missiles and launchers on the island of Cuba. Photoreconnaissance seemed to indicate a quantity of equipment consistent with a larger number of missiles than had been accounted for (cf. McNamara's signed file memo, cited above). By October 27, however, all the launch sites had in fact been identified.

46. Some, such as Maxwell Taylor, expressed concern about the mobility of the missiles. There may have been some fear that the SS-4s could have been moved, set up, and fired quite rapidly. Nitze states that he finds it difficult to imagine that this could have been done, but "the point was, what could you do about it?" (p. 145), indicating an acceptance of the risk. Curiously, though, the mobility issue appears not to have been discussed much in the ExComm, presumably because the intelligence people had informed the President that, as Raymond Garthoff puts it, the SS-4 was mobile in the sense that a small house is mobile. It could be a matter of weeks before it would be ready to use again from a fixed position. (Personal communication, March 6, 1987.)

47. This is strongly, though incongruous, in a way, suggested that all-out invasion of Cuba was less likely to trigger Soviet involvement in local military counteractions than an air strike and graduated military action. See Garthoff, *Reflections on the Cuban Missile Crisis*, p. 31n. Richard Ned Lebow argues that if Kennedy had gone with the air strike, Khrushchev's acquiescence would have entailed considerable costs. He would have suffered a major setback to his foreign policy; he might have inadvertently encouraged further American aggression; and he might have suffered in domestic standing. "In short, some of the very same reasons that made Kennedy ready to risk war when he discovered Soviet missiles in Cuba could have compelled Khrushchev to do the same in response to an American airstrike." Lebow, *Nuclear Crisis Management*, p. 137.

48. P. 148.

49. P. 192.

50. Garthoff, *Reflections on the Cuban Missile Crisis*, p. 51.

51. See chapter 6, pp. 310–312, and Afterword, pp. 338–40.

52. The Soviet armed forces had been told for years that they enjoyed a significant advantage over the United States in strategic nuclear weapons. Roswell Gilpatric's speech of October 21, 1961, which revealed the Amer-

ican government's awareness that the missile gap was a hoax, was not widely reported in the Soviet Union, and there were undoubtedly Soviet officers who continued to believe that they held the winning nuclear cards in their hands. If Nitze is right that nuclear cards mattered, misinformation might have cut the deck both ways.

53. See Abel, *The Missile Crisis*, p. 188.

54. See pp. 236–37.

55. See Blight, Nye, and Welch, "The Cuban Missile Crisis Revisited," pp. 180–81.

56. For a useful discussion of various selection principles for dealing with uncertainty, as applied to the case of nuclear deterrence, see Gregory S. Kavka, "Deterrence, Utility, and Rational Choice," *Theory and Decision*, Vol. 12 (March 1980), pp. 41–60.

57. P. 148.

58. P. 148.

59. P. 152.

60. P. 142. This was also the position of fellow hawk, and Nitze's mentor from the Truman State Department, Dean Acheson. Upon hearing Robert Kennedy's impassioned plea to the ExComm to refrain from recommending the air strike, thus rendering his brother the "Tojo of the 1960s," Acheson "rejected the analogy with majestic scorn." Abel, *The Missile Crisis*, p. 64.

61. P. 155.

62. P. 162.

63. P. 188.

64. McNamara is, in our view, accurately reconstructing his reasoning process. Late in the day of October 27, 1962, he took his fellow ExComm members on a similar exercise in "possibility logic" regarding risk of nuclear war in Europe. See "October 27, 1962: Transcripts of the Meetings of the ExComm," pp. 52–56, 74–75. It is true, as Robert Jervis notes, that "Experiments have shown that subjects avoid judgments of extreme probabilities. Even when the evidence is overwhelming and subjects should give probability estimates of above .95 or below .05, they keep their estimates much closer to .50. Thus they underestimate the probability of extremely likely events and overestimate the likelihood of very unlikely ones." Jervis, *Perception and Misperception in International Politics*, p. 378.) It is plausible to argue that McNamara's probability judgments were following this pattern. Yet he seems not to have operated on the basis of his probability judgments, a fact of some relevance to students of crisis decisionmaking.

65. See chapter 1, p. 80. Cf. General Curtis LeMay's statement: "During that very critical time, in my mind there wasn't a chance that we would have gone to war with Russia because we had overwhelming strategic capability and the Russians knew it." In Kohn and Harahan, eds., "U.S. Strategic Air Power, 1948–1962," p. 94.

66. P. 195. McNamara adds: "And . . . with such adverse consequences, who wants to test it?"

67. Schelling, *The Strategy of Conflict*, p. 16.

68. Information that has only recently become available suggests that President Kennedy was a thoroughgoing dove by the end of the Cuban missile crisis. One must conjecture that the members of the ExComm were not blind to this: that after the first week's intense debates, involving the hawks' ad-

vocacy of the air strike and the doves' advocacy of the quarantine, the President came to know his own mind. By the end of the crisis, as indicated in the Rusk revelation and the transcripts of the October 27, 1962, Ex-Comm meetings, Kennedy was very reluctant to resort to even limited military action—more reluctant, perhaps, than any of his advisors save George Ball. See Welch and Blight, "The Eleventh Hour of the Cuban Missile Crisis," pp. 12–18; and "October 27, 1962: Transcripts of the Meetings of the ExComm," pp. 32–92. It may be that the doves as a whole were influenced heavily by their heightened sensitivity to the President's thinking. They advised him, to be sure; but this strong yet very cautious President may have powerfully affected their own risk aversion.

69. P. 153.
70. P. 169.
71. It should not be forgotten that, in an obvious sense, experience is simply no guarantee against error. For example, it would be correct to say that the hawks were more familiar with the Soviets' traditional patterns of behavior. For this reason, they may have felt that they had a decisive advantage over the doves in assessing the probabilities of various Soviet actions. But the Cuban missile crisis was the result of an atypical Soviet move. The Soviets were not traditionally prone to high-risk adventures; they had never deployed land-based nuclear weapons outside their borders; and the American intelligence community—clearly more experienced in analyzing Soviet behavior than most of the hawks on the ExComm—had concluded with a high degree of confidence in September that there was simply no way the Soviets would deploy missiles in Cuba. The hawks' greater experience in dealing with the Soviets did not prevent them from making significant errors of this kind. Cf. Garthoff, *Reflections on the Cuban Missile Crisis*, p. 26.
72. See *Khrushchev Remembers*, pp. 378–79.
73. On this point, see Richard K. Betts, *Nuclear Blackmail and Nuclear Balance* (Washington, D.C.: Brookings Institution, 1987). At the same time, the historical record surely should have moderated their confidence in the efficacy of nuclear superiority; after all, American nuclear superiority had not prevented Stalin from solidifying his grasp over Eastern Europe, and it had not deterred the Chinese from intervening in the Korean War. Nor had an apparent (but phony) Soviet nuclear superiority prevented the United States from successfully standing up to Khrushchev in Berlin.
74. Acheson, "Dean Acheson's Version of Robert Kennedy's Version of the Cuban Missile Affair," pp. 76–77, 44, 46.
75. P. 185.
76. *Ibid.* (emphasis added).
77. Sorensen, *Kennedy*, p. 724.
78. P. 178.
79. Kierkegaard, *The Concept of Anxiety*, pp. 43, 156.
80. There was, it seems, insufficient information even to identify the type of confrontation the superpowers were engaged in and the degree of cooperation available to the antagonists. Thus, in their attempt to understand the Cuban missile crisis in game-theoretic terms, Glenn Snyder and Paul Diesing note that "the Cuban crisis of 1962 is still too recent to permit a reliable reconstruction. In particular, information about the Soviet estimates of the situation, objectives, preference structure, and decision-making process is weak. On balance, we are inclined to interpret it as

Called Bluff, with the Soviet Union the bluffer, though PD [Prisoner's Dilemma] is a possibility on the assumption that the Soviet Union perceived the United States as intending to take over Cuba." Glenn H. Snyder and Paul Diesing, *Conflict Among Nations: Bargaining, Decision Making, and System Structure in International Crises* (Princeton, N.J.: Princeton University Press, 1977), pp. 114–15. As a result, as Richard Ned Lebow notes: "Blind to the interests that the Soviets might have believed they had at stake, so many members of the Ex Com were also blind to the dangers of pushing the Soviets too far." *Nuclear Crisis Management*, p. 138.

81. This is not to suggest that an appreciation of the possible will be the only factor that enters into deliberation under conditions of radical uncertainty, but merely that it will be the only reliable empirical component. "The requirements for a rational, well-calculated decision . . . are indeed difficult to meet in practice. Not surprisingly, such decisions have a strong subjective element and may be influenced by doctrines and general beliefs that fill the vacuum left by the inability to make more refined calculations." George, Hall, and Simons, *The Limits of Coercive Diplomacy*, pp. 15–16.

82. "The most important lesson of Kennedy's success in this crisis is that it is extremely difficult to apply coercive diplomacy effectively even when one possesses overall military superiority and other advantages as well." *Ibid.*, p. 131.

83. Chapter 1, p. 101.

84. In his interview, for example, Dillon makes the following revealing comment in response to the question, "What difference would it have made if there had been strategic parity in 1962?": "I think that we would have had to do the same thing. We would have had to tell the Soviets that this was unacceptable and we were going to use whatever conventional force that was necessary to get the missiles out. We would want to make it crystal clear that they, not we, would have to start a nuclear war, if there was going to be one. But we would also have to be clear that we were ready. By that I mean it would be obvious that the consequences for the Soviets of going to nuclear war would be the total destruction of the Soviet Union. Going to nuclear alert would accomplish that, just as it did in the missile crisis." P. 165. One searches in vain in this comment for evidence that Dillon's cognitive understanding of nuclear vulnerability is accompanied by the doves' visceral appreciation of its implications.

85. Nikita S. Khrushchev, interview with Norman Cousins shortly after the Cuban missile crisis, *Saturday Review*, October 10, 1977, p. 4.

CHAPTER 5

1. Schlesinger, *A Thousand Days*, p. 769.

2. See, e.g., Richard Bernstein, "Meeting Sheds New Light on Cuban Missile Crisis," *The New York Times*, October 14, 1987, p. A10; Bill Nichols, "Old Foes Meet, Discuss Lessons of 1962 Crisis," *USA Today*, October 14, 1987, p. 7A; Joseph S. Nye and Kurt M. Campbell, "The Soviets Come Clean on Cuba," *The Christian Science Monitor*, December 1, 1987.

3. See David A. Welch, ed., *Proceedings of the Cambridge Conference on the Cuban Missile Crisis, October 11–12, 1987*, CSIA Working Paper 89-2 (hereafter *CCT*, for "Cambridge Conference Transcript"), pp. 1–2.

4. *CCT*, p. 8.

5. *Ibid.*

6. *CCT*, p. 13.
7. *CCT*, p. 14.
8. In the unedited transcript of the Cambridge meeting, Burlatsky says the following: "Let me say some things about my play. Maybe you know I was political advisor to Khrushchev at that time, and I accompanied him on six visits to socialist countries. I prepared some speeches for him, including his speech to the Supreme Soviet after the conclusion of the Cuban missile crisis. On 'Black Saturday' [October 27], I met my friend Balyakov, who asked me, 'Where is your family, by the way? Maybe it would be better if they were in the village rather than in Moscow.' 'Why?' I said to him. 'Because maybe there will be an atomic blow from the Americans,' he said to me. Everyone was shocked, and maybe this is the reason why I tried to explain to our public opinion—not to Americans—what happened. I wrote my play with great sympathy for John Kennedy, who is very popular in the Soviet Union even now, by the way—especially with my wife, for example." Burlatsky also noted that the play, originally called *Black Saturday*, was written before Gorbachev's coming. "I published it first in 1983, twenty years after John Kennedy's assassination. But it was only possible to show it after the Geneva summit, because of the new thinking." *CCT*, pp. 22, 23.
9. *CCT*, p. 19.
10. Burlatsky came back to this theme again later in the discussion. "I was very glad to see the program about Khrushchev. It seems to me well done. It shows sympathy for Khrushchev and shows his psychology well. But what about the picture of relations between Khrushchev and the members of Presidium? Perhaps it is the same in my play with *your* advisors. [Laughter.] I tried to do this correctly, but perhaps I did not succeed. It is not so simple to get the information. But it was not possible for members of Presidium to have open conflict with Khrushchev." *CCT*, pp. 22, 24.
11. *CCT*, p. 25.
12. *CCT*, pp. 23–24.
13. *CCT*, p. 25.
14. *Ibid.*
15. *CCT*, p. 26.
16. Immediately before adjournment, it was announced that Seymour Hersh had written a story in *The Washington Post* that very day discussing an alleged conflict between Cubans and Soviets for control of a SAM site at the height of the crisis. Hersh's article suggested that this alleged struggle might have been related to the shooting down of an American U-2 on October 27, and that Cubans—rather than Soviets—might have been responsible, indicating that Khrushchev had lost control of the military situation in Cuba. While the issue was postponed for discussion on Monday, copies of Hersh's article were distributed to those who had not seen it. See *CCT*, p. 28. Cf. the discussion in chapter 6.
17. Cf. Ulam, *Expansion and Coexistence*, pp. 661–71.
18. Khrushchev was used to nuclear diplomacy and "missile rattling." As early as the Suez affair in 1956, for example, he sent notes to the British and French governments reminding them that it was reckless to start a war with Egypt when the Soviet Union could destroy them both with nuclear weapons. Cf. Dinerstein, *The Making of a Missile Crisis*, p. 58.
19. Khrushchev became First Secretary in September 1953 but did not become Premier until March 1957.

20. Khrushchev was in Bulgaria May 14–20, 1962.
21. Burlatsky is referring to a letter from Khrushchev to Castro given to him to edit by Yuri Andropov in 1963.
22. William F. Buckley, Jr., *See You Later Alligator* (New York: Doubleday, 1985).
23. On January 22–31, 1962, the Organization of American States (OAS) held a conference in Punta del Este, Uruguay. Castro's regime was declared incompatible with the inter-American system, and Cuba was excluded from participating in the OAS. The organization's members were prohibited from selling Cuba arms, and the OAS agreed on collective-defense measures against Cuba.
24. The previous Ambassador to Cuba was Sergei M. Kudryavtsev (July 6, 1960, to May 30, 1962).
25. Khrushchev, Mikoyan, and Kozlov.
26. American intelligence had estimated the number of Soviet troops in Cuba at 4,500 in early October, 1962. The estimate was raised to approximately 10,000 at the peak of the crisis, and again to 12,000–16,000 by mid-November, with the discovery of four mechanized infantry regiments. Retrospective estimates put the figure around 22,000. See Garthoff, *Reflections on the Cuban Missile Crisis*, p. 20n. Mikoyan's figure is therefore much higher than American analysts have hitherto believed, though it is very close to Castro's later recollection of 40,000. (*Ibid.*)
27. With this question, Lebow seeks confirmation of a view he first advanced in 1981: that attempts to deter can be self-defeating because they may stimulate fear which evokes a hostile response. See Lebow, *Between Peace and War*. Lebow, Jervis, and Stein argue the case more recently in *Psychology and Deterrence*. Cf. the critiques by John Orme, "Deterrence Failures: A Second Look," *International Security*, Vol. 11, No. 4 (Spring 1987), pp. 96–124, and James G. Blight, "The New Psychology of War and Peace," *International Security*, Vol. 11, No. 3 (Winter 1986/87), pp. 175–86.
28. The Soviets successfully launched the first man-made satellite, *Sputnik I*, on October 4, 1957.
29. Theodore Sorensen was the principal author of the President's October 22 address to the nation.
30. While Shakhnazarov may be technically correct on this point, it should be noted that there was no attempt on the part of the United States to deploy Jupiter missiles in Turkey secretly.
31. See chapter 1, p. 44.
32. See chapter 6, n. 65.
33. Khrushchev's speech was delivered on December 12, 1962, and printed in *Pravda* and *Izvestia* on December 13. For a translation, see *Current Digest of the Soviet Press*, January 16 and January 23, 1963.
34. This confirms Graham Allison's analysis in *Essence of Decision*, pp. 109–13.
35. Castro acknowledges he accepted missiles to strengthen socialism on the world scale, in an interview with Claude Julien, *Le Monde*, March 22 and 23, 1963; but he has been inconsistent on this point.
36. At the conference itself, Shakhnazarov seemed to be saying that the information he was relating was off the record. He did not, however, alter the text upon review, and it is our belief that Dobrynin authorized Shakhnazarov to make public this fascinating piece of information.

37. Reagan and Gorbachev met in Geneva on November 19–20, 1985.
38. Robert C. Tucker, *Political Culture and Leadership in Soviet Russia: Lenin to Gorbachev* (New York: Norton, 1988).
39. Shortly after the Cambridge conference, in December 1987, General Secretary Gorbachev and President Reagan signed an agreement in Washington eliminating intermediate-range nuclear forces in Europe.
40. Many American students of nuclear crises would agree. See William L. Ury, *Beyond the Hotline* (Boston: Houghton Mifflin, 1985).
41. Shortly before the Cambridge conference, a U.S.–Soviet agreement was signed establishing joint crisis prevention centers in Washington and Moscow. One of the participants at the Cambridge conference, William Ury, was instrumental in the negotiation of the agreement.
42. Mikoyan may be referring here to Robert Kennedy's verbal message to Dobrynin on October 27, or John Scali's meeting with Aleksandr Fomin that same day in which he reportedly stated that "an invasion is only hours away." See Detzer, *The Brink: Cuban Missile Crisis, 1962*, p. 250.
43. See Pope, ed., *Soviet Views on the Cuban Missile Crisis*, pp. 48–49; and Larson, ed., *The "Cuban Crisis" of 1962*, p. 180.
44. *Khrushchev Remembers*, pp. 497–98.
45. Sorensen appears to be correct on this point. Cf. Welch and Blight, "The Eleventh Hour of the Cuban Missile Crisis," pp. 20–22; and "October 27, 1962: Transcripts of the Meetings of the ExComm," pp. 30–92.
46. See Raymond L. Garthoff, *Détente and Confrontation: American–Soviet Relations from Nixon to Reagan* (Washington, D.C.: Brookings Institution, 1985), pp. 828–48.
47. Mikoyan understates his case. During the 1980 campaign, Reagan suggested "that we might blockade Cuba and stop the transportation back and forth of Russian arms, of Soviet military. . . . A blockade of Cuba would be an option." Reagan asked, "Suppose we put a blockade around the island and said, 'Now buster, we'll lift it when you take your forces out of Afghanistan.'" And back in 1972, Reagan had said, "We have seen an American President walk all the way to the barricade in the Cuban missile crisis and lack the will to take the final step to make it successful." Cited in Ronnie Dugger, *On Reagan: The Man and His Presidency* (New York: McGraw-Hill, 1983), p. 360. After becoming President, Reagan continued to make threats. In a February 1982 speech to the OAS, for example, Reagan urged his colleagues to join the U.S. and act "promptly and decisively in defense of freedom" and remove the government of Castro, a "brutal and totalitarian regime." See Robert Dallek, *Ronald Reagan: The Politics of Symbolism* (Cambridge, Mass.: Harvard University Press, 1984), p. 177. The statement to which Mikoyan refers was made on September 4, 1983, to a meeting of American Hispanic leaders: "As far as I'm concerned, that agreement [between Kennedy and Khrushchev] has been abrogated many times by the Soviet Union and Cuba in the bringing in of what can only be considered offensive weapons." In *Public Papers of the Presidents, 1983*, Vol. II (Washington, D.C.: Government Printing Office, 1985), p. 1274.
48. Wayne S. Smith, *The Closest of Enemies: A Personal and Diplomatic Account of U.S.–Cuban Relations since 1957* (New York: Norton, 1987), pp. 82–83. Clement's statement "that there was no understanding or agreement" may be found in *The Report of the President's National Bipartisan Commission on Central America* (New York: Macmillan, 1984), p. 155.

49. Garthoff, *Reflections on the Cuban Missile Crisis*, pp. 98–102.
50. On August 30, 1983, a Soviet Su-15 shot down a Korean Air Lines Boeing 747, killing all 269 people on board.
51. See Garthoff, *Reflections on the Cuban Missile Crisis*, p. 22.
52. Michael MccGwire, *Military Objectives in Soviet Foreign Policy* (Washington, D.C.: Brookings Institution, 1987), pp. 361–62.
53. Reagan and Gorbachev met at Reykjavik, Iceland, on October 11–12, 1986. Burlatsky was present at both Geneva and Reykjavik.
54. See "The Caribbean Crisis: A Most Important Lesson of History," *Latinskaya amerika*, No. 1 (January 1988); Garthoff, "The Caribbean Crisis (Cuban Missile Crisis) of 1962: Reflections of an American Participant," pp. 40–58; Rafael Hernández, "The October 1962 Crisis: Lesson and Legend," pp. 58–67; and Sergo Mikoyan, "The Caribbean Crisis Seen from a Distance," pp. 67–80, 143–44.
55. Ury, *Beyond the Hotline*.

CHAPTER 6

1. Dylan Thomas, "Poem in October." In Arthur M. Eastman, ed., *The Norton Anthology of Poetry* (New York: Norton, 1970), pp. 1107–8.
2. "Adventurism" is an epithet in the socialist diplomatic lexicon. Just after the Cuban missile crisis, the Chinese, for example, accused Khrushchev of adventurism. See the remarks on this in Pope, ed., *Soviet Views of the Cuban Missile Crisis*, pp. 138–40. Gorbachev himself, though regarded as an ambitious reformer, is nonetheless quite aware of the sting carried by the accusation of "adventurism." This, in fact, is the charge he leveled publicly at deposed former Moscow party boss Boris Yeltsin, a Gorbachev admirer, who finally had to be removed because of his ceaseless tirades against those who he felt were holding up the reform movement. (See Mikhail Gorbachev, interview with Tom Brokaw, in *The New York Times*, December 1, 1987, p. A12).
3. The written record of the meeting found in the previous chapter does not fully reflect the sense of astonishment experienced by the Americans in the room. Robert McNamara spoke for all when he said: "Well, this is absolutely fascinating to me, and I am *very* grateful to you for your candor. I, for one, have never heard anyone speak of these matters so openly, and I think it's tremendous." (P. 244.) It is a tribute to the courage and honesty of our Soviet colleagues that not only did they choose to speak with candor in the public sessions following the private meetings in Cambridge but, except for very minor stylistic revisions, they have left *all* of their contributions to the Cambridge conference on the record. As William Taubman said shortly after the conference at a public seminar, this meeting represents "Soviet foreign policy told in a new way." Cited in Bernstein, "Meeting Sheds New Light on Cuban Missile Crisis," p. A10.
4. Gromyko, "The Caribbean Crisis," reprinted in Pope, ed., *Soviet Views on the Cuban Missile Crisis*, pp. 161–226. The original appeared in *Voprosy istorii* (*Questions of History*, No. 7, 1971.
5. See Khrushchev, *Khrushchev Remembers*, pp. 509–14; Khrushchev's speech to the Supreme Soviet, December 12, 1967 ("The Present International Situation and the Foreign Policy of the Soviet Union," reprinted in Pope, ed., *Soviet Views on the Cuban Missile Crisis*, pp. 71–107); and Gromyko, "The Caribbean Crisis."

6. See Kennedy, *Thirteen Days*; Schlesinger, *A Thousand Days* and *Robert Kennedy and His Times*, and Sorensen, *Kennedy*. Of course, Cuban missile crisis "revisionists" have been eager to lay the bulk of the blame directly on President Kennedy. Richard Walton, for instance, concludes the following: "Whatever Russia's share in aggravating the Cuban crisis by installing missiles, the indisputable fact is that the United States by its unrelenting hostility to a weak and isolated Cuba caused the confrontation in the first place." Richard J. Walton, *Cold War and Counterrevolution: The Foreign Policy of John F. Kennedy* (New York: Viking, 1972), p. 112.

7. John F. Kennedy, "Radio and Television Address to the Nation on the Soviet Military Buildup in Cuba," in Larson, ed., *The "Cuban Crisis" of 1962*, p. 61.

8. *Ibid.*, p. 62.

9. Nikita Khrushchev to John F. Kennedy, October 23, 1962, *ibid.*, p. 67.

10. John F. Kennedy to Nikita Khrushchev, October 23, 1962, *ibid.*, p. 68.

11. See pp. 26–45.

12. See chapter 2, pp. 116–17.

13. See, e.g., Pope, ed., *Soviet Views on the Cuban Missile Crisis*, pp. 83–84.

14. Ulam, *The Rivals*, p. 332.

15. Horelick, "The Cuban Missile Crisis," p. 365.

16. Tatu, *Power in the Kremlin*, p. 230. Tatu qualifies his remark almost in the same breath: "It is possible, of course, that Khrushchev believed the rockets would help the defense of Cuba as a deterrent. . . . But this was a minor consideration." In contrast to these dismissive analyses, Richard Walton concludes that the defense of Cuba was Khrushchev's "predominant motive." Walton, *Cold War and Counterrevolution*, p. 121.

17. See p. 238.

18. Pp. 261–63.

19. Khrushchev recalled in his memoirs that, while he was in Bulgaria, "one thought kept hammering away at my brain: what will happen if we lose Cuba? And it would have been a terrible blow to Marxism-Leninism. . . . We had to establish a tangible and effective deterrent to American interference in the Caribbean. But what, exactly? The logical answer was missiles." *Khrushchev Remembers*, p. 493. Burlatsky does not believe that Khrushchev accurately reported his primary concern on that trip. Based on his own recollections and on his reading of some secret Khrushchev materials from that period, Burlatsky believes Khrushchev may have thought of the deployment earlier, on a trip to the Crimea. See p. 235.

20. *Ibid.*, p. 494. Many American commentators maintain that this was what Khrushchev chiefly sought to do. Cf., e.g., Horelick, "The Cuban Missile Crisis," p. 376; William Hyland and Richard W. Shryock, *The Fall of Khrushchev* (New York: Funk and Wagnalls, 1968); and Garthoff, *Reflections on the Cuban Missile Crisis*.

21. Nikita Khrushchev, "Celebration of Fraternal Friendship on Bulgarian Soil" (speech in Varna, Bulgaria, May 16, 1962). In *Current Digest of the Soviet Press (CDSP)*, Vol. 14, No. 20, p. 3 (reprinted from *Pravda*).

22. *Ibid.*

23. Nikita Khrushchev, "Rally of 250,000 Working People in Sofia in Honor of Soviet Party and Government Delegation" (speech in Sofia, Bulgaria, May 19, 1962). *CDSP*, Vol. 14, No. 20, p. 7 (reprinted from *Pravda*).

24. Pp. 233–34. For a particularly lucid and revealing account of Khrushchev's personality and the way in which it probably affected his decisionmaking

in this instance, see Crankshaw, *Khrushchev: A Career*, especially pp. 270, 280–83.

25. A corollary of this conclusion is that we may have to be very careful about what in Soviet statements we have rejected in the past, and what we continue to reject, on the basis of their obvious convenience or their polemical tone. Sometimes, it seems, the Soviets believe what they say.

26. The myriad arguments advanced over the years by Western scholars designed to show that the defense of Cuba hypothesis cannot make sense of the size and nature of the deployment may satisfactorily be answered by the recognition that the deployment makes a good deal more sense if two goals were being pursued simultaneously. See, e.g., chapter 2, n. 13 (p. 361). The main arguments against the defense of Cuba hypothesis are that the deployment was unnecessarily large; that the deployment of two types of missiles was unnecessary for that purpose; and that there were easier, cheaper, and safer ways of providing a guarantee for Castro's regime, such as bringing Cuba into the Warsaw Pact, concluding a formal treaty pledging Soviet support, or stationing a handful of Soviet soldiers on the island as a trip-wire, and so forth. Roger Hagan and Bart Bernstein argue, however, that the main value of the missiles in Cuba was as a deterrent to the invasion of Cuba, and that they were effective means for achieving that end. See Hagan and Bernstein, "Military Value of Missiles in Cuba," *Bulletin of the Atomic Scientists*, February 1963, pp. 8–13.

27. See Ulam, *The Rivals*, p. 329; and *Expansion and Coexistence*, pp. 661–71.

28. P. 251.

29. See, e.g., the Nitze interview, p. 140; "White House Tapes and Minutes of the Cuban Missile Crisis," p. 177; Horelick, "The Cuban Missile Crisis," p. 377; and *Time*, November 2, 1962, p. 15.

30. P. 288.

31. P. 289.

32. P. 237.

33. Cf. Rusk's remarks in the October 16 transcripts: "I must say I don't really see the rationality of, uh, the Soviets' pushing it this far unless they grossly misunderstand the importance of Cuba to this country." In "White House Tapes and Minutes," p. 178.

34. Mikoyan, for example, suggests that Khrushchev may have listened too closely to the optimistic assessments of Marshal Biryuzov—a man the elder Mikoyan thought a "fool." P. 239.

35. Adam Ulam writes that "the Bay of Pigs venture was exactly what the doctor, i.e. Khrushchev, would have ordered. In their discomfiture and guilt feelings, the Americans were less likely to repeat the attempt." *The Rivals*, p. 320.

36. Horelick, "The Cuban Missile Crisis," pp. 378–83. On this last point, Khrushchev would have been correct. In the transcripts of the October 27 ExComm meetings, the President voices concern that if he does not accept Khrushchev's offer of a missile trade, then "maybe we'll have to invade or make a massive strike on Cuba which may lose *Berlin*. That's what concerns me." See "October 27, 1962: Transcripts of the Meetings of the ExComm," p. 55.

37. Horelick, "The Cuban Missile Crisis," p. 383.

38. George and Smoke, *Deterrence in American Foreign Policy*, p. 463.

39. Dinerstein, *The Making of a Missile Crisis*, p. 234. Dinerstein notes, however, that "for Kennedy, it was a new departure." Dinerstein also argues that "Khrushchev believed that U.S. policy was more consistent and had more consequentialness than it indeed had. If the United States and its clients had stayed their hands at the Bay of Pigs, in Laos, and in Brazil in an atmosphere of missile rattling, why should they risk war when presented by concrete evidence of new Soviet nuclear power? In putting missiles into Cuba, the Soviet Union would be doing nothing more than the United States had done in a dozen countries. But Khrushchev failed to realize that Kennedy did not accept a U.S. decline." P. 158.

40. This argument was quite sincerely made by Shakhnazarov at the Cambridge meeting. See pp. 247–48.

41. P. 236. Bohlen's account of the Vienna summit of June 1961 is in many respects complementary to Burlatsky's, which is interesting in itself because of Bohlen's well-known Cold-Warrior reputation. According to Bohlen, "Kennedy made a mistake. He let himself be drawn into a semi-ideological discussion involving Marxian theory," a subject on which, as Bohlen put it gently, "Kennedy had a bowing knowledge," but which Khrushchev knew thoroughly. Charles E. Bohlen, *Witness to History* (New York: Norton, 1973), p. 481. Adam Ulam states: "One cannot endorse Schlesinger's verdict that 'each man came away from Vienna with greater respect for the mind and nerve of his adversary.' " Ulam, *The Rivals*, p. 321. Cf. George and Smoke, *Deterrence in American Foreign Policy*, p. 481; and *Time*, November 2, 1962, p. 15: "At Vienna and later, Khrushchev had sized up Kennedy as a weakling, given to strong talk and timorous action. The U.S. itself, he told poet Robert Frost, was 'too liberal to fight.' Now, in the Caribbean, he intended to prove his point." Cf. also the debate on this point at Hawk's Cay, chapter 1, pp. 34–36

42. Cf. Allison, *Essence of Decision*, pp. 235–37.

43. "It seems likely that the Soviet leaders heavily discounted the President's declarations, perhaps virtually to the point of ignoring them, precisely because they were so obviously motivated by internal political needs." George and Smoke, *Deterrence in American Foreign Policy*, p. 467. George and Smoke cite Hilsman, *To Move a Nation*, pp. 196–97, in support of the claim that Kennedy's main audience was domestic.

44. See Larson, ed., *The "Cuban Crisis" of 1962*, p. 17.

45. *Ibid.*, pp. 21–31.

46. *Ibid.*, p. 32.

47. The ambiguity in this point is intended. The fact that the Kremlin had been threatening nuclear war for a long time clearly indicated that the Soviet standard of an unambiguous warning was different from the American standard—harsher, clearer, and more threatening. In contrast, Kennedy's September statements were mild and vague. At the same time, the fact that the Kremlin had made clear nuclear threats may have led Khrushchev to believe that Kennedy had been deterred by them, and this in turn may have appeared to Khrushchev to be sufficient explanation of the mildness and vagueness of Kennedy's statements. This is consistent with Michel Tatu's observation that Khrushchev evinced unusual self-assurance in September. Tatu, *Power in the Kremlin*, p. 240.

48. Quoted in Allison, *Essence of Decision*, pp. 236–37.

49. The meeting lasted from 5 p.m. until just after 7 p.m. in the Oval office.

Also present were Soviet Ambassador Anatoly Dobrynin, Secretary of State Dean Rusk, Theodore Sorensen, and former Ambassador to the Soviet Union Llewellyn Thompson.

50. There is an interesting passage in *Khrushchev Remembers* which seems to suggest that Khrushchev believed the Americans knew about the deployment all along. See p. 496. Dinerstein argues that the Soviets may have taken over Walter Lippmann's columns—"Cuba: Watchful Waiting," New York *Herald Tribune*, September 15, 1962—as evidence that the United States knew about the Soviet deployment and was prepared to tolerate it. Lippmann began his piece: "We have complete knowledge of what goes on in Cuba. We may not know every missile site in the Soviet Union, but unless the cameras are fooling us, we are completely informed about Cuba." Lippmann was known to be a confidant of Presidents. "A logical interpretation of Lippmann's column was that some influential Americans knew, through aerial reconnaissance, that Soviet missiles were being installed in Cuba and had rejected an attack on Cuba because of the vulnerability of U.S. overseas bases to Soviet pressure. In the weeks that followed, Soviet diplomacy seemed to assume that the United States was prepared to accept the enlargement of Soviet strategic power and negotiate on that basis." Dinerstein, *The Making of a Missile Crisis*, p. 209. Of course, it would not have been possible for American photoreconnaissance to detect the deployment on September 15. Cf. Garthoff's remarks in chapter 1, p. 44.

51. See p. 241, and Afterword, p. 335.

52. Arnold Horelick argues that, had the missiles been operational, the outcome of the crisis probably would have been the same, because the missiles would still have been vulnerable to American attack, and the Soviet Union would still have been reluctant to initiate a U.S.–Soviet nuclear war. But, he notes, the American response might have been different. Horelick, "The Cuban Missile Crisis," p. 381n.

53. See Welch and Blight, "The Eleventh Hour of the Cuban Missile Crisis," pp. 5–29.

54. Dinerstein suggests that Khrushchev may have thought: "In the end, the United States would have no choice, because neither Cuba nor West Berlin was worth the risk of a nuclear war. What was new was that now the United States was in the same situation the Soviet Union had been in for many years. It either had to accept the opponent's military, economic, and political presence in a country or seek to dislodge him by force, thereby risking the consequences of nuclear war on its own territory. Why should the United States behave any differently than the Soviet Union in analogous circumstances?" Dinerstein, *The Making of a Missile Crisis*, p. 188. Of course, the Americans may not have appreciated the parallelism in the same way. One plausible lesson from Turkey, Italy, and Britain was that the Soviet Union makes a lot of noise but backs down in the face of American resolve—an entirely different lesson from the one Khrushchev may have drawn: that the advantage rests with the initiator; and the responder is forced to back down.

55. P. 235. George and Smoke argue that though Khrushchev probably recognized considerable risk in the deployment, he may have seen the risks as deferred—they would arise later, after an intervening series of manipulable events—and according to the Soviets' "operational code," deferred risks are acceptable. See George and Smoke, *Deterrence in American*

Foreign Policy, p. 488; see also Alexander L. George, "The 'Operational Code': A Neglected Approach to the Study of Political Leaders and Decision-Making," *International Studies Quarterly*, Vol. 13, No. 2 (June 1969), pp. 190–222.

56. Edward Crankshaw, Introduction to *Khrushchev Remembers*, p. xvii.
57. For instance, Khrushchev may have been the victim of systematic moti vated and unmotivated biases. Motivated biases are a function of affective interference in the processing of information, and unmotivated biases are a function of the limitations of cognitive processes. On this distinction, see Robert Jervis's introduction to Jervis, Lebow, and Stein, *Psychology and Deterrence*, p. 4.

The most impressive and most useful book on the subject remains Robert Jervis's *Perception and Misperception in International Politics*. See especially his discussions of "irrational consistency," cognitive distortions of information-processing, and mechanisms for preserving attitudes and beliefs in the face of contradictory evidence, pp. 128–42, 195, 291–95.

58. Herbert Dinerstein, for example, argues that "a rational Khrushchev should have anticipated what had happened. . . . The Soviet Union, or at least Khrushchev, failed to entertain the possibility that the United States might risk war to eliminate ground-to-ground missiles from Cuba. Like so many statesmen before and since, Khrushchev believed that what he wanted to happen would happen." Dinerstein, *The Making of a Missile Crisis*, p. 152.

59. Richard Ned Lebow makes this point in the Cambridge meeting, and elicits Sergo Mikoyan's concurrence. See also Lebow, "The Deterrence Deadlock: Is There a Way Out?" in Jervis, Lebow, and Stein, *Psychology and Deterrence*, pp. 189–90.

60. Note that Khrushchev did not *misperceive* the American response to his deployment, as Kennedy had not determined what that response would be at the time Khrushchev made his decision.

61. See pp. 239–40. Curiously, according to Sergo Mikoyan, Anastas Mikoyan did not believe that Castro would accept Soviet missiles on Cuban territory and also did not believe Kennedy would tolerate them. The elder Mikoyan was therefore right about Kennedy and wrong about Castro, even though he was considered to be an "expert" on Cuba. See pp. 238–39.

62. Cf., e.g., pp. 244–46, 260–61.

63. John F. Kennedy, remarks in a televised news conference, December 17, 1962. In Divine, ed., *The Cuban Missile Crisis*, p. 114.

64. One of the perplexities of the Soviet missile deployment is how Khrushchev could have so thoroughly misjudged the character and commitments of Kennedy, while they were engaged in voluminous secret correspondence over Berlin and other issues. Clearly, more is required to avoid crises than mere communication, as this case proves.

At least one reason why a confrontation between the United States and the Soviet Union might have been unavoidable—if not in Cuba in October 1962, then somewhere else at another time—is that the two countries had incompatible interests, and might not have been able to avoid a showdown when their interests directly clashed. But there are those who do argue that this crisis could have been avoided through timely communication. We are inclined to agree on the basis of the evidence, that this was a crisis neither side wanted or expected. But we do not agree with the simplistic arguments of some of the Cuban missile crisis "revisionists." Walton, for example, argues that Cuban President Osvaldo Dorticós's speech to the UN General Assembly of October 8, 1962, in which he said, "Were the United States able to give up proof, by word and deed, that it would not carry out aggression against our country, then, we declare solemnly before you here and now, our weapons would be unnecessary and our army redundant," was fully equivalent to an "offer" to withdraw Soviet missiles in return for a non-invasion pledge—the terms on which the crisis was ultimately resolved. Walton, *Cold War and Counterrevolution*, pp. 114–15. If Khrushchev deployed for two basic reasons, it seems unlikely to us that he would have gone along with such a deal in the absence of an intervening crisis to convince him of the dangers of the alternatives.

65. Joan Didion has conveniently summarized some of the findings of the Senate "Church Committee" that in 1975–76 investigated American covert operations. The figures are astonishing. According to Didion's tabulations, "the CIA's . . . station on the University of Miami campus was by 1962 the largest CIA installation, outside Langley, in the world, and one of the largest employers in the state of Florida. There were said to have been at . . . headquarters between 300 and 400 case officers from the CIA's clandestine services branch. Each case officer was said to have run between four and ten Cuban 'principal agents. . . .' Each principal agent was said to have run in turn between ten and thirty 'regular agents,' again mainly exiles. The arithmetic here is impressive. Even the minimum figures, 300 case officers each running four principal agents who in turn ran ten regular agents, yield 12,000 regular agents, each of whom might be presumed to have contacts of its own. . . ." There was also a fleet of ships, described by one CIA agent at the time as "the third largest navy in the Western hemisphere," several fleets of aircraft, and a great deal of supporting money and other resources. Joan Didion, *Miami* (New York: Simon and Schuster, 1987), pp. 90–91.

66. A clear example of reading too much knowledge and authority into Soviet public statements is Dinerstein's extensive analysis of the September 11 TASS statement. See *The Making of a Missile Crisis*, pp. 195–210. The statement runs: "The government of the Soviet Union also authorizes TASS to state that the Soviet Union does not have to transfer to any other country, Cuba for example, the means it possesses for the repulsion of aggression, for a retaliatory blow. Our nuclear means are of such powerful explosive force, and the Soviet Union possesses missile vehicles for these warheads of such power that there is no need to search for places to site them anywhere outside the Soviet Union." Dinerstein notes that "a statement that the Soviet Union did not have to place missiles outside the Soviet Union did not necessarily mean that she was not doing so," but he claims that "the intention was to mislead" (p. 197). But the government official authorizing TASS to make the statement—unless it was a member of the Presidium—most likely did not know that missiles were being deployed.

67. Schlesinger, *Robert Kennedy and His Times*, p. 544.

68. We certainly agree with George and Smoke that, "the fact that the secret Soviet deployment of missiles would inflict personal and political humiliation on the President could not have escaped Khrushchev's attention when he *planned* the operation as well as while he was carrying it out. Of the several aspects of his bold gambit that show poor judgment on his part, his willingness to inflict such humiliation upon Kennedy is certainly among the most irresponsible." *Deterrence in American Foreign Policy*, p. 469.

69. P. 244. There were some, of course. UN Ambassador Adlai Stevenson raised the issue on October 20, but his views were not taken seriously. See Abel, *The Missile Crisis*, pp. 94–96. Walter Lippmann, in addition, had published a column in *The Washington Post* on October 25 claiming that the Cuban missile deployment was precisely analogous to the earlier Turkish deployment of NATO, a position which squared exactly with Khrushchev's, as he expressed it to Kennedy in his letter of October 27.

70. P. 244. Theodore Sorensen, the primary drafter of the October 22 speech, acknowledged in response to Shaknazarov's questions that there was some appreciation for the Soviet position: that, legally, the Soviets had a perfect right to do what they did, so long as the Cuban government agreed. Kennedy clearly worried that the Soviets might be able to court world opinion by appealing to the canons of international law. So he urged Sorensen, as a practitioner of international law, to put the "emphasis on the sudden and deceptive deployment" (p. 246). Indeed, there is scarcely a paragraph in the speech that fails to mention Soviet deception. But of course Sorensen, in reminding Shaknazarov of this, was not, strictly speaking, answering his question. Perhaps a paraphrase of Sorensen's reply would be: liars relinquish their right to a fair hearing.

The extent to which Kennedy himself seems to have missed the symmetry of the Cuban deployment is clearly shown in an exchange in one of the meetings of October 16:

J.F.K.: . . . It's just as if we suddenly began to put a major number of MRBMs in Turkey. Now that'd be goddam dangerous, I would think.

Bundy?: Well, we *did*, Mr. President. . . .

J.F.K.: Yeah, but that was five years ago.

"White House Tapes and Minutes," p. 190.

71. See the discussion in chapter 2.

72. P. 247.

73. P. 246. Cf. Fyodor Burlatsky, "The Caribbean Crisis and Its Lessons," *Literaturnaya gazeta*, November 11, 1987, p. 14. In *Foreign Broadcast Information Service (FBIS) Soviet Union*, November 17, 1987, pp. 21–24, 23.

74. P. 247.

75. See p. 246. We have no independent confirmation of Burlatsky's judgment, and we appreciate the force of the skeptical views against it advanced at the Cambridge meeting.

76. Gromyko, "The Caribbean Crisis, Part 1," reprinted in Pope, ed., *Soviet Views on the Cuban Missile Crisis*, pp. 182–84. "It was the Soviet side that raised the Cuban question during that meeting. . . . During the conversation, it was said to President Kennedy that solution of the overwhelming majority of international problems was the result of statements and negotiations between states, in which governments set forth their positions on various questions. The American President was thus clearly given to understand that if the U.S. had any 'claims' against Cuba or the Soviet Union, it was necessary to resolve them by peaceful means. This statement by the Soviet government was also ignored by President Kennedy, although the 'problem' which concerned him of the strengthening of Cuba's defenses could certainly have been discussed within the framework of negotiations. . . . 'I do not know where all this may take us,' [President Kennedy] commented on the situation in the Caribbean. This

statement by Kennedy was certainly not in accordance with reality, for it presented a consequence of the exacerbation of the international situation in that region as its cause, which actually originated with the United States. The American President at that time also had a clear idea of the future course of events. At that time he was consciously guiding matters toward a military confrontation between the U.S. and USSR, although all the actions of the Soviet Union in Cuba were in full accord with international law and the sovereign rights of the USSR and Cuba." *Ibid.*, pp. 179–81. The younger Gromyko documents his account of the meeting with references to Soviet Foreign Ministry archives, and so it seems likely that the substance accurately reflects his father's report of the conversation.

77. President Kennedy referred directly to the meeting with Gromyko in his speech to the nation on October 22 and quoted the Soviet Foreign Minister at some length, especially his remarks about the nature of the "defensive" armaments in Cuba. Kennedy concluded by saying that "that statement also was false." Kennedy, "Radio and Television Address on Cuba," October 22, 1962, in Larson, ed., *The "Cuban Crisis" of 1962*, p. 60.

78. Sorensen, *Kennedy*, pp. 690–91.

79. Abel, *The Missile Crisis*, p. 77.

80. Gromyko's memoirs describe his October 18 meeting with Kennedy as "perhaps the most complex discussion" in his diplomatic career. Andrei Gromyko, *Pamiatnoe* (Moscow: Politizdat, 1988), pp. 390–96.

81. Shakhnazarov's confirmation of Dobrynin's innocence gives special poignancy to Dean Rusk's recollection that when he delivered a copy of Kennedy's October 22 speech to Dobrynin, just before the President was to deliver it, the Soviet Ambassador "aged ten years right before my eyes." See p. 185. According to former UN Under Secretary General and Soviet defector Arkady Shevchenko, Zorin was by 1962 often the victim of seizures, lapses of memory, and other indications that "his faculties had begun to fail him." *Breaking with Moscow* (New York: Alfred A. Knopf, 1985), p. 114. It certainly did not help Zorin, in his weakened condition, to have to equivocate in front of Adlai Stevenson and the world as the American Ambassador provided photos of the missile bases in Cuba that Zorin had said did not exist.

82. P. 185.

83. In Pope, ed., *Soviet Views on the Cuban Missile Crisis*, p. 30; and Larson, ed, *The "Cuban Crisis" of 1962*, pp. 67–68.

84. Tatu, *Power in the Kremlin*, p. 261.

85. Roy Medvedev, *All Stalin's Men*, tr. Harold Shukman (New York: Doubleday, 1985), p. 52. As *Time* magazine noted immediately after the crisis, "When Kennedy first made known this plan, there were some complaints that it was not enough. But Kennedy meant it only to give Khrushchev an opportunity to think things over; more precipitant action by the U.S., Kennedy felt, might cause Khrushchev to lurch wildly into a nuclear war." *Time*, November 2, 1962, p. 15.

86. *All Stalin's Men*, p. 52.

87. Robert Kennedy reports the following conversation the morning of October 24, 1962, between the President and McNamara: ". . . I heard the President say: 'Isn't there some way we can avoid having our first exchange with a Russian submarine—almost anything but that?' 'No, there's too much danger to our ships. There is no alternative,' said McNamara. 'Our commanders have been instructed to avoid hostilities if at all possible, but

this is what we must be prepared for, and this is what we must expect.' We had come to the time of final decision." *Thirteen Days*, p. 70.

88. Abel, *The Missile Crisis*, p. 153.

89. Yet Roy Medvedev is, by Western standards, a serious and careful historian. See the fine essay on Medvedev by Stephen F. Cohen, "Roy Medvedev," in *Sovieticus* (New York: Norton, 1986), pp. 112–15.

90. Mikoyan had not realized, prior to our conversation, that Medvedev had in fact written of this episode; for Medvedev's writings are not available in the Soviet Union. Upon hearing of it, however, Mikoyan related that his father had in fact told him the story in detail. Moreover, Mikoyan is convinced he knows Medvedev's source, a man who would have had no motive to exaggerate the elder Mikoyan's role in the conduct of the crisis, and a man who would have had no interest in disparaging Khrushchev.

It should be noted that Sergo Mikoyan, throughout the Cambridge conference, was reluctant to stress his father's role in the crisis because of his concern that doing so would appear immodest. We are therefore inclined to believe Mikoyan's confirmation all the more strongly.

91. It should also be remembered in this regard that UN Acting Secretary General U Thant played a crucial role here by providing Khrushchev with a face-saving way of justifying his order to halt his ships short of the quarantine line. He did so by proposing on October 24 that the United States suspend the quarantine and the Soviets suspend arms shipments for a period of two to three weeks in order to facilitate negotiations. See Welch and Blight, "The Eleventh Hour of the Cuban Missile Crisis," p. 9.

92. President Kennedy is reported by nearly all of those close to him to have reacted initially with anger to the discovery of the Cuban missiles. "He [Khrushchev] can't do this to *me*," was, according to Richard E. Neustadt, one such response. See Neustadt's remarks as moderator of videotaped discussions on the Cuban missile crisis with former members of the ExComm, January and June 1983 (available at the Alfred P. Sloan Foundation, New York City).

93. "I don't think we got much time on these missiles. They may be. . . . So it may be that we just have to, we can't wait two weeks while we're getting ready to, to roll. Maybe just have to just take *them out*, and continue our other preparations if we decide to do that. That may be where we end up. I think we ought to, beginning right now, be preparing to. . . . Because that's what we're going to do *anyway*. We're certainly going to do number one; we're going to take out these, uh, missiles. Uh, the questions will be whether, which, what I would describe as number two, which would be a general air strike. That we're not ready to say, but we should be in preparation for it. The third is the, is the, uh, general invasion. At least we're going to do number one, so it seems to me that we don't have to wait very long. We, we ought to be making *those* preparations." "White House Tapes and Minutes," p. 181.

94. *Ibid.* It is interesting to note Robert Kennedy's report of the President's encounter with congressional leaders on October 22: "He was upset by the time the meeting ended. When we discussed it later he was more philosophical, pointing out that the Congressional leaders' reaction to what we should do, although more militant than his, was much the same as our first reaction when we first heard about the missiles the previous Tuesday." *Thirteen Days*, p. 55.

95. We discuss these matters extensively in chapters 2 and 4.
96. Pope, ed., *Soviet Views on the Cuban Missile Crisis*, p. 29; and Larson, ed., *The "Cuban Crisis" of 1962*, pp. 57–58.
97. Pope, ed., *Soviet Views on the Cuban Missile Crisis*, p. 31; and Larson, ed., *The "Cuban Crisis" of 1962*, pp. 68–69.
98. Pope, ed., *Soviet Views on the Cuban Missile Crisis*, p. 38; and Larson, ed., *The "Cuban Crisis" of 1962*, p. 176.
99. Pope, ed., *Soviet Views on the Cuban Missile Crisis*, pp. 37–39, 48–49; and Larson, ed., *The "Cuban Crisis" of 1962*, pp. 175–76, 180.
100. Tatu, *Power in the Kremlin*, p. 261.
101. Pp. 256–57.
102. P. 256.
103. Schlesinger, *Robert Kennedy and His Times*, p. 554. Ever since Kennedy had come into office, Americans and Soviets had been sparring in Southeast Asia. The question of who was to govern Laos was the heart of the problem. The Soviets provided substantial military supplies and some advisors to friendly Pathet Lao forces, while the Americans provided advisors and flexed their muscles by landing Marines in neighboring Thailand to conduct war games. Finally, the situation was defused when Kennedy accepted a sub-optimal but tolerable arrangement: a neutral Laos led by Prince Souvanna Phouma. See Sorensen, *Kennedy*, pp. 639–48. It seems plausible that the analogy would have been very powerful to Dobrynin during the Cuban missile crisis. In Southeast Asia, a potentially dangerous situation was defused when the U.S. and Soviet Union agreed mutually to withdraw their forces, leaving a neutralist regime intact. Why not, therefore, agree in October 1962 to a mutual withdrawal of their (this time nuclear) forces?
104. *The Washington Post*, October 25, 1962.
105. Detzer, *The Brink: Cuban Missile Crisis, 1962*, p. 250.
106. P. 254.
107. Tatu, *Power in the Kremlin*, p. 268.
108. See, e.g., Mikoyan's remarks, p. 254; Welch and Blight, "The Eleventh Hour of the Cuban Missile Crisis," p. 14; and Afterword, p. 342.
109. The transcript of the ExComm meetings of October 27 reveals that while the news of the U-2 shoot-down was troubling, it still did not distract the President for long from his central concern, which was the Soviet proposal for a missile swap. "October 27, 1962: Transcripts of the Meetings of the ExComm," pp. 62–72.
110. U. Alexis Johnson says, for example, in the October 27 ExComm meeting: "It's a very different thing. You could have an undisciplined anti-aircraft— Cuban anti-aircraft outfit fire, but to have a SAM-site and a Russian crew fire is not any accident." "October 27, 1962: Transcripts of the Meetings of the ExComm," p. 71.
111. Jorge I. Domínguez, *To Make a World Safe for Revolution: Cuba's Foreign Policy* (Cambridge: Harvard University Press, 1989), pp. 40–42.
112. Carlos Franqui, *Family Portrait with Fidel*, tr. Alfred Mac Adam (New York: Vintage, 1984), p. 193.
113. Tad Szulc, *Fidel* (New York: Morrow, 1986), pp. 584–85.
114. Seymour M. Hersh, "Was Castro Out of Control in 1962?" *The Washington Post*, October 11, 1987.
115. Daniel Ellsberg, "The Day Castro Almost Started World War III," *The New York Times*, October 31, 1987, p. 27. See also Adrian G. Montoro, "Moscow Was Caught Between Cuba and U.S.," *The New York Times*,

November 17, 1987. Montoro, former director of Radio Havana (in 1961), appears to corroborate Ellsberg's thesis in a very general way—that Castro was furious about the way Soviets and Americans treated him in October 1962—without saying anything about Ellsberg's specific claim, which appeared earlier in the Hersh piece, that Cubans actually shot down the U-2.

116. See pp. 270–73.

117. Robert Schackne, Special Report on "Sunday Morning," October 25, 1987, CBS News.

118. Garthoff reports that General Statsenko was only forty-five years old at the time, very young for a Soviet general. Garthoff notes cryptically that despite this, a few years after the missile crisis, Statsenko was retired into the reserve. *Reflections on the Cuban Missile Crisis*, p. 5. Moreover, Mikoyan noted at the Cambridge meeting that it took some years to discover the identity of the Soviet officer responsible for shooting down the U-2. Perhaps it was after this interval, and after his connection with the U-2 shoot-down was discovered, that he "was retired," involuntarily. There is some reason to suspect that Statsenko may indeed have tried to cover his tracks. In Seymour Hersh's piece on the U-2 shoot-down, for example, we discover that Statsenko told U Thant shortly after the event that the SAM sites in Cuba were "manned by Cubans. It was a Cuban colonel that shot down our plane." If this line of reasoning is correct, then the downing of the U-2 over Cuba would have been the second such incident in two and a half years to affect the fortunes of the responsible Soviet general. Michael Beschloss suspects that Commander of Soviet Air Defense S. S. Biryuzov's move to Chief of Staff was aided by his responsibility for the shooting down on May Day 1960 of the U-2 piloted by Francis Gary Powers. See *Mayday* (New York: Harper & Row, 1986). Just as Biryuzov's career took off because of that incident, Statsenko's may very well have been destroyed by the other.

119. In his speech to the Supreme Soviet, Khrushchev states that he received information "from Cuban comrades and from other sources" on the morning of October 27 that the U.S. would attack Cuba "in the next two or three days." See Pope, ed., *Soviet Views on the Cuban Missile Crisis*, p. 87. Colonel Bruce Williams, then with the First Armored Division, recalls spending hours toward the end of the crisis in assault ships just off the Florida coast, presumably attempting to look obvious to Cuban spotters. (Personal communication.) And in an interview for WGBH-TV Boston, a former U.S. Naval commander recalled how, when he was skipper of a ship based in Panama, his ship set sail toward Cuba each day, its deck prominently loaded with coffins, and returned each night during the public phase of the crisis. (Zvi Dor-ner and Elizabeth Deane, producers, "War and Peace in the Nuclear Age," a PBS series aired in January 1989.)

120. See Welch and Blight, "The Eleventh Hour of the Cuban Missile Crisis," pp. 19–20; and "October 27, 1962: Transcripts of the Meetings of the ExComm," pp. 66–72.

121. P. 277. Horelick agrees. See "The Cuban Missile Crisis," p. 385.

122. See p. 275; see also chapter 4, p. 160. It should be noted that the Soviets are not currently in a political position to admit publicly that an attack on Cuba would not have been a *casus belli*, though, of course, it may indeed be their sincere opinion that it was. Mikoyan addressed this question with considerable emotion when he said, "I knew Khrushchev very well, and

I met him at home many times and I think I understand his nature and his perception of the prestige of our country. For both reasons, in my opinion, we could not swallow an air strike without a very strong reply. I do not know where or how; but I do not think we would do nothing." P. 278. This seems to have been the President's reading of events. "When the President questioned what the response of the Russians might be, General LeMay assured him that there would be no reaction. President Kennedy was skeptical. " 'They, no more than we, can let these things go by without doing something. They can't, after all their statements, permit us to take out their missiles, kill a lot of Russians, and then do nothing. If they don't take action in Cuba, they certainly will in Berlin.' " Robert Kennedy, *Thirteen Days*, p. 36.

123. See p. 254.
124. Sorensen, *Kennedy*, p. 724.
125. Khrushchev's October 27 and 28 letters, for example, very clearly indicate the responsibility and anxiety he felt, as well as his appreciation of the cooperative aspects of crisis prevention and management. See Pope, ed., *Soviet Views on the Cuban Missile Crisis*, especially pp. 51, 58, 61. In his memoirs, Khrushchev acknowledges that his anxiety during the crisis was "intense." *Khrushchev Remembers*, p. 497.
126. "I think," Kennedy wrote Khrushchev on October 28, "that you and I, with our heavy responsibilities for the maintenance of peace, were aware that developments were approaching a point where events could have become unmanageable." Pope, ed., *Soviet Views on the Cuban Missile Crisis*, pp. 65–66; Larson, ed., *The "Cuban Crisis" of 1962*, p. 194.
127. "Across the Iron Curtain, through the fog of propaganda and the barrage of weapons, Khrushchev, too, had to perceive that he and his opponent were shouldering a responsibility together and that their antagonistic dependence on each other could be tolerable only through mutual respect or even . . . a certain solidarity of purpose." Pachter, *Collision Course*, p. 64.
128. *Khrushchev Remembers*, p. 505.
129. See, e.g., Kennedy, *Thirteen Days*, p. 128.
130. In his speech to the Supreme Soviet on December 12, 1962, Khrushchev raised the issue: "Which side was victorious, who won? Here it can be said that reason won, that the cause of peace and of the security of nations won." In view of his claim earlier in the speech that he had intended for the missiles solely to defend Cuba, he had put himself in a position, if he had wanted to, of painting the resolution of the crisis as a considerable triumph. See Pope, ed., *Soviet Views on the Cuban Missile Crisis*, p. 90. As for the President, "He instructed all members of the Ex Comm and government that no interview should be given, no statement made, which would claim any kind of victory." Kennedy, *Thirteen Days*, pp. 127–28.
131. See Joseph S. Nye, "Nuclear Learning and U.S.–Soviet Security Regimes," *International Organization*, Vol. 41, No. 3 (Summer 1987), pp. 371–402.
132. Kennedy, *Thirteen Days*, p. 111.
133. P. 185.
134. Mikoyan's remarks may be found in Fyodor Burlatsky, Sergo Mikoyan, and Georgy Shakhnazarov, "New Thinking About an Old Crisis: Cuba, 1962," in Graham T. Allison and William L. Ury, eds., with Bruce J. Allyn, *Windows of Opportunity: From Cold War to Peaceful Competition in U.S.–Soviet Relations* (New York: Harper & Row, 1989).

135. *Ibid.*
136. *Ibid.*
137. Theodore C. Sorensen, "Reflections on a Grim but Hopeful Anniversary," *The Miami Herald*, November 1, 1987, pp. 1C, 5C.
138. *Ibid.*, p. 1C.
139. Durlatsky, "The Caribbean Crisis and Its Lessons," pp. 21 24.

EPILOGUE

1. Bundy, "To Cap the Volcano," pp. 9–10.
2. A particularly long and instructive list, assembled by several former ExComm members, appeared on the twentieth anniversary of the crisis in *Time* magazine, October 27, 1982, pp. 85–86.
3. The skeptic's view may be found in George F. Will, "The Lessons of the Cuban Crisis," *Newsweek*, October 11, 1982, p. 120; and in Eliot A. Cohen, "Why We Should Stop Studying the Cuban Missile Crisis," *The National Interest* (Winter 1986), pp. 3–13. Cf. Blight, Nye, and Welch, "The Cuban Missile Crisis Revisited," pp. 170–88.
4. *Thirteen Days*, p. 111. Cf. chapter 6, pp. 313–14.
5. Cf. chapters 1 and 3, pp. 99, 171–72.
6. Bernstein, "Meeting Sheds New Light on Cuban Missile Crisis," p. A10.
7. Susan Glasser, "Invasion Fears Prompted '62 Missiles, Soviets Say," *Harvard Crimson*, October 14, 1987, p. 1.
8. Nye and Campbell, "The Soviets Come Clean on Cuba."
9. Mikhail Gorbachev, *Perestroika: New Thinking for Our Country and the World* (New York: Harper & Row, 1987), p. 150.

AFTERWORD

1. This afterword is based largely on research published in Bruce J. Allyn, James G. Blight, and David A. Welch, "Essence of Revision: Moscow, Havana, and the Cuban Missile Crisis," *International Security*, Vol. 14, No. 3 (Winter 1989/90) pp. 136–72, from which portions of the text are reprinted. (Copyright of MIT Press)
2. Personal communication.
3. All three delegations included a number of scholars and lower-level participants. For details, see Bruce J. Allyn, David A. Welch, and James G. Blight, eds., *Proceedings of the Moscow Conference on the Cuban Missile Crisis, January 27–29, 1989*, CSIA Working Paper, Center for Science and International Affairs, Harvard University, forthcoming (hereafter *MCT*, for Moscow Conference Transcript). Owing to delays in clearance and translation, specific page-number references for the transcript were unavailable as this afterword went to press.
4. Useful and revealing treatments stimulated by the Cambridge and Moscow conferences include Aleksandr I. Alekseev, "Karibskii krizis: kak eto bylo" (The Caribbean crisis: as it really was), *Ekho planety*, No. 33 (November 1988), pp. 27–37; A. I. Alekseev, "Karibskii, Kubinskii, Oktiabr'skii krizis" (The Caribbean, Cuban, October crisis), *Ekho planety*, No. 7 (February 1989), pp. 16–18; A. I. Alekseev, "Uroki karibskogo krizisa" (Lessons of the Caribbean crisis), *Argumenty i fakty*, No. 10 (1989), p. 5; Georgy Bolshakov, "Goriachaia liniia: kak diestvoval sekretnyi kanal sviazi Dzhon Kennedi-Nikita Khrushchev" (The Hot Line: the secret com-

munication channel between John Kennedy and Nikita Khrushchev), *New Times*, Nos. 4–6 (1989); Georgy Bolshakov, "Karibskii krizis: kak eto bylo" (The Caribbean crisis: as it really was), *Komsomolskaya pravda*, February 4, 1989, p. 3; F. M. Burlatsky, "Karibskii krizis i ego uroki" (The Caribbean crisis and its lessons), *Literaturnaya gazeta*, November 11, 1987, p. 14; Fyodor Burlatsky, Sergo Mikoyan, and Georgy Shakhnazarov, "New Thinking about an Old Crisis: Soviet Reflections on the Cuban Missile Crisis," in Allison and Ury, eds., *Windows of Opportunity*; S. Chugrov, "Politicheskie rify karibskogo krizisa" (Political reefs of the Caribbean crisis), *Mirovaia ekonomika i mezhdunarodnye otnosheniia*, No. 5 (1989), pp. 19–32; Andrei A. Gromyko, "Karibskii krizis: o glasnosti teper' i skrytosti togda" (The Caribbean crisis: on openness now and secrecy then), *Izvestia*, April 15, 1989, p. 5; Stanislav Kondrashov, "Eshche o karibskom krizise: v kriticheskom svete glasnosti" (More on the Caribbean crisis: in the critical light of glasnost), *Izvestia*, February 28, 1989, p. 5; S. A. Mikoyan, "A War That Never Started," *New Times*, November 23, 1987; S. A. Mikoyan, "Karibskii krizis, kakim on viditsia na rasstoianii" (The Caribbean crisis: how it appears from a distance), *Latinskaya amerika*, No. 1 (1988), pp. 67–80, 143–44; G. Shakhnazarov, "A Moment of Fear and Revelation," *New Times*, December 11, 1987; and Melor Sturua, "Dialektika karibskogo krizisa" (The Dialectic of the Caribbean Crisis), *Izvestia*, February 6, 1989, p. 5. Interesting Cuban stories include Adela Estrada Juárez, "El general que Dió la Orden de: ¡Fuego!" *Bastión*, March 30, 1989, p. 4; reprinted as "The General Who Gave the Order to Fire," in the *Granma Weekly Review*, April 23, 1989; an interview with Dimitri Yazov by Captain Mario H. Garrido, "I Have My Uniform, Ready to Fight," same issue; and Rafael Hernández, "Es ridículo pretender que teníamos la intención de provocar una guerra nuclear" ("It is ridiculous to pretend that we intended to provoke a nuclear war"), *Granma*, February 26, 1989, p. 9.

5. Allyn, Blight, and Welch interview with Jorge E. Mendóza, director of the Instituto de Historia de Cuba, May 15, 1989, Havana.

6. See *MCT*; and pp. 296–97, above.

7. See pp. 42–50. Gromyko argued that the United States considered the Castro regime "unacceptable" and that this was the "beginning of the whole chain of events." Jorge Risquet also said that Khrushchev told him in August 1964 that the "sole idea" behind the deployment was to defend Cuba. *MCT*.

8. This concurs with Sergo Mikoyan's recollection, p. 241.

9. *MCT*.

10. In a later interview, del Valle claimed that the 270,000 armed and mobilized troops were divided into fifty-six existing divisions, which had been brought up to full strength from reserves. Although they varied considerably in size, each division had on average 4,800 men, considerably smaller than an American division. Twenty-eight divisions deployed on the western side of the island included some of the largest and strongest, since this was where the first wave of an invasion was expected to land. Allyn, Blight, and Welch interview with Sergio del Valle, May 18, 1989, Havana.

11. The commander-in-chief of the Atlantic Command (CINCLANT) prepared three contingency plans for military action against Cuba. Operational Plan No. 312-62 (312 OPLAN) set out air strike options, and Operational Plans 314-62 and 316-62 (314 OPLAN and 316 OPLAN) set out invasion

options. The invasion force, ready on October 27, would initially have involved five Army divisions and one Marine division: the 82nd Airborne, 101st Airborne, 2nd Infantry, 1st Armored, 1st Infantry, and 2nd Marines. The 5th Infantry, 2nd Armored, and 4th Infantry divisions were held in reserve. See Raymond Garthoff's remarks, *MCT*; and *CINCLANT Historical Account of Cuban Crisis* (1963), chap. II, pp. 17 23 (available at the National Security Archive, Washington, D.C.). According to Emilio Aragonés, the Cubans estimated in 1962 that as many as 800,000 people would have died in the event of an American invasion (*MCT*); CINCLANT estimated in 1962 that 316 OPLAN would succeed after ten days and that the U.S. armed forces would suffer between 18,000 and 19,000 casualties. *CINCLANT Historical Account*, pp. 55–56.

12. *MCT*.
13. Cf. p. 251; and p. 382 n. 35.
14. Del Valle interview, May 18, 1989; Blight and Welch interview with Emilio Aragonés, May 19, 1989, Havana. In an interesting inversion of public rationales, Aragonés claimed that "even though it seemed to me that the [Soviets'] main goal of the deployment was to change the correlation of forces, the missiles would have had the effect of protecting Cuba, and so I was very much in favor of the idea."
15. On October 19, the CIA reported that the Soviet Union was installing twenty-four SS-4 launchers in Cuba, each of which could have been equipped with two missiles, for a possible total of forty-eight MRBMs. Twelve SS-5 launchers were observed under construction, suggesting that twenty-four IRBMs could have been deployed to Cuba (including reloads). With one warhead per missile, seventy-two warheads could have been deployed to Cuba. In such a case, the number of land-based missile warheads capable of reaching the United States would have more than quadrupled, increasing from twenty (the ICBMs in the Soviet Union itself) to ninety-two (twenty on ICBMs, seventy-two on MRBMs and IRBMs in Cuba). See CIA memorandum on the construction of missile sites in Cuba, October 19, 1962, National Security Archive, Washington, D.C. According to General Volkogonov, however, the deployment consisted of three SS-4 regiments (eight launchers each for a total of twenty-four) and two SS-5 regiments (eight launchers each for a total of sixteen). *MCT*. Raymond Garthoff claims that only one warhead was to be provided per launcher even though two missiles were assigned to each (to offset reliability problems). Garthoff, *Reflections on the Cuban Missile Crisis*, 2nd ed. (Washington, D.C.: Brookings, 1989), p. 20. If this is so, the deployment would have tripled the number of warheads that Soviet land-based missiles could have delivered promptly on the United States, from twenty (the ICBMs in the Soviet Union) to sixty (twenty on ICBMs, forty on MRBMs and IRBMs in Cuba). American intelligence estimated in 1962 that the Soviets had also deployed 155 cruise and ballistic missiles on submarines, and approximately 200 long-range bombers. Although these were severely constrained operationally (because of geographical, logistical, and technical factors), and although they did not represent a serious first-strike threat, they might have succeeded in delivering some number of nuclear warheads on the United States in the event of war. The missiles in Cuba, therefore, probably no more than doubled the number of nuclear weapons of all kinds that the Soviets could have delivered, though an accurate estimate of this increment is impossible to make. See Sagan, "SIOP-62:

The Nuclear War Plan Briefing to President Kennedy," pp. 27–28; and Garthoff, *Intelligence Assessment and Policymaking*, p. 55.

16. Among those in the West who have viewed the deployment primarily or exclusively as an attempt to redress the strategic nuclear imbalance are Hilsman, *To Move a Nation*, pp. 200–2; Horelick, "The Cuban Missile Crisis," p. 376; Horelick and Rush, *Strategic Power and Soviet Foreign Policy*, p. 141; Tatu, *Power in the Kremlin*, p. 231; and Jerome H. Kahan and Anne K. Long, "The Cuban Missile Crisis: A Study of Its Strategic Context," *Political Science Quarterly*, Vol. 87, No. 4 (December 1972), pp. 564–90. Sergei Khrushchev denied at the Moscow conference that the deployment of missiles to Cuba was a cost-effective solution to the strategic nuclear imbalance, arguing that stationing ICBMs on Soviet soil, requiring nothing extra in the way of conventional defenses and involving none of the added expense of dismantling, crating, shipping, and assembling missiles thousands of miles away, would have been a more sensible solution. He therefore discounts the strategic nuclear rationale behind the deployment of missiles to Cuba. His argument, however, overlooks the difficulties that the Soviets were experiencing in producing three-stage long-range rockets. There was simply no long-range option available in 1962. Cf. Horelick and Rush, *Strategic Power and Soviet Foreign Policy*, pp. 105–6; and Allison, *Essence of Decision*, pp. 20–21.

17. *MCT*. Recall Shakhnazarov's and Burlatsky's remarks at the Cambridge conference, pp. 229, 234, 248, above.

18. Cf. Alekseev's remarks, *MCT*; and n. 40, below.

19. *MCT*.

20. Cf. pp. 293–305, above.

21. See, e.g., James G. Hershberg, "Before the Missiles of October: Challenging Camelot's Line on the Crisis with Cuba," *Boston Phoenix*, April 8, 1988, pp. 8ff.; and Pierre Salinger, "Gaps in the Cuban Missile Crisis Story," *The New York Times*, February 5, 1989, pp. 4–25.

22. "Program review memorandum, subject: The Cuba Project, 20 Feb., 1962," National Security Archive, Washington, D.C.

23. *CINCLANT Historical Account*, p. 39.

24. Bundy, however, said that he viewed American covert operations against Castro as a "psychological salve," and that he had no expectation that they would succeed in their stated goals. Remarks at a new conference at Harvard University, October 13, 1987.

25. See "White House Tapes and Minutes," pp. 171–94.

26. *MCT*.

27. Khrushchev, *Khrushchev Remembers*, p. 493.

28. See p. 238.

29. Gromyko, "Karibskii krizis," p. 5.

30. *MCT*.

31. *MCT*. Cf. p. 238.

32. *MCT*. Otto Kuusinen was a Soviet Presidium member of Finnish origin.

33. Gromyko, "Karibskii krizis," p. 5. Alekseev reports that Gromyko told him privately in August 1962 that he had "strong reservations" about the idea, and that he had expressed them to Khrushchev in private. Allyn, Blight, and Welch interview with Aleksandr Alekseev, April 27, 1989, Moscow; and Alekseev, "Uroki karibskogo krizisa."

34. Alekseev interview.

35. Alekseev interview.

36. *MCT*; and Raymond L. Garthoff, "Cuban Missile Crisis: The Soviet Story," *Foreign Policy*, No. 72 (Fall 1988), p. 66.
37. Alekseev interview; and *MCT*.
38. Mikoyan, "Karibskii krizis," p. 70.
39. Aragonés interview.
40. Although the reasons for Biryuzov's personal optimism are unclear, Sergio del Valle notes that "Cuba's geography lent itself to a secret deployment. Our terrain and our vegetation made it quite simple to hide the missiles effectively." Del Valle interview. Sergo Mikoyan believes that Biryuzov's estimate was influenced by his fervent desire to redress the strategic nuclear imbalance. Allison and Ury, eds., *Windows of Opportunity*, pp. 108–9.
41. *MCT*. Volkogonov noted that a decision was taken to send four motorized rifle regiments to defend the missile sites; air defense forces (including radars, SAMs and MiG-21s); and a coastal defense regiment, including Komar torpedo boats and Il-28 bombers.
42. Medvedev, *Khrushchev*, p. 184.
43. Allyn, Blight, and Welch interview with Othon Montero, researcher at the Instituto de Historia de Cuba, May 15, 1989, Havana.
44. Alekseev interview.
45. *MCT*; and Alekseev interview.
46. Montero interview; Aragonés interview; and *MCT*.
47. Aragonés interview.
48. Aragonés interview. Khrushchev may have believed from the start that the United States would react to the news of Soviet missiles in Cuba with moderation. Alekseev reports that, in May, Khrushchev "said the Americans are a pragmatic people and would not attack if there were missiles in Cuba." Alekseev interview. The Soviet Baltic fleet, however, would have been completely incapable of providing timely or effective naval support, and it is difficult to credit the claim that Khrushchev was serious on this point.
49. When asked at the Moscow conference whether the deployment could have been undertaken openly, Gromyko insisted that a secret deployment was the only viable option. His opinion was widely shared among the Soviet delegation, echoed most forcefully by Viktor Komplektov and Georgy Shakhnazarov, who noted that secrecy was "characteristic of the times." Theodore Sorensen asserted that the President would have found it much more difficult to mobilize world opinion on his side if the deployment had been done openly; McGeorge Bundy strongly agreed. *MCT*.
50. Alekseev interview. This clarifies the rather unclear passage on this point in Alekseev, "Uroki karibskogo krizisa," p. 5.
51. See p. 241; and p. 382 n. 26.
52. Juárez, "El general que dio la orden de: ¡Fuego!" p. 4.
53. Montero interview.
54. See p. 390 n. 66; and Larson, ed., *The "Cuban Crisis" of 1962*, pp. 17–18, 21–32.
55. See n. 4, above.
56. Mendóza interview.
57. Montero interview.
58. See, e.g., pp. 274–76, above; and Ray S. Cline, "Nuclear War Seemed Remote," *Washington Post*, February 5, 1989, p. D-8.
59. See, e.g., Bundy, *Danger and Survival*, p. 425.
60. *MCT*.

61. Del Valle interview. The details of the deployment in Cuba evince a high degree of Soviet self-reliance, and an equally high degree of Cuban deference. There may have been a dearth of trust on the one side, and an excess of trust on the other.

62. *MCT*. American intelligence estimated in 1962 that the fastest an SS-4 missile could have been fired from a cold start was eight hours. CIA memorandum on the construction of missile sites in Cuba, October 19, 1962.

63. *MCT*.

64. *MCT*.

65. See p. 392 n. 80.

66. Gromyko, "Karibskii krizis," p. 5.

67. Cf. John Scali, "I Was the Secret Go-Between in the Cuban Crisis," *Family Weekly*, October 25, 1964, pp. 4, 5, 12–14; and Hilsman, *To Move a Nation*, pp. 217–23.

68. *MCT*.

69. See p. 342, below. Dobrynin reports that Robert Kennedy had asked him on October 26 to disregard other channels of communication because they did not reflect the president's views. *MCT*.

70. See Pope, ed., *Soviet Views on the Cuban Missile Crisis*, p. 48.

71. *Department of State Bulletin*, Vol. LXIX, No. 1795, 11/19/73, p. 640.

72. See Larson, ed., *The "Cuban Crisis" of 1962*, p. 185.

73. "October 27, 1962: Transcripts of the Meetings of the ExComm," pp. 34–44.

74. See pp. 256–67.

75. *MCT*.

76. See pp. 83–84.

77. See Welch and Blight, "The Eleventh Hour of the Cuban Missile Crisis," p. 23, n. 58.

78. Bruce Allyn, discussion at the Soviet Defense Ministry Institute for Military History, July 1989.

79. See p. 311.

80. Juárez, "El General que dio la orden de: ¡Fuego!"

81. Alekseev interview.

82. Del Valle interview.

83. Alekseev interview; del Valle interview. According to both Othon Montero and Sergio del Valle, the Cuban Armed Forces had no surface-to-air missiles, only artillery.

84. Juárez, "El general que dio la orden de: ¡Fuego!"

85. *MCT*.

86. Aragonés interviews.

87. Khrushchev, *Khrushchev Remembers*, p. 499.

88. Personal communication. It is worth noting that Statsenko himself told U Thant that Cubans shot down the American U-2. This, too, may have been part of a cover-up. Hersh, "Was Castro Out of Control in 1962?" p. H2.

89. Kennedy, *Thirteen Days*, p. 108.

90. Personal communication.

91. *MCT*. For earlier written accounts, see Khrushchev, *Khrushchev Remembers*, pp. 497–98; and Pope, ed., *Soviet Views on the Cuban Missile Crisis*, pp. 214–15. At the Moscow conference, Dobrynin revealed that coded

messages from the Soviet Embassy in Washington were transmitted to Moscow via bicycle courier and Western Union.

92. Kennedy, *Thirteen Days*, pp. 108–9.
93. *MCT*.
94. *MCT*.
95. *MCT*.
96. *MCT*.
97. See pp. 309–10.
98. For the text of Khrushchev's October 28 message, see Larson, ed., *The "Cuban Crisis" of 1962*, pp. 189–93.
99. Scali, "I Was the Secret Go-Between in the Cuban Crisis," p. 14. The number of cases where representatives of the governments of the superpowers appear to have conducted freelance diplomacy appears quite striking in retrospect. Fomin, Dobrynin, Robert Kennedy, and Scali all seem to have made important approaches to the other side without prior discussion with their responsible decisionmaking bodies: Fomin in proposing terms for settling the crisis; Dobrynin in raising the issue of Turkish missiles; Robert Kennedy in suggesting a deal (with the President's knowledge, but not the ExComm's); and Scali in delivering an ultimatum. One hears a good deal of discussion in academe about the dangers of unauthorized and inadvertent acts on the part of the *military*; these episodes suggest that a certain amount of effort should be devoted to exploring the dangers and consequences of inadvertent *diplomatic* acts.
100. See, e.g., Garthoff, "The Cuban Missile Crisis: The Soviet Story," pp. 74–76.
101. See, e.g., Bill Keller, " '62 Missile Crisis Yields New Puzzle," *The New York Times*, January 30, 1989, p. A2.
102. This was conveyed to the authors by a knowledgeable source. This passage did not appear in the manuscripts that were delivered to the West in 1970.
103. Alekseev interview; Aragonés interview.
104. Del Valle interview.
105. See Harry Rositzke, *The KGB: The Eyes of Russia* (Garden City, N.Y.: Doubleday, 1981), pp. 197–98.
106. Kennedy, *Thirteen Days*, p. 99.
107. See p. 75.
108. *MCT*; and Alekseev interview.
109. See p. 269n.
110. Dobrynin reported at the Moscow conference that, in a confidential letter to President Kennedy on October 29 or 30, the Soviet Union did raise the issue of Guantánamo, but he added that he doubted that any hopes of American concessions on the base were realistic. Andrei Gromyko further remarked that the agreement concluding the crisis included the crucial concession from the United States: a commitment not to invade Cuba. *MCT*. Alekseev reports that he believes Khrushchev deliberately chose not to consult Castro on the removal of the missiles, because he knew he would not agree. Alekseev interview.
111. Aragonés interview. The Cuban delegation to the Moscow conference added that Khrushchev's explanation for his failure to consult Castro— that there was simply insufficient time—was wholly understandable. Indeed, Castro's telegram may have been largely responsible for convincing Khrushchev that time was so short in the first place. Nevertheless, the

Cuban delegation insisted that Khrushchev should at least have made the October 28 deal contingent upon Cuban agreement. *MCT*.

112. Garthoff, *Reflections on the Cuban Missile Crisis*, 1st ed., pp. 63–64.
113. *MCT*.
114. Del Valle interview; Aragonés interview. Del Valle explains that, between October 24 and 28, fifty antiaircraft batteries were mobilized from the reserves and were assigned to protect the missile sites. On October 28, when the dismantling of the nuclear missiles began, these units started to withdraw.
115. Alekseev, "Karibskii krizis: kak eto bylo," p. 36; Aragonés interview.
116. Allison, *Essence of Decision*, pp. 104–5.
117. Del Valle interview. According to del Valle, the Cubans planned to use their Il-28s in a coastal defense role, primarily against mother ships from which smaller craft would be launched carrying subversives and counter-revolutionaries attempting to infiltrate the Cuban coast.
118. Garthoff, *Reflections on the Cuban Missile Crisis*, 1st ed., p. 73; *HCT*, p. 150.
119. Aragonés interview.
120. Larson, ed., *The "Cuban Crisis" of 1962*, pp. 189–90.
121. *MCT*.
122. See, e.g., the discussion on pp. 127–34, 201–21.
123. Interview with Norman Cousins, *Saturday Review*, October 10, 1977, p. 4.
124. *MCT*.
125. *MCT*.
126. Cf. Bruce J. Allyn, "Toward a Common Framework: Avoiding Inadvertent War and Crisis," in Allison and Ury, eds., *Windows of Opportunity*, pp. 185–219.
127. *MCT*.
128. See pp. 319–21.
129. E.g., Schlesinger, *A Thousand Days*, p. 769.
130. *MCT*.
131. Coral Bell, *The Conventions of Crises: A Study in Diplomatic Management* (New York: Oxford University Press, 1971), p. 2.
132. *MCT*.

Appendix: Chronology

(All times EST)

Entries in the following chronology set in normal type were on the public record prior to this study, and have been compiled from Abel, *The Missile Crisis*; Chang, Rich, and Wallace, *A Chronology of the Cuban Missile Crisis*; Hilsman, *To Move a Nation*; Kennedy, *Thirteen Days*; Khrushchev, *Khrushchev Remembers*; Larson, *The "Cuban Crisis" of 1962*; Sorensen, *Kennedy*; and the collection of documents in the Cuban missile crisis file at the National Security Archive, Washington, D.C. Italicized entries represent information or testimony that came to light in the course of this project.

1959

January 1
- The regime of Cuba's General Fulgencio Batista falls; Fidel Castro assumes power.

1960

December 19
- Cuba openly aligns itself with Soviet foreign and domestic policies and claims solidarity with the Sino–Soviet bloc, issuing a joint communiqué with the U.S.S.R.

1961

January 3
- The U.S. terminates diplomatic and consular relations with Cuba; Cuba reciprocates.

March 31
- President John F. Kennedy (J.F.K.) reduces the Cuban sugar quota to zero.

April 12
- J.F.K. pledges the U.S. will not intervene militarily to overthrow Castro.

April 16
- Describing his regime as socialist, Castro orders general mobilization and accuses the U.S. of scheming to invade Cuba.

April 17
- Backed by the U.S., a group of Cuban exiles invades Cuba at the Bay of Pigs in an attempt to trigger an anti-Castro rebellion. By April 19, the invasion has failed; more than a thousand Cuban rebels are captured by Castro's forces.

June 3–4
- Khrushchev and J.F.K. hold a summit in Vienna. Khrushchev announces a six-month deadline for a resolution of the Berlin situation.

August 12–13
- Soviet forces assist the East Germans in erecting the Berlin Wall.

September 7
- The U.S. Congress bars assistance to any country aiding Cuba, unless the President determines such aid to be in the American national interest.

September 11
- Former President Eisenhower announces that, during his Presidency, no plan was ever made to invade Cuba.

October 21
- Deputy Secretary of Defense Roswell Gilpatric gives a speech in Hot Springs, Virginia, in which he publicly reveals that the U.S. government knows that the alleged "missile gap" in the Soviets' favor is a hoax. Gilpatric's speech acknowledges that the U.S. enjoys considerable nuclear superiority over the Soviet Union.

1962

January 22–31
- The Organization of American States (OAS) holds a conference in Punta del Este, Uruguay. The government of Cuba (under Castro) is declared incompatible with the inter-American system; Cuba is excluded from participating in the OAS, and the organization's members are prohibited from selling it arms; the OAS agrees on collective-defense measures against Cuba; U.S. Secretary of State Dean Rusk declares Cuba a threat to the Western Hemisphere and calls for its isolation.

February 3
- J.F.K. declares an embargo on all trade with Cuba, except for critical medical supplies.

February 20
- Brigadier General Edward G. Lansdale's "Cuba Project" program review details American covert activities in Cuba and specifies October 1962 as a target date for Castro's ouster.

Late April
- *Khrushchev first discusses the idea of deploying nuclear missiles to Cuba with Soviet First Deputy Premier Anastas I. Mikoyan. On April 25, Soviet Press Representative in Havana, Aleksandr Alekseev, receives an urgent cable to return to Moscow.*

May 7
- *Alekseev is informed he will be the new ambassador to Havana, effective May 31.*

May 14–20
- Khrushchev visits Bulgaria, where, according to his memoirs, "the idea of installing missiles with nuclear warheads in Cuba without letting the United States find out until it was too late to do anything about them" occurs to him for the first time. *On the return flight to Moscow, Khrushchev first mentions the idea of the deployment to Foreign Minister Andrei Gromyko.*

Late May
- *A high-level Soviet delegation, including the commander of the Strategic Rocket Forces, Marshal S.S. Biryuzov, travels secretly to Havana to propose to Castro the deployment of nuclear weapons to Cuba. The Cuban leadership unanimously and enthusiastically gives its approval in principle.*

June 10
- *Biryuzov reports the results of the Soviet–Cuban negotiations to the Presidium, which then orders the Ministry of Defense to prepare detailed operational plans for the deployment.*

July 3 and 8
- Khrushchev meets in Moscow with a Cuban delegation led by Defense Minister Raúl Castro to discuss Soviet military shipments to Cuba, including nuclear missiles. *Raúl Castro and Soviet Defense Minister Malinovsky agree on a draft of a treaty governing the deployment.*

July 27
- Castro announces that Cuba is taking measures that would make any direct U.S. attack on Cuba the equivalent of a world war. He claims that the U.S.S.R. and others have invested greatly in jointly resisting the dangers of further imperialist attacks.

Late July
- *The first SAMs and supporting equipment for the construction of nuclear missile sites leave the Soviet Union.*

August 10
- CIA Director John McCone dictates a memo to J.F.K. expressing his belief that Soviet medium-range ballistic missiles (MRBMs) will be deployed in Cuba.

August 23
- In National Security Action Memorandum (NSAM) 181, J.F.K. calls for study and action "in light of the evidence of new [Soviet] bloc activity in Cuba." Highlights include: action toward potential removal of U.S. Jupiter missiles from Turkey; study of the probable military, political, and psychological impact of the establishment in Cuba of missiles capable of reaching the U.S.; study of military alternatives should the U.S. decide to eliminate such missiles.

August 27–September 2
- *A Cuban delegation led by Che Guevara and Emilio Aragonés travels to Moscow with Fidel Castro's revisions to the draft treaty. The Cubans propose*

that the deployment be made public to forestall an American overreaction; Khrushchev successfully argues for continued secrecy.

August 31

- Sen. Kenneth Keating (R–NY) tells the Senate that there is evidence of Soviet missile installations in Cuba. Keating urges J.F.K. to take action and proposes that the OAS send an investigative team to Cuba.

September 4

- Attorney General Robert Kennedy (R.F.K.) meets with Soviet Ambassador Anatoly Dobrynin and expresses J.F.K.'s concern over Soviet military equipment reaching Cuba. Dobrynin conveys a message from Khrushchev that no ground-to-ground or offensive weapons would be placed in Cuba, which R.F.K. relays to Dean Rusk and to Secretary of Defense Robert McNamara. R.F.K. suggests that a statement be issued declaring that the U.S. will not tolerate the introduction of offensive weapons in Cuba.
- J.F.K. releases a statement, drafted by R.F.K. and Assistant Attorney General Nicholas Katzenbach, revealing that surface-to-air missiles (SAMs) and substantially more military personnel have been detected in Cuba by a reconnaissance flight on August 29. The President reassures the American public that the Soviets have deployed no offensive weapons in Cuba and warns the Soviets against such a deployment.

September 6

- Theodore Sorensen, Special Counsel to the, President, meets with Soviet Ambassador Dobrynin at the Soviet Embassy. In a memo on the conversation, Sorensen reports that Dobrynin repeatedly assured him that the Soviets "had done nothing new or extraordinary in Cuba—that the events causing all the excitement had been taking place somewhat gradually and quietly over a long period of time." Dobrynin reiterated his assurances that Soviet military assistance to Cuba was strictly defensive in nature and did not represent a threat to American security. Dobrynin also delivered a message from Khrushchev in which he promised that the Soviets would refrain from any activities that "could complicate the international situation" before the American congressional elections in November.

September 7

- J.F.K. requests congressional authority to call up fifteen thousand reservists.
- Dobrynin assures UN Ambassador Stevenson in New York that the U.S.S.R. is supplying only defensive weapons to Cuba.

September 9

- Chinese Communists shoot down a U-2 reconnaissance aircraft over mainland China.

September 11

- Soviet news agency TASS announces that the Soviet Union neither needs nor intends to introduce offensive nuclear weapons into Cuba.

September 13

- J.F.K. announces that if "at any time the Communist buildup in Cuba were to endanger or interfere with our security in any way . . . or if Cuba should ever attempt to export its aggressive purposes by force or the threat of force against any nation of this hemisphere, or become an offensive military base of significant capacity for the Soviet Union, then this country will do whatever must be done to protect its own security and that of its allies." At the same time, J.F.K. notes that no information to date suggests that military action would be necessary or justified.

September 15
- *The first SS-4 MRBMs arrive in Cuba.*

September 18
- Former Vice President Richard M. Nixon calls for a quarantine to stem the flow of Soviet arms to Cuba.

September 19
- A Special National Intelligence Estimate (SNIE) by the U.S. Intelligence Board, "The Military Buildup in Cuba," asserts that although the Soviets would gain considerable military advantage from establishing medium- and intermediate-range ballistic missiles in Cuba, Soviet policy does not support the establishment of nuclear forces on foreign soil and the Soviets are aware of the risks of U.S. retaliation. It therefore concludes that such a deployment is unlikely.
- The Senate Foreign Relations and Armed Services Committees approve the text of a joint resolution on Cuba (#230, introduced by Sen. John Sparkman, D–Ala.) sanctioning the use of force to defend the Western Hemisphere against Cuban aggression or subversion if necessary.

September 20
- Resolution #230 on Cuba passes the Senate by a vote of 86–1.

September 21
- In a speech to the UN, Soviet Foreign Minister Andrei Gromyko warns that an American attack on Cuba would mean war with the Soviet Union.

September 26
- The House of Representatives passes the joint resolution on Cuba by a vote of 384–7.

September 28
- In Yugoslavia, Soviet President Leonid Brezhnev reiterates Gromyko's warning that an American attack on Cuba would mean war with the Soviet Union.

October 1
- McNamara and the Joint Chiefs of Staff (JCS) discuss contingency planning. Admiral Dennison, Commander-in-Chief of the Atlantic Fleet, is ordered to make preparations for a blockade of Cuba if necessary.

October 4
- Congress passes a diluted version of the Joint Congressional Resolution on Cuba, introduced by Senators Dirksen and Halleck, sanctioning the use of

American forces to defend the Western Hemisphere from aggression or subversion from Cuba, and pledging cooperation with the OAS and "freedom-loving Cubans" to achieve self-determination.

October 9
- J.F.K. approves a U-2 reconnaissance flight over western Cuba, delayed by bad weather until October 14.

October 10
- Senator Keating charges that six intermediate-range ballistic missile bases are being constructed in Cuba.

October 13
- Chester Bowles questions Soviet Ambassador Dobrynin on whether the Soviets plan to put "offensive weapons" in Cuba. Dobrynin repeatedly denies any such intention.

October 14
- Presidential Assistant for National Security McGeorge Bundy appears on ABC's *Issues and Answers*, denying any hard evidence of Soviet offensive weapons in Cuba.
- A U-2, piloted by Air Force Major Rudolf Anderson, Jr., flies over western Cuba. Photographs obtained by this flight provide the first hard evidence of MRBM sites.

October 15
- A readout team at the National Photographic Intelligence Center reviews photos taken during the October 14 U-2 flight, and identifies objects similar to MRBM components observed in the U.S.S.R. scattered about a meadow at San Cristobal.
- (8:30 p.m.) CIA Deputy Director of Intelligence Ray Cline calls Bundy and Roger Hilsman, State Department Director of Research and Intelligence, on a non-secure phone and, in cryptic language, informs them of the discovery of MRBMs in Cuba. Hilsman phones Dean Rusk, who in turn notifies Paul Nitze, Assistant Secretary of Defense for International Security Affairs. Bundy decides to wait until morning to alert the President.
- (Midnight) McNamara is shown photographic evidence of the MRBMs at San Cristóbal.

October 16
- (Early morning) Cline informs Bundy, R.F.K., and Treasury Secretary Douglas Dillon of the MRBM sites under construction in Cuba.
- (8:45 a.m.) Bundy breaks the news to J.F.K., who calls for an 11:45 a.m. meeting of his high-level advisors, a group later to become known as the ExComm.
- (6:30 p.m.) J.F.K. and his advisors discuss possible diplomatic and military courses of action.

October 17
- Georgy Bolshakov, an official in the Soviet Embassy in Washington, brings R.F.K. a "personal message" from Khrushchev to J.F.K., assuring that "under no circumstances would surface-to-surface missiles be sent to Cuba."

October 18
- (Afternoon) Gromyko and J.F.K. meet for two hours. Reading from notes, Gromyko assures J.F.K. that Soviet aid to Cuba "pursued solely the purpose of contributing to the defense capabilities of Cuba and to the development of its peaceful economy. . . ."

October 19
- J.F.K. departs Washington for scheduled campaign speeches in Cleveland and on the West Coast.
- Radio Moscow reports that U.S. naval maneuvers in the Caribbean are in preparation for an invasion of Cuba.

October 20
- (10:30 a.m.) White House Press Secretary Pierre Salinger announces in Chicago that the President is canceling the remainder of his campaign trip because of a "slight cold."
- The chief legal officers of the Departments of State, Defense, and Justice draft the quarantine proclamation prohibiting the shipment of offensive weapons to Cuba.
- (2:30 p.m.) J.F.K. meets with his advisors and orders a defensive quarantine instituted as soon as possible. The full operation is reviewed and approved, and the President's television address is scheduled for Monday at 7 p.m. The draft of his speech is discussed and revised.

October 21
- (11:30 a.m.) J.F.K., R.F.K., General Maxwell Taylor (chairman of the JCS), and McNamara meet with General Walter Sweeney, Jr., Commander in-Chief of the Tactical Air Command. Informed that an air strike could not guarantee to destroy all Soviet missiles in Cuba, J.F.K. confirms that the U.S. will impose a quarantine, rather than execute an air strike.
- J.F.K. calls Orville Dryfoos of *The New York Times*, who cooperates in suppressing a story on the pending crisis. The morning edition of *The Washington Post*, however, runs a story speculating about recent White House activity and surmising that its focus might be Cuba, but mentions the possibility of Berlin.

October 22
- J.F.K. signs NSAM 196, formally establishing the Executive Committee of the National Security Council (ExComm).
- (Noon) Salinger announces that J.F.K. will make an important statement at 7 p.m. and requests air time from radio and television networks.
- (5 p.m.) Congressional leaders assemble at the White House for a meeting with J.F.K., who discloses the photographic evidence of missile sites and

announces his quarantine plans. The congressional leaders express support, but many advocate stronger action. J.F.K. resists.

- (6 p.m.) Dobrynin is brought to Rusk's office at the State Department, where he receives an advance copy of J.F.K.'s forthcoming address, with a covering memo. According to reporters, Dobrynin is "ashen" when he leaves Rusk's office. Virtually simultaneously, American Ambassador Foy Kohler delivers a letter from J.F.K. and the text of his speech to the Kremlin, but he does not meet with any high-ranking officials, and there is no immediate response. At the same time, American UN Ambassador Adlai Stevenson informs Acting UN Secretary General U Thant of the President's speech, and announces that the U.S. will request a meeting of the Security Council.
- (7 p.m.) The President addresses the nation in a televised speech, announcing the presence of offensive missile sites in Cuba.
- The alert level of U.S. forces worldwide is raised from Defense Condition (DefCon) 5 to DefCon 3, coincident with J.F.K.'s speech.
- The U.S. base at Guantánamo in southeastern Cuba is reinforced by three Marine battalions. Dependents are evacuated by the time J.F.K. goes on the air.
- (10:40–11:25 p.m.) McNamara meets with Chief of Naval Operations Admiral George Anderson to discuss quarantine and surveillance procedures.
- *The U.S. Air Force hands over the first of fifteen Jupiter intermediate-range ballistic missile launchers to the Turkish Air Force for maintenance and operation, signaling that they have become fully operational.*
- Soviet Colonel Oleg Penkovsky, a senior officer in Soviet Military Intelligence, is arrested in the Soviet Union on charges of acting as a Western agent (since April 1961).
- (Late evening) British philosopher and pacifist Bertrand Russell sends telegrams to Kennedy and Khrushchev calling on them to halt the course of actions they have undertaken which threaten to plunge the world into nuclear war.

October 23

- (2:41 a.m.) The State Department receives a telegram from Adlai Stevenson reporting Cuba's request for a UN Security Council meeting to discuss the unfolding crisis.
- (8 a.m.) TASS begins transmitting a Soviet government statement accusing the U.S. of piracy, violation of international law, and acts of provocation that might lead to nuclear war.
- (10 a.m.) The ExComm holds its first official meeting.
- The OAS Council meets to consider the proposed U.S. quarantine proclamation. The final vote is 20–0 in favor of condemning the Soviet action and endorsing the U.S. action.
- The U.S.S.R. requests a meeting of the Security Council to examine the "violation of the Charter of the United Nations and threat to the peace on the part of the U.S."
- (11:56 a.m.) J.F.K. receives a letter in which Khrushchev declares: "I should

frankly say that the measures outlined in your statement represent a serious threat to peace and security of peoples. The United States has openly taken the path of gross violations of international norms of freedom of navigation on the high seas, a path of aggressive actions both against Cuba and against the Soviet Union." He adds: "We confirm that the armaments now in Cuba, regardless of the classification to which they belong, are destined exclusively for defensive purposes, in order to secure the Cuban republic from an aggressor's attack."

- (4 p.m.) Adlai Stevenson delivers his opening statement to the specially convened meeting of the Security Council, saying that Castro's regime "has aided and abetted an invasion of this hemisphere," making itself "an accomplice in the communist enterprise of world domination. . . . If the United States and other nations of the Western Hemisphere accept this new phase of aggression, we would be delinquent in our obligations to world peace."
- Valerian Zorin, the Soviet representative in the UN, declares that the U.S. charges are "completely false" and "a clumsy attempt to cover up aggressive actions" in Cuba.
- (6 p.m.) The ExComm meets. J.F.K. reviews and signs the Proclamation of Interdiction.
- (7:30 p.m.) McNamara announces that he has taken the necessary steps to deploy American forces so that the quarantine may take effect at ten o'clock the next morning.
- J.F.K. agrees to preliminary talks with U Thant to explore the possibility of "satisfactory arrangements" for negotiations. Khrushchev agrees to U Thant's appeal for a moratorium on further action, and agrees that if the U.S. ends the quarantine, the U.S.S.R. will suspend arms shipments to Cuba.

October 24

- (Early morning) Soviet ships en route to Cuba with questionable cargo either slow down or reverse their course; one tanker continues on.
- (10 a.m.) The ExComm meets. J.F.K.'s quarantine proclamation goes into effect.
- (2 p.m.) U Thant sends private appeals to Kennedy and Khrushchev to avoid any confrontation that will risk general war. He calls for voluntary suspension of arms shipments to Cuba and for voluntary suspension of the quarantine for two to three weeks, so that a settlement may be negotiated. Khrushchev accepts U Thant's appeal; J.F.K. rejects it.
- Bertrand Russell appeals to Khrushchev for caution and urges J.F.K. to stop the "madness"; Khrushchev responds, stating that the U.S.S.R. will make no "reckless decisions" and warning that if the U.S. carries out its planned "pirate action" the U.S.S.R. will have no choice but to "make use of the means of defense against the aggressor."
- The alert level of the Strategic Air Command is raised to DefCon 2, indicating full readiness for war.
- The State Department cables Ankara, urgently requesting U.S. Ambas-

sador Raymond Hare's assessment of the political consequences of removing Turkish Jupiter missiles outright, in conjunction with the deployment of a Polaris submarine in the area, or with some other significant military offset, such as a NATO seaborne multilateral nuclear force.

- American businessman William Knox is summoned to meet with Khrushchev, who rails against the quarantine and threatens to order the sinking of quarantine vessels if Soviet ships are stopped. Khrushchev states that the U.S. will have to learn to live with Soviet missiles in Cuba, just as the U.S.S.R. has learned to live with American missiles in Turkey. Khrushchev also claims that the SAMs and ballistic missiles in Cuba are under "strict Soviet control," and vaguely proposes a summit.

October 25

- (1:45 a.m.) J.F.K. sends a letter to Khrushchev laying responsibility for the crisis on the Soviet Union. J.F.K. draws Khrushchev's attention to his repeated warnings against the deployment of offensive weapons to Cuba, and to the Soviets' repeated statements that they had no need or intention to undertake such a deployment.
- (10 a.m.) The ExComm meets.
- Austrian Foreign Minister Bruno Kreisky suggests that Cuban bases be withdrawn in exchange for the withdrawal of Jupiter bases in Turkey.
- Walter Lippmann advocates a Cuba–Turkey missile trade in his syndicated column.
- (11:45 a.m.) At a Defense Department news conference, Assistant Secretary of Defense for Public Affairs Arthur Sylvester states that at least a dozen Soviet vessels have turned back. He also announces that the tanker *Bucharest* has been intercepted and permitted to proceed without boarding.
- (5 p.m.) The ExComm meets and considers several political options for resolving the crisis, among them a proposal to withdraw U.S. missiles from Turkey in exchange for the withdrawal of Soviet missiles from Cuba; a proposal to send UN teams to Cuba and Turkey to take control of missiles there, pending the outcome of negotiations; and a proposal for having a Latin American representative in Cuba approach Castro to try to convince him that the Soviets are merely exploiting Cuba.
- The State Department receives a cable from U.S. Ambassador to NATO Thomas Finletter, clarifying Turkey's position on the Jupiter missiles: the missiles are deemed to be of great value, serving "as a symbol of the alliance's determination to use atomic weapons against Russian attack on Turkey whether by large conventional or nuclear forces, although the Turks have been most reluctant to admit the presence of IRBMs [intermediate-range ballistic missiles] publicly."

October 26

- *Castro authorizes his air-defense forces to fire on all American aircraft within range.*
- (7:50 a.m.) A party from the *U.S.S. Pierce* and the *U.S.S. Kennedy* boards the Lebanese freighter *Marucla*, under charter to the Soviet Union, for

inspection. No prohibited material is found, and the *Marucla* is allowed to proceed.

- (10 a.m.) The ExComm meets.
- (1 p.m.) ABC's State Department correspondent John Scali has lunch with Aleksandr Fomin, senior Soviet intelligence officer in Washington, at Fomin's request. Fomin asks Scali to determine from his "high-level friends in the State Department" whether the U.S. would be interested in resolving the crisis on the following terms: (1) The U.S.S.R. would agree to dismantle and remove all offensive missiles from Cuba. (2) The U.S. would be allowed to verify the removal of these weapons. (3) The Soviets would promise never to introduce offensive weapons in Cuba again. (4) The U.S. would promise never to invade Cuba. Fomin suggests that if Stevenson proposed this in the UN, Zorin would be interested.
- (6 p.m.) A private letter from Khrushchev to J.F.K. arrives at the State Department, vaguely proposing to resolve the crisis along the lines suggested more explicitly by Fomin.
- Dean Rusk authorizes Scali to tell Fomin that the "highest levels in the government of the U.S." see real potential in his terms and that the U.S. and Soviet representatives "could work this matter out with U Thant and with each other."
- (7:35 p.m.) Scali meets Fomin to relay Rusk's message. Fomin assures him that the information will be relayed to the highest levels of the Kremlin and to Zorin at the UN.
- U.S. Ambassadors are directed to avoid public comments suggesting any symmetry between the presence of American Jupiter missiles in Turkey and Soviet missiles in Cuba.
- Khrushchev sends a letter to U Thant indicating that Soviet ships will stay away from the quarantine area temporarily.
- J.F.K. sends a statement to the UN Security Council reporting that development of the ballistic missile sites in Cuba is continuing at a rapid pace and that they will soon achieve full operational capability. It concludes that "there is no evidence to date indicating that there is any intention to dismantle or discontinue work on these missile sites. On the contrary, the Soviets are rapidly continuing their construction of missile support and launch facilities and serious attempts are underway to camouflage their efforts."
- *R.F.K. meets secretly with Dobrynin and hints that the United States might accept a missile trade as the basis for a settlement.*

October 27
- (10 a.m.) The ExComm meets.
- (10:17 a.m.) A new letter from Khrushchev arrives, proposing a public trade of Soviet missiles in Cuba for Jupiter missiles in Turkey. Moscow Radio carries Khrushchev's proposal, as well as his statement that Soviet missiles in Cuba are under strict Soviet control.
- (Morning) The SAM network in Cuba becomes operational. An American U-2 is shot down over Cuba, and its pilot killed—Major Rudolf Anderson,

Jr., who flew the reconnaissance mission that originally spotted the missiles.

- A U-2 under SAC's Strategic Reconnaissance Wing at Eielson Air Force Base in Alaska, reportedly on a "routine air-sampling mission," strays into Soviet airspace over Chukotski Peninsula. Though Soviet fighters scramble to intercept it, the plane returns safely to base without drawing fire.
- The Soviet Ambassador to Ankara attempts to persuade the Turks to agree to the missile-exchange deal proposed in Khrushchev's latest letter.
- An anti-submarine barrier is set up southeast of Newfoundland.
- The 5th Marine Expeditionary Brigade sails from the West Coast.
- (4 p.m.) The ExComm meets.
- (4:15 p.m.) Scali and Fomin meet again. Scali has instructions from Rusk to determine what has happened to the previous proposal and why Khrushchev raised the idea of swapping Turkish for Cuban missiles. Fomin tells Scali he will get back to him.
- (7:15 p.m.) R.F.K. telephones Ambassador Dobrynin, requesting a meeting.
- (7:45 p.m.) Dobrynin and R.F.K. meet. In his memoir, R.F.K. recalls telling Dobrynin that the U.S. knew work on the missile bases in Cuba was continuing; that the shoot-down of the U-2 was a serious turn of events; that J.F.K. did not want a military conflict but that his hand was being forced; that the U.S. needed a commitment "by tomorrow" that the Cuban missile bases would be removed by the Soviets, or the U.S. "would remove them"; and that the U.S. would not publicly trade missiles in Turkey for Soviet missiles in Cuba, though the Jupiters were scheduled to be removed in any case.
- (8:05 p.m.) Kennedy sends Khrushchev a carefully worded letter, potentially part of the contractual basis for a settlement. He writes: "(1) You would agree to remove these weapon systems from Cuba under appropriate United Nations observation and supervision; and undertake, with suitable safeguards, to halt the further introduction of such weapon systems into Cuba. (2) We, on our part, would agree, upon the establishment of adequate arrangements through the United Nations, to ensure the carrying out and continuation of these commitments (a) to remove promptly the quarantine measures now in effect and (b) to give assurances against the invasion of Cuba."
- (9 p.m.) The ExComm meets. J.F.K. reads a message from NATO Commander-in-Chief General Lauris Norstad, which presents the difficulty for NATO of any Cuban–Turkish missile trade. Also, J.F.K. tells Stevenson to tell U Thant that a Soviet tanker is approaching the quarantine zone and to remind U Thant of the Soviet statement that their ships would not challenge the quarantine.
- *Khrushchev receives a cable from Castro, via Alekseev, which he interprets as an exhortation for a preemptive nuclear strike against the United States.*
- *(Late evening:) J.F.K. meets with Rusk, whom he asks to send a letter to President Andrew Cordier of Columbia University. Cordier is instructed, upon further signal from the White House, to give U Thant the letter, re-*

questing him to propose the removal of both the Jupiters in Turkey and the Soviet missiles in Cuba. The contingency is never activated.

October 28
- Shortly before 10 a.m., Radio Moscow announces that it will have the text of a new Khrushchev message; when the ExComm convenes at eleven, the full text is available. In part, it reads: "The Soviet Government, in addition to earlier instructions on the discontinuance of further work on construction sites, has given a new order to dismantle the weapons, which you describe as offensive, and to crate them and return them to the Soviet Union."
- J.F.K. hails Khrushchev's decision as "an important and constructive contribution to peace."
- Zorin informs U Thant that instructions to dismantle the missiles in Cuba were received between 1 and 3 p.m., Sunday, October 28, and that dismantling started at 5 p.m.
- *American intelligence notices that troops in Cuban uniform have taken up positions around the Soviet nuclear missile sites.*

October 29
- Adlai Stevenson and John McCloy begin meeting with Anastas Mikoyan and Vasily Kuznetsov in New York to discuss the terms of the settlement.

November 2
- Mikoyan travels to Cuba to smooth over relations with Castro, who is furious at the U.S.–Soviet deal. Mikoyan is asked to discuss verification procedures for the removal of the Soviet missiles, and to enlist Castro's cooperation in complying with the terms of the agreement, which include withdrawal of all Il-28 bombers.

November 3
- *The troops in Cuban uniform withdraw from the area of the Soviet nuclear missiles.*

November 19
- Castro finally agrees to allow the withdrawal of the Il-28s.

November 20
- J.F.K. announces at a press conference that Castro has agreed to permit the withdrawal of the Il-28 bombers within thirty days.
- U.S. forces return to their normal peacetime levels of alert.

November 21
- J.F.K. issues a proclamation terminating the quarantine.

Index

DATE DUE

DEMCO 38-296